The Kansas City Athletics

For
Stan Peterson, my father,
who took me to Kansas City to watch Athletics games;
Linda Peterson, my wife,
whose love and support helped me write this book;
and Dr. Milton Engebretson,
who encouraged me to write this book.

The Kansas City Athletics

A Baseball History, 1954–1967

JOHN E. PETERSON

McFarland & Company, Inc., Publishers
Jefferson, North Carolina, and London

[LIBRARY OF CONGRESS ONLINE CATALOG]

Peterson, John E., 1949–
    The Kansas City Athletics : a baseball history, 1954–1967 / John E. Peterson.
        p.   cm.
    Includes bibliographical references and index.

    ISBN-13: 978-0-7864-1610-3
    softcover : 50# alkaline paper ∞

    1. Kansas City Athletics (Baseball team)—History.
GV875.K3 P48 2003
796.357'64'09778'411—dc22   2003016500

British Library cataloguing data are available

©2003 John E. Peterson. All rights reserved

No part of this book may be reproduced or transmitted in any form or by any means, electronic or mechanical, including photocopying or recording, or by any information storage and retrieval system, without permission in writing from the publisher.

Manufactured in the United States of America

Front cover: 1964 team photograph.
(From the Kansas City Athletics.)

McFarland & Company, Inc., Publishers
Box 611, Jefferson, North Carolina 28640
www.mcfarlandpub.com

Contents

Preface	1
1. Big League Dreams	3
2. A Clever Businessman	8
3. Quest for the A's	12
4. Last-Minute Maneuvering	19
5. Going to K.C.	23
6. How to Buy a Ballclub for Peanuts	29
7. Arnold Johnson's Ultimate Plan	35
8. The 90-Day Wonder	42
9. 1955: Big League Baseball Comes to K.C.	48
10. 1956: Listless and Bad	63
11. 1957: Big Trades Bring New Faces	71
12. 1958: Cerv's Amazing Season	81
13. 1959: Great Expectations	90
14. 1960: A Very Difficult Year	100
15. Who Will Buy the Team?	109
16. Charles O. Finley — The "O" Stands for Owner	118
17. Trying to Outdo Veeck	123

18. 1961: Gordon, Lane and Charlie O.	133
19. Courting Dallas	148
20. 1962: Let Bygones Be Bygones	156
21. 1963: Everything's Green and Gold	168
22. Happiness Is Being Somewhere Else	176
23. 1964: Rocky, Jim and a Pennant Porch	193
24. 1965: Charlie O.—The Man or the Mule?	208
25. 1966: The Dark Ages	224
26. 1967: "A Menace to Baseball"	235
27. "Luckiest City Since Hiroshima"	250
28. A Bad Marriage	263
29. Just a Yankees Farm Team	277
30. No More Trades with the Yankees	289
31. Crop Failure	298
32. Growing a Championship Team	305
Notes	317
Bibliography	333
Index	337

Preface

Why a book about the Kansas City Athletics?

The team did not have a long history. Arnold Johnson purchased the Philadelphia Athletics and moved them to Kansas City in 1954. They were in Kansas City just 13 seasons before Charlie Finley moved them to Oakland in 1968.

The A's were the worst team in modern baseball history. The 1962 New York Mets lost 120 games in their inaugural season, but they won the World Series in 1969. The Kansas City Athletics were consistently bad. They won 829 games and lost 1,224, a winning percentage of just .404, and never came close to a winning record in any season. Only four teams can match or exceed 13 consecutive losing seasons—the Boston Red Sox, the Seattle Mariners, the Philadelphia Phillies and the Philadelphia Athletics—but at least these teams had winning seasons and championships to counterbalance their losing seasons. The Tampa Bay Devil Rays are the only other team in modern baseball history never to have a winning season. The Milwaukee Brewers of 1901 and the Seattle Pilots of 1969 had losing records in their only season of existence before relocating.

Despite this futility the A's had a fascinating and colorful history. Few teams had as many interesting events occur in such a brief period of time. Yet nobody recorded these events in a book. Books written about Oakland Athletics contain little information about the Kansas City years; other books mention the Kansas City Athletics in passing. I felt compelled to write this book so that the rich heritage of the Kansas City Athletics would not be lost.

Besides, the Kansas City A's were my team. I grew up in Omaha, listened to the games on the radio, and heard Monte Moore's glowing descriptions of the great plays made by the A's players. I wondered why such an outstanding collection of players did not win more games. I believed him when he said the team played well (despite the loss), when he predicted some minor league player in Birmingham would soon become an All-Star player in Kansas City, and when he explained why a player obtained in a trade would improve the team. Kansas City A's fans had to be optimistic.

It was always exciting to go to Kansas City to see the A's in person. Sometimes my father drove to Kansas City and parked our car in one of Sam's lots (or in somebody's back yard). Sometimes we rode a train that the Burlington railroad occasionally ran between Omaha and Kansas City especially for A's games. I felt something special every time I walked into the stadium.

Some of my friends were A's fans. We started an unofficial A's fan club called "COFFIN" — Charles O. Finley Fans in Nebraska. Other friends were Yankees fans. They often reminded me that their team was better than my team. One these Yankees fans made a cartoon of A's catcher Doc Edwards with the caption: "He is the classic example of a bad catcher — he can't catch, throw or hit." I wished I had kept the cartoon when the A's traded Edwards to the Yankees a few weeks later!

The A's may have been bad, but they were my team, win or lose — or lose and lose.

1

Big League Dreams

Bill Veeck wanted to move the St. Louis Browns to Baltimore. The American League met in July 1953 to discuss the Browns' future, and Yankees owner Del Webb wanted the team to move to Kansas City. "The Yankees owner's motives were hardly altruistic," wrote James Miller. "Kansas City was a New York AAA farm club. A move to that city would mean financial compensation for his club and the shift of its AAA farm club to a lucrative market in Denver. Moreover, Kansas City's municipal government was preparing to purchase the local stadium from the Yankees and finance a major expansion of its seating. Webb's construction company was bidding for the job." The city would enlarge the seating capacity of the stadium from 17,500 seats to 35,000.[1]

Kansas City Star sports editor Ernest Mehl, John McDermott from the Junior Chamber of Commerce, Alex Levi, president of Macy's Department Store in Kansas City, councilman Joe Nolan, Chamber of Commerce president Karol Koerper and Lester Milgram, owner of Milgram grocery stores, led the city's efforts to obtain a major league team. Mayor William E. Kemp, Milgram, McDermott and city councilman Robert Benson went to the American League meeting in New York before the start of the 1953 World Series. The owners listened to representatives from Kansas City, Los Angeles, Baltimore and other cities before approving the sale to a Baltimore group. The Kansas City delegation realized they needed a person or group with adequate capital to buy and operate a team. They also needed a larger stadium. Previously, all the major league teams except Cleveland built their own stadiums; now, major league teams expected cities to provide stadiums.[2]

Kansas City had another opportunity one year later. The Philadelphia Athletics, owned by legendary Connie Mack, were one of the best teams in baseball until the Great Depression. Since that time they had struggled on the field and at the box office. The team was plagued by family problems that could be traced back to 1901. Benjamin Shibe owned 50 percent of the team (750 shares) and Mack owned 25 percent (375 shares) in the team's first season in the American League. The other 25 percent of the shares went to Sam Jones and Frank Hough, two local newspapermen, who each owned an eighth interest.[3]

Mack was offered the managerial reins of the New York Yankees following the 1912 season. As a counter-offer, Shibe loaned Mack $113,000 to buy the shares owned by Jones and Hough. Mack bought the shares on November 16, 1912. Shibe passed away in 1922 and his family of two sons (Tom and John) and two daughters inherited A's stock, as did two grandsons, Frank and Benny Macfarland. Tom Shibe died on February 16, 1936, and John Shibe died just one year later on July 11, 1937. The John Shibe estate was insolvent and by 1940 Connie Mack purchased 141 shares of stock from the estate. Mack held the majority ownership of the team by a margin of 891 shares to 609 shares still held by members of the Shibe family.

Mack, who married Margaret Hogan in 1887, had three children: Roy, Earle and daughter Marguerite. Mrs. Mack passed away five years after they were married and Mack married Katherine Hallahan in 1910. They raised five children—four daughters and one son, Connie Mack Jr. Mack wanted all three of his sons to join the organization. Earle served a 14-year apprenticeship as a minor league player and manager, coached the A's in 1924 and was appointed assistant manager in 1939. Roy started working in minor league offices in 1915 and became the A's vice president in 1935. Connie Jr. joined the organization in 1935. He wanted to make changes, but his brothers felt his ideas were impractical. The franchise was threatened by intermittent warfare between Earle and Roy on one side and Connie Jr. and his mother on the other. Connie Sr. had grown somewhat indecisive and was swayed first by one side and then the other.

Mack began dividing his shares among his sons in 1946. He transferred 163 shares apiece to Roy, Earle and Connie Jr., and gave 100 shares to his wife Katherine. He kept 302 shares for himself. Connie Jr. formed an alliance with Shibe's grandsons Ben and Frank Macfarland, who controlled 609 shares. Connie Jr. could add these shares to the 163 shares he owned and the 100 shares owned by his mother to outvote his father and his brothers 872 to 628. He was finally able to push through some major changes. The 1950 season would be Connie Sr's. fiftieth anniversary as manager and the theme became "One more pennant for Connie." Connie Jr. fired coaches Al Simmons and Earle Brucker. Connie Jr. and the Macfarlands maneuvered Earle, assistant manager and his father's handpicked heir as manager, out of his job on May 26. Coach Jimmy Dykes replaced Earle as assistant manager and Mickey Cochrane was brought into the front office as general manager.

Connie Jr. planned to sell the team after the season, stay with the new owners for a year or two and then leave. James P. Clark, a local trucking official who organized a syndicate to buy the Philadelphia Eagles football team in 1948, wanted to purchase the team in June. Roy did not want to sell and allied with his brother Earle. They insisted that if Connie Jr. and the Macfarlands wanted to sell their controlling interest they should first give the other Macks a chance to buy their stock. Connie Jr. gave Earle and Roy a 30-day option. If they failed to purchase the stock by July 31, Connie Jr. and the Macfarlands would have 45 days to buy out Roy and Earle. Connie Jr. set the price of $2,000 a share for his group's 872 shares for a total of $1,744,000. He did not think Roy and Earle could raise the money.

By the time the option agreement was formally signed, Roy had worked out a plan to mortgage the ballpark. The Phillies and Eagles leased the stadium from the A's. The Phillies gave the A's 10 cents per admission, an amount between $75,000 and $120,000 a year. The football team gave 15 percent of receipts after taxes, an amount that ranged between $50,000 and $60,000, but had gone as high as $85,000 in one season. The Athletics received approximately $200,000 from concession revenue. The Phillies received only a small portion of the concession proceeds from their games and the Eagles did not receive any. The rent and concession income at Shibe Park would be sufficient to cover the mortgage payments of $50,000 a quarter ($200,000 a year) for both interest and amortization of the principal for the first five years and $40,000 a quarter ($160,000 a year) for the next five at the end of which the principal would be down to $483,000. The $1,750,000 mortgage was approved within three weeks.

The papers were signed on August 28. Roy and Earle arranged for a temporary advance of money from John McShain because they thought they had to buy the club before they would be eligible to receive the mortgage, but it was not necessary. The stock was purchased in the name of the club rather than individuals, and all 872 shares went into the club treasury. The only active shares were the 628 shares previously held by Connie Sr., Roy and Earle. The two sons had the option to buy their father's stock until 1960.

Connie Sr.'s fiftieth anniversary was a disappointment. The "Whiz Kids" Phillies won the National League pennant and captured the hearts of local fans when they while the A's finished in the cellar and lost $315,000. Jacobs Brothers (Sportservice) concessionaires loaned the A's $250,000 to cover the operating loss. In exchange, the Macks signed a 25 year contract on September 25, 1950; the contract followed the club wherever it played and under whatever ownership. It gave Sportservice exclusive rights for scorecards, program advertising, refreshments, novelties and other concession rights, beginning with the 1951 season.

Connie Sr. retired as manager on October 18. Publicly, Earle and Roy maintained that their father could manage as long as he chose, but privately they had applied pressure on him to step down. Jimmy Dykes succeeded Mack. The mortgage payments made it difficult to operate profitably and the team did not have the financial resources to rebuild the organization. The A's operated with few full-time scouts and a sparse minor league operation.

Earle wanted to sell his interest in the team to a Philadelphia group in 1951. The opposition of Roy — and Connie Sr. himself — killed the transaction. One year later Bobby Shantz amassed a record of 24 victories against just seven losses and led the team to a fourth-place finish. Attendance climbed to 627,100 and Roy reported the team "just about broke even" financially during 1951 and 1952. Shantz was injured in 1953, the team tumbled into seventh place, attendance plunged to 362,113, and the A's lost $101,461. The *Saturday Evening Post* reported the A's couldn't "afford even moderate losses for very long.... If things turn out as poorly (in 1954) as they did last year, when home attendance was only 362,000, it is likely that the club will leave Philadelphia, or change ownership — or both."[4]

Roy conceded there were times during both 1953 and 1954 when the A's were short of working capital and had to borrow an additional $150,000 from the Jacobs Brothers (Sportservice). He said it would take between 650,000 and 700,000 in home attendance for the team to break even in 1954. Attendance did not improve. Although both Roy and Earle wanted to retain their ownership, they were barely on speaking terms and it was unlikely that they could work together to save the franchise. The antagonism became so great that if one brother tried to organize a group to save the team, the other brother would veto the plan. By mid-season the *Saturday Evening Post* speculated one of three things would occur at the end of the season:[5]

1. The Macks might move the team to another city. Roy wanted to maintain ownership even if it had to be moved. On the other hand, Earle said, "If the team goes to another city, I won't go with it." Since they held equal ownership, including a mutual option on their father's stock, Earle could prevent any attempt to move the franchise and a move seemed unlikely.

2. The A's could be sold to a Philadelphia buyer. Babe Alexander, an advertising man and ex-publicity director of the Phillies, organized a syndicate to buy the A's. Jim Peterson, a restaurant manager who once pitched

for the A's, headed another syndicate. Two additional newly organized groups were also interested.

    3. Bidders from another city could purchase the A's. Los Angeles, San Francisco, Kansas City, Minneapolis–St. Paul, Dallas, Houston, Montreal and Toronto wanted to obtain a major league team. None of the cities offered an adequate stadium in 1954, and many experts felt it would be at least 1956 before a suitable stadium could be provided by any of these cities.

2
A Clever Businessman

Arnold Milton Johnson was born in Chicago on January 11, 1907. He graduated from the University of Chicago in 1928 and joined Lamson Brothers, a grain and stock exchange brokerage. He left Lamson after six months to join Merrill and Lynch. After the stock market crash Johnson moved to a bond firm to set up a statistical department and assist the manager in charge of underwriting and discovered methods to revitalize run-down businesses.

He joined the City National Bank and Trust Company in 1932. After a few years he capitalized on the first of what he later called "fair opportunities." Northwestern Terra Cotta Company, a manufacturer of tiles and ceramics, owed nearly $2 million and had only $50,000 in assets. Johnson refinanced the firm and reorganized the personnel, and the corporation prospered. He was named to Northwestern's board of directors and became chairman of the board. Johnson remained on the board until he joined the Navy during World War II. J. Patrick Lannan, a Chicago broker who became Johnson's partner in several ventures, filled his position on the board.

Johnson was chief of staff and operations officer of the U.S. flagship *Callaway* before the landing on Luzon in January 1945. He was replaced by another officer and ordered ashore for a more hazardous landing operation. A Japanese suicide plane struck the *Callaway* shortly after he was replaced, killing 42 men, including the officer that replaced Johnson.

When the war ended Johnson stopped in San Francisco and met Carmen Burr. They were married three weeks later. Johnson returned to City National Bank and was promoted to vice president in the banking department. He also returned to the board of Northwestern Terra Cotta.

Joining Bill Tobin's syndicate that purchased the Chicago Blackhawks hockey team from the estate of Major Frederic McLaughlin, Johnson became the team's vice president and treasurer. He later relinquished those positions

2—A Clever Businessman

although he still retained some stock in the team and was listed as a corporate director.

Johnson's most successful venture was with the Automatic Canteen Company of Chicago. Nathaniel Leverone, a Chicago manufacturer, had started the company 25 years earlier to expand the candy vending machine idea to include machines for food, drink and other products. Johnson watched this firm grow and determined that it had a good future. Leverone's brother Louis was a partner and Johnson reasoned that Louis, then in his 70s, might be tempted to retire. J. Arthur Friedlund, a Chicago attorney and director and general counsel for Automatic Canteen, helped John-

Arnold Johnson (National Baseball Hall of Fame Library, Cooperstown, New York).

son form a group that paid $1.5 million to purchase Louis's holdings. Friedlund was general counsel and secretary of the New York Yankees and he persuaded Yankees co-owners Del Webb and Dan Topping to join the group. Johnson became vice chairman of Automatic Canteen.

Johnson became the nominal owner of Arnold Kirkeby's Warwick Hotels in Philadelphia and New York in a capital gains transaction conceived by Johnson to take advantage of capital gains and tax laws. Johnson borrowed almost all of the money to buy the hotels to give Kirkeby his capital gain, and then rented the hotels back to Kirkeby on terms insuring that Johnson would net a worthwhile profit and repay all his obligations.

Johnson organized a group of investors to purchase the Chicago, North Shore and Milwaukee Railroad, an electric interurban train that ran between Chicago and Milwaukee. The North Shore voluntarily reorganized in 1953 as the Susquehanna Corporation. Susquehanna diversified into such activities as mining, uranium processing, chemicals and electronics. The company became profitable writing off the operating losses of the railroad and its subsidiary bus operations against its profits from other operations. The company stood to profit even more in the form of tax credits if the railroad was abandoned. One estimate placed the total gain at anywhere from $17 million to $28 million in addition to profit earned by selling land rights. The North Shore was ultimately abandoned in January 1963.

Johnson applied his capital gains strategies to baseball in 1953. He developed a plan for Topping and Webb to sell Yankee Stadium to Johnson and then lease it back from him. They would benefit from capital gains, elimination of real estate and inheritance tax problems and a write-off of lease rentals under operational expenses. Johnson would benefit on a long-range capital investment basis. Topping and Webb wanted to include Blues Stadium in Kansas City in the transaction. Johnson did not feel it was a sound investment but was compelled to accept it as part of the transaction.

He formed a New York corporation that included his brother Earl to purchase Yankee Stadium and Blues Stadium for a reported $6.5 million in December 1953. Of this total $650,000 was for Blues Stadium. Topping and Webb received capital gains benefits of more than $1 million. Johnson obtained most of the funds from four transactions that added up to $6 million, leaving only a modest balance of $500,000 to be assumed by Johnson's corporation.[1]

After acquiring Yankee Stadium and the surrounding land, he sold the land (but not the stadium) to the Knights of Columbus for $2.5 million because land could not be depreciated for tax purposes. He leased the land back from the Knights for 28 years at annual rentals of $125,000 for the first four years and $181,250 for the final 24 years, for a total of $4,850,000. The Knights would receive a healthy return on their investment because they were tax-exempt and did not pay property taxes. Johnson obtained three successive 15-year renewal options that could extend the lease to a total of 73 years.

Johnson leased the stadium and sublet the land (rented from the Knights) to the Yankees over the same 28 year period beginning at $600,000 a year and gradually descending to $350,000 a year for a grand total of $11,500,000. The difference between the rent he received from the Yankees and the rent he paid to the Knights netted Johnson's corporation a profit of $6,650,000.

Johnson obtained a 10-year first mortgage on the stadium and lease rights for $500,000 from a co-partnership identified only as Atwell and Company. All of Johnson's rights were assigned to Atwell as protection for this loan. Seven weeks later these rights were reassigned to another co-partnership Salkeid and Company.

Johnson then negotiated a 20-year second mortgage on the stadium and lease rights for $2.9 million from Webb and Topping. He also obtained a $100,000 mortgage on the Kansas City stadium from Webb and Topping.

Ernest Mehl invited Johnson to come to Kansas City to look at the stadium. Johnson agreed to sell the stadium for what it cost him if Kansas City obtained a major league team. He told Mehl he was not interested in purchasing the Philadelphia Athletics, if they became available, and moving the team to his stadium in Kansas City, but he would help Mehl find someone who was interested. Before the major league All-Star game in Cleveland in July Johnson changed his mind and decided he'd try to purchase the Athletics. Kansas City leaders assured him the city would buy the stadium, enlarge it for the team, and provide financial incentives that would virtually assure a profitable operation.

Johnson was a director of 20 corporations, chairman of the board of five and vice chairman of the board of Automatic Canteen Corporation when he purchased the Athletics in November 1954. He did not have a great amount of money himself but had a remarkable ability to work out mutually profitable deals involving millions of dollars without any individual investing much of his own money. The purchase of the Athletics was similar to all the other transactions he arranged in which all the parties benefited.

COMPARISON OF CITIES SEEKING A MAJOR LEAGUE TEAM (1954)

City	1950 Population Figures		1960 Population Figures		1954 Attendance
	City Proper	Metro Area	City Proper	Metro Area	
Kansas City	456,622	791,800	475,539	1,025,900	141,905 AAA
Dallas	434,462		679,684		134,955 AA
Fort Worth	278,778		356,268		122,274 AA
Total	713,240	1,005,500	1,035,952	1,527,400	
Houston	596,163	810,400	938,219	1,251,700	310,531 AA
Los Angeles	1,970,358	4,292,000	2,479,015	6,565,000	238,567 AAA
Minneapolis	521,718		484,872		128,187 AAA
St. Paul	311,349		313,411		134,006 AAA
Total	833,067	1,116,700	796,283	1,441,700	
Montreal			1,109,439	1,595,000	195,896 AAA
San Francisco	775,357		740,316		298,908 AAA
Oakland	384,575		367,548		201,922 AAA
Total	1,159,932	2,424,600	1,107,864	3,275,000	
Toronto			667,706	1,450,000	408,876 AAA

3
Quest for the A's

Arnold Johnson began negotiating with the Macks on July 12, although he did not officially announce his plans until Kansas City passed a $2 million bond issue to purchase and enlarge Blues Stadium. There were some objections as bonds for a new stadium were passed in a 1947 election in the amount of $1.25 million. The city purchased 134 acres of property north of downtown Kansas City along the Missouri river for $400,000 for the stadium but felt there was no need to build a new stadium at that time. Supporters of the bond issue contended it was necessary to rebuild Blues Stadium to reimburse Johnson for the $650,000 he spent to purchase it. The New York Yankees, in an attempt to protect Johnson's investment, indicated they would not transfer their Kansas City Blues franchise unless the city purchased the stadium. The election was held on August 3, 1954, and the bond issue passed with an overwhelming four-to-one majority. Johnson formally announced his plans to purchase the team and move it to Kansas City on the same day. But Johnson was not the only bidder.[1]

Louis Jacobs from Sportservice met with Minneapolis area businessmen on July 4. The Athletics owed Sportservice approximately $400,000 and Jacobs said he could deliver the team to Minneapolis and St. Paul if they raised $1.6 million as down payment for the estimated overall cost of $3.2 million. The team would be kept in Philadelphia until a stadium could be built in the Twin Cities. Dick Burnett headed a group of Texas millionaires that reportedly pledged $5 million to purchase the team and move it to Dallas. Bill Veeck, the former owner of the Cleveland Indians and St. Louis Browns, wanted to buy the team and move it to Los Angeles. Clint Murchison, a wealthy Texas businessman who later purchased the Dallas Cowboys football team, also wanted move the team to Los Angeles. Jack Kent Cooke, owner of the Toronto franchise in the International (AAA) League, wanted to move the team to Toronto.[2]

Philadelphia mayor Joseph S. Clark announced plans to organize a

75-man group to launch a "Save-the-A's" campaign on July 1. The campaign set a goal to sell enough tickets to reach an attendance of 600,000 by the end of the season so the debts could be paid and the Macks could retain the franchise. Roy Mack wanted to purchase his brother's stock. "I'm going to battle for all-out control of this club," he said. "Especially since the 'Save-the-A's' campaign has gotten going." Roy reportedly offered Earle $300,000, but Earle countered with a bid of $500,000 to purchase Roy's stock. Both brothers declined to sell their stock to the other.[3]

Several Philadelphia business leaders expressed interest in the franchise: John McShain, the builder who temporarily loaned Roy and Earle Mack the $1.7 million that enabled them to gain control of the team in 1950; Matthew McCloskey Jr., a wealthy builder; Albert M. Greenfield, a real estate broker; and a syndicate headed by Harry Sylk, a 51-year-old magnate of the Sun Ray Drugstore chain. McShain and McCloskey each submitted an offer, but no agreement was reached.

Sylk organized his group on August 6 with Greenfield and 14 other investors. They offered to purchase the team for $2.5 million. Between $1.5 and $1.7 million would be used to pay off the debts with the remainder going to the Macks. They would invest an additional $2 million to rebuild the team, acquire players, hire a new general manager and add parking at the stadium. Roy Mack would be retained as executive vice president on a salary basis and Connie, Roy and Earle Mack each would be given the option to reinvest in the team and become stockholders. Roy Mack and John McShain attempted to organize a different group. The group would buy the stock owned by Connie and Earle Mack and reorganize the management.[4]

The financial condition of the Macks worsened. A quarterly payment of $50,000 for the stadium was owed, along with other debts— unpaid federal admissions tax, bills on uniforms, long-overdue hotel bills and a large note for advances made by Sportservice. Roy Mack tried unsuccessfully to borrow $750,000, and Mayor Clark's "Save-the-A's" appeal failed. The mayor stated "the economic situation made it almost impossible to keep the club here." Johnson and his attorney, Edward L. Vollers, met with the Roy and Earle to try to persuade them why they should sell the team to him, but neither brother was anxious to sell.[5]

Opposition to Johnson arose from some American League owners. Detroit owner Walter "Spike" Briggs Jr. said he was opposed to the transfer of the Athletics to Kansas City, primarily because of Johnson's relationship with the Yankees. He also felt Johnson's ownership of Yankee Stadium reflected a conflict of interest. Washington owner Clark Griffith also questioned the landlord relationship and felt the shift of the team would affect the Senators' schedule. Teams in the eastern part of the league (Washington, New York, Boston and Philadelphia) played more games against each other than against teams in the western part of the league. (Chicago, Cleveland, Detroit and Baltimore). Griffith did not want the Orioles shifted to the eastern part of the league to make room for Kansas City in the west, as that might result in the Senators and Orioles playing games at home at the same time.

American League rules required a three-fourths majority approval for any change of ownership or to move a franchise. Briggs and Griffith would oppose the transfer so Johnson needed the approval of the other six teams. Johnson knew he had the support of the Yankees, Orioles president Clarence Miles, White Sox general manager Frank Lane and White Sox co-owner Chuck Comiskey. American League president Will Harridge supported Johnson because he felt the Phillies were the dominant team in Philadelphia and the Athletics would never attract sufficient support. In his opinion relocation was the only solution.

Harridge called the first of what would eventually be four meetings to decide the fate of the Athletics on September 28 at the Commodore Hotel in New York City. The meeting lasted part of the morning, all of the afternoon and extended into the evening. They listened to a plea by Los Angeles officials before the Kansas City delegation made its presentation. Several owners wanted the Athletics to move to the West Coast. Tommy Richardson, president of the class AA Eastern League and a member of the Athletics board of directors since 1951 attended the meeting. He represented a group that offered to match Johnson's bid and keep the A's in Philadelphia at least through the 1955 season. "But then if the operation does not prove satisfactory, we would be willing to move the franchise to whatever city would be acceptable to the rest of the American League," he said.[6]

Connie and Earle Mack reportedly wanted to sell to Johnson, but Roy wanted to keep the team. He felt he could get the organization back on its feet if was given additional time and was encouraged by Tommy Richardson's proposal. After discussing the matter for six hours, the American League owners gave Roy a two-week extension after Earle agreed to sell his stock to Roy for $450,000. Roy also had to buy his father's 302 shares for $604,000 ($2 a share) and demonstrate to the league the ability to defray approximately $310,000 in past-due debts.

The announcement stunned Johnson and the Kansas City delegation. They felt the two-week delay could result in other bidders. It would also delay the start of the stadium reconstruction. Engineers said it would require six months at the minimum to complete the work. The Kansas City delegation boasted of the city's enthusiasm and fan loyalty but it had not been enough to influence the American League owners. They sponsored a ticket drive before the next league meeting. The response exceeded all expectations as more than one million tickets were requested. There was no guarantee that those who sent in the ticket pledges would honor them, but organizers had no doubt that the Athletics would draw more than one million spectators if the team moved to Kansas City.

Roy Mack worked hard to raise the money required to save the franchise but it was difficult. John McShain had been rebuffed in his efforts to organize a group by Earle Mack and was no longer interested. There had been some offers by other groups or individuals but they hinged on an agreement by both brothers to drop out of the organization and Roy wanted to remain in some capacity.[7]

The second league meeting was held at the Blackstone Hotel in Chicago on October 12. Earle Mack was anxious to sell because the team owed approximately $1.9 million to creditors: $1.2 million for the mortgage on Connie Mack Stadium, $300,000 in current bills and $400,000 to Sportservice. Johnson felt confident the league would approve his bid because he would pay cash and was "willing to keep Roy Mack in the picture if that is what he wants" but with Detroit and Washington almost certain to oppose the sale and with Boston and Cleveland doubtful, the vote to approve the sale to Johnson was not guaranteed.[8]

Johnson hoped to meet with Roy Mack before the meeting but did not have the opportunity because Roy's train was delayed by floods and the meeting began three hours late. Roy met with Tommy Richardson and Washington vice president Calvin Griffith when he arrived. Roy Mack told the owners he failed to raise the money. The Kansas City delegation was not required to make a formal presentation because they had their opportunity at the first meeting; nine individuals or groups still appeared.

Dallas millionaire Dick Burnett headed a Dallas group that reportedly was ready to offer $5 million. They would pay $1 million as a down payment and the remainder in notes over a three-year period.[9]

Bill Veeck obtained an option for the territorial rights to Los Angeles from Phil Wrigley. Veeck organized a group that included hotel owner Conrad Hilton and industrialist Henry Crown, the largest stockholder in General Dynamics.

Veeck claimed to have the support of three owners, which in effect would give him an absolute veto since nobody else could obtain the franchise without the approval of six of the eight owners.[10]

Clint Murchison wanted to move the team to Los Angeles. He offered $3,375,000, the same amount as Johnson.[11]

Calvin Griffith claimed to represent a third Los Angeles group that wanted to buy the team.[12]

Jack Rensel, an advertising representative and a former front office employee with the Phillies, was organizing a group of 20 Philadelphia investors who each pledged $150,000 to keep the team in Philadelphia. The group offered to pay $2,500,000 for the team and assume the mortgage on Connie Mack Stadium.[13]

Tommy Richardson represented a second group of Philadelphia investors. He pledged his group would match Johnson's bid of $3,375,000 and keep the team in Philadelphia for another season. After that, unless conditions improved, he would move it to one of six cities: Toronto, Montreal, Los Angeles, San Francisco, Houston or Minneapolis–St. Paul. He was accompanied by Charles O. Finley, a Chicago insurance broker. Finley brought a certified check for $450,000. "He was the only one to bring a certified check to the meeting," Calvin Griffith recalled.[14]

Roy Mack and Finley entered the meeting room shortly after Richardson's presentation and said that the group had reorganized and Richardson was out. Mack and Finley joined efforts and Finley's $450,000 check would be used to buy out Earle. Veeck recalled that Finley offered to "permit innocent bystanders—like me—into his syndicate."[15]

C. Leo DeOrsey, a Washington lawyer, and Joe Tucci, a retired Washington plumbing contractor, wanted to purchase the team for $2,856,000 and keep the Athletics in Philadelphia. Roy Mack would be retained in an executive capacity.[16]

Minneapolis and St. Paul interests were invited to bid by some American League owners who questioned the ability of Kansas City to support a major league team. Louis Jacobs supported the Minneapolis group.[17]

Johnson and Vollers were summoned after a long wait. They presented their case, offered the total of ticket pledges as proof of Kansas City's sincerity, and assured the owners that the stadium could be built in time for the start of the 1955 baseball season.

Johnson, Murchison, Finley and Veeck emerged as the serious bidders. Finley had money but lacked support among owners such as Topping and Webb. Veeck had a similar problem even though Webb pledged his "unswerving support to the old hometown, Los Angeles." Veeck discovered he could not obtain additional votes and dropped out of the bidding rather than force the Macks to remain in an impossible situation in Philadelphia.

This left Johnson and Murchison as the remaining bidders. Murchison's bid, although matching Johnson's bid on paper, fell short in actual cash. He bid $1 million in cash with the remainder in notes. Baseball commissioner Ford Frick expressed misgivings about Murchison's connections with the Del Mar racetrack and asked for an investigation into his background. "Frick, it seemed to me, was just doing his supporter, Webb, a favor," wrote Veeck. "With the Macks sinking fast and the Yankees pushing for a vote, there wasn't a great deal of time to wait for a report to come in. Murchison saved them the trouble by withdrawing his offer."[18]

Chronology of A's move to Kansas City, 1954

July 12	Roy Mack says the A's positively will not be sold or transferred to another city.
August 3	Arnold Johnson says he wants to buy the A's and move them to Kansas City.
August 9	Two groups, headed by John McShain and Matthew McCloskey, seek to buy the team but no agreement is reached.
August 16	Harry Sylk forms a syndicate and offered $2.5 million for the team, allowing Macks to keep stock.
September 28	League owners meet in New York without decision.
October 8	Tommy Richardson pledges more than $3 million to purchase the team.
October 12	American League approves the sale to Johnson and relocation of the franchise to Kansas City.
October 15	Rensel's Philadelphia group publicly pledges sufficient funds to buy the team and keep it in Philadelphia.
October 25	Roy Mack balks at deal to sell the team to the Philadelphia group.
October 28	American League rejects sale to Philadelphia group.
October 29	Connie Mack says A's will go to Kansas City.
November 4	Arnold Johnson completes deal, subject to league approval.
November 8	American League owners approve Johnson's purchase and relocation of the team to Kansas City.

"Del (Webb) didn't have to worry too much about me, of course," wrote Veeck. "He did have to worry about offending Hilton and Crown. He also had to worry about the newspapers. In every city that has won a big league franchise, a single newspaperman has led the campaign. In Los Angeles it was Vincent X. Flaherty, who conducted the greatest one-man campaign over a period of years I have ever seen. Webb walked into the meeting still vowing to support Flaherty and as soon as the door was shut behind him, he got up and announced that Los Angeles wasn't ready for big league baseball. That left me sitting with my three votes, as I knew I was going to be. Here's where it gets funny. As soon as the franchise was voted to Kansas City, Webb dashed out of the conference room, rushed to a phone and called Flaherty in Los Angeles to assure him he had done his best to get the franchise for Los Angeles but that Clark Griffith, out of his old friendship to Connie Mack, had been hot for Kansas City. Old Uncle

Clark, said Mr. Webb to Mr. Flaherty, had been too strong for him. What made it so outrageous was that Griffith had led the battle against Kansas City.... This is the kind of thing that makes Webb so transparent. He cannot realize that a columnist like Flaherty has his own sources of information. Flaherty had known everything that had been going on in that presumably secret meeting, and he knew very well — and told Webb so — that it had been Del himself who had killed Los Angeles."[19]

The meeting recessed several times as different owners took Roy Mack into a private room and spoke to him. The owners pointed out the sale meant a considerable sum to him, his father and his brother and that it was futile to continue in Philadelphia without adequate funds due to decreasing attendance and increasing debts. The meeting lasted into the evening and Spike Briggs returned to Detroit. Roy finally yielded. Will Harridge accompanied Mack into the room and announced he agreed to sell the A's stock to Johnson with the proviso that he and his brother be given until 10 A.M. on October 18 to complete the sale. Roy explained he needed to talk to his wife and obtain her formal consent before notifying the league office of his final decision.

Harridge announced that by unanimous vote of the American League directors the transfer of the Philadelphia Athletics to Kansas City had been approved. The vote was actually 6–0, with no ballot cast by Philadelphia or Detroit. Mack's decision to sell changed the Philadelphia tally to yes and Spike Briggs had given his proxy to Harridge before he left. Even though Briggs stipulated this to be a negative vote, it was felt that under the circumstances the result might as well be announced as unanimous.

4

Last-Minute Maneuvering

Roy and Earle Mack had until Monday, October 18, to sell their stock to Johnson. Jack Rensel followed Roy from the meeting room after Harridge announced the sale. He contacted his group and they met with Roy when he returned to Philadelphia. They convinced him that he owed it to the city to make every possible effort to keep the team in the city, at least temporarily. The group, which had dropped from 20 members to eight, was organized on Friday October 15. Each man wrote a check for $150,000 to form the syndicate. They pledged to commit additional funds to operate the team and keep it in Philadelphia.[1]

Two other groups wanted to purchase the team and keep it in Philadelphia. Harry Sylk tried to organize a syndicate with Charles Finley. They felt they could raise $1.9 million. "I have enough financial backing to match Johnson's offer of $3,375,000," said Sylik. "Finley is awaiting word from two other associates who are ready with money. If he is able to get them we will be able to go into the A's office with a check for $2 million and talk business." Washington attorney C. Leo DeOrsey also wanted to purchase the team. He announced that he and Roy Mack had "some unfinished business dealing with a proposition to keep the Athletics in Philadelphia." Adding to the confusion was a report that Earle Mack might not sell his stock to Johnson. Earle previously had not indicated any problem with the sale to Johnson. Although the league dealt almost exclusively with Roy Mack, both brothers had to agree to the sale.[2]

The league had already approved the sale of the stock to Johnson and approved the transfer of the team to Kansas City. Johnson returned to Chicago and intended to remain there to wait for a call from Harridge on Monday. Rensel's group met with the two Mack brothers on Sunday, October 17th, the day before the deadline. Johnson and Vollers became concerned and flew to Philadelphia.

While Johnson and Vollers were en route to Philadelphia, Roy Mack

19

telephoned Harridge 18 hours before the deadline and told him he would sell to Rensel's syndicate. The last minute maneuver to save the team in Philadelphia apparently succeeded because both Roy and Earle agreed to sell to the group. "I have notified William Harridge, president of the American League, that we have agreed to sell to this fine group of civic-minded Philadelphia businessmen," said Roy Mack at a press conference. "I have requested league approval. Our lawyers are now meeting and are drafting the necessary legal documents. I am very, very happy to be able to keep the A's in Philadelphia. That has always been my goal."[3] Members of the group were Jack Rensel, advertising representative and former front office employee with the Phillies; Arthur Gallagher, executive at a trucking firm and former Olympic rower; Ted R. Haniff, investment broker; Barney Fischer, oil and automobile industrialist; Isadore Sley, president of the Racquet Garage Corporation; Morton Liebman, son of a Philadelphia department store magnate; Arthur Rosenberg, vice president of Food Fair Stores grocery store chain; John P. Crisconi, automobile dealer; and Roy Mack, son of Connie Mack and current part owner of the team.

Roy insisted on retaining both his stock and a leadership position. This caused some delay but an agreement was reached before the press conference was called. Rosenburg, speaking on behalf of the group, said they would invest $4 million in the team. They would match Johnson's offer to buy Connie Mack's 302 shares for $604,000. Earle would be paid $450,000 for his 163 shares, and Roy would receive $200,000 because he would re-invest $250,000 for a one-ninth share in the new ownership. He would be executive vice president of the team and receive an annual salary of $25,000. The group agreed to assume the $1.2 million mortgage held by Connecticut General Life Insurance Company and would pay other debts totaling $500,000. They planned to hire a new general manager and field manager.

Several reporters met the airplane when Johnson and Vollers arrived in Philadelphia. They informed Johnson that the syndicate obtained signed contracts from the Macks, the deal had been closed and all that remained was approval by the league. Johnson and Vollers still held hope as they headed for a hotel in downtown Philadelphia. The American League owners might not approve the purchase by the Philadelphia group. Johnson felt Roy might change his mind if he compared Johnson's proposal to that of the Philadelphia group, but Roy refused to speak with Johnson or Vollers on the telephone. They finally sent a carefully worded telegram to Roy F. McGillicuddy at 423 Fishers Road in Bryn Mawr, Pennsylvania. Johnson instructed the telegram company not to read the telegram over the phone because it had to be sent directly to the house.

4—Last-Minute Maneuvering

"Dear Roy," Johnson wrote. "Unbelievable that you would not talk to me or let me see you before you went off the deep end." Johnson stated there were certain changes in the situation he wanted to discuss with Roy. These changes would make it possible for Roy to have a stock interest in the team, a substantial sum of cash and a position in the organization not only for himself but also for his son, Connie Mack III. "Would appreciate courtesy of your calling me at Warwick in the morning. Suggest you do not sign until you get all the facts. Your future and your son's future are at stake."[4]

The telegram was sent at 12:08 on Monday morning. Roy and his wife read the telegram and compared the offers. "We had, I suppose, only the faintest hope that the telegram would have any effect," said Johnson, "But we had to do something.... After it was all over and we had the club, Roy mentioned to me that this telegram had turned the trick. It had stated exactly what I was prepared to do. He and his wife talked over the matter and they agreed that as far as their own interests were concerned, there were great advantages to my proposition as compared to the one which the Philadelphia group had made." A meeting was arranged between Johnson and the Mack interests in Huntington Valley. The Mack family found themselves in the middle of a battle between Johnson and the Philadelphia group, with the creditors closing in.[5]

The Philadelphia group hoped for quick approval by the league. After the papers were signed on October 25, an attorney for the group flew to Chicago to obtain Harridge's approval. Harridge wanted to inspect the agreement before he called a meeting. The Philadelphia group asked the Macks for an extension until the league gave its approval but Roy would not grant an extension. He switched his allegiance to Johnson although Earle still favored the Philadelphia group. Roy found himself legally bound to the deal made with the Philadelphia group, even though he felt the Philadelphia group's offer was inferior.

The American League held the third meeting at the Waldorf-Astoria Hotel in New York City on October 28 to vote on the Philadelphia group's offer. Johnson arrived at the meeting early and saw Connie Mack appear from the back seat of a limousine at the hotel's side entrance. His chauffeur assisted him to a room near the meeting room. Mack apparently wanted to keep the team in Philadelphia and the Philadelphia group hoped his presence would create sympathy for him and the Philadelphia group. Mack's chauffeur, Chuck Roberts, escorted him to the door of the meeting room, and then awaited his return. "I don't like what they've done to my boss," he told Johnson. "They made him come over here today.... They called our house eight times yesterday. They insisted that he make the trip.

He's real old, you know, and a trip like this won't do him any good. I don't think they were very fair in insisting that he do this." Mack made two appearances during the meeting. Then Roberts assisted him as left the hotel.[6]

The meeting lasted six hours. Roy no longer favored the sale even though he was still a member of the group. The league also discovered the syndicate did not have as much money as had been reported, although a spokesman assured the league more money was forthcoming. The votes were deadlocked at 4–4 when the votes were taken. The Philadelphia group was stunned and glared at the league directors when the decision was announced. The syndicates contract to purchase the team was voided when the league did not grant its approval and the Athletics were now back in the hands of the two brothers and their father. Harridge stated no further meetings were scheduled. "It seems," said one owner, "that the family can't make up its mind and until it does I'm not coming back to any meetings."[7]

5

Going to K.C.

"No matter what the Macks say or do, the answer will be Kansas City," Connie Mack said from his bed in his Germantown apartment on October 29, the day after the third meeting. Johnson returned to Philadelphia on October 30 to meet with Roy and Earle at the Warwick Hotel, a hotel owned by one of Johnson's corporations. Roy encouraged Earle to sell to Johnson. Earle held out until 2 A.M. before he signed a tentative agreement, subject to his father's approval. Johnson needed the consent of both brothers before he could bid for Connie Mack's stock.[1]

Four of the members of the Philadelphia group withdrew from the syndicate following their failed bid. The four remaining members, John P. Crisconi, Ted Haniff, Morton Liebman and Isadore Sley, formed a new group to make another bid. The stock might be worth more than Johnson would be willing to pay. If they prevented the transfer for a few weeks, it might make it impossible for Kansas City to build the stadium. Charles Finley also wanted to bid for Connie Mack's stock. He felt that if he could buy Mack's stock he could either become part of the Philadelphia syndicate or form his own.

Connie Mack had not eaten since the league meeting and was confined to his bed most of the time because he began falling with increasing frequency. Some reporters described him as "shattered." The Philadelphia group went to his apartment in Germantown on November 3 with checks that totaled $604,000, but Connie was too ill to speak with them. Johnson also went to the apartment and said every day the sale was delayed made it more difficult to build the stadium in Kansas City. "Johnson played his trump card," wrote Art Morrow. "He threatened to withdraw the offer, and in a panic lest they be forced into bankruptcy, the Macks weakened."

"We will make a decision one way or the other at 12 o'clock noon (tomorrow)," Mrs. Mack told Johnson. "At that time we will decided whether to sell our stock to you or to the four businessmen here in Philadelphia."[2]

Johnson went to the apartment at 9 A.M. with Frank O. Schlipp, an attorney representing Connie Mack. That was a wise decision because there was a misunderstanding about the time and Mrs. Mack intended to meet with the groups at 10 o'clock. Charles Finley also arrived early. "I thought I'd be cute and show up 10 minutes before the scheduled time," he said. "But Johnson was even cuter. He showed up an hour before. I had a check just as big as Johnson's, but I never got the chance to wave it."[3]

Johnson and Schlipp saw Chuck Roberts in the lobby. "I remember you," Johnson said. "You're Connie Mack's chauffeur. I think we talked with you outside the meeting room in New York last week."

"That's right," Roberts answered. "That was the day they insisted my boss drive over there from here. I was afraid that day it wouldn't do him any good. I didn't like what those men did to him that day. I was afraid then that something like this would happen ... and you know what, I sorta hope you get it [the team]."

"I'm glad to hear you say that," Johnson answered. "It's been a long struggle. And I'm afraid the four men who will be here at noon may have the inside track." Johnson handed him a $50 bill and added: "You're a fine gentleman and to prove it, I want you and your family to have a nice, big dinner on me."

"Why don't you take your check to my boss right now," Roberts suggested. "I'll bet if you did that you might get his stock before those other men get here. There's another way up to his bedroom and I can show it to you, follow me."[4]

Johnson followed Roberts to the bedroom to meet with Connie and Mrs. Mack. Earle Mack phoned Isadore Sley. "Where are you fellows?" Earle asked. "I thought you'd be up here first thing this morning." Sley said he understood his group had until noon and they arranged to meet at 11:30 to drive to Mack's apartment together with their checks totaling $604,000. "No, no, no," Earle replied. "Mrs. Mack says the appointment's for 10 o'clock — and the first one here with the money gets Dad's stock. You better get your group together and get out here. Arnold Johnson and an attorney already are here. In fact they are with Connie and Mrs. Mack. If you want this stock you'd better not waste any time." Sley reached Samuel Goldberg, an attorney for the group who had the checks, and the two rushed to the apartment.[5]

Johnson and Schlipp told Connie and Mrs. Mack they came early because they wanted to impress upon them why they should accept his offer. It guaranteed financial security for Connie for the remainder of his life and Connie would be made the honorary chairman of the board of directors in the new organization. They repeated Johnson's threat to withdraw the offer if it was not accepted. Johnson reminded them that the American League had already approved his offer, while the league rejected the offer made by the Philadelphia group. His offer seemed to be the only safe way to avoid bankruptcy. Connecticut General Life Insurance Company, the company that held the mortgage on Connie Mack Stadium, informed the club lawyers that a representative would call later in the day to inquire into certain phases of the transaction. The Macks were up to date in amortization payments, but the insurance company wanted details with respects to other bills, particularly taxes. The indebtedness of the team was staggering. The team had not even paid for the uniforms worn by the players during the previous season.

"All right," Mrs. Mack finally told Johnson. "Give us the check for $604,000 and we'll sell. After all, you got here ahead of the other men and you've worked hard all through this thing. I guess you're really entitled to the stock." Mrs. Mack handled all the details for her husband and she handed the pen to Connie to sign the agreement. The transaction was completed and Johnson was now the sole owner of the team because he had already purchased an option to buy the stock held by Roy and Earle. The Macks sent a letter to Harridge. "This letter is being sent to you by Cornelius McGullicuddy, Earle T. McGullicuddy and Roy F. McGullicuddy to inform you we have made an agreement with Arnold M. Johnson to sell all of the stock of the Philadelphia Athletics," they wrote. "This agreement contemplates the transfer of the franchise to Kansas City. All are now united in our desires and we would appreciate that this be done at the earliest date."[6]

Johnson emerged from Mack's apartment and announced he had completed the deal. Liebman and Crisconi joined Sley and Goldberg and they waited in the lobby, but Johnson already purchased the stock by the time all four members of the syndicate arrived. Finley never had the opportunity to meet with the Macks. "Johnson offered too strong a proposition," said Mrs. Mack. "There was nothing else we could do. Mr. Johnson is a nice man and he won out. We said whoever got here first would be the buyer. Mr. Johnson was here at 9 o'clock; the Philadelphia group came at 10. The Philadelphia group dilly-dallied."[7]

Johnson wanted to meet with Vollers to exercise his option and purchase the stock held by Roy Mack. He also contacted Harridge. Harridge summoned the club owners to a meeting at the Commodore Hotel in New York on November 8.

Johnson needed the approval of six of eight owners and he knew Spike Briggs and Clark Griffith were still opposed. Briggs was upset by what he considered were the manipulations of the Yankees; Johnson saw little hope he would approve the transfer. Griffith wanted the league to finance the Athletics in Philadelphia until such time as a suitable site was found for the team. "As far as I am concerned," he stated, "the club is not going to Kansas City. I have been against it all along and I am not going to retreat now.... Mind you, I've got nothing against Kansas City. But I just think there are bigger towns with more population that would give our league better balance. Under no circumstances will I change my position."[8]

One owner, presumably Griffith, contacted *Minneapolis Star* sports editor Charles Johnson on Friday November 5 and asked if anyone in the Twin Cities could come up with $1.6 million down payment before the Monday meeting. If they raised the money, the owner was confident the league would approve a deal whereby the Athletics would remain in Philadelphia through the 1955 season and move to the Twin Cities in 1956. "See if your people can raise $1.5 million by Monday," the owner said. "I won't guarantee that your cause will get the franchise but I'm sure you'll get a hearing with a good chance the league as a whole will go for it." They raised $800,000 but felt they could have raised the whole amount if they had been given more time.[9]

Although Briggs and Griffith opposed the sale, Johnson assumed the Yankees, Orioles, Red Sox, and White Sox were on his side. He also had the vote of the Athletics, although technically Roy Mack still represented the club since Johnson had not yet been approved. This made Cleveland the crucial vote. Hank Greenberg, who represented the Indians, said Cleveland would be "open-minded."

Some owners felt Johnson's ownership of Yankee Stadium violated baseball regulations because Major League rule number 20 stated: *No club or stockholder of official of a Club shall, directly or indirectly, own stock or have any financial interest in any other Club in its league.* Johnson was the corporate owner of Yankee Stadium, the Kansas City Stadium, as well as the prospective owner of Connie Mack Stadium. Dan Topping attempted to explain Johnson's position regarding the Yankees. "We hold a long-term lease with him and it is on a flat rental basis. A percentage arrangement might cast a different light on the lease."

"I don't see anything wrong with Johnson retaining ownership of Yankee Stadium and leasing it to the Yankees," said Commissioner Ford Frick. "Of course he can have nothing to do with the club and the lease must be passed by the league and commissioner's office."[10]

Arnold Johnson asked the men who would be associated with him to accompany him to the meeting. These men would purchase stock and be on the corporate board of directors. They were Nathaniel Leverone, Chairman of Automatic Canteen Corporation; J. Patrick Lannan, principal

5—Going to K.C.

owner of the Chicago, Milwaukee, St. Paul and Pacific railroad and senior partner at Kneeland and Company, an investment firm; Joseph H. Briggs, President of H.M. Byllesby and Company investment firm; Earl Johnson, Arnold Johnson's brother; Ed Vollers, Johnson's attorney.[11]

The meeting convened on November 8, five weeks after the first meeting was held in the same hotel. Civic leaders from Kansas City made the trip to support Johnson. The meeting lasted throughout the morning while Johnson and his associates waited in a small room across the corridor. It recessed at noon and no decision had been reached even though Roy Mack urged that the sale to Johnson be approved and that the new owner should be permitted to move the team to Kansas City. Johnson left the group to try to find out what was happening. "I've got some bad news," he said when he returned. "I've just talked with Hank Greenberg of the Cleveland club and he has told me he definitely will vote against Kansas City. It looks as though Cleveland, Washington and Detroit will vote against us." Greenberg did not think Kansas City was large enough to support a major league team. He reportedly wanted to keep the team in Philadelphia until Los Angeles was ready to obtain the franchise. He may have had ulterior motives, as he was a close friend and former associate of Bill Veeck, who waited at the nearby Biltmore Hotel.[12]

Johnson and Vollers were called into the room at the start of the afternoon session. Johnson said he felt Kansas City could support the Athletics better than what anyone in the room expected. He told them city officials promised that he would not be held to the terms of the five-year lease unless the attendance reached a minimum of one million people for each of the first three years. "This as much as anything indicated tremendous confidence," Johnson said, "and I am confident we can draw at lease a million yearly." Since the visiting teams received approximately 29 cents per admission for traveling expenses, the other American League teams would be assured of much higher income in Kansas City.[13]

Harridge asked Johnson if he would be willing to sell Yankee Stadium if the league approved the purchase. Briggs was concerned that Topping and Webb held Johnson's note for $2.9 million in a debtor-creditor relationship that could reflect on the integrity of baseball competition. Briggs's objections would be eliminated if Johnson sold the stadium and removed any hint of possible collusion. Johnson asked for time to talk it over with his partners. He re-entered the meeting room a short time later and agreed to sell asking for three months to complete the deal. He felt that if he were given that much time he could succeed, although such a deal involved between $6 and $7 million and represented considerable problems.

He wanted to introduce the men who would be associated with him in Kansas City. "Gentlemen," he said, "I am quite proud of the men I have chosen as my associates in this deal. One of the great civic leaders in Chicago is Nathaniel Leverone. He is here with me. Pat Lannan, a director in many companies, is another. My brother Earl. Joseph Briggs, who is in the investment banking business in Chicago...."

"Just a minute, Mr. Johnson," broke in a voice from the side of the room. "Did you say one of your partners will be a man by the name of Briggs?"

Johnson smiled, "That's right, Joe Briggs."

"That's good enough for me," shouted Spike Briggs. "Anybody with the name of Briggs has to be all right. Mr. President, I move that the American League approve the purchase of the Athletics by Mr. Johnson and their transfer to Kansas City."

From another part of the room Chuck Comiskey of the White Sox jumped up and said: "I'll second that motion, Mr. President."[14]

Six clubs, including the Athletics with Roy Mack casting that vote, approved the transfer of the A's to Kansas City and their sale to Johnson, the majority required for approval. The two factors that helped win the approval were Johnson's promise to sell Yankee Stadium and the attendance guarantee made by city leaders. It was late in the afternoon when Earl Halligan, secretary to Harridge, called a press conference. "I have an announcement to make," he stated. "The American League has approved the transfer of the franchise to Kansas City by a three-quarters vote. Mr. Briggs made the motion and it was seconded by Mr. Comiskey. The league also has unanimously approved the sale of the stock to Mr. Johnson." (The approval of the sale to Johnson was conditional on his promise to sell Yankee Stadium in 90 days.)[15]

The other owners welcomed Johnson and told how, after Johnson left the room Chuck Comiskey and Clarence Miles made speeches advocating the transfer to Kansas City. Roy Mack's face was covered with smiles. He planned to spend a great deal of time assisting the new owner.

Phillies owner Bob Carpenter purchased Connie Mack Stadium for $1,675,000. The negotiations started before Johnson purchased the team. Johnson wanted to sell the stadium and attempted to get a binding commitment from Carpenter. Johnson reportedly warned Carpenter he would double the rent if Carpenter did not buy the stadium and would also require payment for the maintenance expenses previously covered by the A's. Carpenter did not want to buy the stadium but was given no alternative after the American League approved the transfer of the Athletics. He also realized the value of the Phillies would increase if they were the only major league franchise in the city.[16]

6

How to Buy a Ballclub for Peanuts

Arthur Mann wrote an article for the *Saturday Evening Post* in which he examined some of Arnold Johnson's previous financial transactions, including the purchase of Yankee Stadium, and concluded he was an individual who could arrange mutually profitable deals involving millions of dollars through the ingenious use of lease-backs, second mortgages, large cash loans and special stock issues without any individual investing much of his own money. "Only a handful of insiders were in a position to appreciate what a really remarkable deal (purchase of the A's) Johnson had brought off.... The fans haven't known, for instance, how little the ball club actually cost Johnson and the men behind him," he said. "It was publicized as a $3.5 million transaction, and Johnson did push a lot of money across the table — but large sums also were pushed in his direction. His net cash outlay in becoming a big league baseball owner was practically nothing.... In Chicago financial quarters the talk was that Johnson swung his Athletics deal without a dollar of fresh money appearing on the table."[1]

Mann stated Johnson paid $1,504,000 for the Mack stock ($604,000 to Connie Mack and $450,000 each to Roy and Earle Mack). Johnson also had to settle the $1,225,000 mortgage balance the A's still owed to Connecticut General Life Insurance Company, and $800,000 in other debts. This made the total obligation nearly $3.5 million. "That was one side of the picture," he said. "Here is the other. Connie Mack Stadium was conveyed to Bob Carpenter's Phillies for $1,675,000 — and the mortgage retired three days later. Johnson also got a reported $650,000 from Kansas City for Blues Stadium. As for the $800,000 in other debts, it was easy enough to get an extension on most of this, since it was owed to the Jacobs Brothers, who had a long-term concession lease. They would be happy enough to accept repayment out of future proceeds in Kansas City. That left only a few hundred thousand dollars to be accounted for, and Johnson picked up the bulk of this through sales of minority stock interests in the new baseball corporation. Roy Mack has said that he plowed back a sizable chunk of his $450,000 into stock, and then there were the Chicago investors."[2]

"[Mann] implied that Arnold Johnson had done some slick maneuvering in juggling of figures, properties, and accounts in order to acquire the Kansas City Athletics franchise," wrote Ernest Mehl. "With utter and complete abandon and disregard of facts he concluded that the Kansas City Athletics represented a net investment of roughly $400,000. How ridiculous this is! How can more than $1.5 million be overlooked in making computations...? The story left the impression with some that the Chicagoan merely had turned a slick promotional deal, that he expected to profit from the enthusiasm engendered in Kansas City, and then dispose of his new holdings for a profit.... All bills of every kind were paid in cash as soon as the amounts could be ascertained. No creditor was asked for an extension.... The facts are that the sale price [of the stadium] to Kansas City was within a few thousand dollars of Johnson's actual cost of the stadium, so that it was a return of Johnson's investment, not a gift and not a windfall. Mann, however, blithely disregarded the facts, deducted all the sale price of the stadium from Johnson's investment." Mehl said the new organization spent more than 500,000 in reorganization including more than $100,000 paid by Johnson for the huge scoreboard that was acquired from Braves Field in Boston. "From the foregoing," Mehl concluded, "it can be seen that considerably more than peanuts was involved in the purchase and transfer of the Athletics from Philadelphia to Kansas City."[3]

In retrospect Mann was fairly accurate, even though all the figures were not available at that time. Johnson paid approximately $100,000 to the American Association for the loss of the Kansas City franchise. This included $56,843.75 to reimburse the class A Western League for the loss of the Denver franchise. The Yankees waived reimbursement for the loss of the Kansas City territorial rights, but in return, Johnson agreed to reimburse the Western League because the Yankees moved their AAA team to Denver. Johnson did not repay the $400,000 loan to the Jacobs Brothers. Sportservice obtained the concession rights in Kansas City under the terms of the agreement signed with the Macks in 1950. Since the Macks arranged to repay the loan out of future proceeds, Johnson merely continued the arrangement. Johnson signed a five-year contract with Schlitz Brewery for the radio and television rights. The contract would pay the team $250,000 a year but instead of receiving the payment each year Johnson received a five-year advance payment of $1,050,000.⁴ As a result, Johnson paid the following:

To Connie Mack	$604,000.00	
To Roy F. Mack	$450,000.00	
To Earle T. Mack	$450,000.00⁵	
Total	$1,504,000.00	$1,504,000.00
		$1,504,000.00
Mortgage on Connie Mack Stadium	$1,231,969.35	
Territorial Rights to the American Association (and Western League)	$100,000.00	
Taxes and creditors ($861,458.28 less approximately $400,000 owed to Jacobs Brothers)	$461,458.28	
Total	$1,793,427.63	$1,793,427.63
		$3,297,427.63
Less proceeds from the sale of Connie Mack Stadium	$1,675,000.00	
Less five-year advance from sale of radio and television rights	$1,050,000.00	
	$2,725,000.00	$2,725,000.00
NET COST		$572,427.63

Johnson retained 52 percent of the stock and sold stock to finance the remainder of the purchase. The Kansas City Athletics were chartered as a Missouri Corporation with a $1 million capitalization. Application for the charter was filed in the Missouri secretary of state's office on November 10, 1954, with authorization granted on November 12. Nathaniel Leverone, J. Patrick Lannan, Joseph H. Briggs, Ed Vollers, Roy Mack and Earl Johnson joined Arnold Johnson on the board of directors, although Briggs and Vollers did not purchase stock. Parke Carroll, a Kansas City native and former sports editor, employee of the Yankees and general manager of the Kansas City Blues, became the eighth member of the board when he was appointed vice president and business manager of the A's. Johnson was named president of the board, Carroll vice president and business manager, Ed Vollers secretary and Earl Johnson treasurer. The team issued 10,000 shares of stock with a par value of $100 per share, capitalized as follows:

5,200 shares	Arnold Johnson	$520,000⁶
2,000 shares	Roy Mack	$200,000
1,500 shares	Nathaniel Leverone	$150,000
1,000 shares	Patrick Lannan	$100,000
300 shares	Earl Johnson	$30,000

Mann's assertion was essentially correct. The net cost of the team was approximately $570,000. With a total investment of $1 million by the five investors they acquired a team worth at least twice that amount. Charles Finley paid approximately $4 million for the team in 1960. That gave these investors a 400 percent return on their investment in just six years.

Johnson also received favorable concessions that virtually guaranteed profitable operations in Kansas City. The city guaranteed a minimum attendance of at least one million during the first three years in Kansas City and Mann estimated that would result in a net of $750,000 to the club. When concession income and road receipts were added the team would earn a profit of approximately $1 million during each of the first two or three years. The club received an additional benefit when the stadium rental was reduced to just $1,000 a year for the first two years, with an additional $24,000 paid if the attendance exceeded one million. (The team paid $25,000 each year to rent the stadium for both the 1955 and 1956 seasons because the attendance exceeded one million.) Without the reduced rates the normal rent would have been approximately $205,000 in 1955 and $155,000 in 1956. This enabled the A's to save nearly $360,000 in rent payments. The team paid $138,012 to rent the stadium in 1957, $135,635 in 1958, and $148,604 in 1959.[7]

"The American Baseball Club of Philadelphia has been dissolved and is no longer in existence," wrote Mehl. "Had it been possible to preserve the old corporation Johnson could have taken advantage of more than $300,000 in income tax carry-over. This he chose not to do, preferring to start a brand-new Missouri corporation to operate the Athletics in Kansas City." This was not as noble as Mehl believed. Johnson dissolved the old corporation because it was financially advantageous to form a new one. Bill Veeck discovered the value of depreciating the value of player contracts a few years earlier. "The conniving genius of Bill Veeck saw that there was nothing in the tax code to stop a new owner who took over a team, from reorganizing the team as a new business, and then assigning most of the purchase price of the team to the player contracts the team owns," wrote James Quirk in his book *Pay Dirt*. "Organizing as a new business was crucial, because if the owners did not reorganize, then, under the tax code, the new owners would be bound by the book values assigned to the player contracts by the previous owners, who had already expensed their acquisitions of players, so that the book value of contracts would be negligible. Veeck saw that players contracts acquired by the new organization could be treated as depreciable assets, which means that after reorganization and assigned a value to the player contracts acquired, the new team could now deduct from its income a (noncash) player contract depreciation cost, to reduce its income for tax purposes."[8]

The Treasury Department ruled that a new corporation could depreciate the player contracts at fair value and extend recapture of that valuation through five years. The A's owned 200 player contracts. The total cost of the Athletics was $2,079,271.28 (the amount paid to the Macks plus the amount to pay off the outstanding debts, less the sale of Connie Mack stadium). If $250,000 of that sum was allocated to the cost of the franchise approximately $1.8 million could be applied to the player contracts. The first $1.8 million in profits during the first five years would be *tax-free*. Since the tax on corporate earnings was 52 percent at that time this meant the team would save $936,000 in taxes compared to $300,000 Johnson would have received from the income tax carry-over.

ATHLETICS PROFITS 1952–1956

Income

Year	Home	Road	Exhibition	Radio-TV	Concession	Interest, Ads, Etc.
1952	648,420	257,355	2,769	168,595	235,696	224,068
1953	387,181	202,667	3,054	292,850	232,778	200,685
1954	345,634	187,936	8,436	300,035	191,117	167,502
1955	2,214,445	198,218	23,554	210,000*	242,589	112,689
1956	1,702,959	183,415	81,894	210,000*	200,233	118,899

Expenses

Year	Player Salaries	Player Bonuses	Player Deals	Officer Salaries	Farm Clubs	Taxes	Dividends	Other Expenses	Net Profit or Loss
1952	387,758	19,000	31,201	70,000	40,089	none	none	1,039,390	- 51,437
1953	392,097	none	(8,000)	70,000	31,474	none	none	936,083	- 102,461
1954	357,329	none	(22,500)	64,583	127,688	none	none	891,496	- 217,936
1955	375,457	10,000	419,100	64,063	(9,705)	none	none	2,105,765	+ 28,214
1956	345,257	none	189,500	67,500	none	none	none	1,892,867	+ 1,657

Notes

*The Athletics radio and television income of $210,000 in 1955 and 1956 was actually received in an advance payment of $1,005,000 in 1955 covering the 1955 through 1959 seasons. The income is shown as a yearly payment in the financial statements.

During a Congressional hearing in 1957 all 16 major league teams had to provide their income and expense figures for the 1952 through 1956 seasons. In 1955 the A's reported $2.2 million in home attendance revenue. Kansas City, Milwaukee and the New York Yankees were the only teams to exceed $2 million in home revenue for any season during this time period. Despite this large revenue the team reported net profits of just $28,214 in 1955 and $1,657 in 1956. This was due to "other expense" listed at $2.1 million in 1955 and $1.9 million in 1956. This other expense is significantly higher than any other team and was primarily caused by the player depreciation expenses. In reality the team earned approximately $1 million a year.

The only financial hardship Johnson encountered was the forced sale of Yankee Stadium. He was unable to sell within the 90-day limit and was given the extension to complete the transaction. He sold Yankee Stadium to John W. Cox, a business associate from Texas. The deal was announced while the Athletics were in spring training before the start of the 1955 season.

7

Arnold Johnson's Ultimate Plan

Some American League owners questioned the long-term ability of Kansas City to support major league baseball. They feared that once the novelty wore off, the attendance would drop and the city could not support the team. "In two years we made two shifts and in each case we moved out of good baseball towns where our clubs owned the ballparks, and turned them over to the National League," said Hank Greenberg. "We thus made the other league stronger in each instance. Any new franchises, for a year or two or three, will draw well. This is the near-sighted attitude. If we want immediate gains, we could be shifting teams each year.... We must take the long view in regard to attendance, and attendance is based on population. In regard to Kansas City I sincerely believe it will outdraw Philadelphia three to one next year and also the following year. But for how long? I voted against Kansas City for only one reason: it simply doesn't have enough people. When you have areas holding 3,000,000 to 5,000,000 people it is wiser to take your product where the market potential is the greatest."[1]

Why did Johnson move the A's to Kansas City when there were larger cities without major league baseball? Johnson's motives are apparent when compared to the other options available.

Option One: Keep the Franchise in Philadelphia

Some owners wanted Johnson to operate the team in Philadelphia for at least one additional year and then, if the situation did not improve, he could move the team to another city. The Athletics made modest profits in the 1940s, but lost $51,437 in 1952, $102,461 in 1953, and $217,936 in 1954. Fans were disgruntled and it was unlikely attendance would improve.

Continued operation in Philadelphia would mean substantial financial losses for the foreseeable future. Johnson's financial resources were not sufficient to support these losses. He formed a new corporation to take advantage of the substantial tax benefits after he purchased the team but "there is one catch to the write-offs," said Bill Veeck. "You have to make those profits before they become tax-free. If you make no profits you save absolutely nothing."[2]

Johnson acquired Connie Mack Stadium when he purchased the team. He wanted to sell the stadium to the Phillies for approximately $1.7 million. The mortgage had been reduced to $1,225,000 and this would give Johnson a $425,000 profit. Phillies owner Bob Carpenter was not eager to buy it. The Phillies had a favorable lease and were content to rent the stadium as long as the A's played in Philadelphia. The only way to force the sale of the stadium would be to relocate the A's. After Johnson moved the team he sold the stadium to the Phillies for $1,675,000.

Option Two: Move the Franchise to Los Angeles

Before a team could relocate in Los Angeles, the nation's third largest city, territorial rights had to be purchased from Phil Wrigley, who owned the class AAA Los Angeles Angels and 20,500-seat Wrigley Field in Los Angeles. Wrigley wanted to protect his investment and asked $3 million for the territorial rights ($2 million for Wrigley Field and $1 million for the franchise). He eventually sold the rights to the Dodgers for an estimated $2.5 million in 1957. Although it was less than he wanted, Wrigley also acquired Brooklyn's profitable Fort Worth franchise and ballpark in the Texas League as part of the transaction.[3]

Wrigley Field was too small for major league baseball and was located in a deteriorating neighborhood in Los Angeles. A $4.5 million bond issue to erect a new Los Angeles stadium failed to pass in 1954, just a few months before Johnson purchased the Athletics. If a team moved to Los Angeles it would be necessary to use Wrigley Field (or another site) for an indefinite period of time without any guarantee that a bond issue would pass. It would take at least two years to construct a new stadium once a bond issue passed.

In addition to territorial rights and stadium problems, a large indemnity would be paid to the Pacific Coast League, as a major league team in Los Angeles would affect both the Los Angeles and Hollywood franchises. (The Dodgers paid $450,000 to the Pacific Coast League when they moved to Los Angeles in 1957.) It would have cost Johnson approximately $3.5 million to move the Athletics to Los Angeles in 1954 ($3 million for the territorial rights and stadium and $450,000 for the indemnity), the team would not be profitable until it moved into a new stadium, and he would be forced to purchase a stadium that would become worthless after a new stadium was completed. Johnson did not have the financial resources he needed to move the team to Los Angeles.

There were also problems with transportation and scheduling. Both the American and National leagues gave visiting team approximately 29 cents per admission (30 cents for grandstand seats and 20 cents for bleacher seats) for travel expenses. The figure was not adequate to cover expenses but this was not a problem as long as the teams were all located in the East Coast and upper Midwest regions. Transportation costs would be substantially higher if visiting teams traveled to Los Angeles. Nearly half of all travel by baseball teams was by air by 1954, but commercial air travel was expensive, only a limited number of flights were offered to Los Angeles and virtually none of these flights were offered following night games.

"Los Angeles and San Francisco ... would have to come in together, because of schedule and travel expense considerations," said Dan Topping. The most likely American League team to move to San Francisco was Washington, but Clark Griffith stated, "They'll never move the Senators out of Washington as long as I'm alive." Griffith was 80 years old and in failing health. (He died in the fall of 1955.) Control of the Senators team would pass to his adopted son, Calvin, and his daughter Thelma Haynes when he died. Many observers predicted Calvin he would be eager to move the team to a new location once he obtained control.[4]

Option Three: Move the Franchise to Another City

American League officials felt Houston, Toronto, Montreal, Minneapolis–St. Paul, Los Angeles and San Francisco offered greater potential than Kansas City, but none of these cities had a suitable major league stadium and only Minneapolis had plans to build one. Minneapolis began constructing a new stadium in 1955. Johnson did not consider moving the Athletics to any of these cities because none of them had a suitable stadium or offered financial benefits similar to the ones Johnson obtained from Kansas City.

Option Four: Move the Franchise to Kansas City

Kansas City was the logical choice because Johnson owned Blues Stadium, the city offered financial incentives and Yankee owners Dan Topping and Del Webb benefited if the A's moved to Kansas City.

"It is ... doubtful that Johnson would be there (in Kansas City) except for personal business considerations," stated Arthur Mann. "His motive boiled down to this: Johnson's business dealing with the Yankees' Topping and Webb had left him owning Blues Stadium in Kansas City. It wasn't too much of an asset, with just American Association ball being played there.... He [expected] the city to pay him a good price for the ballpark, and then enlarge and revamp it for him." Johnson could recapture his $650,000 investment by purchasing the Athletics and moving it to Kansas City if the city agreed to purchase the stadium and enlarge it into a major league ballpark.[5]

Kansas City offered attendance guarantees and monetary benefits. "For Arnold Johnson there were all sorts of favorable conditions—if he could get the franchise to Kansas City," wrote Mann. "Local leaders such as Ernie Mehl, sports editor of the *Kansas City Star* had assured Johnson he could write his own ticket if he brought a big league team to Kansas City. Minimum attendance of 1,000,000 would be assured. That sort of home attendance would return a net profit of $750,000 to the club. Adding items like radio rights, concession profits and road receipts, Johnson could see a $1 million profit easily in each of his first two or three years."[6]

Johnson signed a favorable lease with minimal rent to use Municipal Stadium during the first two seasons. The lease contained an attendance clause that allowed the Athletics to terminate the lease on March 31, 1958 if paid admissions during the first three years failed to reach a total of three million. This was the only lease in the major league with an attendance clause.

Topping and Webb also benefited by the move to Kansas City. The Yankees owned the territorial rights to Kansas City because they owned the Kansas City Blues. The team was no longer profitable and it was unlikely the Yankees would remain in Kansas City much longer. After the A's moved to Kansas City the Yankees sold the franchise to Denver interests for $78,000. Although the Yankees did not require Johnson to pay for the loss of the Kansas City territorial rights, he agreed to pay $56,843.75 to the class A Western League for the loss of the Denver franchise. By endorsing the move to Kansas City, the Yankees sold an unprofitable minor league team and Johnson paid the indemnity to the Western League.[7]

They also benefited from the sale and reconstruction of Blues Stadium. Kansas City had to reconstruct Blues Stadium in just four months. Johnson wanted to choose a construction company and convinced the city the best one was the Webb Company. They also received $100,000 when the mortgage they held on the stadium was liquidated.

What was Johnson's ultimate plan? First, Johnson moved the team to

Kansas City because it guaranteed large short-term profits. He made money in all his business transactions and he may have been one of the first owners to recognize the significant profits available in short-term ownership. Prior to Johnson's acquisition of the Athletics the majority of the owners were people like the Macks who owned their teams for many years. A trend of short-term ownership emerged in the 1960s as owners purchased a team, depreciated the value of the players and then sold the team for a profit. This emerged because Veeck discovered an idea a few years earlier that "completely changed the economics of team ownership, not just in baseball but in all team sports," wrote James Quick in his book *Pay Dirt*. "The boom in franchise prices, league expansions, and the creation of rival leagues in team sports in the post–World War II period are all beholden to Veeck's idea of converting team ownership into a tax shelter. An average playing career in baseball is around five years, so a reasonable length of time to depreciate the player's contracts would be five years. At the end of five years, the player contracts would be completely written off, and now the team would find itself subject to taxes on its entire income, of course. But at the end of five years, the team can be sold to someone else, who then proceeds to do the same thing and writes off most of his or her purchase price over five years. If each succeeding owner sells out when the tax advantages are exhausted, there is no end to the tax sheltering associated with the franchise." Veeck described these owners as "carpetbaggers." Johnson may have been one of the first carpetbaggers. He moved the team to Kansas City to receive the short-term profits and then intended to sell the team to the highest bidder.[8]

Veeck predicted Johnson would operate the team in Kansas City for a few seasons and then move to Los Angeles. "I have always been sure that Webb's primary interest in Kansas City, even above the sale of the park and the construction work, was in getting control of a franchise which he could eventually move to Los Angeles himself," he wrote. "There's no way of proving it, of course, but it's one of those things your nerve ends tell you has to be true because it's the logical explanation.... When I say there's no way to prove it, I'm leaning over backward. I did read later that he told Connie Hilton the Kansas City franchise was going to be moved to Los Angeles after a couple of years, but I'd hate to cite that as any kind of proof. It has to be true, though, because there was no other possible explanation for moving a team into Kansas City. By moving to Kansas City after having already moved to Baltimore, the American League had, to all intents and purposes, taken two relatively small, constricted cities and invited the National League into the two booming western cities, Los Angeles and San Francisco—*unless the Kansas City franchise jumped again in a hurry.*"[9]

Evidence supports Veeck's theory. The unfavorable conditions that made it impossible to move to Los Angeles in 1954 were rapidly changing. Johnson could move the Athletics to Kansas City, recapture his investment in the stadium and enjoy large profits for the first few seasons that would provide the capital needed to finance a move to the West Coast. After the novelty wore off, the team would be ready to relocate, transportation would no longer be a major problem, and a new stadium would be available in Los Angeles. The attendance clause enabled Johnson to cancel the lease if Kansas City did not have a total of three million admissions during the first three seasons. Chicago (Cubs), Cincinnati, Philadelphia (Athletics and Phillies), Pittsburgh, Baltimore and Washington all failed to sell three million tickets during the three-year span prior to 1955 and it seemed unlikely Kansas City would reach this mark.

The first public indication Johnson might move the team again came in 1957. City Councilman Charles C. Shafer wanted to add a 5 percent license fee on the gross of professional sporting events, bringing in an additional $125,000 a year from Athletics' games and other athletic events. Johnson objected and said the Athletics would either have to stop their efforts to strengthen the team or move the franchise to another city. "[The] lack of cooperation by public officials could be the only apparent reason for the possible transfer of the Athletics to another city," he said. This threat was eliminated when the city council failed to pass the ordinance. Johnson became one of the first owners to threaten to move a team to coerce the city to provide financial benefits, something that became common practice in later years.[10]

By the end of the 1957 season rumors circulated that either the Athletics or Washington Senators would move to Los Angeles. The American League wanted to beat the National League into Los Angeles because the New York Giants already announced they would move to San Francisco. Despite these rumors it would have been virtually impossible for American League owners to approve a bid to move the Athletics. The A's sold over one million tickets in each of the team's first three years. They sold approximately 3,590,000 tickets, well above the required three million required to maintain the lease. Even if Johnson had been able to cancel the lease and tried to move to Los Angeles, it was unlikely he could have done so because the Dodgers purchased the territorial rights on February 21, 1957. Walter O'Malley eventually moved the Dodgers to Los Angeles on October 18, 1957.

The stadium lease in Kansas City expired following the 1959 season. Johnson wanted a two-year extension, claiming he did not want to be saddled with a long-term lease if conditions changed that made it unprofitable

7—Arnold Johnson's Ultimate Plan

to operate the team in the future. A four-year lease was signed on January 8, 1960, that contained a clause specifying it could not be cancelled before two years passed, and then a year's notice was required. The city felt this guaranteed the team would remain in Kansas City at least three years. The new lease also contained a new attendance clause, inserted at Johnson's request, stating the lease could be cancelled if total ticket sales failed to reach 850,000 in any season. This satisfied Johnson's desire not to be saddled with a long-term lease if attendance dropped to the point where the team became unprofitable. The city did not consider this a problem because the team sold over one million tickets in each of the previous five seasons.

It was not in Arnold Johnson's best financial interests to operate the team in Kansas City over the long term. After a few seasons in Kansas City he could sell the team or move the A's to Los Angeles, possibly in conjunction with the Senators moving to San Francisco. The Dodgers and Giants ended the speculation when they moved to the West Coast after the 1957 season. Johnson's short-term lease and the inclusion of the attendance clause in 1959 gave him the flexibility to either move the team to whatever city offered him the greatest financial benefits or sell the team to the highest bidder. The team was valuable if the lease did not bind the A's in Kansas City. Johnson's ultimate plan for the team was never revealed because he died on March 10, 1960.

8
The 90-Day Wonder

George Muehlebach, a local brewer who owned the Blues, built Muehlebach Field at a cost of $400,000 in 1923. It had a capacity of 16,000 in the single deck stadium and 1,500 bleacher seats that had a poor view and were seldom used. The right field wall was 450 feet from home plate with a 60-foot-high fence. The New York Yankees purchased the Blues franchise for $117,500 and the ballpark for $117,500 in 1937 and renamed the stadium Ruppert Stadium. A 12-foot-high fence was installed across the outfield, reducing the dimensions to 350 feet down the lines and 406 feet in center. The name of the stadium was changed to Blues Stadium in 1946.[1]

The city passed a $2 million bond issue to purchase and enlarge the stadium if Johnson moved the Athletics to Kansas City. The city council would not sell the stadium bonds unless Johnson purchased the Athletics and construction of the stadium would not begin until the purchase was finalized. The council authorized the sale of $2,775,000 in bonds after it appeared likely Johnson would obtain the Athletics, $2 million from the bonds approved in the August election and $775,000 from what remained from the $1.25 million stadium bonds approved in 1947.

The council planned to add a second deck over the existing stadium. It was estimated it would take six months to complete the stadium expansion. The lower deck would be extended from the point along the third base line where it presently ended all the way to the left field fence but the new second deck would not be built over these seats. The measurements down the left and right field lines would be cut from 350 feet to 312 feet. The cost of the additions would be $2,275,000 and would increase the capacity to 37,000. If the need for additional seats arose, bleachers could be added behind the outfield fence that would increase the capacity to 45,000.[2]

Sam Gould operated the parking lots outside the stadium. He opened

8—The 90-Day Wonder

Kansas City's Municipal Stadium as it looked in 1955. (National Baseball Hall of Fame Library, Cooperstown, New York.)

his first lot in 1950 and bought an additional lot at Twenty-fourth and Brooklyn during Ernest Mehl's campaign to bring major league baseball to Kansas City in 1953. These lots did not provide adequate parking. The city wanted to purchase three square blocks across the street south of the stadium to provide an additional 2,500 parking spaces. The school board owned the land and construction of R.T. Coles Vocational and Junior High School had been started on the site. Graham Watt, assistant city manager, estimated it would cost $1,005,000 to reimburse the Board of Education for the site and to terminate construction contracts, $92,000 to improve the land for parking, and $230,000 to purchase a new site for the school and other expenses. The city estimated the annual revenue from parking would produce $50,000 (estimating a profit of 30 cents on each car space for each game). This would service only about $700,000 of general obligation bonds, slightly more than half the estimated cost of the land. The city felt they could not afford to purchase this property. City officials felt there would still be parking spaces available in this area that could be used for the baseball games. *Sports Illustrated* reported there were 3,800 parking spaces in 1957.[3]

On November 18 the city council approved a five-year lease, with options to renew up to December 31, 1974. The city would receive $1,000 a year for the first two years. In the event ticket sales exceeded one million during these two seasons, the city would receive an additional $24,000. For the last three years, the city would receive $1,000 a year plus 5 percent of the gross receipts of paid admittances after deduction for taxes, shares payable to visiting baseball clubs. In addition, the city would receive 5 percent of the gross receipts, less sales taxes at the stadium (concessions of food and beverages); 20 percent of other concessions. If paid admissions exceeded one million, the team would pay an additional $24,000. The Kansas City Athletics, Inc., could terminate the lease on March 31, 1958, if the paid admittances (total ticket sales) totaled less than three million in the first three years. However, the corporation would have to notify the city in writing of its intention on or before November 15, 1957.

The team would be given the option to renew the lease under the same rental terms from January 1, 1960, through December 31, 1964, and had the option to extend the lease another five-year period, from January 1, 1965, through December 31, 1969, upon rental terms to be renegotiated on or before January 1, 1965. An option to extend the term for another five-year period, from January 1, 1970, through December 31, 1974, was also granted. Rental would again be renegotiated on or before January 1, 1970. The city estimated rental income from the Athletics would produce between $100,000 and $150,000 a year beginning in the third year of the lease.[4]

The bonds were sold on November 17 but it was discovered the bond funds to purchase and enlarge the stadium would not be available for nearly one month. Because construction needed to start as soon as possible, Les Milgram, John McDermott and William G. Austin organized a nonprofit organization named the Kansas City Stadium Association. The Stadium Association borrowed $900,000 from the Commerce Trust Company and temporarily bought the stadium for $650,000. They entered into contracts for the renovation using the preliminary plans and specifications that were submitted to the city council, paid for the construction costs, and acted as owners of record until the stadium was deeded to the city. The original intent was for the Association to construct the stadium until December 31, 1954. At that time or before, the city would receive the $2,775,000 from the sale of the bonds, pay off the bank loan and the Association would turn over the stadium to the city. The city council approved the plan at its November 18 meeting, and unanimously adopted a resolution expressing the city's intent to buy the stadium for $650,000 and spend $2,110,000 to add the second deck and 6,000 uncovered seats.[5]

Johnson wanted to use the Del E. Webb Construction Company of Phoenix, Arizona. "Johnson's deal with Kansas City ... was that the city would buy the minor league park from him (remember that Webb and Topping still held that $2,900,000 mortgage note on the two parks) and then pay for a complete reconstruction job," wrote Veeck. "Johnson was to award the contract to a construction company of his own choosing and, by sheer coincidence, the best possible construction company, as it later turned out, happened to be Del Webb's." Johnson told members of the Stadium Association that Webb's advice and active participation would be invaluable. Webb worked with the Winn-Senter Company of Kansas City and formed the Webb-Winn-Senter Corporation to build the stadium.[6]

When construction began engineers discovered the under piling was not strong enough to support the second deck and was barely strong enough to support the single deck of the original stadium. A substantial part of the old stadium would have to be torn down, the understructure rebuilt, the footings replaced and new pilings drilled and filled before the second deck could be added. All the steel from the old stadium was removed by January, and construction began on the new 35 feet high and five feet wide footings. More than 200 of these supports had to be poured and each one contained enough concrete to make basements for three homes.[7]

The added cost of the footings meant the bond issue was no longer sufficient and the 6,000 uncovered seats down the left field line would have to be eliminated, decreasing the seating capacity to 31,000. The city council proposed another $2.5 million bond issue to "make the stadium one of the finest in the major leagues and provide necessary street and parking improvements." Under their plans the second deck would be extended to the left field fence and additional bleacher seats would be added increasing the capacity to 40,000. Funds from the bond issue would also be used for additional meeting rooms and a room to display trophies won in the past by the Athletics. These features were in the original plans, but dropped due to a lack of funds.[8]

On January 21 City Manager L.P. Cookingham submitted an alternative plan to use $650,000 in general obligation bond funds to rehabilitate and enlarge the stadium to a seating capacity of 30,716 and provide traffic relief projects in the area. The city could use $400,000 from a $6 million bond issue approved in 1954 to purchase the riverfront stadium site because the city charter permitted the city to sell land when it was no longer needed for the purpose for which it was intended. Approximately $376,000 could be used to complete Municipal Stadium with 30,000 seats and $24,000 that could be used to improve parking. Money for traffic improvements, estimated at $250,000, would come from traffic and highway bond funds to widen Twenty-second Street between Paseo and Prospect Avenue and Woodland Avenue from Eighteenth to Twenty-seventh Street.[9]

Mayor William Kemp and the city council voted to use these funds and dropped the proposal for another bond issue. "The stadium with 30,000 seats and limited street improvements may be sufficient to meet demands the first year," the mayor stated. "If the facilities are not adequate, then I am sure the people will vote a bond issue to make them adequate next year." Johnson reluctantly agreed. He told Cookingham the 30,000-seat capacity would be sufficient during the first year, but felt the capacity would have to be increased for the second year.[10]

The city continued the relationship Kansas City Stadium Association past the original December 31 deadline. The city checked the bids and paid the money to the Stadium Association. The Association became a liaison between the city and the various companies engaged in the stadium construction. The Association acted as the owner of record of the stadium until it deeded it to the city prior to opening day.

Construction was hampered by one of the worst winters in Kansas City history. At the peak of construction there were nearly 400 men employed, including the subcontractors. They devised methods to beat the weather and the time. They borrowed the huge cylinder used to roll the infield tarpaulin as a shoot for sand and built a toboggan slide with an engine at the top to pull up the chairs. The playing field lay under a heavy blanket of snow and was frozen almost to the consistency of rock three weeks before the opening game. Huge machinery had left deep indentations. Workers used portable heaters to remove the ice and snow from the field.[11]

Johnson purchased the 80 x 40 foot scoreboard from Braves Field in Boston for an estimated $100,000 in February. The scoreboard cost $80,000 when it was erected in 1948. Braves owner Lou Perini wanted to take the scoreboard when the Braves moved to Milwaukee in 1953, but Milwaukee brewer Fred Miller insisted on a new scoreboard. Johnson paid $10,000 to have the board dismantled and transported to Kansas City. It took two weeks to remove 2,600 silver switches, 4,000 lamp sockets, file miles of wiring, and 2,000 feet of neon tubing. The board, and all 54,000 pounds of structural steel, was ready for shipment in March. The 40-foot base weighed 36,000 pounds and the board itself weighed an additional 10,000 pounds. Four trailer trucks were used to move the larger sections of the board.[12]

"Of course we forgot a few things," said city engineer Jim Neville. "On the day we finished, on the day before the 1955 baseball season was to start, we made an inventory. We checked this and that. The numbers on the backs of the seats ... we hadn't forgotten them. We were just about ready to call it a job, to sit back and relax. And then it occurred to someone ... we hadn't numbered the sections. That would have been a confusing situation for the opening game, no numbered sections. But we got it done and that frightened us so much we made another inspection."[13]

Even though the most hectic conditions existed, the stadium was rebuilt at the smallest per-seat cost of any major stadium in the country. Most stadiums at that time were constructed at a cost of $120 to $150 per seat, but the cost to rebuild Municipal Stadium was only $80 per seat. The total cost was $3,219,759. The deed to the property was transferred from the Kansas City Stadium Association to the city on the day before the first game. Kansas Citians called the stadium the "90 day wonder."[14]

9

1955: Big League Baseball Comes to K.C.

Some people felt Arnold Johnson should change the name Athletics because it would always be associated with Philadelphia. There were suggestions for new names, such as Cowboys. "We will keep the name," Johnson said. "I like the name, and besides it stands for something that has been great in baseball. It also stands for a man who started from the bottom and built an institution." The traditional white elephant emblem was modernized and the elephant now balanced on a large baseball with a baseball bat in his trunk.[1]

Johnson hired Parke Carroll as vice president and business manager on November 15. Carroll, who had been one of two candidates for the position, was signed to a three-year contract. Carroll hired Ray Kennedy as director of personnel, Bill MacPhail as director of public relations and Bob Wachter as director of stadium operations. Kennedy, who served as minor league director for Pittsburgh and Detroit, had been out of baseball for three seasons. Connie Mack III, the son of Roy Mack, was hired to help with promotions and sales. Dave Keefe, who served as traveling secretary in Philadelphia, accepted the same position in Kansas City.

Bernie Guest, the minor league director in Philadelphia, was hired for the same position in Kansas City and Hank Peters was hired as his assistant. Peters was the assistant minor league director for the St. Louis Browns from 1949 until the team moved to Baltimore in 1953. The A's minor leagues consisted of "100 nondescript players who had no chance of playing in the major leagues." Their immediate tasks were to hire scouts and prepare for the major league draft held in New York on November 22. The A's had virtually no information on players from other organizations but the A's spent $35,000 to purchase three players: Art Ceccarelli, a young left-handed pitcher who pitched in class AA Birmingham in 1954; Robert

9—1955: Big League Baseball Comes to K.C.

Spicer, a pitcher who pitched for class AAA Los Angeles; and Cloyd Boyer, a pitcher from the St. Louis organization.[2]

Guest resigned after only a few months to return to Philadelphia. Peters replaced Guest and began assembling what would become one of the best scouting staffs in baseball. Instead of hiring men with extensive scouting backgrounds, Peters preferred younger people who had managed a year or two in the lower minors because he felt they would be able to determine which players had the skills to move up in the Kansas City system. Peters's duties were expanded after his first year.[3]

Johnson met with Red Sox general manager Joe Cronin during the second league meeting and discussed Lou Boudreau's managerial abilities. "I've got a spot for you to manage," Cronin told Boudreau after the meeting. "It will be Kansas City if you want it, but we can't say anything about it now." Johnson called Boudreau after he purchased the A's. He assumed the unexpired portion of Boudreau's contract for the 1955 season and made a verbal agreement to rehire Boudreau for 1956. He was paid $25,000 a year.[4]

Boudreau selected Oscar Melillo and George Susce for his coaching staff. Melillo was a former major league second baseman with the St. Louis Browns and Boston Red Sox. He coached for the Browns in 1938, and for the Indians in 1939–40, 1942, 1945–48, and 1950. Boudreau wanted him to work with the infielders and coach third base. Susce was a former major league catcher with the Phillies, Detroit, Pittsburgh, St. Louis Browns and Indians. He coached in Cleveland from 1941 until 1949 and then moved with Boudreau to the Boston Red Sox where he coached from 1950 until 1954. He served as the Athletics' bullpen coach and let Boudreau know when the pitchers were ready to enter the game. Boudreau also hired Harry Craft, a former major league outfielder for Cincinnati. He managed six seasons in the Yankees minor league system, including the previous two seasons (1953–54) in Kansas City. He coached the outfielders and served as first base coach. Boudreau completed the staff on March 24, 1955, less than three weeks before the opener, by naming Burleigh Grimes pitching coach. Grimes was a former major-league pitcher for Pittsburgh, Brooklyn, New York Giants, Boston Braves, St Louis Cardinals, Chicago Cubs and New York Yankees. He managed Brooklyn in 1937 and 1938, and served as a scout.

More than $600,000 of tickets were sold by the middle of January. Blueprints were used to show customers where their seats would be located, but tickets could not be ordered until the seat locations were assured. The Athletics sold 4,836 season tickets by the start of the 1955 season. With 73 dates on the schedule, this meant 353,247 tickets had been sold, more than the entire attendance in Philadelphia in 1954.

The Athletics signed a contract with the Joseph Schlitz Brewing Company of Milwaukee to broadcast all of the games on radio and build a network of out-of-town stations. Schlitz paid $250,000 a year for five years, although the team actually received $210,000 a year because it took a five-year advance payment of $1,050,000. This represented the first venture for Schlitz in the area of sports broadcasting. Kansas City radio station KMBC (980) would originate the broadcasts and feed the accounts to a network of stations in Missouri, Kansas, Iowa, Oklahoma and Nebraska. Johnson did not televise any games in order to build a larger radio network. Schlitz hired Larry Ray and Merle Harmon as play-by-play announcers. Ray had broadcast the Kansas City Blues on radio for the previous six seasons. Harmon previously served as the play-by-play announcer for football and basketball games at the University of Kansas. He moved to Kansas City in 1954 and assisted Ray with the Blues' broadcasts during the 1954 season. Harmon would also be in charge of the station relations for the Schlitz Baseball Network.

"Our goals are the first division in three years and a pennant contender in five, over a million in attendance this year, and a million average the first three years—a million is about the break-even point for a baseball club," said Johnson. "The A's never had the capital in recent years for big-player purchases. From now on, they will. We are ready to spend $1 million in the next three years.... We can't expect much the first year or the second ... by the third year perhaps we will show some improvement, by the fifth year I can promise you that we will be stronger.... I am going to take every possible step I can to make sure that we have the finest team I can build. I am going to work this year to build up a strong farm club organization that will help us in providing good young players in the years ahead."[5]

Spring training began in West Palm Beach on March 1. All but two players were signed. Jim Finigan and "Spook" Jacobs felt their 1954 seasons warranted more money than they

Lou Boudreau (National Baseball Hall of Fame Library, Cooperstown, New York).

were offered in the initial contract offers. The Athletics made few personnel changes in the off-season and were a unanimous choice to finish in the cellar. Only a few players who were considered solid major league players and Jim Finigan and Arnold Portocarrero were the only players sought by other teams in trades. Several offers were made to Johnson but he felt none of the offers provided comparable talent in exchange. "In the history of the American League there hasn't been an outfit this impossible," wrote one sportswriter. "Boudreau needs just about everything. He has no pitching, no outfield, and a very questionable infield. The manager is trying to adopt an attitude of optimism but he isn't fooling anyone, not even himself."[6]

Boudreau knew about challenges. In 1942 the slick-fielding shortstop became the youngest manager in the history of major league baseball when the Cleveland Indians named him player-manager at the age of 24. The popular "boy-manager" guided the Indians to the World Series championship in 1948. He was voted the American League's Most Valuable Player that year as he batted .355 with a career high 18 home runs, scored 116 runs and drove in 106 runs.

He managed the Indians through the 1950 season. By that time he was no longer the starting shortstop but remained on the roster as a utility infielder. He was replaced as manager on November 10, 1950, and released as player 11 days later. He signed to play with the Boston Red Sox for the 1951 season and was named player-manager of the Red Sox in 1952. He played in just four games for the Red Sox in 1952 before he retired as a player. He managed the Red Sox through the 1954 season.

Boudreau was named manager of the Kansas City Athletics on November 17, 1954. He signed a new two-year contract during the 1956 season that began with the following season but was fired midway through the season with the team in last place. An Illinois native, Boudreau became a member of the Chicago Cubs radio broadcasting team in 1958. He teamed with Jack Brickhouse and became a fixture in the broadcasting booth, with the exception of a managerial stint with the Cubs in 1960. In 16 seasons as manager he won 1,162 games and lost 1,224.

Boudreau was named to baseball's Hall of Fame in 1970. He died on August 10, 2001.

LOU BOUDREAU'S MANAGERIAL RECORD

Year	Club	Won	Lost	Position
1942	Cleveland	75	79	4
1943	Cleveland	82	71	3
1944	Cleveland	72	82	5

Year	Club	Won	Lost	Position
1945	Cleveland	73	72	5
1946	Cleveland	68	86	6
1947	Cleveland	80	74	4
1948	Cleveland	97	58	1
1949	Cleveland	89	65	3
1950	Cleveland	92	62	4
1952	Boston	76	78	6
1953	Boston	84	69	4
1954	Boston	69	85	4
1955	Kansas City	63	91	6
1956	Kansas City	52	102	8
1957	Kansas City	36	67	8
1960	Chicago Cubs	54	83	8

Connie Mack, who was spending the winter in Fort Meyers, attended the Kansas City Athletics' first spring training game in 1955. The crowd, which included several hundred Kansas City fans that made a trip to Florida to watch the Athletics play their first game, greeted Mack with loud cheers. Unfortunately, Washington spoiled the party with a 12–1 win. The A's finished spring training in Florida and came north for a two-game exhibition series against the Phillies. The games with the Phillies were the traditional close for the exhibition season but were now a mere formality because the A's now belonged to Kansas City. The A's finished the series with a 10–2 victory over the Phillies in Wilmington, Delaware.

Johnson purchased three pitchers from the Yankees before the end of spring training: Ewell Blackwell, a 34-year old veteran who pitched for a number of seasons in Cincinnati, Tom Gorman and Lou Sleater. Gorman was used exclusively in relief and became one of the bright spots on the team. Blackwell pitched in the opening game but was released a few weeks later. Johnson spent more than $700,000 to purchase players during the 1955 season.

April 12 was the official start of major league baseball in Kansas City. The pressure to obtain tickets became for the opening game became intense and management attempted to resolve the problem by scheduling a second season opener the following day with a repetition of all the ceremonies. The team arrived at Kansas City Municipal Airport aboard a TWA Constellation charter flight and Boudreau introduced each player over the speakers as they stepped off the plane. The team rode into the city as part of a large parade with 20 flowered floats and 10 marching bands. Connie Mack rode near the head of the parade. Other members of the parade included governor Fred Hall and lieutenant governor James Blair Junior of Missouri, baseball commissioner Ford Frick, Detroit Tiger president

Walter Briggs, Yankees co-owner Del Webb, and mayors from surrounding cities. The players rode in private convertibles through the downtown section where an estimated crowd of 200,000 applauding and cheering fans lined the streets or threw confetti from office windows above the street. The children and adults wore A's baseball caps and held up friendly signs of welcome.

There was concern that the opener might be rained out, but the weather cleared up in the morning and the game between Kansas City and Detroit went on as scheduled, even though the outfield was soft and mud puddles were visible along the foul lines and behind home plate. Connie Mack occupied a front-row box. Ford Frick and Will Harridge attended the game and Missourian and former president Harry S Truman threw out the first ball. The Athletics provided the capacity crowd of 32,844 with a 6–2 victory. The score was tied 2–2 after five innings before the A's scored three runs in the sixth. Boudreau sent outfield Elmer Valo to hit for pitcher Alex Kellner with the bases loaded. Before drawing a walk Valo watched a wild pitch sail by that put the A's ahead 3–2. Boudreau went to the bench again and sent Don Bollweg to hit for leadoff hitter Vic Power. "Ned Garver threw me a slider," Bollweg recalled. "I hit the ball good and it went in the hole (between first and second). I was supposedly a pull hitter … he was pitching me away. The second baseman was playing toward second base." Bollweg's hit drove in two runs. Bill Wilson hit a home run over the left field fence in the eighth for the A's final run. Ewell Blackwell came out of the bullpen and survived the final three innings. The A's had a double play in each of these innings. [7]

The A's lost to Detroit in the second opening game and then failed to win a game on a road trip to Chicago and Detroit, finishing with a 16–0 loss to Detroit on April 17. Al Kaline hit three home runs, two of them in the sixth inning. The A's arrived back in Kansas City and the airport was filled with nearly 5,000 fans who turned out to welcome the players and encourage the team. The players were astonished. They heard of championship teams cheered at the airport but there was no report of any team welcomed so warmly after a road trip in which the team had not won a single game.

The home field advantage failed to help and the A's suffered an embarrassing 29–6 loss to the White Sox on Saturday afternoon, April 23. Sherman Lollar hit two home runs and three singles and became only the third player in baseball history to collect two hits in one inning twice in the same game. The Sox had seven home runs, one short of the record. A gale-like wind helped the Sox but the weather almost became their worst enemy. Rain began to fall in the fourth inning with Chicago holding a 14–5 lead.

1955 team — Front row: Lopez, DeMaestri, Slaughter, Melillo (coach), Boudreau (manager), Craft (coach), Susce (coach), Portocarrero, Power. Middle row: Finigan, Kellner, Gorman, Wilson, Zernial, Renna, Cloyd Boyer, Simpson, Astroth, Valo, Ewell (trainer). Back row: Bobby Shantz, Herbert, Harrington, Raschi, Ditmar, Littrell, Bill Shantz, Ceccarelli, Clete Boyer. (Photograph from the Kansas City Athletics.)

9—1955: Big League Baseball Comes to K.C.

The A's ended their first long home stand on May 4. Gorman pitched three innings and was the winning pitcher in a 6–5 victory over Baltimore that was highlighted by Gus Zernial's sixth home run. That evened the A's record at 9–9 and was the last time in the season they had a record of .500. The team headed to Cleveland to start a 19-day road trip that carried them to six cities. After one of the games Boudreau accused the Cleveland pitchers sitting in the right-center field bullpen of stealing the signs from the A's catcher. The army had staged a display of some of its tanks between the games of the doubleheader and a telescope had been part of the equipment. Boudreau claimed the pitchers in the bullpen borrowed the telescope to steal the signs and relay the information to the Indians batters. If the designated Cleveland pitcher in the bullpen sat with his legs crossed, that meant a fastball was to be thrown. If he sat with the legs uncrossed, that meant a curveball signal had been given. Boudreau said he was familiar with the tactics since he used a similar strategy when he managed the Indians. Similar charges were made against the A's at the end of the season. A New York writer wrote that Kansas City had stolen pitching signs from teams that visited Municipal Stadium. Relief pitchers in the center field bullpen used binoculars and relayed information to the batters by use of a towel. It was waved to indicate a fastball would be thrown. When it was laid over the low fence in front of the bullpen, that indicated a curve ball would be thrown. The writer claimed this was the primary reason why the Athletics, picked to finish in last place, achieved more success than anyone predicted. Boudreau denied the story and said anyone waving a towel in the bullpen in full view of the crowd and visiting players would have aroused everyone's suspicions.

The Athletics finished the road trip with a 5–12 record. The A's slumped to 17 games below .500 on June 23rd but

Vic Power (National Baseball Hall of Fame Library, Cooperstown, New York).

then the A's won 10 of their next 12 games and had a 34–42 record midway through the season on July 5. "Being where we were halfway into the season I think I had a meeting every other day just to keep them up to the attitude where they were professionals." Boudreau said. "At the time it did work. But then when they hear you so much, you run out of things to say." The A's lost their final three games before the All-Star break, paused for the break, then they dropped their next nine games—all at home.[8]

Kansas City celebrated Hall of Fame Night on July 20. Connie Mack returned to Kansas City along with some of his best players: Al Simmons, Mickey Cochrane, Jimmie Foxx, Frank "Home Run" Baker, Bing Miller, Jack Barry, Lefty Grove and Mule Haas. Six of these men had played on Mack's championship teams of 1929, 1930 and 1931. Two others had been members of the championship teams of 1911 and 1914. These players could not influence the 1955 version of the team. Vic Power led off the A's first with a single but that was their only hit of the game.

Baltimore's Vic Schallock made only one pitch in his role as a starting pitcher yet lost the game in an unusual development on August 3. Vic Power, the A's leadoff batter, tagged his one and only pitch for a single to left field. Schallock asked to be replaced because of pain in his shoulder. Harry Dorish replaced him and Kansas City scored three times before he was able to retire the side. Baltimore was unable to catch up and Schallock was charged with the 5–1 defeat.

Boudreau installed Power at first base in spring training. He led the league in hitting for the first several weeks of the season and finished the season with a .319 average, trailing only Al Kaline's .340. He had 19 home runs, drove in 76 runs and was a substitute on the American League All-Star team. Boudreau called him a "magician with his defensive ability." He liked to showboat, made many one-handed catches, and habitually covered first base late. "Vic never lacked confidence," said Joe Astroth. "He knew he could play ball and he knew he could hit the ball. He always had a favorite expression when he'd go up to hit in spring training. He would look out there with that big bat and the way he'd swing (while he waited for the pitched he held just his right hand on the bat while he waved it below his waist) and in his Spanish accent he would say: 'Hey peecher, I have a s'prise for you. I'm going to get a heet.'"[9]

Hector Lopez had been tried in all infield positions for Ottawa in 1954. "We'll give Lopez a chance at second base," Boudreau announced in spring training. "If he can make it there we will have Jim Finigan at third and either Joe DeMaestri or Jack Littrell at short." Lopez opened the season in Kansas City but was optioned to Columbus (AAA) to work on his fielding. Veteran Pete Suder moved to second base but was released a few weeks later and signed as a scout. Lopez was recalled and Boudreau made what he considered the most important move of the season shortly before the All-Star game in Milwaukee. He moved Lopez to third base and Jim Finigan to second. Lopez showed immediate improvement, both in the field and at the plate. He finished the season with 15 home runs, 68 runs batted in and a .290 batting average.[10]

Finigan was selected as the American League's starting third baseman in the All-Star game even though Boudreau had already moved him to second. He went hitless in three attempts at the plate in the game. He finished the season with a .255 batting average with nine home runs and had 68 runs batted in. The infield showed such improvement that by the end of the year Boudreau claimed he possessed one of the best infields in the league. Moving Lopez and Finigan "gave us a first-class infield," Boudreau boasted.[11]

Joe DeMaestri played shortstop until he was sidelined by an injury late in the season and was one of the most valuable players on the team. "We had two solid positions in the infield, shortstop and first," said Boudreau. "DeMaestri was a very adequate shortstop; he kept that infield together."

"Boudreau helped me more than anybody," said DeMaestri. "He taught me how to play shortstop. Even though I had the arm to play deep, he told me how to shorten up and cut off a lot of the ground balls and how to play the hitters. And that really helped.... He'd set up plays that were incredible that he'd pulled off when he was playing. He made it a little more fun. He put more into the game for us."[12]

DeMaestri was not known for his hitting, but finished with a respectable .249 average. He set a team record going 6-for-6 with six singles in an 11-inning game in Detroit on July 8. "You don't forget the kind of nights like that," he said. "The reason that night sticks in my mind so much is my first time up I remember hitting a line drive to right field. The ball was a good solid line drive. Al Kaline came running in and he stopped. He decided to play it on one hop. He could have caught it. After that, the five other were real complete singles. There wasn't any doubt." Despite his hitting, Detroit won the same 11–9 on Earl Torgeson's three-run home run.[13]

Joe Astroth and Wilmer Shantz shared the catching duties. Astroth caught 100 games but drove in only 23 runs with a .252 batting average. Shantz caught in 78 games but knocked in only 12 runs with his .258 average.

The team opened the season with four veteran outfielders: Gus Zernial, Elmer Valo, Bill Wilson and Bill Renna. Enos Slaughter and Harry

Simpson joined the team during the season. They were all good hitters with limited defensive abilities. "Zernial and Valo were out there without gloves," Boudreau said. "Slaughter no longer had the ability to play regularly in the outfield and was used primarily as a pinch hitter and neither Wilson nor Simpson could cover enough ground to adequately play center field. "We never cut off anything in the outfield," Boudreau said. "Singles became doubles, doubles became triples."[14]

Zernial, a 32-year-old left fielder, led the team with 30 home runs and 84 runs batted in. "I was the type of hitter that primarily I would be flatfooted," he recalled later. "And I could wait on a ball an awful long time. I remember I had very quick wrists and a quick bat. And a lot of comments were made by the catchers that they were waiting for the ball to hit the mitt, then all of a sudden I hit it." Kansas City fans loved the way he played the game. "There were times when this stalwart lofted the ball over the fence and there were times when he struck out," wrote Ernie Mehl, "but perhaps no one of the players tried any harder." [15]

Zernial felt that he would have had a better season if he had not been platooned in left field. "I really believe in my own mind that I lost a lot through Boudreau's managing," he said. "I hit 30 home runs, which was second in the league, and I didn't play. I only went to bat 400 times.... If I would've played, Mantle wouldn't have led the league that year. I could've hit 45–50 home runs. I went to Boudreau in Baltimore one day. I was driving in runs. I was hitting home runs. I was never a great outfielder. I was never going to win a Gold Glove award. He knew that. I knew that. Everybody knew that. But I was doing the job. And I went to Boudreau and I said, 'Lou, what do I have to do? What is it you want? What do you want from me as a ballplayer?' And one of the worst comments that could ever come from a human being, especially the intelligence of Lou Boudreau. He said, 'You're not colorful.' That's all he said. Boudreau — as a player-manager relationship, we never had a close relationship. He two-platooned. We had Valo, Bill Renna. Wilson was there. Slaughter, Simpson. So we had some pretty good ballplayers, but he two-platooned. But I was not one of his favorite ballplayers, and so I understood that."[16]

Boudreau disputed Zernial's claims. "Because of the kind of players we had, I felt compelled to do a lot of shuffling to get the best out of each of them, and earned — unfairly, I believe — a reputation for being a 'platoon manager,'" he wrote. "I know a lot of players resented my strategy and thought that I overmanaged sometimes. But what I did was play the percentages. I felt I knew my personnel better than anyone else and what I tried to do was match up my hitters against the other team's pitchers according to strengths and weaknesses. It wasn't simply a matter of left vs. right and vice versa. Gus Zernial, our best power hitter, was one who didn't hide his belief that he should play every day, against all pitching, and it bothered him when he didn't. Gus pointed out that he hit 30 home runs in 120 games and 413 at-bats, which averaged out to one homer every 13.7 trips to the plate. That same season Mickey Mantle led the American League with 37 homers in 517 at-bats, or one every 13.9 trips to the plate. Zernial's argument was that—at least theoretically—he could have hit as many homers as Mantle if I had let him play every day. My rebuttal was that Zernial did as well as he did because of the way I matched him against some pitchers and kept him away from certain others. I did the same with guys like Elmer Valo and Enos Slaughter, who were also getting up in years, and got the best out of them, too."[17]

Two of the best outfielders were acquired in separate transactions on May 11; the day major league teams cut their roster to the required 25-man player limit. The A's purchased Harry "Suitcase" Simpson from Cleveland. He was once regarded as one of the most promising players but he was not used regularly in Cleveland. Boudreau placed him in the cleanup spot in the batting order. He batted .301 for the A's with 52 runs batted in. He played both center and right fields.

The A's also acquired veteran outfielder Enos Slaughter from the Yankees. Although he could not play on a regular basis, he played with enthusiasm and fans always felt he gave it his best. His first hit for the A's was a dribbler in front of home plate that he beat out for a single. He came to bat for the last time as a pinch hitter in the closing game after he had been presented with a new Chrysler Imperial for being voted the team's most popular player. He sent a rolling grounder to the first baseman, who tossed the ball to the pitcher covering first. Slaughter raced down the line, the pitcher was knocked into right field and Slaughter ran to second base with smug look on his face as the large crowd screamed its approval. He finished the season with a .315 batting average.[18]

The A's finished fourth with a team batting average of .261, but ranked last in pitching with a 5.35 ERA. "We had to use a lot of pitchers that year," remembered Bobby Shantz. "We never got anybody out. There was always somebody on base. Most guys were run-of-the-mill guys. We didn't have any stars. We were all about even."[19]

Veteran southpaw Alex Kellner won the opening day game in Kansas City, pitching the first six innings. He picked up his second win with a five-hit shutout against the White Sox. He pitched a one-hitter against Baltimore on June 26, winning the game 1–0. The only hit was a ground single up the middle in the second inning by Hal Smith. He faced only 30 batters. "The only one they got went right through me," said Kellner. "Not between my legs but a little to the side. A good-fielding pitcher would have had it, but I was a little bit too slow.... That day I had exceptional stuff. I didn't throw but seven to 10 curves; the rest were fastballs and changeups. There was a feeling you get. The hitter comes up, and you just know he's not going to hit you.... You have it that day, and ain't nothing they can do. It's a wonderful feeling."[20]

Mickey Mantle hit one of the longest home runs in Yankee Stadium history off Kellner on June 21. Mantle drove one of his pitches 486 feet, clearing the 30-foot screen in dead center field and into the stands. It was the first home run hit to that part of Yankee Stadium. "I threw him a changeup," Kellner said. "He didn't hit it out of the ballpark like a changeup. It went by my head on a line shot. I turned around and it started climbing, climbing, climbing like a golf ball. It went straight into the bleachers. Joe Astroth was catching. He came out to the mound. The only thing he said—very serious—was, 'I'm glad we didn't throw him a fastball.' I laughed at that." Astroth had called for a fastball. Kellner finished the season with an 11–8 record and a 4.20 ERA.[21]

Art Ditmar, a 26-year-old right-hander, was not impressive in spring training but showed steady improvement and by the end of the season he was one of the leading pitchers on the staff. He finished with a 12–12 record and a 5.04 ERA. He pitched a two-hit shutout against the White Sox on May 20, winning the game 1–0.

Bobby Shantz made his first start against the White Sox on April 23 and failed to survive the second inning. This was the game the Sox won 29–6. In his second start a crowd of 33,471 sat spellbound as the lefthander held the Yankees to just three hits and won a 6–0 shutout. In between innings Shantz wrapped a hot water bottle next to his pitching arm on the theory that his arm would give him no trouble if it were kept warm. The Yankees threatened in the ninth inning with a base on balls and an infield hit, but the next batter for the Yankees hit into a double play. Shantz had three victories by the end of May, but he had shoulder pain throughout the season and he finished with a 5–10 record and a 4.54 ERA.[22]

Arnold Portocarrero finished with a 5–9 record and a 4.78 ERA. Vic Rashi, a veteran pitcher released by the St. Louis Cardinals and signed by the Athletics on April 28, started 18 games and finished with a 4–6 record and a 5.44 ERA. The Athletics purchased Ray Herbert from the Tigers on May 11. He was just 24 years old but had pitched in the major leagues since 1950. He appeared in 23 games with the A's, and had a 1–8 record and a 6.04 ERA before he injured his arm. Veteran Johnny Sain was successful in his first appearance with the A's in Boston. He entered the game with the bases loaded and nobody out. He had a 3–0 count on each of the next three batters and then retired each of them without any runs scored.

Tom Gorman was the only dependable member of the bullpen. He appeared in 57 games, had 18 saves and made an almost daily relief appearance. The bullpen was located behind the center field fence and he rode to the mound in a new convertible. By the end of the summer it was estimated that he had spent a fair share of his summer in the car and a fund was suggested to purchase it for him. "It came around the track and brought you close to the fans," Gorman said. "I remember them shouting at you and rooting you on. It really got the adrenaline going. Then it would let you out at the dugout and you'd walk to the mound. I guess sometimes if you had a lousy day, you'd wish it had kept going instead of dropping you off." Through one torrid stretch through mid–June and early July he pitched 20 2/3 scoreless innings in which he allowed only 11 hits and struck out 10 batters.[23]

"There have been times when I've suffered," said Boudreau near the end of the season. "Times when the heart has stopped momentarily. Times when it appeared as if we might have trouble winning another game. Now I check off the remaining dates of the season on my calendar in the office and I get a shock when I think this season is nearing an end. There isn't much left. And frankly I'll be sorry when it's over."[24]

The A's ended their home schedule with a weekend series against Chicago. More than 90,000 fans turned out and there would have been more if the stadium were larger. Kellner won his eleventh game on Friday night, beating Chicago 13–7 before 28,875 fans and aided by three innings of relief from Gorman. The victory enabled the A's to clinch sixth place. The A's lost 12–8 in 10 innings the next afternoon before 31,587 fans. Ditmar beat the Sox 8–1 on Sunday before 31,034 fans as Zernial hit his second grand slam home run in five days. The fans were invited on the field after the game to shake hands with the players and many had note pads for autographs and cameras to take pictures. Enos Slaughter was chosen as spokesman for the players. "Speaking for the players we want you to know that we will never forget your attitude toward us," he said. "If we were able to do better than many persons expected us to do, it is due to the faith and support of all you fans. We have enjoyed playing here because you have been behind us. All of us want to be back next season and we hope we can do better."[25]

The A's finished the season with six straight losses on the road. The A's suffered 4–0, 7–3, and 10–1 losses in Detroit then moved to Chicago where they lost 12–4, 4–0 and 5–0. Home plate umpire Bill Sommers ejected Valo in the fifth inning in the final game. "I don't know who was mad at him, and they hollered 'Applehead,'" Valo said. "Boudreau let me drive in from Kansas City to Chicago. Sommers knew that I drove in from Kansas City and I was going to drive home (to Pennsylvania), so he thought, 'Well, I'll get Valo so he can get an early start.' And I said to him, 'I want to tell you something, Bill. You know, dang-gone-well right — I said it worse than that — I didn't holler at you. I respect you, but thanks a lot for getting me an early start.' And I shook his hand and he said, 'Have a good winter.'"[26]

"It was a tough team to manage, a hard team," Boudreau later recalled. "There were no outstanding individuals that you could depend on or know they were going to be consistent for you." The A's floundered in seventh place for most of the first two months of the season, but took over sixth place on June 18 and remained there for the remainder of the season.[27]

The enthusiasm of the Kansas City fans inspired the team. The A's toppled their opening day attendance six times. The team drew 1,393,054 fans for the season, second highest in the league and just 100,000 less than league champion New York. Kansas City exceeded the all-time season records of Washington, Baltimore, Cincinnati, the Chicago White Sox, the Phillies and the Athletics. The city fulfilled the pledge it made at the league meetings to draw at least one million fans when attendance passed one million on August 12. The Kansas City A's attracted visitors from a wide area, including 26 states. The Athletics felt it was important to recognize visiting groups and were the first major league team to have the public address announcer acknowledge these groups between innings: "We welcome tonight a group of fans from Salina, from Omaha, from St. Joseph, from Pittsburg, Kansas...." There were often so many groups that he needed the time between every inning to finish reading the entire list.[28]

10
1956: Listless and Bad

"I have learned there is a great deal which goes into the make-up of a big league club. Most important of all, it seems to me, is organization," said Arnold Johnson, reflecting on his first year as owner. "Some clubs succeed and some fail because of the presence or lack of a good organization. The competency of the scouts, the public relations department, the efficiency of the farm club operation, are all very important. It's very easy to make mistakes and the mistakes can be very costly. Baseball is a perfection sport, as I see it. Details can't be overlooked. When we took over in Kansas City we had to accept the fact we had a team run down at the heels. It had been neglected because there had been no money available by which to strengthen it. There was no adequate personnel in the office and no organization. The equipment, the uniforms, these had been neglected. We had to start absolutely from scratch and it was obvious we would need at least a five-year program for rehabilitation. We not only had to acquire young players who might be developed but had to stabilize what we had as quickly as possible.

"I asked myself the question: How can I hope to accomplish something quickly when other owners of major league teams have been trying for years? It can be, I learned, an extremely frustrating business in which the best intentions often are not enough. The American league seemed to be split between those clubs which had and those which didn't have. Those which had had first the advantage of a strong organization. They depended very little on guesswork in a business where guesswork has to play some part. A scout, when he signs a youngster, can't be entirely sure. He is backing his own judgment. But then he is dealing with the human factor and it quite often is unreliable. So I felt I had to learn and the best way to do this was ask questions of those who had succeeded. That is why we chose the Detroit club as a model operation and why we made a thorough check of it. We wanted to learn what was best in the other clubs and copy from these.... We had nothing when we started and we still have very little in comparison with the majority of the clubs. But we may be said to have one great asset: we know we have a steep hill to climb and we can never afford to let down."[1]

The A's averaged 20,189 during the inaugural season with 23 games sold out. City manager L.P. Cookingham reminded city officials that the city promised the American League that they would build a stadium with a seating capacity of 35,000. The lack of time and funds necessitated the change in plans prior to the start of the season. Mayor Bartle referred the question to a newly appointed a baseball committee. They reported it would cost between $550,000 and $750,000 to enlarge the stadium and only $87,000 remained in the stadium bond fund account. Council members did not want to hold an election to authorize the sale of additional bonds at that time and felt the capacity could be increased when the need arose in the future. The council approved the following expenditures totaling $85,500 using the remainder of the available funds:[2]

Rebuild the field, including new drainage and new sod	$63,000
Raise certain box seats to improve visibility	$20,100
Plant trees and shrubs in the center and right field areas	$2,400

The Athletics agreed to pay for construction of a new underground sprinkler system in the rebuilt playing field.[3] Their main concern for the off-season renovation, however, involved doing something to help their pitchers: keeping the ball in the park. The A's wanted to move back, but a light tower and an equipment shed behind the fence would have to be moved. Although a respectable 330 feet down the line, the fence did not break out sharply and the distance to straight away left was comparatively short. Prevailing winds to left field that aided the home run hitters and resulting in 180 home runs hit in Kansas City. The A's decided to raise the height of the fence six feet from the left field foul pole to left center field instead of moving the fence, making the fence 20 feet high in that area compared to 14 feet high for the remainder of the fence.[4]

Lou Boudreau signed a new one-year contract on September 10, 1955. Johnson stated the club policy was to sign a manager for only one season ignoring Connie Mack's half century as field boss—but added that he was very satisfied with Boudreau as manager. He gave Boudreau credit for what had been accomplished in 1955 and said he was happy to have him back for the following season. Harry Craft, George Susce and Oscar Melillo returned as coaches, but Burleigh Grimes did not. He became a scout. William MacPhail resigned as director of public relations on October 31 to become director of sports at CBS and was replaced by Gordon H. Smith. Ray Kennedy resigned as director of player personnel one month later.

Johnson held several staff meetings at the conclusion of the 1955 season to determine how to improve the team. The sixth-place A's decided to retain the nucleus of the team. The Athletics would not be active in the trade market, but Johnson contacted other teams and tried to buy some of their players. During the winter meetings he asked Detroit owner Spike Briggs what he wanted for Al Kaline, the league's batting champion. "I can't sell Kaline," Briggs said. Johnson then offered a substantial amount of money. "Well, I still couldn't do it," Briggs answered.[5]

The A's purchased pitcher Lou Kretlow and catcher Joe Ginsberg from the Seattle (AAA) club for $90,000. Kretlow was named the outstanding pitcher in the Pacific Coast League. The A's purchased three players from the San Francisco Seals (AAA) of the Pacific Coast League: relief pitcher Bill Bradford, outfielder Dave Melton and infielder Mike Baxes. Kansas City also purchased two AAA Most Valuable Players: pitcher Jack Crimian, the MVP in the International League, and third baseman Rance Pless of the Minneapolis Millers, the MVP in the American Association. Pless led the league in hitting, with a .337, plus 26 home runs and 107 runs batted in. The Athletics hoped to select pitcher Jack McMahan at the winter meetings. When he was selected by Pittsburgh Kansas City selected pitcher Bill Herriage, who had a 15–7 record at Montgomery (A).

The Athletics spent a considerable sum of money to purchase these players. Without making a trade, Johnson hoped Crimian, Bradford, Herriage and Kretlow would improve the weak pitching staff, Pless and Baxes would contend for infield positions, Melton would fill the center field position and Ginsberg would solve the problem behind the plate. There was no guarantee that Johnson had strengthened the team by all the transactions, but Ernie Mehl commented, "Within a year's time (Johnson) had made what everyone agreed was remarkable progress." [6]

The A's obtained 33-year-old catcher Charley (Tim) Thompson from Brooklyn in exchange for outfielder Tom Saffell and pitcher Leroy Wheat on April 16. They purchased outfielder Johnny Groth from Washington on the same day. Thompson had appeared in just 10 major league games because the Dodgers had Hall-of-Fame catcher Roy Campanella behind the plate. Groth, a 29-year-old outfielder, started his major league career with Detroit in 1949.

The baseball world mourned the death of Connie Mack on February 8, 1956. He passed away in the home of his daughter, Mrs. Frank Cunningham, in Germantown, Pennsylvania. Mack was 93 years old and the honorary chairman of the Kansas City Athletics board of directors. He fractured his hip while getting out of bed on October 1, 1955, and was unable to walk.

Although saddened by the death of Mack, A's fans were optimistic as the team opened the 1956 season. Most of the players from 1955 were back and the team appeared to be better because of the new faces. The optimism quickly faded and the A's fell into seventh place and struggled with Washington to stay out of the cellar.

The Athletics had defensive problems in the infield as Boudreau tried to find a regular position for Hector Lopez. Lopez played at third most of the season, but also played some games at second and in the outfield. By the end of the season Boudreau felt that third was his best position. He finished with a .273 average with 18 home runs and 69 runs batted in.

Vic Power hit .309 with 14 home runs and 63 runs batted in and played well at first base. He had two five-hit games during the season. Power and Tim Thompson both had five hits in six trips to the plate in a 13–4 victory over Washington on June 13. Power and Lopez each had five hits in a 10–9, 14-inning loss to the Yankees on July 27; Power had five hits in seven trips to the plate while Lopez was five out of six in the contest. Power and teammate Harry Simpson were named to the American League All-Star team that played in Washington on July 10. Power entered the game in the sixth inning and played the remainder of the game the National League's 7–3 victory. Simpson appeared as a pinch hitter.

Second base was a problem spot throughout the season. Clete Boyer was not ready to assume a regular playing position, hitting just .217 in 67 games. Jim Finigan played in just 91 games. "Spook" Jacobs played at second before being traded to Pittsburgh for pitcher Jack McMahan and minor league infielder Curt Roberts on June 23. The A's acquired veteran first baseman Eddie Robinson and outfielder Lou Skizas from the Yankees on June 14 in exchange for pitcher Ed Burtschy and outfielder Bill Renna. Robinson played some games at first for Kansas City, allowing Power to play 47 games at second base. Robinson hit just .198 with the Athletics.

Joe DeMaestri was less effective at shortstop than he had been during the 1955 season. He slumped in the field although much of the blame could be attributed to the unsettled situation in rest of the infield. Thompson began the season behind the plate and batted .272 in 92 games. The A's traded Joe Ginsberg to Baltimore for catcher Hal Smith on August 17. The 25-year-old Smith assumed the starting role in Kansas City and batted .275 for the A's. The A's pitching staff improved after Smith arrived because of his ability to handle pitchers.

The Athletics continued to have defensive problems in the outfield.

The outfielders were slow and Boudreau even tried Lopez in the outfield to improve the speed. Gus Zernial hit 16 home runs but was injured much of the season and batted just .224. "The year was a disaster," Zernial said later. "(Boudreau) never played me at all. I don't know whether they made any attempts to trade me or what. I do know that Harry Craft was the coach. And I used to share with Harry. I'd say, 'Harry, what do I need to do? Help me. What does he want from me?' It became frustrating when I couldn't play when I thought I should be playing."[7]

Hector Lopez (from Jay Publications and the Kansas City Athletics).

Simpson played in the outfield and filled in at first base when Power was injured. He finished the season batting .293 and became the first Kansas City Athletic to hit a "Brooklyn Avenue" home run. His tape-measure blast on June 24 cleared the outer right field wall before it landed on the street. Larry Stahl was the only other Athletic to ever hit a home run onto Brooklyn Avenue, hitting his home run in 1965. Simpson's 21, however, home runs and 105 RBI in 1956 established him as one of the better sluggers in the league. He tailed off toward the end of the season, however, as the result of playing everyday took its toll.

Skizas, a 24-year-old outfielder, hit .316 with 11 home runs after being obtained from the Yankees. Skizas became known for his poor fielding, his unorthodox batting stance, and his elaborate routine before he entered the batter's box. He finished the routine by putting his hand in his hip pocket before approaching the plate. Enos Slaughter hit .278 in 91 games. He was sold to the Yankees on August 25. Veteran Elmer Valo appeared in just nine games before he was released on May 22.

Art Ditmar was the ace of the pitching staff. He led the A's pitchers with 12 victories but also led the league with 22 defeats. He set a Kansas City A's record with 14 complete games. Ditmar had a one-hitter, a 15–1 victory over the White Sox on April 21. Ed Burtschy was one of the team's

1956 team — Front row: Lopez, Finigan, Susce (coach), Craft (coach), Boudreau (manager), Melillo (coach), Skizas, Pilarcik, Shantz. Middle row: Ewell (trainer), Baxes, Boyer, Herriage, McMahan, Ginsberg, Crimian, Santiago, Slaughter, Thompson. Back row: Robinson, Zernial, DeMaestri, Kellner, Gorman, Simpson, Burnette, Ditmar, Groth, Kretlow, Power. (From the Kansas City Athletics.)

best pitchers in the first part of the season. He had a 3–1 record in 21 games with a 3.98 ERA before he was traded to the Yankees. Veteran Alex Kellner appeared in 40 games both in starting and relief roles. He had good control with a fine assortment of curveballs and finished with an 8–6 record and a 4.28 ERA. Tom Gorman also appeared in both starting and relief roles. He started the season slowly, but finished with a 9–10 record and a 3.84 ERA.

A sore arm plagued hurler Bobby Shantz, who finished with a 2–7 record and a 4.37 ERA. Tom Lasorda, who later achieved fame as manager of the Los Angeles Dodgers, was purchased from Brooklyn before the start of the season. The 28-year-old left-hander was a 0–4 with a 6.20 ERA. The A's purchased the 27-year-old knuckleball hurler Wally Burnette on July 11. He held Washington scoreless on only six hits in his first start for the A's on July 15, and defeated Boston 8–4 in his next start. He finished the season with a 6–8 record and 2.90 ERA. None of the pitchers purchased from minor league teams significantly helped the A's. Crimian and Kretlow both pitched over 100 innings but finished with ERAs over 5.00. Rookie Bill Herriage epitomized the A's mound woes. He had a 1–13 record (.071 winning percentage) in his only major league season.

The A's tried to improve the team through trades and almost made baseball history with a blockbuster mid-season trade. "Back in 1956 Paul Richards, then manager and general manager of the Baltimore Orioles, walked into the office of the late Parke Carroll, who was then the general manager of the A's," wrote Joe McGuff. "The Orioles and the A's had played a night game and the trading deadline was less than an hour away (on June 15). Richards said he wanted to make a deal. Carroll said he would listen to the offer, although he was scarcely prepared for what followed. Richards said he would trade the entire Baltimore club for the entire Kansas City club. Carroll was interested, but couldn't make a deal of that magnitude without approval of the A's owner, the late Arnold Johnson. Carroll tried to reach Johnson but failed and the deal fell through."

Although the A's struggled on the field, they rewarded manager Lou Boudreau with a new two-year contract on June 30. "This action reflects our confidence in our manager," said Johnson. The new two-year contract would start in 1957 and extend through the 1958 season and continue to pay him $25,000 a season.[8] Boudreau's new contract failed to affect the play of the A's on the field. The A's tumbled into the cellar after the All-Star game.

Yankees ace Whitey Ford equaled an American League record (since broken) on July 20 when he fanned six consecutive Kansas City batters to lead the Yankees to a 6–2 victory in Yankee Stadium. The streak began in the second inning when Ginsberg took a called third strike. DeMaestri, Boyer and McMahan struck out in the third inning. The first two batters in the fourth inning, Lopez and Pilarcik struck out before Slaughter was hit by a pitch to end the spree.

    The A's failed to rebound in the second half of the season and finished in last place with a 52–102 record. Despite the disappointing record, 1,105,154 fans attended the games in Kansas City. The A's fielded basically the same team in 1956 as they did the previous season because the minor league players purchased by the A's failed to help the team. The few minor trades made during the season did little good. The team was plagued with the same problems they had the previous season: they had decent hitting but were plagued by poor defensive play and poor pitching. Veteran players like Gus Zernial and Enos Slaughter were a year older and did not play as well as they did the previous season. *Sports Illustrated* stated the team was "listless and bad," and then analyzed the problem by concluding the Athletics are "not a team at present, but merely a collection of players."[9]

11
1957: Big Trades Bring New Faces

The A's retained Harry Craft but fired coaches Oscar Melillo and George Susce. Bob Swift and Spurgeon "Spud" Chandler took their places on the coaching staff. "Oscar Melillo and George Susce were nice guys and good friends of Boudreau's, but they were little help to him, to my way of thinking, in running a ball club," stated Bill Veeck. Swift was a former major league catcher who coached for the Tigers in 1953 and 1954 and managed at Albuquerque (A) in 1956. Chandler spent his entire major league pitching career for the Yankees. He joined the A's as a scout in 1956 and worked with the club's pitchers at the 1956 spring training camp in West Palm Beach. This convinced the A's to hire him as pitching coach in 1957. Former major league outfielder and minor league manager George Selkirk joined the Athletics on October 17 as supervisor of player personnel. Ed Edwards replaced Larry Ray as radio broadcaster. He broadcast games for the Cleveland Indians in 1954 and 1955.[1]

The A's purchased outfielder Bob Cerv on waivers from the Yankees at the conclusion of the 1956 season. The 30-year-old was fondly remembered in Kansas City for tape-measure home runs hit while a member of the Blues.

The A's made a major trade involving eight players on December 3, 1956. The A's traded pitchers Jack Crimian and Bill Harrington, first baseman Eddie Robinson and infielder Jim Finigan to Detroit in exchange for pitchers Ned Garver, Gene Host, Virgil Trucks and first baseman Wayne Belardi. Finigan was the only player that played regularly for the A's in 1956. Garver, a 32-year-old right-hander, won 20 games with the St. Louis Browns in 1951 on a team than won just 52 games during the entire season. He missed most of the 1956 season with arm problems but was considered the key man in the trade. Trucks, a 38-year-old right-hander, pitched two no-hitters for Detroit in 1952. He was projected to be a spot starter and relief pitcher for the A's. Host, a 24-year-old southpaw, was a promising rookie.

The A's completed a 13-player swap with the Yankees on February 18. The A's sent pitchers Bobby Shantz and Art Ditmar and four other players to New York for pitchers Mickey McDermott, Tom Morgan, Jack Urban and Rip Coleman, second baseman Milt Graff, shortstop Billy Hunter, and outfielder Irv Noren. "We have just made by far the most important deal since the Athletics were transferred to Kansas City," said Arnold Johnson. "(The trade) changes the entire complexion of the Athletics. We needed certain playing positions filled with talent who could do the job now. We wanted youth, ability and experience and believe we obtained it."[2]

Ditmar was the A's leading pitcher in 1956, but Shantz had been a disappointment in both 1955 and 1956. McDermott, a 28-year-old southpaw, pitched for Boudreau in Boston and won 18 games with the Red Sox in 1953. Morgan, winner of 41 games by the age of 26, and Coleman, a 27-year-old southpaw, were primarily used in relief in New York. Hunter was expected to challenge Joe DeMaestri at shortstop and Graff, a 26-year-old second baseman, was one of the best prospects in the Yankees organization. Noren, a 32-year-old outfielder, was hampered by knee problems in 1956 and appeared in only 39 games with the Yankees. Urban, a 29-year-old right-hander, was the "player to be named later" and was acquired a few days before the close of spring training.

Sports Illustrated felt all the off-season player transactions "brought the Athletics a cluster of players who could move the team to sixth place in the standings. The A's entered spring training with new pitchers, better infield defense and more power in the outfield."[3]

Kansas City made its second major trade with the Yankees a few hours before the midnight trading deadline on June 15. The A's sent outfielders Harry Simpson and Jim Pisoni, infielder Milt Graff and pitcher Ryne Duren to the Yankees for infielder Billy Martin, pitcher Ralph Terry, and outfielders Woodie Held and Bob Martyn. The A's hated to lose Simpson, who was batting .296 at the time of the trade, but none of the other players traded would be missed. Graff played well defensively at second but was batting only .181. Pisoni, tailed off after a strong start and was batting just .237. Duren appeared in 14 games, but was 0–3 with a 5.23 ERA.

Martin, the Yankees' starting second baseman, was considered the key player in the trade. He became expendable because the Yankees felt he was a bad influence. Six members of the Yankees—Hank Bauer, Mickey Mantle, Whitey Ford, Yogi Berra, Johnny Kucks, and Martin—held a party that lasted past midnight and ended in a brawl observing Martin's twenty-

11—1957: Big Trades Bring New Faces

ninth birthday on May 16. Held, a 25-year-old outfielder, was considered an outstanding prospect. He began his career as a shortstop, but was transferred to the outfield because of his strong arm and great speed. He would be given the opportunity to fill the center field position for the A's. Terry, a 21-year-old right-hander, pitched a shutout victory for the Yankees before being obtained by the Athletics.

The early season optimism quickly faded as the team had several losing streaks and fell into seventh place on June 9. The team seemed disorganized and Boudreau said his biggest disappointment was the failure of the trades to improve the team. "The Kansas City club hasn't started to work as a unit," he said, "but I'm confident it will. We received many players from the Yankees, and with every one of them, there is a mental problem. Coming to a team such as the Athletics, they know they are giving up $5,000 to $8,000 a year in World Series money. It isn't easy to forget."[4]

Parke Carroll accompanied the team during a long eastern road trip during the end of July and the first week of August. The A's lost 11 games in a row to drop their season record to 36–67. Carroll and Arnold Johnson knew the A's had deficiencies in talent but still felt the team should have a better record. The team traveled to Chicago and Johnson summoned Carroll, Boudreau and coach Harry Craft to his Chicago office for a meeting on August 6. "Lou, I've talked with Mr. Johnson and we think it's best to make a change," Carroll said. "I hope you understand." Boudreau was upset because he felt nobody could have done a better job with the players he had been given. He blamed Johnson and Carroll because he felt they scrapped the building program. He was offered another position in the organization but also had other job offers.[5]

"Managers of second-division clubs always have to accept more than their share of the blame for the misfortune of their teams, but in recent weeks the efforts of the Athletics had become so futile that a change was inevitable, regardless of where the blame rest for the A's failures," wrote Joe McGuff. "As a tactical manager, we firmly believe that Boudreau is as efficient as anyone. He played sound percentage baseball and although he was severely criticized for his handling of pitchers, it should be remembered that this is the most common of all complaints made against managers. Disregarding strategy, however, it was obvious that there was something basically wrong with the Athletics. Somewhere along the line the club had lost its way and the manager had been unable to rally it."[6]

Craft was offered the managerial position but was reluctant to take the job out of loyalty to Boudreau. He changed his mind after talking to Boudreau.

Craft had paid his dues to get to this position. Born on April 19, 1915,

Harry Craft (from Jay Publications and the Kansas City Athletics).

in Ellisville, Mississippi, he joined the Reds in 1937 after spending seven years in the minor leagues. Craft had his best year in 1938 when he batted .270, hit 15 home runs and had 85 runs batted in. Craft retired as a player in 1948 and started his managerial career in the New York Yankees organization in 1949. He spent six years with the Yankees, including two years as manager of the Kansas City Blues. He became a coach for the Kansas City Athletics in 1955.

When Craft replaced Boudreau as manager of the Athletics on August 6, 1957 the team was 31 games below .500; he guided them to a 23–27 record the rest of the way. He led the team to their best season in Kansas City in 1958: a 73–81 record. The team struggled to a 66–88 mark in 1959 and he was replaced as manager at the end of the season.

Craft joined the Chicago Cubs as a coach in 1960 and split his time as head coach of the Cubs, San Antonio, and Houston under the Cubs revolving coaching system. He was named the first manager of the Houston Colts (later Astros) expansion team in the National League in 1962. He managed the team nearly three seasons before being replaced by Luman Harris on September 10, 1964. He was named field coordinator of the Baltimore Orioles a few months later. He scouted for the Yankees in 1968. Craft died on August 3, 1995.

Craft's first move was to add former Cincinnati teammate Jimmy Gleeson to the coaching staff on August 13th. Gleeson was a former major league outfielder and had been a scout for the A's. Craft's contract would expire at the end of the season, but club officials promised to rehire him if the team improved. The *Sporting News* reported that Marty Marion, former

Harry Craft's Managerial Record

Year	Team	Class	Won	Lost	Position
1949	Independence	D	71	53	1
1950	Joplin	C	90	46	1
1951	Beaumont	AA	84	77	4
1952	Beaumont	AA	77	84	7
1953	Kansas City	AAA	88	66	2
1954	Kansas City	AAA	68	85	7
1957	Kansas City	Major	23	27	7
1958	Kansas City	Major	73	81	7
1959	Kansas City	Major	66	88	7
1961	Chicago Cubs	Major	13	15	
	San Antonio	AA	12	5	
	Houston	AAA	32	24	
1962	Houston	Major	64	96	8
1963	Houston	Major	66	96	9
1964	Houston	Major	61	88	9

manager of the Cardinals, Browns and White Sox, was the leading candidate to manage the A's if they did not rehire Craft.[7]

Craft talked with the players after he took over and asked for their hustle and cooperation. Craft removed veteran pitcher Trucks from the starting rotation because he felt Trucks was more valuable out of the bullpen. He benched the team's leading hitter, Hector Lopez, placed Billy Martin at third base and returned Hunter to second base to improve the infield defense — Lopez had made several costly errors at third base. The A's played with more spirit and enthusiasm and won the first game Craft managed against the White Sox. After losing the next two games, the A's swept Cleveland in four games and climbed within percentage points of Washington in seventh place.

Vic Power enjoyed another solid year defensively at first and had a streak of 69 consecutive games (625 chances) without an error, but his batting average dropped to .259 with just 42 runs batted in.

Hunter shared second base with Graff during the first part of the season. He played well defensively but batted just .191. Martin moved to second when he joined the A's and also played 20 games at third. He stabilized the infield and finished the season with a .257 batting average and nine home runs in games he played with the A's. By the end of the year, however, he was not playing with the same enthusiasm. He later admitted the trade and the defeatist attitude of the A's shocked him.[8]

Joe DeMaestri fought off a challenge by Hunter for the shortstop position and enjoyed a good season. He led all American League shortstops in fielding average while batting a respectable .245. He was named to the

American League All-Star team, Kansas City's lone representative at the game in St. Louis on July 9.

Lopez played third base until Martin replaced him for defensive reasons at the end of the season. Lopez led the team in hitting with a .294 average and established a Kansas City record with a 22-game hitting streak.

Held took over in center field after he was obtained from the Yankees. He finished the season with a .239 batting average with 20 home runs and 50 runs batted in despite appearing in only 93 games. "He could become one of the great major league hitters because he has great wrist action," commented Lou Boudreau. "He reminds me somewhat of Ted Williams in this respect."[9]

The remainder of the outfield was weak defensively. Cerv injured his ankle early in the season, was somewhat overweight, and hit .272 with just 11 home runs and 44 runs batted in. Gus Zernial played sparingly in left field under Boudreau but became a starter under Craft. "Harry Craft became manager and he said 'You can play left field,'" Zernial recalled. "Now I'm reaching 33, 34 years old. We had a bad ballclub that year. I hit 27 home runs, but I didn't hit for any average." (Zernial batted .238 with 69 RBI.) Martyn had good speed, an adequate throwing arm and occasional signs of power but hit just one home run and had 12 runs batted in. Irv Noren appeared in 81 games and hit just .213 before being sold to St. Louis.[10]

Hal Smith was the only catcher in the league to hit .300, finishing the season batting .303 with 13 home runs. Reserve catcher Tim Thompson hit just .203 in his part-time role.

Although none of the pitchers won more than nine games, the staff lowered its earned run average to 4.19 as the newcomers improved the pitching staff. Trucks was one of the league's most effective relief pitchers during the first part of the season. He was forced into a starting role following a number of injuries and finished the year with a team leading 9–7 record and a 3.03 ERA. Morgan matched Trucks's 9–7 record in a relief and spot-starting role. He had a perfect 3–0 record against Detroit and finished the season with a 4.63 ERA. Garver overcame the arm problems that plagued him in 1956 and pitched two two-hit games, defeating Cleveland 7–0 on August 11 and Detroit 2–1 on September 22. He finished the season with a 6–13 record and a 3.85 ERA.

Terry, obtained from the Yankees in June, was the tough-luck pitcher on the staff. He had an impressive 3.38 ERA with the A's yet finished the year with a 4–11 record because he lost more heart breakers and low-score battles than any other pitcher. He pitched a two-hitter against the Yankees two weeks after the A's acquired him but lost the game 2–1. Urban started the season on loan to AAA Denver. He won his first game against Washington, did not surrender a hit in the last nine innings of a 13-inning victory over the White Sox and finished the season with a 7–4 record and a 3.35 ERA. He was named to *The Sporting News* All-Rookie team. McDermott pitched in 29 games with a 1–4 record and a 5.48 ERA. He became the first A's pitcher to hit a pinch-hit home run. He batted for pitcher Wally Burnette in the seventh inning against Cleveland on August 10 and hit a home run off Indians hurler Mike Garcia.

Joe DeMaestri (from Jay Publications and the Kansas City Athletics).

Four holdovers also made important contributions to the pitching staff. Tom Gorman had a sore arm but finished with a 5–9 record and a 3.82 ERA in relief and starting roles. Wally Burnette had arm problems in spring training that hampered his knuckleball and caused control problems. He finished with a 7–12 record and a 4.30 ERA. Alex Kellner had another good year as a starter. He could not pitch in a regular rotation due to back and arm problems but still finished with a 6–5 record and a 4.26 ERA. Arnold Portocarrero rebounded to a 4–9 record and a 3.91 ERA after two disappointing seasons battling arm problems and a loss of self-confidence. He was used in relief during the season but was given the opportunity to start a game against Detroit in the last series of the season.

A rare occurrence symbolized the futility of the season. On August 18, Indians outfielder Gene Woodling was credited with two runs batted in on a sacrifice fly in the fourth inning in Cleveland's 9–2 victory over Kansas City. Pitcher Cal McLish opened the inning by drawing a walk and went to second on Al Smith's single. Roger Maris's sacrifice enabled both runners to advance a base. Woodling came to bat and belted a long drive to the right field corner where Cerv made a running catch. Both runners tagged up on the play and Smith raced home from second ahead of the relay.

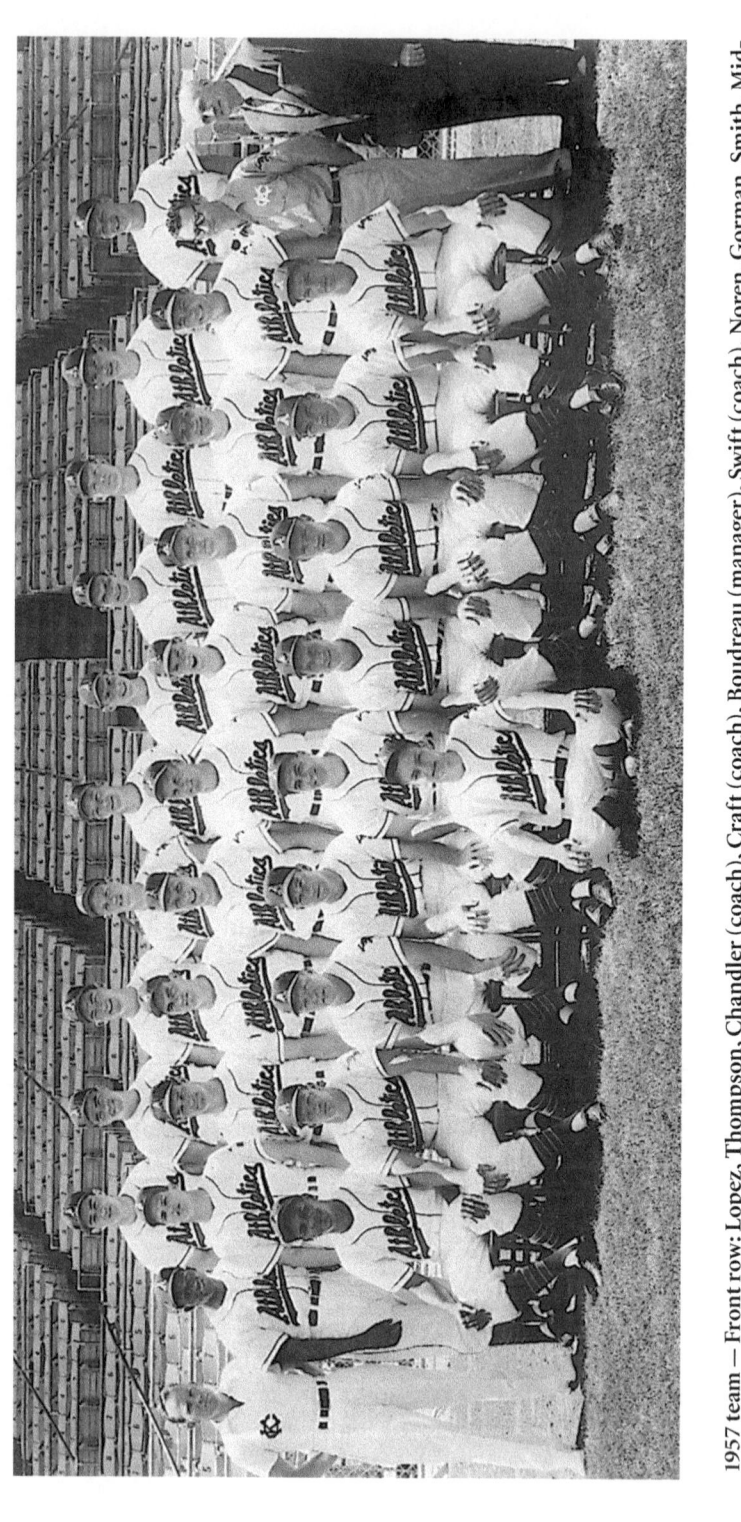

1957 team — Front row: Lopez, Thompson, Chandler (coach), Craft (coach), Boudreau (manager), Swift (coach), Noren, Gorman, Smith. Middle row: Ewell (trainer), Power, Terry, Portocarrero, Morgan, Zernial, McDermott, Trucks, Kellner, Cox, Reid (equipment manager), Keefe (traveling secretary). Back row: Skizas, Garver, Burette, Hunter, DeMaestri, Held, Groth, Martyn, Martin, Urban. Seated in front: Jay (batboy). (From the Kansas City Athletics.)

The team played more spirited baseball under Craft. They finished with a 23–27 record under his leadership, although they never climbed higher than seventh except for a one-day tie for sixth. The A's rewarded Craft with a one-year contract to manage the team for the 1958 season on October 11. Although the attendance in Kansas City slipped to 901,067, the first time in the three years that the turnstile count failed to reach one million, the actual paid attendance was 1,001,542. This enabled the city to exceed the three-million-person attendance guarantee in each of the first three seasons. The total paid attendance during the three seasons was 3,509,000 for an average of 1,170,000 each year.

Head groundskeeper Eddie Dick submitted his resignation on August 13 to accept a position with a fertilizer company in Kansas City. Kansas City hired 27-year-old George Toma to replace him. "(The stadium) was known as one of the worst playing fields in the majors in 1955, 1956 and 1957," Toma said later. He transformed the field into one of the best conditioned fields in the major leagues and became widely acknowledged as one of the finest groundskeepers in major league baseball.[11]

During the 1957 season rumors surfaced that the New York Giants would move to either Minneapolis or San Francisco and the Brooklyn Dodgers would move to Los Angeles. The league owners met in May and told the Dodgers and Giants they would have to declare their intentions of drafting the cities by October 1, 1957. Under baseball law, the period for major league teams to draft minor-league territory was October 1 through October 31 each season.

Reports indicated that the American League wanted to thwart the National League plans and allow either the Washington Senators or Kansas City Athletics to move to Los Angeles. Senators owner Calvin Griffith had been in contact with Los Angeles officials. One radio station reported on August 15 that the Giants would move to Minneapolis and that the A's would be in either San Francisco or Los Angeles in 1959.[12]

Giants owner Horace Stoneham announced his team would move to San Francisco for the 1958 season on August 20, while Dodgers owner Walter O'Malley negotiated with Brooklyn and Los Angeles. The Dodgers did not meet the October 1 deadline and the National League granted them a two-week extension until October 15. The delay made it possible for the American League to draft the Los Angeles territory and Washington and Kansas City were still mentioned as the possible franchises that would move.

"There have been from time to time those bland predictions that the Athletics will be moved in a year of two," wrote Ernie Mehl. "We asked Arnold Johnson one day about those reports. He grimaced. 'I couldn't live with myself,' he said, 'if I were to do a thing like that. I stated at the outset that I intended to build a pennant contender for Kansas City and that's exactly what I still intend to do.' Obviously, if after the A's are strengthened to the point where they can compete on even terms with the other clubs in the American League and the attendance here doesn't keep pace with the improvement, the owner would consider moving. He isn't primarily interested in making money, but at the same time he wouldn't want to lose a great deal. But right now he feels that Kansas City has exceeded his expectations in support of the A's. He believes the fans have stood by a loser and so are entitled to a winner.... The reports probably will persist, but he doesn't pay any attention to them." The Dodgers ended all speculation when they announced they would move to Los Angeles on October 18.[13]

12

1958: Cerv's Amazing Season

The A's hired Don Heffner as a coach at the close of the 1957 season to replace Jimmy Gleeson. Heffner was a former major league second baseman for the Yankees, Browns, Athletics and Tigers. Craft and Heffner had been rival managers in the Texas League. This was his first opportunity to coach in the major leagues.

Kansas City continued to make trades to improve their pitching and defense. The Athletics completed their second 13-player trade in nine months on November 20, 1957: The A's sent second baseman Billy Martin, and pitchers Tom Morgan and Maury McDermott, outfielders Gus Zernial and Lou Skizas and catcher Tim Thompson to Detroit in exchange for outfielders Bill Tuttle and Jim Small, pitchers Duke Maas and John Tsitouris, catcher Frank House and first baseman Ken Hadley. The Tigers sent first baseman Jim McManus to Kansas City on April 3, 1958, to complete the trade. "I was convinced the deal would help us," said Craft. "The way I look at it we have strengthened ourselves in three positions. Tuttle and Small give us a better outfield. Maas is a pitcher of great promise and House should help our catching. I don't know too much about Tsitouris, but our reports on him are good. We gave up an outstanding ballplayer in Billy Martin and a good relief pitcher in Morgan, but you have to give up something to get something. I hated to see Martin go, but I feel we improved our club."[1]

Billy Martin refused to report to Detroit unless he received a cash settlement from the A's. That would have voided the trade because Martin was the player Detroit sought in the transaction. He changed his mind and consented to the trade. *Sports Illustrated* stated the trade helped Kansas City because the A's "got rid of some of their low-batting-average power hitters to add speed and better defense to a team that was probably the slowest in baseball last year." The A's insisted that both Tuttle and Small had to be included in the trade. Tuttle, a 28-year-old outfielder, had been the Tigers starting center fielder since 1954 and had good speed and a good throwing arm. Small, a 20-year-old outfielder, who signed for a $35,000 bonus with the Tigers in 1955, was considered an outstanding prospect. Maas, a 26-year-old right-hander, had a 10–14 record and a 3.29 ERA with Detroit in 1957. House, a 27-year-old catcher, had been a Tigers starter in 1954. The A's felt he had the potential to challenge Hal Smith for the catching duties. Tsitouris, a 21-year-old right-hander, pitched in Charleston (AAA) in 1957 and Hadley and McManus were minor league first basemen.[2]

The A's purchased 25-year-old catcher Harry Chiti in the major league draft on December 3. They signed veteran knuckleball pitcher Murry Dickson on January 28. The 41-year-old right-hander had been released by St. Louis

The A's almost completed another trade with Baltimore near the close of spring training that would have made baseball history. The trade, almost identical to one trade proposed by the two teams in 1956, would have traded the entire 25-man playing rosters of both teams.

"The Baltimore and Kansas City clubs almost traded their 25-man rosters," wrote Jerome Holtzman. "This was prior to the 1958 season when both clubs were struggling. Paul Richards, then the Baltimore general manager and the late Arnold Johnson, who owned the KC franchise, had agreed to the swap. But, at the eleventh hour, Richards remembered the Orioles had a young third baseman named Brooks Robinson and told Johnson, 'But there is one player we'd like to keep....' Replied Johnson, 'Well, as a matter of fact, there are two players on my club I want to keep, too.' And so what would have been the biggest and most unusual trade in baseball history wasn't consummated."[3]

Although the two teams did not complete the blockbuster trade, they completed a trade a few days after the start of the season. The A's traded pitcher Arnold Portocarrero to Baltimore for 24-year-old knuckleball hurler Bud Daley. Daley pitched for Cleveland in 1957 and had a 2–8 record with a 4.45 ERA. The A's felt he could be either a starting pitcher or a relief pitcher.

Kansas City was one of the most surprising clubs during the first half of the season and was in second place most of the time from May 27 to the All-Star game recess. They were in second place on June 21; just 8 1/2 games back, and were still in second on July 7. They occupied second place for 52 days during the season. The team faded in the second half and wound up in seventh place for the second consecutive year, but still exceeded Craft's goal of 70 victories. The primary reason for their fast start was the

12—1958: Cerv's Amazing Season

stellar play of left fielder Bob Cerv. "At long last Kansas City fans can point to an authentic star," wrote *Sports Illustrated*. "In Bob Cerv they have a hero in the classical mold who can bust up any ball game with one swing of his bat."[4]

Cerv started the season with a hot bat and won the left field position. He was batting .344 on May 17 and led the American League with 11 home runs and 30 runs batted in when he broke his jaw in a collision at home plate with catcher Red Wilson in the seventh inning of a night game against Detroit. Cerv tried to score from second base, but as he approached the plate he realized he would be out. Instead of sliding, he crashed into Wilson in the hope the catcher would drop the ball. Cerv broke his jaw in two places when the left side of his face collided against Wilson's shoulder.

"If I was ever going to show anything, it would have to be this year," said Cerv. "I'm 32 years old and reaching the now-or-never stage. The way I started the season it looked like now. From opening day one I had a hot bat.... And now here I was, flat on my back at St. Luke's Hospital in Kansas City, waiting for them to set my jaw and listening to a nurse tell me it might be six weeks before I could play ball again. The last thing I remember just before going to sleep was thinking over and over to myself, *Not me! They won't keep me out six weeks—or even six days!*"[5]

His jaw was wired shut and his diet consisted of chicken broth, gruel and milk shakes in the hospital. Doctors refused to predict when he could return to action although one doctor reluctantly said, "Maybe after a week or so you can try." Cerv left the hospital on May 19 and discovered he could eat steak and other solid foods after a kitchen blender reduced the food to a liquid. "I wouldn't mind sitting around if I had a broken leg and couldn't move," said Cerv. "But all I've got wrong with me is a broken jaw. I don't see why I can't play.... At first the doctor flatly refused to consider the idea. 'It's only three days since you jaw was set,' he pointed out. 'You need more time.' '...Let me try,' I said. The next day was Thursday.... I went to the hospital. The doctor was no more enthusiastic over the idea of my playing than he was the day before. But when I kept insisting he finally gave me permission to try. 'You've got to get it out of your system,' he said, 'but I don't think you'll last very long. Whoever heard of a man on a liquid diet playing big league baseball any length of time? You won't get enough nourishment to make up for the energy you use up. Besides, you'll have trouble breathing. You'll be ready to take a rest in less than a week.'"[6]

Cerv returned to the lineup against Boston after missing just three games. He did not get any hits and discovered his jaw throbbed with

1958 team — Front row: Herzog, Davis, Herbert, Swift (coach), Craft (manager), Chandler (coach), Heffner (coach), Urban, Baxes, Dickson. Middle row: Ewell (trainer), Grim, Smith, Carrasquel, Simpson, Ward, Terry, Chiti, Daley, Keefe (traveling secretary), Reid (clubhouse attendant). Back row: Garver, Lopez, Craddock, Maris, Tomanek, Tuttle, DeMaestri, Martyn, Cerv, Gorman, House. Seated in front: Close (batboy). (From the Kansas City Athletics.)

12—1958: Cerv's Amazing Season

pain whenever he swung and missed, tried sliding or even threw from the outfield. He played every day and although his hitting fell off at first, it gradually improved. He got stronger every day despite the liquid diet. When the temperature warmed up Cerv had trouble breathing and Jim Ewell, the trainer, gave him oxygen. The doctor removed the wires from Cerv's jaw on June 16. Despite the liquid diet Bob Cerv lost only four pounds and still led the American League with 17 home runs and 51 runs batted in. His batting average dropped from .344 to .310, but in the 28 games he played with his jaw wired shut he managed to hit six home runs.

Bob Cerv (National Baseball Hall of Fame Library, Cooperstown, New York).

Cerv fractured a toe on July 1 but still started in left field in the All-Star game in Baltimore a week later. Despite the A's surprising success, Cerv was Kansas City's lone representative on the All-Star team. By the end of the season Cerv suffered a broken jaw, a broken hand, two broken toes along with an injured knee and ankle, but still finished with a .305 average with 38 home runs and 104 runs batted in. He battled Boston's Jackie Jensen and the Yankee's Mickey Mantle for the home run honors before fading in the final weeks of the season because of his injuries. He finished fourth behind Jensen in the final balloting for the American League's Most Valuable Player award, but he finished ahead of Mantle and Red Sox legend and batting champion Ted Williams in the voting. The A's held a special night to honor Cerv on July 22.

The A's continued to make trades during the season. They traded infielder Billy Hunter to Cleveland on June 12 for veteran Alfonso "Chico" Carrasquel. Carrasquel played 32 games at third base for the A's before Hal Smith took over the position.

Cleveland general manager Frank Lane wanted to acquire Vic Power and Woodie Held. Kansas City was willing to deal but wanted either Rocky

Colavito or Roger Maris in return. Arnold Johnson preferred Colavito because he felt he could hit 50 home runs for Kansas City. Lane proposed a seven-for-one trade in June that would have sent Colavito to Kansas City in exchange for Power, Held, Hector Lopez, Dave Melton, Bill Tuttle and Duke Maas. Kansas City felt Cleveland wanted too much in return for Colavito.[7]

Lane proposed another trade a few days later. He substituted Maris for Colavito and on June 15 the A's traded Power and Held to Cleveland for Maris, first baseman Preston Ward and pitcher Dick Tomanek. Maris, a 23-year-old right fielder, was considered an outstanding prospect with good speed, a good arm and great power. He was hitting .315 in May 1957, led the league with seven home runs was being touted as the rookie of the year when he slid into Kansas City's Milt Graff trying to break up a double play. Graff broke two of Maris's ribs when he came down with both knees on the runner's chest. Maris missed a month and finished the season batting .235 with 14 home runs and 51 runs batted in. Maris platooned with Colavito during the first part of the 1958 season, but Colavito earned the position full-time and Maris was benched. He had a .225 batting average with nine home runs and 27 runs batted in when he came to the A's. Tomanek, who was a 26-year-old left-hander, had a 5.62 ERA at the time of the trade.

The A's made another trade on June 15, trading pitchers Virgil Trucks and Duke Maas to the Yankees for Harry Simpson and pitcher Bob Grim. Simpson fractured his wrist in spring training and was hitting just .216 with six runs batted in for the Yankees in a part-time role. "He got off to a poor start and never did get straightened out," said Craft. Grim had an impressive and a 2.63 ERA for the Yankees in 1957, but had pitched just 16 innings for New York with a 5.51 ERA at the time of the trade.[8]

Power began the season at first base. He and was batting .302 on June 15 and was in the midst of a 22 game hitting streak when he was traded to Cleveland. The A's acquired Simpson the same day they traded Power and installed Simpson at first base. He batted .264 with seven home runs and 27 runs batted in with Kansas City.

Mike Baxes, a good defensive player, clinched the second base position during spring training but was forced out of the lineup with an injury. Craft shifted Hector Lopez to second on an emergency basis. When Baxes recovered, Craft decided to keep Lopez at second because he felt his offensive talent outweighed his defensive liabilities and Baxes was confined to a utility role. Lopez was one of the best hitters on the team and he finished the season with a .261 average with 17 home runs and 73 runs batted in. Lopez hit three home runs against Washington on June 26. He hit a solo home run in the fourth inning, a two-run blast in the eighth, and then ended the game with a decisive home run in the twelfth inning with one runner on base to give the A's the 8–6 victory.

Joe DeMaestri was one of the most dependable shortstops in the league with a strong and accurate arm. Offensively, he hit just .219 with six home runs and 38 runs batted in. Hal Smith was pressed into action at both first and third base, even though he had been a catcher throughout his career. He moved to third base when Lopez shifted to second. The more Smith played at third, the more adept he became. He finished the season with a .273 batting average and 45 runs batted in.

Chiti was as a valuable draft choice for the A's. He backed up Smith behind the plate until Smith moved to third. Chiti did the bulk of the catching during the last half of the season despite an injured finger on his glove hand. He finished the season with a .268 batting average and 44 runs batted in.

Held played center field until he was traded to Cleveland. Tuttle started the season in right field, but moved to center after Held was traded. Tuttle, a valuable team player, had a number of timely hits even though he batted just .231 with 22 home runs and 51 runs batted in. He tied a major league record with two assists in the second inning when the A's defeated Cleveland 5–0 on April 15.

Maris quickly became a fan favorite. He had one of his best games against Detroit on August 15. He hit a home run, set off a three-run rally with a single in the fifth inning and had hit in the seventh to lead the A's to a 12–5 victory. "Have the Athletics found in Roger Maris the outstanding performer they have been searching for ever since the franchise moved here?" wrote Ernie Mehl. "It has been said of Maris by no less an authority than the former great outfielder George Selkirk, personnel director for the Kansas City club, that Maris had unusual potential. 'He could have used another season in a top minor league to get the experience he needs,' Selkirk commented, 'But there is no telling how far he can go. He has all the tools to be great.'"

Maris ended the season batting .240 with 28 home runs and 80 runs batted in for both Cleveland and Kansas City. He batted .247 with Kansas City with 19 home runs.[9]

Utility players also made important contributions. Whitey Herzog was purchased from Washington on May 14 and played all three outfield positions while batting .240. Preston Ward played both first base and outfield and batted .254 with six home runs and 24 runs batted in. He hit three consecutive home runs against Baltimore in Kansas City to lead the A's to an 8–6 victory on September 9.

The A's pitching was a key factor for the team's improved record. Kansas City ranked seventh in the league with a 4.15 team ERA. Veteran Ned Garver was the club's biggest winner and an important factor in the early success. He had seven victories in his first eight decisions through Memorial Day, including a two-hit, 4–0 shutout over Baltimore on May 25. He finished the season with a 12–11 record and a 4.02 ERA.

Ray Herbert developed into one of the most dependable pitchers on the staff. Herbert pitched in the minors in 1957 and reported to spring training with the enthusiasm of a rookie. "I was 27 years old and this might be my last chance," he said. "I don't think I would have been given another shot if the Athletics didn't want me. I just had to make good." He appeared in 42 games, both as a starter and a middle relief pitcher. He finished the season with an 8–8 record and a 3.50 ERA with 108 strikeouts.[10]

Ralph Terry had an 11–13 record and a 4.23 ERA. He pitched a one-hit, 1–0 shutout at Washington on August 22, permitting just one base runner. He started the game retiring the first eight batters. Pitcher Russ Kemmerer lashed a single for the only Washington hit with two outs in the third inning. Terry retired the next 19 batters in order for his third shutout over the Senators. Bud Daley spent the first month of the season at Buffalo in the International League to work on his knuckleball. He was recalled by Kansas City and became a spot pitcher, working mostly middle relief. Despite limited activity he was effective in tough situations and walked only 19 men in 71 innings. He finished with a 3–2 record with a 3.30 ERA.

Jack Urban, considered one of the three "certain starters" at the beginning of the season (with Garver and Terry), was injured in a collision at first base early in the season and did not pitch effectively after that. He finished with a disappointing 8–11 record and a 5.93 ERA. Grim, acquired in the Simpson trade, started slowly. He began to find himself and had a 6–2 record in August and September. He finished the season with a 7–6 mark for the A's with a 3.56 ERA. Maas was one of the team's leading pitchers during the first part of the season before being sent to New York in the Simpson trade. He had a 4–5 record and a 3.90 ERA. Maas threw a two-hitter against Detroit on May 18 and won the game 2–0.

Tom Gorman was the top relief pitcher. He finished with a 4–4 record with eight saves and a 3.50 ERA even though a sore arm hindered him during part of the season. Tomanek was obtained in the Maris trade and had a 5–5 record with a 3.61 ERA for Kansas City. One of his most impressive relief appearances came against his old team. He entered the game with the bases loaded and nobody out and struck out all three Indians.

Murry Dickson was an important addition to the pitching staff. He appeared in both starting and relief roles and had a 9–5 record and a 3.27 ERA when he was traded to the Yankees for a "player to be named later" on August 22. The Yankees were in first place at the time of the trade, but both Whitey Ford and Don Larsen had arm problems and the Yankees wanted Dickson to strengthen their pitching. Although the A's had fallen into sixth place at the time of the trade, they were only two and a half games out of fourth and just six and a half games out of second place. The A's not only lost a valuable member of the pitching staff, but they received virtually nothing in return. The "player to be named later" was not obtained until after the season: outfielder John "Zeke" Bella.[11] Bella batted .207 in 82 at bats with Kansas City in 1959.

Baltimore manager Paul Richards listed three pitchers in his starting lineup in Kansas City on September 11. In addition to southpaw Bill O'Dell, who was to pitch and bat in the usual ninth sport, was Jack Harshman, who was listed as the center fielder batting fifth, and Milt Pappas, who was listed at second base and batting seventh. Richards's plan was to remove Harshman and Pappas for pinch-hitters if the Orioles had a big first inning and then send his regular center fielder, weak-hitting Jim Busby and his second baseman, Billy Gardner, into the game. The situation worked out somewhat as Richards planned. Baltimore had two runners on base with two out when Harshman's turn to bat came up. Gene Woodling batted for him and flied out. Busby then took over in center field and Gardner at second when Kansas City came to bat for the first time. The managerial maneuvering was hardly worth it. The A's, with Ned Garver firing a four-hitter, won the game 7–1.

Kansas City registered its finest season in its four years of major league baseball when the season ended. Bob Cerv emerged as the team's first star and Roger Maris demonstrated the potential to become a star player. The A's had a good blend of young talent and seasoned veterans, some good pitchers and improved defense in the outfield. Although they faded in the final months of the season, the exciting season rekindled the interest of Kansas City baseball fans. Attendance increased by nearly 25,000 over the 1957 season. The A's finished in seventh place with a 73–81 record and a turnstile count of 925,000.

13
1959: Great Expectations

Harry Craft signed a one-year contract with an increase in salary to return as manager on September 29, 1958. "Harry Craft has done an outstanding job as manager of the Athletics and we are happy to announce that he will return next season," said Arnold Johnson. "I am highly pleased with the improved showing of the club and I am confident that we will have an even better team next season. Naturally we had hoped to finish higher than seventh, but obviously our position in the standings doesn't reflect the improvement which the club had made. To me the important thing is that we won 73 games this season compared to 59 last season. This represents an improvement of more than 20 percent. We have some outstanding young players on our club. They have made progress this season and we have every reason to believe that they will be better next year." This optimism was reflected in the box office. The 4,800 season tickets sold represented an increase of nearly 5 percent over the previous season.[1]

Arnold Johnson also promoted Parke Carroll to executive vice president and general manager. He previously was vice president and business manager. Coaches Bob Swift and Don Heffner returned but Johnny Sain replaced Spud Chandler as pitching coach. Sain was appointed following the 1958 season and worked with A's pitchers in the winter instructional league. He was a former major league pitcher who spent most of his career with the Braves and Yankees and ended his career in Kansas City in 1955.

Schlitz sold a portion of their broadcasting rights to the Skelley Oil Company and the A's broadcasting network was renamed the Schlitz-Skelley Baseball Network. Merle Harmon and Bill Grigsby broadcast the games. Ed Edwards, who shared the A's broadcasts with Harmon since the start of the 1957 season, had been released from his contract on July 29, 1958 due to an illness. Bill Grigsby, sports director at KCTY-TV in Kansas City, was hired to replace him the following day. "When you broadcast for a losing baseball team you get a lot of hate mail," Grigsby later explained. "Ed started reading his mail and took it too seriously. It got to him so much, he stopped eating. The public criticism caused Edwards to lose weight. By mid-season he couldn't continue." [2]

WDAF (610 AM) replaced KMBC (980) as the originating station. Games would be telecast for the first time in 1958. Ten games would be shown on WDAF-TV. Harmon and Grigsby announced the televised games, also under the sponsorship of Schlitz-Skelley.

"For the first time we're in a position where we don't have to make trades, so we can afford to be a little choosy," said Craft. "We won't make any deals just for the sake of dealing but if we see a chance to improve our club we'll be ready to act." The A's made two minor trades. Utility infielder Chico Carrasquel was traded to Baltimore for infielder Dick Williams and pitcher Jack Urban was traded to the Yankees for pitcher Mark Freeman. The A's made another trade a few days after the start of the season, trading utility infielder Mike Baxes and reserve outfielder Bob Martyn to the Yankees for infielder Tom Carroll and outfielder Russ Snyder. Carroll, a 22-year-old shortstop, was a bonus player who spent 1955 and 1956 on the Yankees roster. Snyder, a 24-year-old outfielder, was considered a good prospect with good speed and excellent range in the outfield. [3]

Carroll and Craft wanted to increase the height of the left field fence to 34 feet. Johnson agreed and a 14-foot-high wire fence was installed on top of the fence. "Naturally I think the higher fence will help us or I wouldn't have given my approval for it," Craft said. "I feel it will be of considerable benefit to our pitchers. It should increase their confidence and nearly all of the cheap home runs should be eliminated.... We have a few men who may be handicapped to a certain extent, but on the whole I think we are sure to benefit."[4]

The press box was renovated before the start of the season. Entrance to the press box had been through two entrance hatches and writers had to walk through the upper deck to reach them. Water leaked through the entrance hatches during heavy rainstorms. During a rain-shortened game on July 30, 1958, 4.17 inches of rain fell and ankle-deep water filled the press box. Yankees announcer Mel Allen held his microphone near a stream of water pouring into the press box and commented: "Just like Niagara Falls." The entrance hatches were covered with steel plates and the top of the press box was waterproofed. Access was provided by new catwalk at the rear of the press box with an entrance stairway from one of the ramps leading to the upper deck. The press box was also enlarged with additions from both ends of the main press box to the two small flanker booths behind first base and third base. The flanker booths were now incorporated into the main press box to create a single press box. Capacity increased from 40 to 50 in the old press box to approximately 100 in the completed structure. The cost of the renovation was $24,267, but ownership hoped the improvements would be adequate for the All-Star game that the city hoped to host in 1960.[5]

The A's were involved in a salary dispute with Bob Cerv during the off-season. He wanted $30,000, a large contract in the 1950s. (Reports circulated that Cerv asked for between $40,000 and $50,000.) He reported to spring training, negotiated with Carroll and received the amount he wanted, but it was not announced for a number of days. "When I got to training camp, Parke Carroll told me I was getting the $30,000," Cerv said. "He said there was no rush to sign me because the club was getting a lot of stories in the papers about the holdout and that would help sell tickets. He knew I had been working out on my own and was in good shape."[6]

The A's appeared to have a solid team as spring training ended. Bill Tuttle and Roger Maris were good defensive outfielders compensating for Cerv's lack of speed in left field. All three were good hitters and Maris and Cerv had home run power. Cerv, plagued with injuries in 1958, theoretically could have an even bigger year in 1959. Harry Simpson, Hector Lopez, Joe DeMaestri and Hal Smith formed an infield that was strong offensively. DeMaestri led the league's shortstops in fielding in both 1957 and 1958 but neither Simpson nor Lopez was a good fielder and Smith had limited experience at third. The team had a promising quarter of starting pitchers in Ned Garver, Ray Herbert, Ralph Terry and Bob Grim. The bullpen was unsettled, but Craft hoped solid relief pitchers would emerge.

The season started well. The A's played at .500 or better throughout the first 43 games and were in the first division most of that time. The team was only three games under .500 on June 15 with a 26–29 record. They fell to 31–39 on June 30 and to 36–48 on July 15. The A's got hot, won 15 games in a 17-day stretch, and evened their record at 50–50 on July 31 to climb to third place only 9 1/2 games out of first place. Craft was absent during most of the winning streak. He was fighting a virus, collapsed from exhaustion and was hospitalized when the A's returned to Kansas City on July 21. Coach Bob Swift was placed in charge during Craft's absence and the team won 11 games in a row and climbed into third place. Craft returned on August 4 and the club went into a tailspin. The A's lost 11 of its next 13 games, including an eight-game losing streak

Maris was the team's best player during the first four months of the season. He signed a $16,000 contract in February, calling it the "best contract I ever signed." He was batting .328 with 10 home runs and 26 runs batted in on May 22 before going hitless in Boston. He felt sick on the plane ride back to Kansas City, went home, and was taken to the hospital with an appendicitis attack. He spent 30 days on the disabled list but hit well when he returned. "On the morning of July 27 American League batting averages revealed a new name at the top," wrote the *Sporting News*. "Roger Maris ... boosted his average to .344, one point higher at that date than Harvey Kuenn. This climaxed the comeback by a youngster now generally accepted as one of the brightest stars in the major leagues. Parke Carroll ... refers to Maris as the most exciting player in the American league and many will agree with him. Maris is a gambler on the bases and it is no uncommon sight to see him snatch an extra base or, failing, find himself in a rundown from which he emerges after a throwing error." Maris started the second All-Star game in Los Angeles on August 3. There were two All-Star games each year from 1959 until 1962. Maris had a 16-game hitting streak but then fell into a major batting slump, batting just .165 from July 27 through the end of the season, with just two home runs and 19 runs batted in. He finished the year batting .273 with 16 home runs and had 72 RBI.[7]

"I don't know what happened," Maris said. "Nothing seemed to work. My timing was off and I had no luck. When I hit a line drive, it was right at somebody. I wasn't sure I'd have enough nerve to show up for my day [Roger Maris Day on August 21]. I came into it with exactly three hits in my last 65 at bats. There was a doubleheader that day and they were having the ceremonies between games. In the first game I came up with the bases full and two out in the ninth. I struck out. I wanted to climb into a hole and pull it in after me." He sat on the bench during the second game. "I had that operation," he said. "I just ran out of gas."[8]

Left fielder Cerv had knee problems and could not duplicate his 1958 totals. He managed a 17-game hitting streak and a number of long home runs. He hit a grand slam off Barry Latham in the third inning on April 15 to help lead the A's to a 10–8 victory over the White Sox, their first victory of the season. He hit three home runs in Kansas City against Boston on August 20, but the A's lost the game 11–10. He finished the season with a .285 batting average, 20 home runs and 87 runs batted in.

Tuttle made many great catches and threw out runners with his strong arm. He led the team with a .300 batting average and had seven home runs and 43 runs batted in. He set a Kansas City record with 10 stolen bases. Rookie Russ Snyder started the season with Portland (AAA) before being recalled to Kansas City. He hit .313 in 73 games and was named to *The Sporting News* Rookie team.

Kent Hadley, a 24-year-old rookie, beat out veteran Simpson at first base during spring training. He appeared in 95 games and batted .253 with

1959 team — Front row: Herbert, Terwilliger, Bella, Heffner (coach), Craft (manager), Swift (coach), Sain (coach), Dickson, Herzog, Garver. Middle row: Ewell (trainer), Daley, Lumpe, Grim, Hadley, Ward, Chiti, Kucks, Coleman, Reid (equipment manager), Keefe (traveling secretary). Back row: Sturdivant, Smith, Boone, Snyder, Tomanek, Williams, Tuttle, DeMaestri, Tsitouris, House, Cerv, Maris. Seated in front: Close (batboy). (From the Kansas City Athletics.)

10 home runs and 39 runs batted in. Simpson appeared in just eight games before he was traded to the White Sox on May 2 for 35-year-old Ray Boone. Boone was acquired to serve as a back up at first and pinch-hit.

Lopez started the season at second and had a .281 average with six home runs and 24 runs batted in on May 26, the day he was traded to the Yankees along with pitcher Ralph Terry for pitchers Tom Sturdivant and Johnny Kucks, infielder Jerry Lumpe, and a player to be named later. Lumpe, a 25-year-old infielder, was the key player in the trade for the A's. He moved to second base in Kansas City and became one of the best defensive second basemen in the league. He finished the season with a .243 batting average.

Roger Maris (from the Kansas City Athletics).

In Terry, however, the Yankees received a solid pitcher who went on to win 23 games and pitch a Game 7 shutout to capture the 1962 World Series. In 1960 Terry allowed Bill Mazeroski's famous Series-ending home run. (The trade was one of several deals with the Yankees that seemed to be one-sided, in favor of New York.)

DeMaestri played shortstop for the fifth consecutive season. By the end of the season he was the only member of the team who had been on the 1954 Philadelphia team. Lumpe also played 56 games at shortstop when DeMaestri was sidelined with a pulled ligament in his side. Smith and Williams shared the duties at third base. Smith hit .288 with 31 runs batted in. Williams finished the season with a .266 average with 16 home runs, 33 double and 75 runs batted in.

Harry Chiti was the catcher until he was sidelined by finger injuries. Frank House assumed the duties following Chiti's injury. House tied a major league record when he scored two runs as a pinch-hitter as the A's scored eight runs in the eighth inning of a 9–4 victory over Cleveland on April 21.

Craft spoke to sports writers during spring training and pointed to Bud Daley. "That guy," he said, "could be my sleeper."

"Some sleeper," commented one writer. "He looks like the same guy who won only three games in 1958. He's been bouncing around for nearly 10 years without impressing anyone."[9]

Daley proved his manager right. He emerged as the ace of the pitching staff. The 26-year-old became a starter in May, more out of desperation than anything else, and developed into the team's most dependable pitcher. He won his fifteenth game by mid–August and seemed to be certain to win 20 games with eight starts remaining, but the A's went into their late-season tailspin during the final month and he won just one more game. He finished with a 16–13 record and a 3.17 ERA.

A's pitching coach Johnny Sain convinced Daley to mix a slider with his knuckler and assortment of curves. "I'd been working with Sain but I still wasn't sure I had the stuff to win big up here," Daley said. "I didn't have any fastball any more and I was getting older.... Then one day I went all the way against Boston early in the 1959 season and I felt good. Each game I felt better and more confident. Now that I knew I could pitch I started to think on the mound, not just throw the ball up there." He defeated every team in the league at least once and was particularly effective against Baltimore, winning six games and losing just one. Orioles manager Paul Richards realized he might be making a big mistake when he traded Daley to the Athletics in 1958. "I thought Daley would make it if he kept up his work," Richards said, "but I had a staff of young pitchers and I needed some experience. I knew Portocarrero would help me immediately."

Daley represented Kansas City in both All-Star games played in 1959 and pitched in the first game at Pittsburgh. Daley was brought into the game after the National League took a 5–4 lead in the bottom of the eighth inning with just one out and a runner on third. He retired the next two batters to end the inning. The American League was unable to score in the top of the ninth and lost the game. Daley did not pitch in the second game.[10]

Craft expected Ray Herbert to be his pitching ace. Herbert won six games in a row with shutouts over Detroit and Baltimore. "I might have won 15 or even as many as 18 games that year," said Herbert, "if I hadn't come up with that cold in my back. I couldn't follow through well and I wasn't getting as much on the ball as I should have." He finished the season with an 11–11 record and a 4.84 ERA.[11]

Ned Garver finished with a 10–13 record and a 3.72 ERA. Ralph Terry, the pitcher with perhaps the greatest potential, had a disappointing 1–4 record and a 5.24 ERA when he was traded to the Yankees with Lopez for Kucks and Sturdivant. Kucks, a 25-year-old pitcher, assumed Terry's starting role and finished with a respectable 8–11 record with the A's and a 3.87 ERA.

Kansas City had trouble with relief pitching. This was apparent early on, most notably when the White Sox defeated the A's by a score of 20–6 on April 22. Kansas City jumped to a five-run lead in the bottom of the second. Ned Garver was replaced at the start of the seventh inning but the bullpen could not hold the lead and the Sox accomplished the unique feat of scoring 11 runs with just *one hit* in that inning—an inning that lasted 45 minutes.

Tom Gorman came in to pitch the nightmarish top of the seventh inning. Ray Boone was safe when DeMaestri fielded his grounder and threw wide of first. Al Smith sacrificed Boone to second but was safe when catcher Hal Smith fumbled the ball. Johnny Callison singled to right for the only hit. Boone scored on the play, and when Maris fumbled the ball, Smith scored and Callison took third. Luis Aparicio walked and stole second. Chicago pitcher Bob Shaw, the beneficiary of Kansas City's generosity, walked to fill the bases. Mark Freeman came in to pitch for the A's. Earl Torgeson walked, forcing in Callison. Nellie Fox walked, forcing in Aparicio. Landis bounced one back to Freeman who threw to the plate forcing out Shaw. Sherman Lollar walked, forcing in Torgeson. George Brunet came in to pitch for the A's, and immediately walked Boone, forcing in Fox. Smith walked, forcing in Landis. Callison was hit by a pitch, forcing in Lollar. Lou Skizas ran for Callison. Aparicio struck out. Bubba Phillips pinch hit for Torgeson and drew a walk, forcing in Smith. Fox walked, forcing in Skizas. Landis grounded out to Brunet to mercifully end the inning. Eleven runs, one hit, three errors. Three Kansas City pitchers, Tom Gorman, Mark Freeman and George Brunet, gave up 10 walks, surrendered one single and hit one batter

Tom Gorman appeared in just 17 games and pitched 20 innings. He spent most of the season with AAA Portland and was dropped from the A's roster at the end of the season. Bob Grim pitched a two-hitter in the second game of a doubleheader against the Yankees on May 17, but later lost his starting position and was used primarily in relief. He finished with a 6–10 record and a 4.10 ERA. John Tsitouris finished the season with a 4–3 record and a 4.99 ERA. Kansas City reacquired veteran Murry Dickson from the Yankees on May 9. Dickson, who was 43 when the season ended, finished with a 2–1 record and a 4.94 ERA.

Kansas City played Pittsburgh in the annual Hall-of-Fame game in Cooperstown, New York on July 20. The game ended in a 5–5 tie. It was halted due to rain after the A's rallied to tie the score.

Pitching coach Johnny Sain resigned on August 24 and Parke Carroll accepted the resignation four days later. "I regret he is resigning because we feel he has done a good job with the pitchers," Carroll said. "I thought he did a fine job for us. He's a conscientious worker and as far as I know there was no personal trouble between John and myself or any other members of the coaching staff. He simply was dissatisfied with the organization."

When he joined the team in spring training, Sain had already worked out his own plan for how the pitchers should be rotated and what type of staff the A's should assemble. Many of his ideas were followed, but others were rejected. He disagreed with management about how pitching injuries were treated, about being stationed in the bullpen instead of on the bench during the game, and about how much voice he should have regarding the pitching. "I feel that my ideas do not fit in with those of the organization," said Sain. "When I came here I thought they were in a building program, but after what I observed, I kind of wonder. Things that I had spent years learning and convincing myself about, they dismissed in two seconds without giving them any real consideration." Sain became one of the best pitching coaches in baseball and developed many 20-game winners during his tenure as a coach for the Yankees, Minnesota, Detroit, White Sox and Atlanta. The team chose not to replace him because it was late in the season. Murry Dickson worked with the pitchers on an unofficial basis and some expected that he would be named as pitching coach after the season ended.[12]

The A's never recovered from the losing streak that occurred when Craft returned. Kansas City lost 22 of its last 29 games and finished in seventh place for the third consecutive season. The team was plagued by a wave of injuries to key players such as Maris, Chiti and Herbert, a failure of relief pitching and a lack of power. The erratic play of the team baffled everyone, including the manager, players and coaches. "I've never seen a club that could look so good for a while and then turn around and look so bad," stated one of the players. "Right now we aren't hitting and everyone has dropped off at the same time. If one or two guys would stay up while the others were down it would be all right but it seems like we all go together." The team attracted 963,683 to the stadium (turnstile count) with a total of 1,042,075 tickets sold, the A's largest attendance in three seasons. Attendance, however, plunged during the latter part of the season as hopes diminished and the team floundered.[13]

Carroll met with Craft met after the season. Craft did not want to quit, but he realized something had to be done to pacify the fans. Neither Carroll nor Johnson found any fault with the manner in which Craft handled the team and could not blame him for the injuries, the failure of the relief pitching or the lack of power. Carroll had tears in his eyes when he told Craft he would have to replace him on September 28, one day after the season ended. Carroll offered him a scouting position with the team. Craft took the position and served as a scout for a brief period before joining the Chicago Cubs organization as a coach.[14]

Carroll said it was a combination of things that led to the decision not to renew Craft's contract. Public opinion turned against him when he was hospitalized and the team won 11 games in a row and moved into third place. Interest was high and the hopes, while unrealistic, were even higher. Kansas City fans began to think the team could finish the season with a winning record and perhaps even challenge for the pennant. The A's started to lose when Craft returned and many fans concluded the trouble with the team was the manager. While this was not true it was difficult to combat the feeling. As the number of losses mounted the dissatisfaction grew even greater.

14

1960: A Very Difficult Year

The Kansas City Athletics and the City Council baseball committee began negotiations to renew the lease at Municipal Stadium during the 1959 season. The city wanted at least a five-year lease but Johnson wanted no more than two years, renewing rumors that he wanted to move the franchise. The Dodgers were setting attendance records on the West Coast and the *New York Post* speculated Johnson wanted to move to Los Angeles and share the Coliseum with the Dodgers. Johnson denied these rumors and said he wanted a short-term lease because he did not want to be "saddled with something which might prove costly if the bottom were to drop out."[1]

The parties finally agreed on terms for a new four-year lease with two four-year renewal options. The contract was ratified by the City Council on November 19, but Johnson did not sign it until January 8, 1960. The lease was similar to the previous lease with a flat $1,000-a-year rental and an additional $24,000 if ticket sales exceeded one million. The city would receive 5 percent of the ticket sales and 7½ percent of the concession sales. The A's would pay the city an extra $5,000 if they finished fourth, $15,000 if they finished third, $40,000 if they finished second, and $75,000 if they won the pennant. Johnson hoped this lease would eliminate any rumors the franchise would be moved. "We are well satisfied with Kansas City," he said, "and we have every intention of remaining."[2]

Johnson insisted on an escape clause that enabled the owner to cancel the lease if paid admissions fell below 850,000 in any season. This was lower than the figure than in the previous lease (one million) and continued to refer to paid admissions (total tickets sold) rather than attendance. If a home game was televised the minimum total would be reduced from 850,000 to 800,000. The city granted this request because the A's exceeded one million season admissions in each of the previous five years. The lowest total had been 1,001,542 in 1957. The A's also had the right to cancel after three years by notifying the city by October of the third year and paying for the fourth year.

The city would spend $115,000 to improve the stadium. The A's bullpen would be moved from behind the center field fence to a location adjacent to the right field foul line. A tunnel-like entrance with restrooms and concession stands would be built from behind home plate to Twenty-second Street to provide an entrance for people seated in the lower areas of the stadium. Approximately 400 to 500 box seats would be lost but they would be replaced by 747 box seats added down the left field line. Additional seats could be added behind the new box seats in the future. The A's and Sportservice would each contribute $30,000 for these improvements with the remainder coming from the $30,000 that rest in the city's stadium maintenance fund and $25,000 that would be placed in the fund during the 1960-61 fiscal year. (The A's lease payments met just the interest and principal payments due on the stadium bonds and left nothing for stadium improvements.)[3]

The A's ended a seven-week search for a new manager when they hired Bob Elliott on November 18, 1959.

Elliott, who turned 53 shortly after he was hired, had played either third base or in the outfield for 14 consecutive years in major league baseball. He was a member of the 1948 National League champion Boston Braves. In 1947 he became the first third baseman to be named a league Most Valuable Player. He was also a member of the *The Sporting News* All Major League team from 1944 through 1948.

Elliott started his managerial career with San Diego in the Pacific Coast League in 1955. He remained there until he was replaced early in the 1957 season. He was out of baseball in 1958. He signed a contract to manage Sacramento in the Pacific Coast League in 1959 and he led

Bob Elliott (from Jay Publications and the Kansas City Athletics).

them to a surprising fourth place finish. The Athletics signed Elliott to a one-year contract to manage the team on November 18, 1959.

BOB ELLIOTT'S MANAGERIAL RECORD

Year	Club	League	Won	Lost	Position
1955	San Diego	AAA	92	80	2
1956	San Diego	AAA	72	96	7
1957	San Diego	AAA			
1959	Sacramento	AAA	78	76	4
1960	Kansas City	Major	58	96	8

Elliott retained Don Heffner as third base coach and hired Fred Fitzsimmons and Walker Cooper a few weeks later. Fitzsimmons would be the pitching coach. He pitched for the Giants, managed the Phillies for three years and coached for the Braves, Giants and Cubs. Cooper, a former catcher, played for the Braves, Reds, Pirates, Cubs, Cardinals and Giants. He managed Indianapolis (AAA) in 1958 and 1959. Dick Challinor was named director of promotions for the team, replacing Connie Mack III. Challinor had been executive secretary of the Kansas City Chamber of Commerce until he accepted the position with the team.

Team officials felt the team was weak in pitching and catching and in the infield. The A's purchased 29-year-old relief pitcher Bob Trowbridge from Milwaukee after the World Series to complete the transaction in which they sold veteran infielder Ray Boone to Milwaukee during their pennant drive. Kansas City traded catcher Frank House to Cincinnati for 30-year-old relief pitcher Tom Acker and traded pitcher Tom Sturdivant to Boston for catcher Pete Daley. Daley had been Boston's second-string catcher for five seasons. The A's drafted 24-year-old infielder Bob Johnson and 22-year-old catcher Lou Holdener in the major league draft on November 30.

Parke Carroll and Pittsburgh general manager Joe Brown discussed a trade during the winter meetings that would have sent Roger Maris to Pittsburgh in exchange for shortstop Dick Groat. The Athletics wanted to acquire a shortstop because Joe DeMaestri did not figure prominently in their plans. The 29-year-old Groat was one of the best shortstops in the National League, but the Pirates would consider a trade because they were impressed with Ken Hamlin, a 24-year-old shortstop with their Columbus (AAA) team. The Athletics settled on the deal, but Brown asked for time to think it over. Pirates' manager Danny Murtaugh turned to Brown after they left the A's suite and said: "I hate to give up Groat." Brown nodded and cancelled the trade. The trade could have impacted both teams as Groat and Maris were named the Most Valuable Players in the National and American leagues respectively in 1960.[4]

The Athletics traded Maris, DeMaestri and first baseman Kent Hadley to the Yankees on December 17 for outfielders Hank Bauer and Norm Siebern, pitcher Don Larsen and first baseman Marv Throneberry. "Carroll knew that Maris, at 25, was a highly desirable ballplayer," wrote Leonard Shecter. "He already had demonstrated power, speed and defensive skill. But the thought of Roger's woefully weak bat in August and September plagued Parke like a nightmare. He felt that another bad year would eliminate the possibility of trading the youngster for front line strength and he would simply wither on the vine in Kansas City. Arnold Johnson, considered Maris a hot and cold hitter and approved Carroll's trade. Johnson, although a comparative newcomer to baseball, subscribed to the Branch Rickey theory that the worst thing you can do with a player is to wait another season to see if he will snap out of it. Then it may be too late."[5]

"If Maris hadn't slumped in '59," said Yankees general manager George Weiss, "I doubt whether Johnson would have traded him." Carroll and Johnson misjudged Maris's potential. Maris shocked the baseball world by breaking Babe Ruth's single season home run record when he hit 61 home runs in 1961.[6]

Siebern, a 26-year-old outfielder, played left field in Yankee Stadium where the sun and shadows posed threats to the fielders and was remembered for defensive mistakes in the 1958 World Series caused by the sun. "We gave up a good deal in that trade," said Weiss. "We were reluctant to give up Siebern and wouldn't make the trade at first. But we finally came to the conclusion he had outlived his usefulness. He's a left-handed hitter, but not the power hitter we felt we needed in Yankee Stadium."

Bauer, a 37-year-old veteran outfielder, had been the Yankees right fielder since 1949 and was near the end of his career. Throneberry, a 26-year-old first baseman, was considered a good fielder despite his later fame as a poor fielder with the New York Mets. He hit many tape-measure home runs in the minor leagues but was unable to dislodge Yankee first baseman Moose Skowron. Right-hander Don Larsen became the first pitcher to pitch a perfect game in the World Series in 1956 but never had an outstanding year in five seasons with the Yankees.[7]

Hamlin became expendable when the Pirates kept Groat. The Pirates traded Hamlin, minor league pitcher Dick Hall, and a player-to-be-named later, to the A's traded for infielder-catcher Hal Smith. Hamlin was a good fielder but there were questions whether he could hit in the major leagues. New manager Bob Elliott recommended Hall because the 29-year-old pitcher was the leading pitcher in the Pacific Coast League (AAA). The A's obtained catcher Hank Foiles on December 15 to complete the trade.

The A's were optimistic when spring training began. The outfield was solid, the infield and pitching seemed to be improved, and the presence of Hank Bauer seemed to inspire the team. Some predicted the team could finish as high as fifth place.

Vice president Roy Mack, the last member of the Mack family associated with the team, died on February 9. He retained partial ownership of the team when he purchased shares from Johnson in 1954.

Arnold Johnson died one month later. He arrived in West Palm Beach on March 9 and went to Connie Mack Stadium to watch an intra-squad game. He left at 2 P.M. but drove only six blocks before becoming ill. He pulled his car over to the curb and collapsed against the wheel, pushing down on the horn. He was taken by ambulance to Good Samaritan Hospital, but lost consciousness after he arrived at the hospital. The 53-year-old Johnson suffered a cerebral hemorrhage and was pronounced dead at 12:45 the next morning. His wife Carmen arrived from Chicago only 30 minutes before he died. "It just seems like a dream," said Carroll. "One minute he is here and the next minute he's gone. It just seems impossible."

Carroll said the team would wear black armbands throughout the 1960 season in honor of Johnson. "This will be a jolt to everybody," stated Bob Elliott. "We are going to miss him."[8]

The remaining members of the board of directors, headed by Nathanial Leverone, held an emergency meeting on March 15. They gave Carroll a new two-year contract as executive vice president and general manager to provide stability until the ownership situation was settled. The directors took no action to fill the two board positions left vacant by the death of Johnson and Mack.

Everything seemed to go wrong for the A's, starting with Johnson's death. The team suffered from a lack of hitting and had virtually no power. Players squabbled with manager Bob Elliott and many players seemed lackadaisical. One front office official commented: "It seemed sometimes like they were making outs on purpose." The A's avoided the cellar during the first half of the season, but dropped into the basement on July 10 and never emerged. Just 774,944 fans attended the games at Municipal Stadium, the lowest attendance in six seasons. Although poor weather early in the season was partly to blame, many fans were disenchanted with the poor performance on the field.[9]

Throneberry had a disappointing season at first base. He swung and missed regularly, hitting just 11 home runs. Siebern played 69 games at first, mostly near the end of the season. Jerry Lumpe led the team in hitting during the first part of the season and played well defensively at second base. Hamlin inherited the shortstop position but was not as polished in the field as the A's had been led to believe and suffered defensive lapses. The A's wanted to replace him as the season drew to a close.

Dick Williams began the season at third base. He started slowly at the plate and was hitting just .242 in the middle of July. The A's traded Bob Cerv to the Yankees for veteran third baseman Andy Carey on May 19. Carey became the A's third baseman and strengthened the infield, despite some physical problems. After Williams returned to a utility role he became one of the hottest hitters in the league. He had a 16-game hitting streak that included a 5-for-5 game against Washington on August 8 in Kansas City. He finished the season with a .288 batting average with 12 home runs and 65 runs batted in.

With the exception of Siebern, none of the outfielders hit well. Siebern won the left field position in spring training, hit .279 and led the team with 19 home runs and 69 runs batted in. Bill Tuttle had another fine year in center field. Cerv led the team with six home runs in his first 23 games before he was traded to the Yankees. The A's were reluctant to trade Cerv, but they needed to strengthen the third base position and the A's had an abundance of outfielders. Bauer was unable to play right field on an everyday basis and appeared in just 69 games. Russ Snyder and Whitey Herzog were dependable utility outfielders.

Harry Chiti won the catching position in spring training and Hank Foiles was traded to Pittsburgh on May 31 for catcher Danny Kravitz. Kravitz unseated Chiti and Chiti was sold to Detroit on July 26. Kravitiz and Daley shared the catching duties for the remainder of the season.

Lefty Bud Daley had a 12–4 record at the All-Star break and was Kansas City's lone representative on the American League All-Star team. His 12 victories by mid–July were more than any other pitcher in the major leagues and it appeared he would win 20 games, but Daley struggled after the All-Star break. "I got tired," he said. "It was just one of those things. I wasn't feeling well for a while, they boys weren't helping me too much and then there's that Kansas City heat in August. I still think I was throwing pretty good at the end." He finished the season with a commendable 16–16 record and a 4.56 ERA. Daley tied the record he set the previous season for most victories by a Kansas City pitcher.[10]

Elliott expected on Ray Herbert to be one of the top hurlers. Herbert tried to add a more controlled and deceptive changeup to mix with his fastball in spring training. "I still felt my fast ball was the big one," he said. "It didn't move as fast as it used to, but now I can usually put it where I

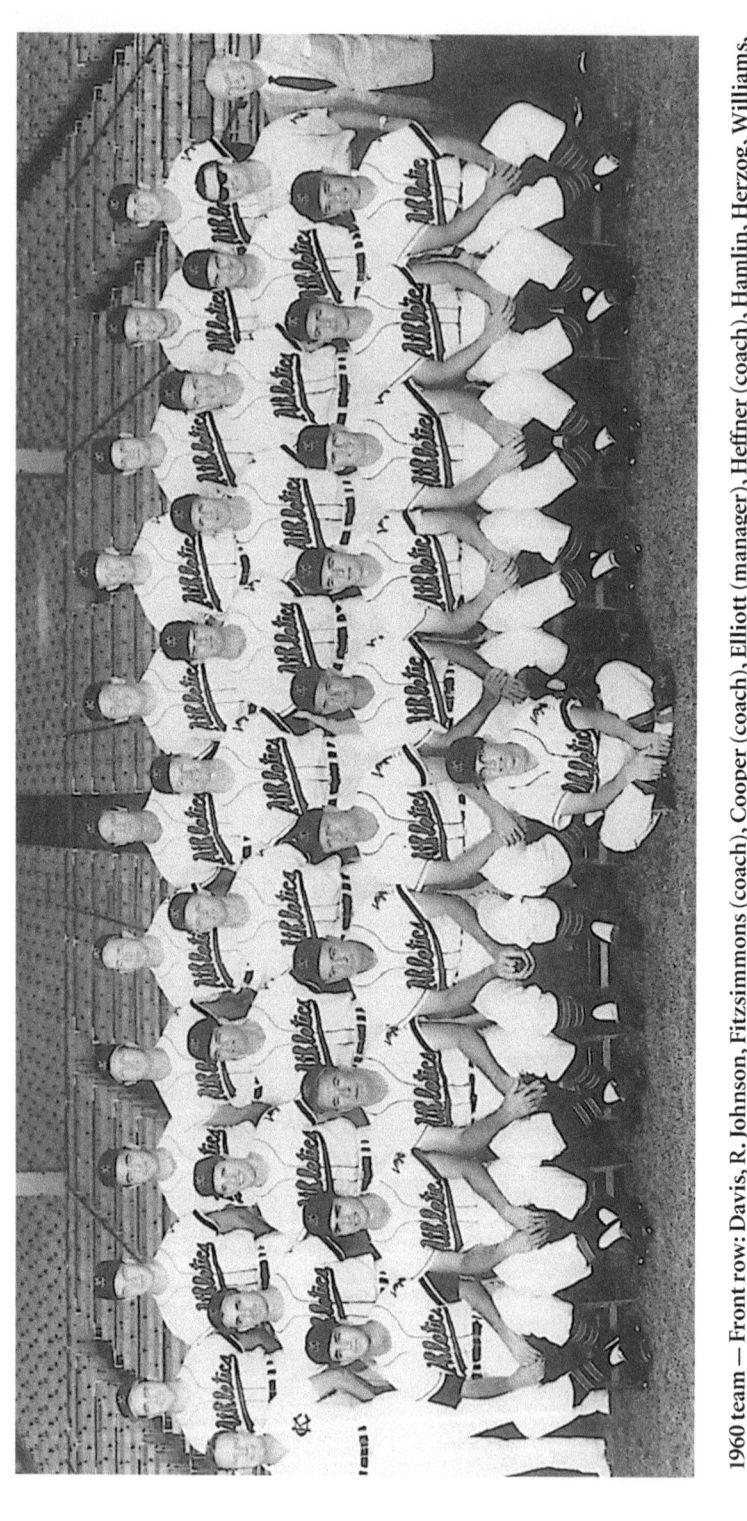

1960 team — Front row: Davis, R. Johnson, Fitzsimmons (coach), Cooper (coach), Elliott (manager), Heffner (coach), Hamlin, Herzog, Williams, Briggs. Middle row: Ewell (trainer), Herbert, Snyder, Kiely, K. Johnson, Hall, Larsen, Kucks, Siebern, P. Daley, Reid (equipment manager), Keefe (traveling secretary). Back row: Garver, Carey, Jablonski, Throneberry, Tuttle, Bauer, Kutyna, Lumpe, Kravitz, B. Daley, Tsitouris. Seated in front: Krimse (batboy). (From the Kansas City Athletics.)

want it. That's what counts." He opened the season with two wins but then lost six straight games. He broke the span with a victory over Boston but then lost three more games in a row before the All-Star break. The A's had a 29–48 record at the All-Star break and would have traded Herbert if any team made a reasonable offer. "I had a fair ERA," Herbert said, "which at 3.80 was better than my 3–9 record. I could only hope that things would start failing my way pretty soon."[11]

Herbert lost another game following the All-Star break, his fourth in a row, but then became one of the hottest pitchers in the league. He won four straight games, regained his confidence, and by mixing his changeup with his fastball, he enjoyed a

Bud Daley (from Jay Publications and the Kansas City Athletics).

good second half of the season. He defeated Detroit 2–1 in the final game of the season to finish the season with a 14–15 record and a 3.27 ERA. He had an 11–6 record after the All-Star break.

Hall was the third starting pitcher. He walked just 38 batters in 182 innings and finished the season with an 8–13 record and a 4.05 ERA. The A's had difficulty finding a fourth starter. Don Larsen hurt his back, was out of shape, and finished with a 1–10 record and a 5.36 ERA. Ned Garver started 15 games and had a 4–9 record and a 3.84 ERA. The A's struggled in the bullpen. Marty Kutyna appeared in 51 games, finished 30, and had a 3.92 ERA. Rookie knuckleball pitcher Ken Johnson appeared in 42 games, finished 18 and had a 5–10 record and a 4.28 ERA.

The highlight of the season was the All-Star game at Municipal Stadium on July 11. It fulfilled Arnold Johnson's quest to bring the game to Kansas City. He had submitted a bid in January 1958 and renovated the press box the following year. Two All-Star games were held and Kansas City hosted the first game. The stadium was decorated with bunting on the railings in front of the boxes. The streets in the downtown area, between Tenth and Twelfth streets, were decorated with 70 banners. Out-of-town writers occupied a temporary press box installed in the lower deck behind the boxes behind the home plate. Four long tables were constructed on top of rows of seats, leaving one row of seats between each table where the writers sat.

The National League won 5–3. Despite a heat wave that sent the temperature soaring to 101 degrees, a capacity crowd of 30,619 attended the game. The National League scored all their runs in the first three innings off pitchers Bill Monbouquette and Chuck Estrada. Willie Mays opened the game with a triple and Bob Skinner followed with a single. Monbouquette retired the next two batters before Ernie Banks hit a home run to give the National League a 3–0 lead. Del Crandall hit a home run in the second inning. Estrada yielded the final National League run in the third inning on a double by Banks and singles by Joe Adcock and Bill Mazeroski.

The American League was blanked for five innings but then jumped on Mike McCormick for a run in the sixth. They had the bases loaded with just one out yet failed to score additional runs. Bob Buhl yielded the American League's other runs in the eighth inning when he served a two-run home run to Al Kaline. Bud Daley pitched the ninth inning for the American League. He yielded a walk and struck out two batters. The American League had the tying runs on base with one out in the bottom of the ninth, but failed to score.

Work did not begin on the stadium improvements until August 11, after the All-Star game. A new grade with a new concrete base had to be built before the construction on the new box seats could begin. It would take six months to complete the project.

The disappointing season ended on October 2. The team was torn by dissension and finished in eighth place with a dismal 58–96 record. Parke Carroll fired Bob Elliott and members of his coaching staff on October 3. "I have a lot of respect for Elliott," he said. "The move was made for obvious reasons and because we feel that the new owners should have a voice in naming the manager.... This has been a very difficult year. Nothing went right from March 10 [the day Johnson died] on. Bob didn't get a single break all year."[12]

Elliott was not offered another position in the organization, but Carroll said he was a highly qualified baseball man and he felt Elliott would remain in baseball. Elliott did not manage again, although he served as a coach for the expansion Los Angeles Angels in 1961. He died in San Diego on May 4, 1966.

15

Who Will Buy the Team?

The future of major league baseball in Kansas City was cast into doubt by Arnold Johnson's sudden death on March 10, 1960. Carmen Johnson wanted to be placed on the Athletics board of directors following the death of her husband, but the other directors refused. She wanted to keep Johnson's stock while the other stockholders wanted to sell. The stockholders, felt the value of their holdings would decrease if the majority shares were not put up for sale. Roy Mack's widow Margaret McGillicuddy held the largest share of the minority stock (20 percent). Nathaniel Leverone owned 15 percent of the shares; J. Patrick Lannan owned 10 percent and Earl Johnson owned the remaining 3 percent. Ed Vollers stated they were "interested in seeing the club sold to Kansas City and retained there."

Kenneth and Leonard Berg, real estate developers from Metuchen, New Jersey, headed an eight-person syndicate that wanted to acquire a major league team and move it to the Middlesex County (New Brunswick) area of New Jersey. The group wanted to build a stadium on 300 acres near the New Jersey Turnpike and hired an architect to design a $30 million all-weather stadium. The new stadium would have a roof that would unfold "like a tulip." The Bergs contacted the A's and Vollers told them to put the offer in writing.[1]

Other groups and individuals wanted to bid for the team, some of them had been seeking a franchise in the Continental League, a proposed major league circuit. Groups were actively raising money in Minneapolis–St. Paul, Dallas and Houston. Some Kansas City groups were interested, but were either under-financed or unwilling to commit themselves to such a large investment. J.W. Putsch, a local restaurateur and chairman of the Kansas City Chamber of Commerce baseball subcommittee, and *Kansas City Star* sports editor Ernest Mehl were appointed co-chairman of a committee to find local investors. "We will proceed immediately with a plan to seek 10 investors at $200,000 each to raise $2 million in earnest money," said Putsch on June 23. "We know we now have four such investors and anticipate one more before the end of the day. Between the $2 million and the actual purchase price, we want to get as wide a spread of ownership as we possibly can among those in the Kansas City trade area." Putsch said they would approach Vollers and one of the minority stockholders "so that we can go ahead with an inspection of the property preparatory to making a bid."[2]

Putsch and Mehl reported back to the Chamber of Commerce on June 30. They said the group had nine investors who pledged $200,000 each but did not reveal the names. A tenth person was considering the investment. Some of the investors were individuals while others represented syndicates or groups, including interested parties in Wichita and Topeka. One of the potential investors was St. Louis Cardinals executive Bill Bergesch. He wanted a front-office position with the team in exchange for his investment and would invest $100,000 of his own money and $100,000 obtained from friends. "It was a consensus that a group of not larger than 10 people be represented in owing a substantial majority of the stock in the Athletics," said Putsch and Mehl, adhering to the league requirement that a majority of the stock had to be held by a small group. "However, this does not preclude widespread participation in ownership of the Athletics, which we would encourage." Putsch and Mehl reported 12 other individuals or groups expressed interest in purchasing the team.[3] Four Kansas City individuals or groups wanted to keep it in Kansas City. One was Alex Barket of the Civic Plaza National Bank. Three "outside" groups (people outside Kansas City) wanted to keep it in Kansas City. Five groups wanted to move it to another city. Two represented Dallas interests; the others represented Houston, Minneapolis–St. Paul and Trenton, New Jersey (probably the Berg group).[4]

A few weeks later a New York real estate group offered Milton Cooper, an executor for the Johnson estate representing City National Bank of Chicago, $4.5 million for the team. The New York group consisted of Morris Karp, president of Realty Equities company; Jerry Dautch, vice president of the company; and Saul Finkelstein, a realtor from New Rochelle, New York.[5]

Attendance at the first 33 games through mid–June 1960 was 319,179, a decline of 107,522 from the previous season. It appeared the final number of tickets sold would be approximately 750,000, and the attendance clause stipulated that if it fell below 850,000 the lease could be cancelled. The large New York offer and similar offers reported from other cities made it imperative for the city to sell enough tickets to reach

15—Who Will Buy the Team?

850,000 tickets to avoid a bidding war and assure the team would remain in Kansas City for at least one additional season. "They are not interested in buying the club if they have to keep it here," stated Mehl. This would enable the Kansas City investors to acquire the team at a reasonable price.[6]

Mehl organized a ticket campaign on July 20. The *Kansas City Star* purchased 25,000 tickets to start the drive. Hallmark Cards also purchased 25,000 tickets. The Building and Construction Trade council reserved 3,000 tickets for the September 9 game and said 35 affiliated local unions would be asked to purchase tickets. More than 100 firms set up special nights. The ticket drive reached its goal of on September 14, 1960, assuring the team would remain in Kansas City for the 1961 season. Approximately 894,000 tickets were sold by the end of the season.

Leverone and the other minority stockholders felt that every effort should be made to keep the team in Kansas City. "We have discussed the situation at length with Mr. Vollers and he shares the feeling that any sale of the franchise should be delayed until the Kansas City civic leaders have had every opportunity to get their funds together," he said. "It is also our understanding that the trustee of the City National Bank and Trust company of Chicago also shares this feeling about the Kansas City interests with Mr. Vollers and those of us who are minority stockholders in the A's."[7]

The executors of Johnson's estate and the minority stockholders officially put up the team for sale on July 31, 1960. Leverone challenged the Kansas City group to organize and come up with enough funds to purchase the team. "I want to say again and I have said it several times before that it would be the height of dishonesty on our part if Kansas City were not given the first chance to buy the franchise," he said. "I have promised to do everything in my power and help in any way I can to further the Kansas City interests even though I am not in a position to make the final decision. I have felt all along that in the light of the magnificent manner in which Kansas City and its area have supported the Athletics there must be men willing to assume the responsibility of the purchase of the franchise. From what I have heard of the efforts begin made there may be need for some one strong figure to step to the front to give some momentum to the drive for the money required to make the bid."[8]

The Continental League collapsed on August 2, 1960, coupled with an announcement the two existing major leagues would each add an additional two teams. New York and Los Angeles were virtually assured of gaining two of the franchises, eliminating the New York groups bidding for the A's. Houston and either Minneapolis–St. Paul or Toronto were the probable locations for the other two franchises. The Houston group, with its large financial resources, presented the greatest challenge to Kansas City. That threat would be eliminated if Houston obtained one of the new franchises.[9]

Byron Spencer, an attorney who was on the board of Power and Light and Pickering Lumber, represented the Kansas City group and met with Vollers and Harry L. Stover, an accountant with Arthur Anderson and Company, in Kansas City on September 14. Spencer said the group exceeded $2 million in pledges and still aimed to reach $3 million. Vollers explained the business operations of the team, including player contracts, leases and other matters.[10]

Parke Carroll wanted to hire a manager for 1961 as the 1960 season came to the close. He was afraid that by the time the ownership question was settled, the best managers would be committed to other teams, especially with the four expansion teams seeking managers. Joe Gordon was interested but had another year left of his contract to manage Detroit. This made it impossible for Carroll to contact him, so Mehl contacted Gordon about working in Kansas City under Carroll and the new local ownership group.

The A's dismissed manager Bob Elliott one hour after Gordon resigned in Detroit October 3. Both Gordon and Carroll denied reports that Gordon had agreed to terms to manage the A's. This prompted speculation that the Kansas City group had reached an agreement to purchase the team. Carroll said the sale was not completed but the present owners were working in cooperation with the Kansas City group on certain matters. "As far as the Athletics are concerned," he said, "Our policy is business as usual. The present ownership will continue to run the club until such a time as it is sold. The present management will sign the new manager of the Athletics unless, of course, the club should be sold first. The action taken today only indicates that we're still operating the ballclub." Gordon signed a two-year contract to manage the Athletics on October 5, 1960. Terms were estimated at $30,000 a year with a bonus clause. This deal, Gordon said, would give him the opportunity he had long wanted—to manage a major league club without front office interference.[11]

The Kansas City group, which ultimately consisted of eight men, finally incorporated and deposited $250,000 in earnest money. The Kansas City group would form a new corporation named Athletics of Kansas City, Incorporated, to take advantage of the tax benefits if its bid was successful. The present name of the team was the Kansas City Athletics, Incorporated. Some members of the group contacted Yankees manager Casey Stengel to see if he was interested in the general manager position. "There is no denying he would be tremendously popular here," said a spokesman for the group. Parke Carroll had another year left on his contract and they would have to buy out his contract in order to offer the position to Stengel.[12]

By the end of October a group from St. Louis headed by Elliott Stein was the only other group bidding for the team. Stein was a St. Louis investment broker, a minority stockholder in the White Sox and former treasurer of the St. Louis Browns. Other members of his group were Gordon Schirk, Stein's partner in the investment brokerage business; Charles Baxter, a investment banker in Cleveland who formerly owned 30 percent of the debentures in the Cleveland Indians; and Lester Crown, a Chicago businessman who was chairman of the board of the Material Services Corporation of General Dynamics. They deposited $200,000 in earnest money. Both groups submitted written bids of $3,500,000 for the team, with $1,800,000 going to the Johnson estate. The bids would be presented in Probate Court in Chicago where Judge Robert J. Dunne would hear both offers and decide which bid was better.

Carmen Humes (Johnson's widow married Warren Humes on June 22 1960) submitted a surprise third bid. She met with Judge Dunne in closed hearings on November 3. She purchased the option to buy the shares for $1,800,000 a few weeks before the court hearing, posted a $100,000 bond, and had until December 14 to complete the transaction. She wanted to keep Johnson's shares for her 10-year-old son Jeffrey, so he could have it when he came of age. Vollers said Arnold Johnson intended to give the stock to Jeffrey, but he died before the changes were made in his will.[13]

According to the terms of Johnson's will, both Mrs. Humes and City National Bank and Trust of Chicago, as co-executors, had to be in complete agreement before a sale could be consummated. A large part of Johnson's $5 million in assets was invested in the A's and the bank wanted to sell those shares to pay the federal estate taxes of $750,000 and Illinois inheritance taxes of $500,000. Judge Dunne heard attorneys representing Mrs. Humes and the bank; the judge ruled against Mrs. Humes because she did not own the stock.[14]

Dunne opened the hearings on the merits of the bids from the Kansas City and St. Louis groups. He approved the sale of the team to Stein's group on November 15 after an out-of-court agreement by the co-executors. He explained that even though the Kansas City group submitted a bid that was slightly larger, other factors made the St. Louis deal preferable so far as the interests of Mrs. Humes were concerned. She reached an out-of-court agreement to sell the stock to Stein, join Stein's group, and retain 20 percent of the stock. "The court had made up its mind," said Dunne, "after taking into consideration the position of Mrs. Humes."[15]

The minority stockholders were not bound by the ruling and favored the Kansas City group. The Kansas City group said they would make a strenuous effort to purchase the stock held by the minority stockholders to prevent Stein's group from moving the team or draining money from the club. Without this stock Stein would not obtain the tax advantages accruing to anyone with 100 percent of the assents or 80 percent of the stock needed to reorganize a team. Stein might be forced to withdraw his offer.[16]

Stein's group did just that on November 18th. Stein explained he did not realize unfavorable opinion against out-of-town ownership in Kansas City until he met face-to-face with Putsch and Irvin Fain. "We know that despite any assurance we might make, there would always be a concern in the community that the club might be moved," he said. "Certainly this feeling of local fans is understandable.... (The) representatives of the Kansas City ... (arranged) a meeting with me to present and urge their viewpoint. Such a meeting was arranged ... for this morning and held with J.W. Putsch, chairman of the Kansas City Chamber of Commerce baseball committee and Irvin Fain, attorney of Kansas City. A thorough consideration of all the factors presented by them resulted in my decision to give the Kansas City group the opportunity to acquire the baseball club without competition from me. This, of course, does not mean that the Kansas City group has clear sailing, but so far as I am concerned it does remove one of the obstacles in the way of that group achieving its purpose. Promptly after reaching this conclusion and advising the Kansas City people of it, I communicated with all of the interested parties and advised them of my position." The Kansas City group would now have the opportunity to acquire the team "without competition from me."[17]

"Elliott Stein found he was going to have trouble buying enough of the minority stock in Kansas City to get his 80 percent," explained Bill Veeck. "The minority stockholders were not particularly disposed to cooperate with Johnson's widow.... Elliott's feeling was that if he bought the majority interest he could — with a lot of effort and at great expense — work something out. I didn't think that I, in good conscience, could recommend that he lock himself in without being sure of that 80 percent.... To be stuck in a marginal operation like Kansas City without tax benefits would be murder. I had to advise him to drop the option."[18]

The Probate Court hearing would be reopened although the Kansas City group now appeared to be the only bidder. They purchased an option to acquire the 48 percent held by the minority stockholders to eliminate any incentive for any outsider to bid on Johnson's stock. Mrs. Humes still had the option to buy the controlling 52 percent, but there was some question whether she could raise $1,800,000 needed to purchase it. The Kansas City group agreed to permit Mrs. Humes to purchase 20 percent of the stock, similar to the agreement she had made with Stein's group.[19]

The unsettled ownership prevented the club from starting its season ticket sale. The sale usually had been initiated by November. Despite the late start the Kansas City group, business and civic leaders in the city, had little doubt that with a concentrated effort on the part of all of them they could have a minimum of 5,000 season box and reserved seat tickets sold before the start of the 1961 season.

The American League met in St. Louis on December 5 and granted conditional approval for the Kansas City group to purchase the team. It took considerable effort by officials of the Athletics to win the league's endorsement because the financing by the group was considered marginal. The group raised $2.6 million in cash and pledges. The largest amount invested by any individual was $50,000. The largest amount invested by a corporation was $100,000, with the exception of $200,000 invested by Schlitz Brewing Company. Schlitz was a Milwaukee corporation, but it had a brewery in Kansas City and held the broadcast rights for the games. Although the group had not raised the full $3 million, they expected to raise additional money through a public sale of the stock.

A conditional contract to purchase of all assets of the Athletics except cash and certain receivables for $3.5 million was signed following the action by the American League. Eight men were identified as the leaders of the Kansas City group and all except Irving Fain would serve on the board of directors of the new organization. They were Barney Allis, president and general manager of the Muehlebach Hotel; Irving Fain, attorney at law; Ed Hogueland, vice-president and treasurer of Harzfield's Department stores; Robert Ingram, a manufacturer representative at Robert Ingram Company; Davis K. Jackson, vice-president of J. C. Nichols Real Estate developers; Bill Morris, executive with the Hotel Phillips; Guy Patterson, director of Majestic Advertising Agency in Milwaukee and the Schlitz Baseball network (Athletics broadcasting network); and Byron Spencer, attorney at law, who represented the group.

The group celebrated at the Park Plaza Hotel in St. Louis. Approval had to be obtained from the present stockholders of the Kansas City Athletics, Inc., before the sale could be completed, but all stockholders had already approved with the exception of Mrs. Humes. An ongoing feud between Mrs. Humes and the minority stockholders made that difficult. Vollers felt the matter would be settled within two or three days, but there could be no action taken until a written commitment had been received from Mrs. Humes to release her option. "I have sent the necessary papers to Mrs. Humes and her lawyer for their signatures," he stated. "To my knowledge they have offered no objections and I have every reason to believe that they are in agreement [with the sale to the Kansas City group]." He felt she would withdraw her bid and in that event he would petition the Cook County Probate Court to approve the Kansas City offer. Approval would be a mere formality because there were no other bidders.[20]

Charles O. Finley submitted a bid for $1,850,000 for Johnson's stock before the Kansas City group completed the transaction, topping the Kansas City bid by $50,000. He sent telegrams on December 6th to Vollers and Milton Cooper, a co-executor for the Johnson estate from the City National Bank of Chicago. Vollers previously contacted him three times and encouraged him to bid for the Athletics. "I was interested," Finley said, "but I couldn't move then because I had this option to buy the [White Sox] stock held by [Bill] Veeck and [Hank] Greenberg."[21]

Mrs. Humes still held the option to purchase Johnson's stock and Finley encouraged her to remain in the negotiations because she appeared to have the ability to determine who would purchase the team. Since he made a firm offer for the stock he did not have to negotiate through her, but he still might try to work out a deal with Mrs. Humes. There were now four possible outcomes:

1. Mrs. Humes could purchase Johnson's stock. The court had already awarded this stock to her after she purchased an option to buy this stock. This was considered unlikely because of the money required.

2. Mrs. Humes could purchase Johnson's stock and sell it to Finley. Finley could finance the transaction and then buy part or all of it from her.

3. Mrs. Humes could withdraw her bid and back Finley. In that event Finley could win approval from the court.

4. Mrs. Humes could withdraw her offer without committing herself to Finley and the Probate Court would approve the Kansas City offer.[22]

The final hearing was held in the Cook County Probate Court on December 16, 1960. Mrs. Humes withdrew her bid, leaving the Kansas City group and Finley as the only bidders. The Kansas City group matched Finley's offer of $1,850,000 and Dunne gave both parties until December 19 to increase their bids. Byron Spencer was given authority to bid as high as $1.9 million for Johnson's stock. "I don't care how high you go," Finley told Spencer, "I'm prepared to go higher." He indicated he would go as high as $2,500,000 because this was his last chance to acquire a major league team and he intended to go all out to get it.[23]

Finley increased his bid to $1,975,000 on December 19, and the Kansas City group withdrew its offer. He also paid $200,000 in back debts owed by the estate as part of the transaction and paid Mrs. Humes a premium price to purchase nearly 30,000 shares of Johnson's stock in Automatic Canteen. He considered this part of the price he had to pay to gain controlling interest in the team. Dunne issued a court order approving the sale of the stock to Finley. Joe Cronin, president of the American League, adhering to a poll of league owners, announced approval of the sale the following day.

"With adequate financing, home ownership could have been achieved, but no one here came forward with enough money to ensure the success of the campaign," wrote Joe McGuff. "The sad facts of the case are that in seven months of intensive campaigning, Kansas City was able to raise only $2.6 million toward the purchase price of the franchise. Undoubtedly additional money could have been raised through a public stock offering, but the American League does not regard this as a desirable form of financing.... Many individuals, most notably Byron Spencer, did heroic work on behalf of the home ownership project and contributed heavily of their time and money. But help from the top was not there."[24]

16
Charles O. Finley — The "O" Stands for Owner

Charles Oscar Finley was born on a farm in Ensley, Alabama, on February 22, 1918. His family moved to Gary, Indiana, in 1934, where he graduated from Horace Mann High School in 1936. He worked at a steel mill and enrolled at Gary Junior College. He transferred to the Indiana University Extension School in Gary, where he met Shirley McCartney in 1940. They married in May 1941.

Finley tried to enlist in the Marines after the Japanese attacked Pearl Harbor but was declared medically unfit due to a perforated ulcer. He left the steel mill to work at the Kingsbury Ordnance Plant where he became superintendent of one of the plant's five divisions. He often worked 10 hours a day, seven days a week. He also played first base for the semipro Gary Merchants baseball team on weekends and evenings.

Finley met Louis Duke, a Gary insurance agent, at the plant. He helped Finley get a part-time position selling insurance at night for the Equitable Life Insurance Company. At the end of World War II Finley became a full-time agent at the Travelers Insurance Agency in Gary. He worked as many as 20 hours a day and established a sales record, writing $15,450 in accident insurance premiums plus an additional $2,412 in health and life insurance premiums in 1946. Finley pushed himself too hard and developed a persistent cough. One evening he had a severe coughing spell after climbing a flight of stairs to see a physician about an insurance policy. The doctor examined him and discovered he had an advanced case of pneumonic tuberculosis. It was incurable. There were no effective antibiotics and he was given a 50–50 chance to live. Finley entered the James O. Parramore Hospital in Crown Point, Indiana, in December 1946. His weight dropped from 160 to 97 pounds. "I was determined not to die," Finley said. "I'd lose my food and I'd push that button and get the nurse back with another tray. I found that anytime you toss your cookies, if you go ahead and force food down, you don't toss 'em a second time.... Sometimes I had to reorder twice."[1]

Shirley and the couple's two children moved in with Charlie's parents in Gary where she got a job as a proofreader for the *Gary Post-Tribune* and made $30 a week. The children supplemented their income doing odd jobs. "Here I was selling health insurance and I didn't have any myself," Finley said. "I'd told myself I'd buy some when I was 40. But I was only 29. Here I was, just a guy in an ordinary job and when this TB hits me, my wife has to work to make ends meet. I was the living proof that professional men needed it. My kids were the living victims."[2]

Finley recovered and was discharged from the hospital in March 1948. He devised a group insurance plan for doctors but needed financial backing from a large insurance company to implement it. Insurance executives did not want take a multi-million dollar risk by increasing the length and cutting the price of health and accident policies for medical professionals. Finley finally received backing from the Provident Life and Accident Insurance Company. He formed Charles O. Finley and Company to administer the insurance and set up his office on the tenth floor of the Gary National Bank Building. He sold his first group policy to the Lake County Medical Society; it provided $100 a week in disability income plus other benefits for an annual premium of $176.60.

Finley wanted to create a nationwide plan. He negotiated with companies for nearly two years before he convinced Continental Casualty Company to underwrite the plan. "His first really big customer was a national professional organization of doctors, the American College of Surgeons," recalled one of his friends. "Sometime in 1951, they were holding a meeting in San Francisco, and Charlie was dying to get out there. But he didn't even have the price of an air ticket out west. So he went out and got another loan on his car—an old DeSoto I think it was. Well as soon as Charlie got that two thousand dollar loan, he ran out and bought two suits, and got his first manicure. Then he sped off for the airport. His car broke down on the way, but he still got there in time to buy his ticket and board the plane." Finley sold them a group policy and earned $441,563 in commissions, according to the U. S. Tax Court.[3]

Finley's business expanded rapidly and he made his first million within two years. Finley added the Southern Medical Association in 1953, a group with doctors in 17 states and an eventual premium yield of more than $3 million. He added the American Medical Association in 1961. Charles O. Finley and Company became one of the country's most successful health insurance brokers. By the mid–1960s it covered 53

Charles Finley (National Baseball Hall of Fame Library, Cooperstown, New York).

different associations that included 70,000 doctors and handled over $20 million in business every year. Finley invested his substantial profits in the stock market and became a multi-millionaire.

Finley was now in a position to fulfill his lifelong dream to purchase a major league baseball team. He attempted to purchase the Athletics in 1954 after he accumulated a personal wealth of approximately $5 million. "I remember Charlie saying that the Internal Revenue had told him to spend some of that money that he had hoarded up, or else declare a dividend," recalled Calvin Griffith. "And of course if he declared a dividend, he'd just be declaring it for his wife and all his kids. So I got the impression that the IRS gave him two or three years to go out and buy something." Johnson bought the A's and Finley tried to purchase the Detroit Tigers in 1956. He said he had the financial support of such prominent Midwest business names such as Storer, Goldblatt and Armour. Finley bid $5 million, but it was only the fifth highest offer. The Tigers were sold to a syndicated headed by Fred Knorr.[4]

The Chicago White Sox were Finley's favorite team. Mrs. Dorothy Comiskey Rigney wanted to sell the 54 percent majority of the stock she owned in 1958. "I had written some stories about (Bill) Veeck being in town putting together a syndicate to buy the White Sox," wrote Jerome Holtzman. "He had taken an option to buy the majority interest from Dorothy Comiskey Rigney (for $100). A couple of days after I wrote the story I got a phone call from a guy who says to me, 'I'll tell you why Veeck isn't going to buy Dorothy's interest. You just get a pencil and paper and listen.' And this guy gave me all kinds of figures. It was the first time I'd ever heard of the possibility of depreciating ballplayers. Well, this conversation went on 45 minutes and I asked the guy his name. He wouldn't tell me. I kept pushing and he finally told me. It was Finley. First time I'd ever talked to the man. I checked out his information and thought that maybe he was put onto me by Chuck Comiskey, who was feuding with Dorothy, his sister, about selling the club. I asked Chuck. He said he wasn't working with Finley but that he'd heard of him."[5]

Finley called Veeck and asked to join his group. Veeck included Finley until he learned about his call to Holtzman and discovered that he went to Dorothy's attorneys and signed a purchase agreement for $500,000 that would be exercisable if Veeck let his option lapse. "Being rather narrow-minded about having people in my own syndicate working the other side of the street, I informed Finley that he had disqualified himself (from being part of the group)," Veeck said. "One thing you have to say for Finley, he's not a man to nurse a grudge; he promptly offered to buy my $100 option for $250,000."[6]

The American League would expand to 10 teams in 1961 and Finley felt this was his opportunity to acquire a team. Hank Greenberg was a member of the expansion committee. He investigated Los Angeles for the committee with the understanding he would be granted an option for that franchise. "Finley is sitting in Chicago reading about all this in the papers," said Holtzman. "He'd been anticipating that Greenberg would get L.A. and that Veeck would go with him. And that would leave the White Sox for sale." Finley purchased an option to buy Veeck's shares and offered him $4.2 million for the White Sox.[7]

American League expansion plans received a setback when baseball commissioner Ford Frick ruled that the Los Angeles franchise would have to indemnify the Dodgers $350,000 for invasion of the Los Angeles territory. Dodgers owner Walter O'Malley also demanded that the new team play in Wrigley Field and sign a contract to become tenants at Dodger Stadium when that stadium was completed in 1962. Greenberg felt this made it impossible to operate profitably and was no longer interested. Finley assumed this meant Veeck would not sell the White Sox. "He was wrong, of course," said Veeck, who had health problems and sold his shares to Arthur Allyn six months later, "a mistake that cost him his golden opportunity to end up with a contending team. Charles O. was hot for the franchise that was available at the moment, though, and for that I couldn't blame him. I had to warn him, however, that on the unlikely chance he did get the Los Angeles franchise, he could only get hurt." Veeck also informed Finley that the Kansas City Athletics were available, but Finley wanted to buy the Los Angeles franchise and thought he had the blessing of Del Webb.[8]

Webb also supported other candidates. He wanted to build the stadium for whoever acquired the franchise. Finley offered $5 million for the franchise and traveled to San Francisco to offer the manager's job to Casey Stengel. Finley felt that if he could present Stengel as his manager, the other owners would approve his bid. Stengel was not interested and had already turned down offers to manage other teams.[9]

Kenyon Brown's syndicate emerged as the front-runner to acquire the Los Angeles franchise. Gene Autry, the movie cowboy, and Bob Reynolds, Autry's partner in a radio chain, were part of Brown's group. "When Charlie heard that Autry was in a group bidding against him, he stopped off in Scottsdale, Arizona to try and find Roy Rogers and get him in his syndicate," Holtzman said. "He was going to match the opposition, cowboy for cowboy." Brown dropped out and Autry became the leader of the Los Angeles group. Finley decided to seek the Kansas City franchise when it became apparent Autry's group would obtain the Los Angeles expansion franchise. Veeck told Finley he could buy the majority interest from Arnold Johnson's widow and he could probably buy the minority interests with a little work.[10]

Finley purchased the Athletics and moved the team to Oakland following the 1967 season. He owned the Athletics for 20 years through stunning failure and remarkable success, while remaining both colorful and controversial. He sold the A's to Levi Strauss and Company on August 23, 1980 for $12.7 million. He died on February 19, 1996.

17
Trying to Outdo Veeck

"My intentions are to keep the A's permanently in Kansas City and build a winning ballclub," Finley said after he purchased the team. "I have no intention of ever moving the franchise. I will spend any reasonable amount of money to get in the first division.... I believe the Athletics can be built up, but that will take money. And I will spend money.... I am not interested in capital gains, nor am I a fast-buck man." He repeated the promise on numerous occasions. "I have said and want to say again I have no thought of moving the franchise. I have liked the manner in which the fans of Kansas City have supported the Athletics. They have proved to me this is a fine major league city." The promises continued. "This ball club is going to stay in Kansas City.... When I was chasing the Detroit Tigers I wasn't going to move the Tigers out of Detroit. When I was chasing the White Sox I wasn't going to move the White Sox out of Chicago. And when I got a place to roost in Kansas City — brother, I mean to tell you, I'm here to stay!"[1]

Finley said he might move his family to Kansas City after his oldest son, Charles Jr., graduated from high school in Gary, Indiana. "Charlie has two more years to go," he said. "He's on the football and track teams and I definitely wouldn't move until he's ready for college." A few weeks later he added: "Wherever I've gone I've met with nothing but the most enthusiastic treatment. I told one group the other night that I felt I couldn't possibly move to Kansas City until my son had been graduated from school in Gary, but the way I feel right now, after what has happened to me in the last week, I feel inclined to make the move right away."[2]

Kansas City would no longer "be regarded as a Yankee farm team," he promised. "We will have no alliances with any other club in the American League. There will be no such trades as have been made in the past. When we develop stars we are going to keep them." Finley said manager Joe Gordon would be retained but did not promise to retain general manager Parke Carroll. "I will need the best baseball brains to help me," he said. "But I am not going to be an absentee owner. I am in a position to spend a great deal of my time running the Athletics. At the same time I will have to lean on men who know a lot more about this thing than I do." Finley wanted to hire Yankees general manager George Weiss if he purchased the White Sox. He made a similar offer after purchasing the A's. Weiss, who was named Major League Executive of the Year by *The Sporting News*, confirmed Finley offered him a position with the A's. "Finley was very kind," he said, "but I failed to develop interest in his offer."[3]

Finley planned to increase season ticket sales through a large direct-mail campaign similar to the way he sold insurance. He also devised a nine-game ticket plan. He thought this would assure a near sellout for every game before the season opened and talked about breaking the all-time Kansas City attendance record. "I am going to spend the month of January in Kansas City and I have in mind engaging in the advance ticket sale myself," he said. "I like that sort of thing. It will enable me to meet a lot of people and it's always better that way."[4]

Finley introduced 65-year-old Frank Lane as general manager of the Athletics in Kansas City on January 3, 1961. *The Sporting News* called him one of the game's most exciting personalities, a baseball doctor who has specialized in rehabilitating sick clubs. "I had several men in mind, but Lane was my first choice," Finley said. "We had several conferences on the phone and finally came to terms. I wanted, for one thing, something to arouse the baseball fans in Kansas City … and I think Lane can help me. I know what he did to revive the interest in the White Sox and what he had done at Cleveland, and I believe he can do as much or more for Kansas City. In Lane I believe we have secured one of the top executives in baseball." Lane reportedly signed a four-year contract with a salary of $100,000 a year. "I can't think of anyone who could do a better job of pumping life into a ball club than Frank Lane," Finley said. "He'll give the club a transfusion — and that's what it needs. I know it isn't going to be easy building a club into a contender. But we'll be wheeling and dealing. That's one of the primary reasons I sought Lane: I wanted an experienced baseball man and especially one who has an outstanding record as a trader. To me Lane is the best trader in baseball.... Even at $100,000 a year Lane is an exceptional bargain. We won't be cheap. I believe in hiring the best men — regardless of their price."[5]

"I have a very high regard for [former general manager Parke] Carroll," Finley said. "We had a fine meeting in Chicago at which time I told him we would like for him to remain in the organization. I have been told

17—Trying to Outdo Veeck

what a tremendous job he has done since Johnson's death in keeping the organization together. The fact that I have hired Lane should not be taken as any reflection on Carroll." Carroll had a contract covering the 1961 and 1962 seasons and Finley was obligated to pay his $25,000 salary unless he found another job at a comparable salary. "Finley told me that since he would have to pay Carroll he would stick him in an office and force him to clip items out of papers for his pay," Lane said a few months later. "And he would have to work from 9 to 5 each day."[6]

Frank Lane (National Baseball Hall of Fame Library, Cooperstown, New York).

"I moved from Cleveland to Kansas City because the offer was too good to turn down," Lane claimed. In actuality he needed to find another position. Cleveland fans were upset because Lane traded popular Rocky Colavito before the 1960 season and attendance dropped more than 500,000. Lane asked Cleveland's board of directors for a new contract even though he still had two years remaining on his current contract that paid him $50,000 a year. They refused. Finley contacted Indians owner Nate Dolin regarding Lane and he told Finley: "You need a general manager. Frank will help you learn the business." Finley offered Lane the position, but he was reluctant to join the A's until Dolin advised him: "I'm trying to tell you that your days (in Cleveland) are numbered and to take that job."[7]

Lane, who was born in Cincinnati on February 1, 1896, began his career by writing about baseball for the *Cincinnati Commercial Tribune*. He was instrumental in bringing Larry McPhail to Cincinnati as general manager of the Reds in 1933. McPhail appointed Lane assistant general manager of the team later that year. Lane was the director of the Reds' minor league operation from 1937 through 1941.

Lane became a Navy commander during World War II. He returned to baseball as director of the New York Yankees western division farm clubs and general manager of the Kansas City Blues in 1946. He was elected president of the American Association in 1947 and served in that position class AAA for two seasons.

Lane was hired as general manager of the Chicago White Sox in November 1948. The Sox lost 101 games in 1948 and finished in last place. Lane acquired the reputation as a man who would trade anyone on the team in order to build a winning team and became known as "Trader Lane." He made 241 trades involving 353 players during his seven seasons with the Sox and built them into a contending team. Lane had repeated conflicts with Sox minority owner Chuck Comiskey and resigned on September 21, 1955.

Lane joined the St Louis Cardinals and immediately made trades to rebuild the team that finished in seventh place in 1955. One controversial trade sent Cardinals second baseman Red Schoendienst to the Giants in 1956. Lane placed popular Stan Musial on the trading block until Cardinals owner August Busch assured local fans that Musial would not be traded. The Cardinals finished in second place in 1957, just eight games behind the pennant winning Milwaukee Braves. Lane asked Busch for an extension on his contract. Lane resigned when Busch refused.

Lane accepted an offer to become general manager for the Cleveland Indians, a team that finished in sixth place in 1957. Lane's trades enabled the Indians to finish in second place in 1959, just five games behind the White Sox. Lane's popularity declined the following year after the trade of Colavito, the league's home run champion, to Detroit for Harvey Kuenn. He made a historic managerial trade later in the season, trading manager Joe Gordon to Detroit for manager Jimmie Dykes.

Finley contacted Cleveland on December 22, 1960, three days after he purchased the Athletics, to seek permission to speak to Lane. Finley offered Lane the position as general manager in Kansas City and Lane accepted the offer on December 30. Lane made nine trades involving 36 players as general manager of the Athletics. Finley fired him on August 22, 1961, although he remained on the A's payroll for the remainder of his contract.

Lane could not work in baseball while he was under contract with Kansas City. He served as general manager of the Chicago Zephyrs basketball team in 1962-63 before the team moved to Baltimore. He returned to baseball as director of baseball operations for the Milwaukee Brewers in 1971 and 1972.

He died on March 19, 1981 at the age of 85. He made over 400 trades during his career as a major league general manager.

The A's named Pat Friday executive vice president and, like Finley, he drew no salary from the club. "As president and vice president of the team, I suppose we could pay ourselves fancy salaries," Finley said, "but I don't want to take any money unnecessarily. Not only that, but we're going to plow every cent of profit back into the club. Our main objective is to build the team into a contender — and we'll spend every cent we can get." Friday had been in charge of one of Finley's insurance offices.[8]

Bill Bergesch became assistant general manager. He worked with Lane in St Louis and had been part of the Cardinal organization for 14 years. He had been an executive at several minor league teams and served as field coordinator in the scouting and minor league departments. He wanted to invest $100,000 in the Athletics during the previous summer when the local group tried to buy the team. Fred Finley, Finley's brother, would work with the team's promotional ventures. James Schaaf replaced Dave Keefe as traveling secretary. Keefe returned as traveling secretary during the 1961 season when Shaaf was named director of public relations. Finley retained minor league director Hank Peters, player personnel director George Selkirk, and stadium operations director Bob Wachter. He did not retain either public relations director Gordon Smith or promotions director Dick Challinor. Finley felt the team had not been marketed well.

The Kansas City group indicated they would exercise their option to purchase the remaining 48 percent of the stock unless Finley agreed to keep the club in Kansas City for at least four or five seasons. "I'd love to have 100 percent control, but that isn't necessary," Finley said. "I'd be happy to work with the other stockholders and I'm sure we could have an excellent and amicable relationship. I know the minority stockholders are anxious to improve the club." If he obtained complete control, Finley promised to eliminate the attendance clause from the lease as a pledge he would keep the team in Kansas City. The Kansas City group waived their rights to purchase the stock in favor of Finley.[9]

The board of directors voted to dissolve at a held a meeting on January 12, 1961. The board, down to five members since the death of Johnson and Roy Mack, consisted of Nathaniel Leverone, Parke Carroll, Ed Vollers, Earl Johnson and J. Patrick Lannan. They gave approval for Finley to exercise the option he obtained from the Kansas City group, enabling Finley to acquire full ownership and reorganize the team. Carroll officially resigned and severed his ties to the team. "Carroll deserves a great deal of credit for the manner in which he kept the organization intact," Vollers stated. Vollers, who served as secretary of the board and its general counsel, also resigned. The last official act of the board before voting to dissolve was to vote a bonus to Carroll and Vollers.[10]

A new board of directors was appointed: Charles Finley, president and chairman of the board of directors; Thomas Keane, secretary and general counsel; Pat Friday, vice president and treasurer; and Fred Finley, vice president.

Leverone, Lannan and Earl Johnson, the three remaining members from the previous board, still owned stock and temporarily remained on the board. They would resign after Finley purchased their stock so Finley could replace them with men of his own choice, hopefully at least one or two of them from the Kansas City area.[11]

Carroll died of a sudden heart attack on February 4, 1961, less than one month after he resigned at the age of 56. Carroll's widow asked Finley for the $50,000 that was owed for remaining two years of the contract. Finley refused and forced her to sue. She ultimately lost.[12]

Finley purchased the 28 percent of the stock owned by Leverone, Lannan and Earl Johnson and gained control of the 80 percent of the stock he needed to reorganize the team. He called a press conference in his Chicago insurance office because Leverone, Lannan and Earl Johnson all lived in the Chicago area. Finley had a Kansas City baseball cap flown there for him to wear. After the press conference Finley realized it would have looked better had he held the event in Kansas City. He called the wire services and demanded that the caption under the picture be changed to state the event took place in Kansas City. They refused to change the caption.[13]

He became full owner on February 16, 1961, after he purchased the stock from Mrs. Margaret Mack. He paid an estimated $1.9 million to purchase the stock from the minority stockholders, making his total investment nearly $4 million. Finley called a press conference in the office of Mayor H. Roy Bartle to fulfill his promise to burn the lease. He invited an official from the fire department, the press, members of the city council and interested citizens. "I gave my word that once I had obtained the full 100 percent this clause in the contract would be stricken," he said. "We're going to accomplish this with a little drama. Maybe at heart I am an arsonist. At any rate I'm going to strike a match and set fire to the contract. Then I will sign a new contract. This will prove I am not in the slightest concerned about the 850,000 minimum. I am not concerned, as a matter of fact, with the attendance at all."[14]

Leverone, Lannan and Earl Johnson resigned from the board after Finley purchased their stock. Finley replaced them with J.W. Putsch, Earl Smith and Byron Spencer. Smith was vice chairman of the Smith-Grives Printing Company and all were members of the Chamber of Commerce baseball committee. The appointments turned out to be non-existent. The board never met because Finley, not a corporation, operated the team. The board was quietly dissolved following the 1961 season.[15]

Finley's popularity was such that during January, February and March, he and his new front office team made more than 150 personal appearances. Finley made approximately 125 of those appearances. He gave hundreds of speeches to civic and social functions, fraternities and sororities, meetings of politicians and the public, sometimes making as many as five speeches a day. "I don't think I can outdo Veeck," he said, referring to Veeck's reputation for giving speeches on behalf of his team, "but I am going to try. There is no substitute for going out and meeting people. The more speeches the better." His theme was always the same: "This is Kansas City's team. I will keep it in Kansas City. I will make it a winning team. If the city will only support me while I am building the team, we will all win."[16]

"I poured a half a million dollars of my own money into improvements on a municipally owned stadium," Finley says. "And now I've got the sexiest-looking ballpark in the country.... You must spend money to make money. The ballpark looked like a pigpen. I asked the council to fix it up. They pleaded poverty but told me they would give me credit if I did something.... They gave me nothing."[17] Finley actually spent $411,670.74 to improve the stadium. The expense broke down as:

Fan-A-Gram	$121,141.86	Dugouts, box seats	$20,575.02
Painting	$92,969.80	Auxiliary scoreboard	$18,173.25
Move left field fence	$50,015.96	Picnic area	$16,508.53
Exterior Lighting	$31,749.39	Ball lift, plate duster	$4,876.03
Left field seats	$27,951.83	Restrooms, neon lights	$2,669.29
A's share of tunnel	$22,553.11	Radio, PA system	$2,486.57

Some of the improvements were completed before he bought the team, such as the addition of box seats along the left field foul line and the relocation of the A's bullpen along the right field foul line, but construction on the tunnel was held up following Johnson's death. Finley and Sportservice shared the $95,000 cost of the tunnel that provided access to box seats and additional restrooms and concession stands. Construction on the tunnel started in January.

The relocation of the A's bullpen made it possible to move the fence. The light tower in left field was moved back and the sheds behind the fence that stored the grounds keeping equipment were relocated to the former bullpen area enabling the left field fence to be moved back 40 feet. Finley added 1,200 bleacher seats behind the new left field box seats and repainted the stadium. The box seats were painted yellow, the reserved seats and bleachers desert turquoise, and the upright beams yellowish orange. The wall outside the park was sandblasted and painted yellow. Finley felt the area was too dark outside. He had quartex lights that shed an amber glow installed every 50 feet around the stadium.

A picnic area was built behind the left field new bleachers, shaded by 10 sugar maple trees and illuminated by carriage lights at night. A Fan-A-Gram was installed adjacent to the center-field scoreboard to display messages. Radio broadcasts of the games were piped into the restrooms. The dugouts were lengthened and lowered and had fluorescent lights installed so that fans could see what the team at bat and its manager were doing during night games. "I look at it from the fans' point of view," said Finley. "I like to see what's going on in the dugout — the strategy being planned and so on. So I figure everybody would like to see, too."[18]

Two sheep replaced the goats that stadium manager Bob Wachter used on the hill behind the right field fence. "What we had in right center field was (not) a hill," Finley recalled. "It was more like a small mountain. You couldn't cut the grass out there, it was too hilly and rocky." The goats were replaced because they ate everything except the grass.[19]

"Finley's two most interesting innovations are a device for supplying the plate umpire with baseballs when he needs them and a mechanism that saves him the bother of bending over and dusting off the home plate," wrote

Kansas City's Municipal Stadium in 1961 (after Finley's "improvements"). (Photograph courtesy of the Kansas City Royals.)

Rex Lardner. "The first is a rabbit with blinking eyes, wearing an A's uniform, that rises from an invisible spot in the grass to the right of the plate umpire. Between the ears of the rabbit, who is called Harvey, is a cage of baseballs. The cover magically flings itself open and the umpire helps himself. The ascent of the rabbit is accompanied by as ascending whistle, while his disappearance into the ground is accompanied by a descending whistle. Simultaneously the organist plays 'Here Comes Peter Cottontail.' The other innovation is a compressed-air device whose spout is in the center of the plate. When needed, air jets out to blow dirt off. A few enemy batters have been startled by Little Blowhard or Harvey the first time they encountered them, one of them leaping nearly a foot in the air."[20]

Finley used Bill Veeck as a model for these changes. One of Veeck's first priorities after he acquired a team was to improve the ballpark. After he purchased the White Sox in 1959, Veeck painted the green seats blue and red and paid $150,000 to paint the exterior of the park. The restrooms were renovated and additional restrooms were added in the bleachers. Veeck installed his famous "exploding scoreboard" the following year with fireworks after every White Sox home run and a "Sox-O-Gram" for messages. A picnic area was built under the left field stands and a ball lift was placed behind home plate. Bright lights were placed around the stadium to dispel fears about the safety of the neighborhood. Some of Finley's improvements were original ideas but most were identical to Veeck's improvements at Comiskey Park:

Veeck	Year Completed	Finley	Year Completed
Sox-O-Gram	1960	Fan-A-Gram	1961
Painting seats	1959	Painting seats	1961
Exterior lighting	1959	Exterior lighting	1961
Picnic Area	1960	Picnic Area	1961
Additional restrooms	1959	Additional restrooms	1961
Radio, PA system	1959	Radio, PA system	1961
Ball lift	1960	Ball lift	1961

"Bill Veeck provided Charlie with a behavioral model of significant proportions—and a lot of new ideas," wrote Tom Clark. "He observes Veeck's famed promotional methods with great interest. Once he gets his own ballclub Charlie does his best to emulate the master showman's tactics, putting into motion a secondhand promotional circus patterned on Veeck's modes as he understands—or misconstrues—them. But he's never able to duplicate Veeck's results, i.e., soaring attendance totals. 'Finley does things without class,' Veeck himself will comment after observing Charlie in action in Kansas City."[21]

Finley changed the team's uniforms, the first change in style since the team moved to Kansas City. The new uniforms had pinstripes, similar to the uniforms worn by the White Sox and the Yankees. He decided to televise the home opener to show off the new team, uniforms, and improved stadium and to accommodate the fans that would be unable to attend the opening game. The number of televised games during the season was increased to 30 selected road games. Merle Harmon and Bill Grigsby continued to announce the games both on radio and television, but Skelley no longer co-sponsored the games. Local participating sponsors shared the network with Schlitz.

Finley won the acceptance of Kansas City baseball fans and many considered him the savior of Athletics baseball. In an appearance on the *Insight* program on WDAF radio, interviewer Monte Moore asked Finley: "You've mentioned earlier to me that you wanted to do one thing above all else in Kansas City in the next few months. That was to instill in the people of Kansas City the confidence that you hoped you could. Do you feel you've achieved that goal?"

"I felt it would take about six months to get the faith and confidence of the fans in this area," Finley answered. "They have been so exceedingly nice to me that I have their faith and confidence already."[22]

"Charlie was liked immediately in Kansas City," said Frank Lane. Mayor H. Roy Bartle expressed the sentiments of the city when he said: "Charlie Finley has put more spirit into the city than anyone [in the past decade]. He holds the heart of the city in the palm of his hand." One of the members of the Kansas City group that nearly bought the team said that every few weeks he and his colleagues got together just for the purpose of thanking God for Charlie Finley.[23]

A'S STADIUM LEASES 1955–1963

1955–1959 Lease

1955–1956	$1,000 a year with an additional $24,000 if paid admissions exceeded one million.
1957–1959	$1,000 a year plus 5 percent of gross receipts (after taxes, visitor's and league's shares) with an additional $24,000 if paid admissions exceeded one million. Five percent of food and beverage concessions and 20 percent of other concessions. Attendance clause enabled franchise to terminate lease on March 31,1958, if paid admissions were less than three million.

1960–1963 Lease

1960	$1,000 plus 5 percent of paid admissions. An additional $24,000 would be paid if paid admission exceeded one million. Seven and one-half percent of all concessions. Attendance clause enabled franchise to be moved if attendance fell below 850,000.
1961–1963	Same as 1960 with the 850,000 attendance clause deleted.

18

1961: Gordon, Lane and Charlie O.

"I have talked to both Lane and Gordon before I made any moves," Finley said, "and I am sure we will have no trouble. I have a high regard for Gordon.... There is no bitterness between the two and I am sure they can work in harmony.... We have the greatest general manager in baseball in Frank Lane. We've got a great field manager in Joe Gordon. You take Lane, you take Gordon and the trades we've already made and I can see fifth place."[1]

Despite Finley's statement, recent history made it unlikely Lane and Gordon could work together. Lane hired Gordon to manage the Indians in 1958. The Indians finished in second place in 1959, but Lane felt the team should have won the pennant. Lane talked with former Dodgers and Giants manager Leo Durocher. Chicago defeated the Indians to clinch the pennant on September 22 and Lane announced that "as of now" coach Mel Harder would manage for the remainder of the season. Lane's negotiations with Durocher broke down when Durocher demanded a better deal. Lane rehired Gordon and gave him a two-year contract with an increase in salary.

The Indians were plagued by a series of injuries in 1960 and fell to fourth place with a 49–46

Joe Gordon (from Jay Publications and the Kansas City Athletics).

record on August 3. Lane contacted Detroit president Bill DeWitt and traded Gordon to Detroit for Tigers manager Jimmie Dykes. Gordon discovered it was almost as difficult to work with DeWitt as it was with Lane. He did not want to return to Detroit in 1961, even though he had another year remaining on his contract. He wanted to work with Parke Carroll and the local ownership group in Kansas City because he felt it would be an opportunity to manage without front office interference. Gordon resigned as manager of the Tigers at the end of the season and the A's signed him to a two-year contract on October 5.

His 26–31 record, in two months with Detroit marked his first below .500 mark as a major league manager. He had a successful playing career, becoming the Yankees' regular third baseman in 1938 and being named the American League Most Valuable Player in 1942. He was traded to Cleveland in 1947 and played with the Indians through the 1950 season.

He began his managerial career as player-manager for Sacramento in the Pacific Coast League in 1951. He held that position for two years. He scouted for Detroit from 1953 until July 6, 1956, when he was named manager of San Francisco in the Pacific Coast League. Gordon became manager of the Cleveland Indians on June 27, 1958, beginning his stormy relationship with Lane.

Gordon later served as a scout and minor league batting instructor for the Los Angeles Angels from October 6, 1961 through 1968. He returned to Kansas City when was hired as the first manager of the expansion Royals in 1969. He managed for one season and then became a scout and instructor for the Royals until 1972. He died in Sacramento, California, on April 14, 1978, at the age of 63.

JOE GORDON'S MANAGERIAL RECORD

Year	Team	League	Won	Lost	Position
1951	Sacramento	AAA	75	92	7
1952	Sacramento	AAA	66	114	8
1956	San Francisco	AAA	33	29	6
1957	San Francisco	AAA	101	67	1
1958	Cleveland	Major	46	40	4
1959	Cleveland	Major	89	65	2
1960	Cleveland	Major	49	46	4
1960	Detroit	Major	26	31	6
1961	Kansas City A's	Major	26	33	8
1969	Kansas City Royals	Major	69	93	4

Gordon selected Ed Fitzgerald, Dario Lodigiani, Jo Jo White and Ted Wilks as coaches in Kansas City. They were all part of the Cleveland organization in 1960. Fitzgerald was a former major major-league catcher who coached under Gordon and Dykes at Cleveland in 1960. Lodigiani, a former major league infielder, scouted for the White Sox from 1955 through 1958 and for Cleveland in 1959 and 1960. White, a former major-league outfielder, managed minor league teams for 10 seasons before he began coaching in Cleveland in 1958. Wilks was hired as pitching coach before spring training. The former St. Louis Cardinals relief pitcher was a minor league pitching coach for the Indians in 1960.

Lane and Gordon had to rebuild a team that lost some players at important positions in the 1961 expansion draft. The league held the draft on December 14, just a few days before Finley purchased the A's. Each existing team submitted a list of 15 players from its 40-man roster that could be selected for a price of $75,000 each. The Los Angeles Angels drafted pitchers Bob Davis and Ned Garver and shortstop Ken Hamlin from Kansas City and the expansion Washington Senators (the original Senators moved to Minnesota and became the Twins) drafted catchers Pete Daley and Henry Dotterer and infielders Chester Boak and Bob Johnson. The A's were now shorthanded in the catching and infield positions. Daley was the A's starting catcher and Hamlin was the starting shortstop. Garver was expected to be one of the starting pitchers for the A's in 1961. Dotterer was obtained in a trade with Cincinnati in exchange for catcher Dan Kravitz following the season. A few days before Lane replaced him, Parke Carroll traded pitcher Marty Kutyna to Washington for catcher Haywood Sullivan to bolster the depleted catching staff.

"I know the catching is almost nil," Lane said after he became general manager, "and we aren't certain we have a major league shortstop. But our outfield is good and we have a pair of outstanding pitchers in Bud Daley and Ray Herbert." He traded outfielders Whitey Herzog and Russ Snyder and a player-to-be-named-later to the Orioles on January 24 for catcher Clint Courtney, outfielder Al Pilarcik, infielders Wayne Causey and Bob Boyd, and pitcher Jim Archer. Archer, a 28-year old left-hander, was considered a possible starter for the A's. Causey, a 24-year-old infielder was a former bonus player with the Orioles and would compete for the starting position at shortstop and third base. Boyd would provide depth at first base and pinch-hit for the A's. Pilarcik had been the Orioles' regular right fielder from 1957 through 1959. Lane later returned Courtney to the Orioles as the player-to-be-named later.[2]

The A's traded pitchers John Tsitouris and John Briggs to Cincinnati for 32-year-old southpaw pitcher Joe Nuxhall the following day. Nuxhall was plagued by injuries in 1960 and had a disappointing 1–8 record with a 4.42 ERA. "I think he needs a change of scenery," said Lane. Lane purchased catcher Joe Pignatano from the Los Angeles Dodgers on January 31.

During spring training Finley told the players to come to him if they had any problems, treated them to dinner in one of Palm Beach's most expensive clubs, gave them a $150 clock radio and said he would tear up their contracts and give them retroactive salary increases if they finished in first division. He invited all their wives and sweethearts to accompany the team to Chicago and attend a cookout at his farm in LaPorte, Indiana, in May. He rearranged the schedule to give the players Monday off and changed all Saturday night home games to the afternoon. "You have to appreciate what Charlie's trying to do," commented a player.[3]

Finley's kindness did not extend to Lane or Gordon. Finley demanded to know about trades before they were made. "Lane has not been shorn of any authority," stated Finley. "I leave the discussions to making a trade to him and then he makes a recommendation to me. Then we discuss the possibilities." The *Saturday Evening Post* reported that whenever Lane suggested a trade, Finley would "deflate him by calling Bill Veeck to find out what he thought of it."[4]

Finley held a press conference at Municipal Stadium in February to announce the A's would no longer make any trades with the Yankees. He purchased an old school bus and said it symbolized the old shuttle bus to Yankee Stadium. Gasoline was poured on the bus and Lane set it aflame in the parking lot behind the left field fence. Kansas City fans "have not wanted to be known as a farm club of the Yankees," he said. "They have resented the many deals that have been made between these two organizations. It's not my place to say whether they were good or bad, but I can say they won't happen in the future. I don't mean we won't make deals when we believe they will help us, when we are trying to strengthen one position. But a new era will start in Kansas City and that I can promise.... no more deals with the Yankees." He added he would not trade the A's batboy to the Yankees for Mickey Mantle.[5]

Finley told Lane he wanted to shift the spring training camp to Arizona in 1962 and Lane went to Chandler, Arizona, to negotiate with city officials. He was ready to sign a contract when he heard a radio report that Finley signed a five-year contract to remain in West Palm Beach. Lane called Finley and asked: "Are we both working for the same club?" Finley told him to see if Chandler would top the West Palm Beach offer but Lane refused. West Palm Beach negotiated a long-term lease with Milwaukee, beginning with the 1963 season. The A's held spring training in West Palm Beach in 1962, but moved to Bradenton, Florida, in 1963.[6]

There were rumors Lane might resign due to ongoing conflicts with Finley. "There have been reports that Frank might be offered a job as general manager of the White Sox," Finley said. "But don't forget, he has a four-year contract as general manager of the Athletics and he couldn't go if I didn't want him to. I wouldn't want Frank to go because he's doing a great job for me."[7]

Minor league director Hank Peters was fired early in the season. Al Zarilla, one of Peters's best scouts, called him during spring training about Bill Landis, a promising left-handed pitcher in a California Junior College. "His last game is on Thursday. I'm going to be there and I think I can sign him Saturday or Sunday night," he told Peters. It would cost $25,000 to sign him and Peters needed Lane's approval for the expenditure. Peters telephoned the A's training camp but nobody could locate Lane. He finally reached George Selkirk, the team's director of player personnel. "Unless you feel otherwise I'm going to tell Al to sign this guy," Peters said. Peters informed Lane the following week and Lane approved. Finley telephoned Peters one month later. "Who gave you the authority to spend my money in signing this pitcher?" Finley demanded to know. Lane had not told Finley that he had approved the expenditure. Finley fired Peters and Bill Bergesch assumed Peters's duties as minor league director. Peters joined Cincinnati as assistant minor league director.[8]

Gordon's problems with Finley began after Finley arrived at the George Washington Hotel, the club's spring training headquarters, at one in the morning and spotted Bill Grigsby and Jo Jo White having a drink at the bar. Finley told White, "Call your boss up [Gordon] right now. I wanna talk to him about the players." White knew Gordon was sleeping and did not want to disturb him. "Mr. Finley, no disrespect, but I think you'd better be the one to call him up," he said. Finley called Gordon and ordered him to join him and a group of his friends for a drink and to discuss some player personnel matters. Gordon told him he would not talk about players in a bar and would speak to Finley at the stadium the next day. "Look, get your ass down here or you're fired," replied Finley.

Gordon was furious and told Finley not to leave because he would be right down. He showed up 10 minutes later in a tee shirt and his stocking feet. Finley told him he was fired if he was too busy to speak with him. Gordon grabbed Finley by the neck. "Look, you phony son-of-a-bitch, I just work for you," he said. "You bought my contract, Mr. Finley, but you don't own me. And if you wanna pay me my $25,000 for the year, let's just get this thing over right now." Before any blows were exchanged Finley, choking and trying to regain his breath, said: "I just love a fighter, Joe! I want you as manager."[9]

Lane and Gordon wanted to send pitcher Ken Johnson to Toronto (AAA), but Finley wanted to give him another chance. Johnson pitched against Baltimore and failed to get past the first inning. Lane fumed: "If we're going to continue spring training into July, we'll drop so many games it won't be funny." Johnson was sent to Toronto and Finley responded: "Lane was right, but I was right too. I want to give our ballplayers every possible chance to make this team."[10]

The team had to cut a player from the roster in May and Lane and Gordon wanted to send pitcher Norman Bass to Shreveport (AA). Finley wanted to give him another chance and outfielder Leo Posada was sent to Shreveport. Bass pitched well against Chicago in his next outing even though he lost the game. Bass won the following game, prompting Lane to remark: "Well, if this team can't experiment, who the hell can? Finley has sunk four and a half million into the club; if he thinks he's protecting his investment by disregarding the advice of experts, I can't argue."[11]

Finley ordered Gordon to take pitcher Jim Archer out of the bullpen and use him as a starter. Gordon told reporters that it was hard to be a manager when you were not permitted to manage. Finley replied he had faith in Gordon's ability to manage and only offered suggestions. "Mr. Finley's statement clarifies the situation for me," Gordon said. "I'm pleased. If he and Frank Lane are only offering suggestions to me, then I'm free to accept or reject them as I see fit."[12]

Finley ordered Gordon to manage some games from the press box because Lane felt it was a better place to observe what happened on the field. Finley requested permission from the league to install a telephone line between the plate umpire and the press box so Gordon could dial the umpire instead of going down to the field if he disagreed with a decision but the request was denied. Gordon tried to manage from the press box twice but decided the disadvantages outweighed the advantages. "He never gave it a chance," complained Lane.

Lane and Finley used the telephone in the dugout whenever they wanted to talk with Gordon and Gordon resented their frequent interference. One evening he turned in a lineup card to the umpires with the notation, "Approved by C.O.F." at the bottom. One of the players wrote it on the card and Gordon thought it was funny. Finley called Gordon when the story appeared in the newspapers and demanded to know whether he put that on the card. Gordon answered no. He probably had an idea who put the inscription on the card, but Finley did not ask and the point was not pursued.[13]

"I gave the fans in Kansas City my word we would not trade with the Yankees and my word is bond," said Finley on June 9. Five days later Lane traded Bud Daley, the A's best pitcher in 1959 and 1960, to the Yankees for pitcher Art Ditmar and infielder Deron Johnson. Ditmar pitched in Kansas City in 1955 and 1956. He had a 15–9 record and a 3.06 ERA with New York in 1960. Johnson, a 23-year-old minor league infielder, was considered a good prospect with power that could play either third base or in the outfield. "When he (Finley) pulled that bush-league trick of burning the charter bus to Yankee Stadium and announcing he wouldn't even trade the A's batboy for Mickey Mantle, I was determined to make a deal if I could," Lane later explained. "I told Finley at the start not to make those stupid promises that he would never deal with the Yankees. I deal with any club and always have.... And if he hadn't interfered, I would have made a better deal with the Yanks than the one we finally made."[14]

"Maybe I ought to blame this on my father," said Finley. "My father told me one day that a wise man changes his mind but a fool never does. I was thinking of that after I okayed the deal Frank Lane was working on for a week.... I've never gotten into such a business where you make a concrete statement, repeat it a hundred times and then suddenly change your mind ... I know I religiously tried to live up to the promise until today. I didn't want to trade with the Yanks. I felt the fans in Kansas City were fed up with that exchange back and forth ... put it down to baseball being a screwy business. That's the best I can do."[15]

Finley began to look for an opportunity to replace Gordon, but he had to wait because the A's won six of eight games on the road. During this streak the A's hit three consecutive triples in a five-run third inning to give the A's a 9–6 victory over New York in the second game in a double header after losing the first game 6–1 on June 8th. The A's returned to Kansas City on June 15th.

Finley informed Lane and Gordon that Lew Krausse Jr. would make his professional debut on Friday, June 16. The 18-year-old had a remarkable career at Chester High School in Pennsylvania, where his teams lost just one game in which he pitched from the time he entered the ninth grade. He pitched 19 no-hit games in high school and struck out 24 batters in one game. His father scouted for the A's and pitched for the Philadelphia A's 30 years earlier. This did not guarantee his son would pitch for Kansas City as he said his son would sign with the highest bidder. Finley brought him to Washington to pitch batting practice. "I don't know much about baseball, but you look like you throw the ball pretty hard," commented Pat Friday. Friday took him to the Shoreham Hotel to finalize the deal with Finley. Finley signed Krausse for a reported $125,000 bonus, the highest bonus paid to any player at that time.[16]

Krausse started the game on a hot, humid night just 10 days after his high school graduation. He did not disappoint the large crowd of 25,869, throwing a three-hit shutout and defeating the Los Angeles Angels 4–0. All three hits were singles. He struck out six, walked five, and even collected two hits when he came to bat. "This is the greatest pitching per-

Lew Krausse (from Jay Publications and the Kansas City Athletics).

formance by a youngster I've ever seen in the majors," Gordon said. Ted Kluszeski, one of the Angels who went hitless in the game, compared him to a "young Bob Feller, a young Robin Roberts," and an editorial in the *Kansas City Star* compared his talent to that of "Walter Johnson and Bob Feller combined."[17]

Finley fired Gordon three days later. Gordon was fishing and was unaware of his dismissal until Lane reached him twenty minutes after the hastily called press conference began. "I was the man behind the move," Finley stated. "Lane told me a thousand times during spring training that Gordon is no good.... It was a cinch to happen because he (Gordon) and Lane had proved they couldn't get along together."[18]

"Charlie told me he was gonna fire Gordon," Lane said later. "And he did it right after we had our best road trip ... but Joe had done a few things to upset Charlie, like the lineup card thing, and you just don't do that. So I made no real strong fight to keep Joe.... Finley's conversation about Gordon and I being enemies was a lot of hogwash. Sure, Joe and I had had some difficulties in the past, but Joe has always known I have liked him and he has liked me. I told Joe after he was fired that as soon as I could get another job, he would be the first one I would hire. And his response was that, if this happened, he would be glad to work for me for nothing."[19]

Finley introduced Hank Bauer, the popular 38-year-old outfielder as the new manager. "He will make a great manager," Finley predicted. "He is tough and he is a winner." Rumors had been circulating that he would be released because he was no longer able to play on a regular basis and his $30,000 salary was too high for a part-time player. Shortly before the press conference Finley and Lane asked him, "How'd you like to go down to the minor leagues and manage?" Bauer said no. Then Lane asked, "How would you like to manage the Kansas City ballclub?" Bauer said he would like to do it and they said: "You're the manager." Bauer had been a U.S. Marine during World War II, and later played with the Kansas City Blues in 1947 and 1948. He first appeared in the major leagues with the New York Yankees at the end of the 1948 season. He remained with the Yankees through the 1959 season when he was traded to Kansas City. He had played on nine pennant winners in New York and was named to three All-Star games.

Hank Bauer (from Jay Publications and the Kansas City Athletics).

After two ninth-place finishes as manager of Kansas City, he landed in a better situation in Baltimore. He signed a one-year contract to manage the Orioles on November 18, 1964. He led the team to a four-game sweep of the Los Angeles Dodgers in the 1966 World Series and was named Major League Manager of the Year by *The Sporting News*. Earl Weaver replaced Bauer as manager on July 11, 1968. Finley hired Bauer to manage the Oakland Athletics for the 1969 season. He became the first manager to be hired and fired twice by Finley when John McNamara replaced him as manager on September 19, 1969. He managed Tidewater (AAA) in 1971 and 1972 and later was hired by a scout by the New York Yankees.

HANK BAUER'S MANAGERIAL RECORD

Year	Team	League	Won	Lost	Position
1961	Kansas City	Major	35	67	9
1962	Kansas City	Major	72	90	9
1964	Baltimore	Major	97	65	3
1965	Baltimore	Major	94	68	3
1966	Baltimore	Major	97	63	1
1967	Baltimore	Major	76	85	6
1968	Baltimore	Major	43	37	3
1969	Oakland	Major	80	69	2
1971	Tidewater	AAA	79	61	2
1972	Tidewater	AAA	78	65	3

Bauer signed a contract that extended through the 1962 season and would be a player-manager until he was replaced on the roster. Terms were not announced but Lane said it was an increase over his salary as a player. Bauer said the present coaching staff would be retained and that he planned no immediate changes in the A's line-up or pitching rotation. "I'm going to take it easy for a while until I get my feet wet," he commented.[20]

Bauer made his managerial debut six hours later. The stadium public address announcer said: "Hank Bauer, your playing days are over. You have been named manager of the Kansas City Athletics." Bauer left the dugout, walked to home plate and submitted the lineup card to Yankees manager Ralph Houk and the umpires. There were a few boos in memory of Gordon, but the boos were replaced by cheers from the 16,715 fans. Jim Archer allowed only seven hits and pitched a complete game. Bauer used his first pinch hitter, Wes Covington, in the bottom of the ninth with the score tied. Covington hit a home run off Luis Arroyo to win the game for the Athletics.[21]

Bauer played until July 21. He threw out Rocky Colavito at the plate, had two hits and drove in the winning run in the A's 3–2 victory over Detroit. Frank Lane got on the public address system in the seventh inning and announced: "This is Frank Lane. Hank Bauer, you're wanted on the bench." Bauer left the field and retired as a player. John Mize was added to the coaching staff on July 7 to assist Bauer for the remainder of the season. Mize had played for the Cardinals, Giants and Yankees during his 20-year Hall of Fame career.[22]

The roster was unsettled most of the season as Lane purchased, sold and traded players. The A's purchased Ed Rakow, a 24-year-old right-handed pitcher from the Dodgers, on March 30. He traded pitcher Dick Hall and infielder Dick Williams to Baltimore on April 12 for Jerry Walker and Chuck Essegian. Walker, a 22-year old right-handed pitcher, was as a member of the 1959 American League All-Star team but was bothered by allergies in 1960 and finished the season in the bullpen with a 3–4 record and a 3.74 ERA. Lane sold Essegian to Cleveland on May 3 and traded center fielder Bill Tuttle to Minnesota for Reno Bertoia and Paul Giel on June 1. Lane wanted Bertoia, a 26-year-old infielder, to replace aging Andy Carey at third base.

Lane traded first baseman Marv Throneberry to Baltimore for veteran centerfielder Gene Stephens on June 7 and made three player transactions on June 10: He sold first baseman Bob Boyd to Milwaukee, signed 39-year-old outfielder Jim Rivera, who had been released by the White Sox, and traded pitchers Ray Herbert and Don Larsen, Carey and outfielder Al Pilarcik to the White Sox for Wes Covington, Stan Johnson, Bob Shaw and

Gerry Staley. Shaw, a 27-year-old pitcher, was a dominant pitcher for the Sox in 1959 when he had an 18–6 record and a 2.69 ERA. He slipped to a 13–13 record in 1960 with a 4.06 ERA. Staley, a 40-year-old relief pitcher, had a 13–8 record and a 2.43 ERA in 1960. Covington, a 29-year-old outfielder, had good power but was not good defensively. Lane traded Covington to Philadelphia for center fielder Bobby Del Greco on July 2. Bertoia and Staley were traded to Detroit on July 31 for infielder Ozzie Virgil and pitcher Bill Fischer. Virgil was a good defensive player and Fischer was acquired to strengthen the bullpen.

Dick Howser was a surprise success. He was not on the major league roster when spring training began on March 1, but he felt he had good chance to make the roster when Gordon walked over to him during infield practice on the first day and said, "Show me some of the same kind of ball you played in the minors last season and shortstop is yours." Two weeks later the Athletics purchased his contract from Shreveport for $25,000.

Dick Howser (from Jay Publications and the Kansas City Athletics).

The 23-year-old Howser set Kansas City records for runs scored (108), bases on balls (92), and stolen bases with 37. Bill Tuttle held the previous team record with 10 stolen bases in 1959. He played 157 games at shortstop and finished with a .280 batting average, the third highest average on the team. He became the first product of the Kansas City minor league system to advance to the A's starting lineup. Paul Richards named Howser to the American League All-Star team, the only member of the Athletics named to the squad and the only rookie chosen for the team. The crowning achievement came at the end of the year when he was selected the American League Rookie of the Year by *The Sporting News*.[23] Howser was second by one vote to Boston's pitcher Don Schwall in the Rookie voting by the Baseball Writers.

Howser's ability to steal bases placed him in a tight battle with Luis

Aparicio. Howser stole two bases in a game against Boston. Boston Red Sox catcher Joe Ginsberg said to him, "Look, Howser, Aparicio's gonna lead the league anyway. Why don't you leave me alone?" Howser smiled at him. "I'm warning you," Ginsberg razzed, "the next time you get on base and go, I'm gonna throw the ball straight up in the air and holler infield fly." Howser got on base and stole second.

Howser trailed Aparicio by just one stolen base midway through the season before falling behind in the final months. "It's becoming more and more apparent," he said to a reporter in early July, "that Kansas City's best hitting is being done by the left-handers, Siebern and Lumpe. We're going to see more and more left-handed pitching the rest of the season. That's going to cut my chances to go." Howser finished second in the league with 37 stolen bases. Aparicio had 53.[24]

One of Bauer's first official managerial acts was to appoint Howser team captain. This surprised Howser because he had just turned 24 one month earlier and had played in just 59 major league games. "Frankly I was just trying to keep a job in the major leagues," Howser said. "My first reaction was an uneasy one. I thought they might be expecting too much from me. I went to our owner, Mr. Finley, and to Hank also and discussed the appointment with both of them. They didn't expect me to do anything different than I had done in the first 59 games. They wanted me to continue hustling and to set an example. They really seemed impressed with my hustle."[25]

Norm Siebern began the season in left field but moved to first base after Throneberry was traded. He led the team in virtually every offensive category: batting average (.296), home runs (18), and runs batted in (98). He also broke the Kansas City record with 36 doubles. Second baseman Jerry Lumpe held the infield together with solid defense and led all major league second basemen with a .293 batting average. Lumpe was credited for aiding the quick development of Dick Howser at shortstop and Siebern at first. Howser and Lumpe became one of the better double play combinations in the league as the season progressed.

Andy Carey started at third base and played in 39 games before being traded to the White Sox. Reno Bertoia and Deron Johnson were tried at third but neither was effective. Johnson moved to the outfield. Bauer gave Wayne Causey his first starting assignment at third base on July 2, and he did not relinquish the position. He led the team in hitting with a mark over .300 at one period after he broke into the starting lineup and made some outstanding plays. He finished the season batting .276 with eight home runs and 49 runs batted in.

Kansas City had a solid young infield by the end of the season. "These boys—Siebern, Lumpe, Howser and Causey—are real major leaguers," said Bauer. "They were the backbone of the club. If the rest of the club can measure up to the infield we will have a greatly improved team in 1962." Unfortunately, the A's had one of the worst outfields. Bill Tuttle, Siebern and Bauer were the starting outfielders at the beginning of the season. Tuttle played in 25 games before he was traded to Minnesota, leaving a void in center until Lane obtained Del Greco. Bauer played in 43 games before retiring. Leo Posada, a 23-year-old rookie, was the only outfielder to appear in more than 100 games. He led the A's outfielders with a .253 batting average and finished third on the team with 53 RBI. Del Greco played in 73 games but batted just .230.[26]

Haywood Sullivan and Joe Pignatano shared the catching responsibilities. Sullivan was the team's leading hitter during the first half of the season but tailed off in the second half and finished with a .242 average in 117 games. Pignatano appeared in 92 games and batted .243.

Pitching problems plagued the A's during the first part of the season. Starting pitchers Bud Daley and Ray Herbert were both traded and Joe Nuxhall and Art Ditmar were major disappointments. Nuxhall finished with a 5–8 record and a 5.34 ERA. Art Ditmar struggled with a poor 0–5 record and 4.31 ERA. Bob Shaw, a 27-year-old right-hander obtained in the trade that sent Ray Herbert to the White Sox, finished with 9–10 record and a 4.31 ERA. Jerry Walker had an 8–14 record and a 4.82 ERA. By the end of the season pitching improved as veterans Shaw and Walker were joined by six young pitchers that showed potential: Jim Archer, Norm Bass, Lew Krausse, Bill Kunkel, Ed Rakow and Dave Wickersham.

Archer, a 28-year-old rookie left-hander, was the A's leading pitcher in the first half of the season. He finished the season with a 9–15 record and a 3.20 ERA. He led the club with 110 strikeouts, nine complete games and ranked ninth among American League pitchers in earned run average. Bass, a 22-year-old right-hander, was the biggest surprise. His record for the class B Sioux City team in 1960 was not impressive, but he jumped to the A's and finished with an 11–11 record and a 4.68 ERA. He relied primarily on his fastball at the beginning of the season and began throwing other pitches as the season progressed.

Krausse nearly duplicated his successful debut in his next start and extended his scoreless string to 15 innings. The streak ended when Boston's Gary Geiger tagged him for a three-run home run in the seventh inning, the first home run Krausse had ever given up. "Gary Geiger hit a home run off me," Krausse recalled. "And he hit it on a 3–0 pitch. First of all, I had never had anyone swing on a 3–0 pitch before because they were always hoping for a walk. So it was a double shock for me. I thought 'I've lost it. It's over. I've given up a home run.'" Boston won the game 5–4.

1961 team — Front row: Archer, Howser, Walker, Wilks (coach), White (coach), Bauer (manager), Lodigiani (coach), Fitzgerald (coach), Shaw, Prescott. Middle row: Keefe (traveling secretary), Lumpe, Rivera, Johnson, Sullivan, Nuxhall, Stephens, Bass, Ditmar, Siebern, Reid (equipment manager). Back row: Jones (trainer), Pignatano, Covington, Bertoia, Krausse, Kunkel, Staley, Rakow, Causey, Klimchock, Posada. Seated in front: Turley (batboy), Woods (batboy). (From the Kansas City Athletics.)

A's pitching coach Ted Wilks tried to teach him some new pitches. "Apparently my arm wasn't mature enough to handle those things," Krausse said. "I felt my arm burning late that season, but I didn't want to tell anybody. I was disappointed in myself that I didn't do better that first year. After a while I began to get intimidated. I was going out there when I had no business being out there pitching.... I really needed to regroup. If I had had any say in it, I would have liked to have gotten some seasoning in the minor leagues. By the end of the season my confidence was shattered." He did not win another game until he hurled a complete game victory against Washington in the final month of the season. He ended the season with a 2–5 record and a 4.82 ERA.

Relief pitching improved with the addition of 24-year-old Bill Kunkel. He finished the season with a 3–4 record and a 5.16 ERA. He faded in the second half of the season but still established a Kansas City record with 58 appearances. Rakow was used both as a starter and in relief. He finished with a 2–8 record, a 4.75 ERA, and 81 strikeouts in just 125 innings. Wickersham, a 26-year-old rookie, came up through the A's minor league system and appeared in 17 games with a 2–1 record with a 4.91 ERA. Veteran Gerry Staley appeared in 23 games with a 3.60 ERA before he was traded to Detroit for Bill Fischer. Fischer appeared in 15 games, all in relief, and had a 1–0 record and a 3.86 ERA.

The A's were in eighth place when Bauer assumed the reins on June 19 and occupied the cellar during most of July and August. "Charles wanted to fire Bauer," Lane said. "I said 'Charlie, you can't do that. You just got through the firing of Gordon a couple of months ago. And this is Bauer's backyard [he lived in nearby Prairie Village].... It would be a horrible thing.'" Bauer finished the season and returned to pilot the team in 1962. It took a victory on the last day of the season against Washington to enable the A's to tie the expansion Senators for last place. Both teams finished with identical 61–100 records, 47½ games behind the Yankees. The expansion Angels finished in eighth place. Lane's numerous transactions created an unsettled situation as players came and went throughout the season and failed to improve the team. Before he was fired, Lane admitted his trades actually hurt the team. He thought the team "as it is now constituted is at least 25 percent inferior to the one which began the season.... The pitching staff quite possibly is better but the other departments are not as strong and the outfield is hardly of top minor league caliber." In an unusual move, Finley signed every player on the roster to a 1962 contract before the 1961 season ended.[27]

19

Courting Dallas

One month after the lease-burning ceremony, a reporter asked the city legal department about the attendance clause and was informed it was still in effect because the old lease had not been cancelled. Finley actually burned a standard printed contract purchased from a stationery store. Finley claimed he thought everybody understood it was a publicity stunt and admitted the clause had not been deleted. He said he intended to keep the franchise in Kansas City and the ceremony demonstrated his intent without actually burning the lease. Ernie Mehl began to suspect Finley wanted to move the A's out of Kansas City. He checked rumors that Finley wanted to move the Athletics to Atlanta or San Diego where C. Arnold Smith, the owner of the San Diego Padres (AAA) team, announced he was ready to spend $5–6 million to enlarge Westgate Park to seat between 40,000 and 48,000 fans.[1]

Hank Bauer informed Mehl that Finley and American League supervisor of umpires Cal Hubbard went to the Cotton Bowl to measure the field and determine whether a baseball field could be configured in the stadium. When Finley returned to Kansas City he strolled into the clubhouse at Municipal Stadium and threw a 10-gallon cowboy hat down on the desk of manager Hank Bauer and said: "Well, what would you boys think about playing down in Dallas?" Mehl contacted Hubbard, who confirmed the trip.[2]

Finley became interested in Dallas–Ft. Worth when he found a pamphlet in the A's files describing the area's potential as a major league market. The pamphlet was one that Dallas and other aspiring major league cities sent to all the major league teams when they sought a franchise. The population of the Dallas–Fort Worth area was nearly twice that of Kansas City and a new 50,000-seat stadium would be built on a 137-acre site adjacent to the Texas Turnpike in Arlington, a city located midway between Dallas and Fort Worth. The Dallas–Fort Worth area offered the potential for significant radio and television revenue as sizeable Texas cities could become part of a large radio and television network. This appealed to Finley because the radio and television revenue in Kansas City was among the lowest in the major leagues. The importance of media revenue was the primary reason the Milwaukee Braves moved to Atlanta in 1966.[3]

"Finley is considering a move of the franchise to Dallas," Mehl wrote in the August 17 edition of the *Kansas City Times*. Finley talked to four of his players about moving the team and told them an old baseball stadium, presumably Burnett Field in Dallas, would be rehabilitated until the new stadium was ready. "Most suspicious of all has been his failure to sign a new lease with Kansas City for the use of the Municipal Stadium, although he made a great to-do about signing a new one at the start of the season," he wrote. "At his suggestion, the 850,000-attendance clause was stricken out at a ceremony held at the city council meeting at which time a picture was taken of Finley setting fire to the old lease. The old lease, however, wasn't burned and the owner's lawyer is said to have criticized him for having even suggested the change. Since then the council has made repeated attempts to get Finley to sign and on numerous occasions he has promised he would attend to the task. But as of now the club is operating under the old lease that stipulates that in the event the (total) ticket sales fall below 850,000 the owner of the franchise can exercise the option to move by so notifying the city before October 15." (It was actually 800,000 because the home opener had been televised but even that figure seemed unattainable). Mehl projected the final home attendance would not exceed 700,000. "The results of all this has been the spreading of these rumors and the feeling that the owner might believe he can recoup some of his losses by moving the franchise," Mehl concluded.[4]

Mehl said Bauer was doing an acceptable job, but he "has had to bow to repeated suggestions on whom to play, on whom to pitch.... His decisions on the field have been criticized, fault found with his judgment. He has been second-guessed by the very men who should have been sympathetic with him. He has had to alter his pitching rotation to satisfy the whim of the owner, make line-up changes against his better judgment. He has had his authority usurped and knows that knowledge of this had penetrated to the players themselves, thus making his job all the more difficult.... What now has so seriously affected the team is that there is no spirit. The players have reacted to the front office discord and they play now as if they no longer cared. Get the season over with as quickly as possible. Several are not hustling and this affects the others. There is a listlessness which very clearly illustrates the state of mind of the athletes. They look back upon how they felt in March and how they feel now, and they find it hard to realize the transformation."[5]

Mehl claimed Finley no longer promoted the team or tried to improve it because he wanted the A's to do poorly so attendance would decline. "Had the ownership made a deliberate attempt to sabotage a baseball operation, it could not have succeeded as well," he concluded. "It is somewhat the sensation one has in walking through a hall of mirrors, where everything appears to be out of focus. There never has been a baseball operation such as this, nothing so bizarre, so impossibly incongruous."[6]

Finley was in Dallas for a meeting of the Texas Medical Association, an organization insured by his firm, when Mehl reported the story. "I know nothing about the rumors [about the A's moving to Dallas]," he said. "They're rather disgusting. No one has offered me any deal to move and I haven't asked for one.... It's just a coincidence that I'm in Dallas. All I'm going to say is that I've spent heavily on what I've got in Kansas City. I've certainly indicated a desire to operate in Kansas City."[7]

The *Dallas News* reported Finley toured the area and added that "despite his denials with a wry grin, the day wasn't entirely devoted to making a personal survey of the Dallas–Fort Worth area's potential as regards to operating a major league baseball franchise." The paper stated Finley was not obligated to remain in Kansas City because the present lease still contained the attendance clause that allowed the lease to be cancelled. Finley told the paper he could move the team even if the attendance was reached. "I would have to pay the remaining two years rental on the stadium if I decided to move the club," he said. "The contract or the attendance would not have any influence on me if I decided to move the club ... a team here (in Dallas) would be a tremendous asset to major league baseball." He said he was confident in the future of the Athletics "if not in Kansas City, then somewhere else ... but that does not mean I will move the club."[8]

"Mehl's stories were based on rumor and not fact," Finley said. "Never once did he call me to check out what he was writing about. He was laboring under misapprehension. The truth is what I have said and I will stand behind it.... It makes me so sick it almost makes me want to take the club out of here."[9]

Finley claimed Mehl's accusation that Finley's operation was "incongruous, incompetent and bizarre" was a response to policy changes that affected Mehl. "The previous owner, the late Arnold Johnson, paid all travel expenses of Mehl and Joe McGuff, baseball writer," Finley said. "The books showed it. I was amazed, being a rookie owner, that this was permitted and when I asked other clubs about such a situation I was told it was not generally done. So I did not permit this to be continued — to me it was nothing but payola." He said the previous owners also paid Mehl

$1,000 to edit the yearbook and claimed Mehl criticized Gordon's dismissal because "Gordon was hired — before I bought the ballclub — on the recommendation and negotiations of Mr. Mehl."[10]

"Finley never paid any of Mehl's traveling expenses," said *Kansas City Star* editor John W. Colt. "It was my decision, not Finley's," Mehl said. "It is true that when Johnson owned the club, Joe McGuff received some expenses when he was keeping statistics for the club on the road. There is nothing wrong with that. They didn't have anyone to do it. I did edit the yearbook and was paid for it. There is nothing wrong with that, either. Incidentally, I did it while I was on my vacation. But I paid my own expenses at the training camp and elsewhere."[11]

Finley wanted Merle Harmon and Bill Grigsby to criticize Mehl during the radio and television broadcasts. "He badgered us for a couple of weeks," said Grigsby. "He wanted us to take out after Ernie, even Joe [McGuff]. He said, 'By God, I'm gonna get rid of that son of a bitch.' I told him, 'Well, sorry Charlie, but that's not my job. I'm the play-by-play guy and I don't do that kind of stuff. I don't want to hurt anybody.' 'You'll do it or you're through,' fumed Finley.... Lane pleaded, 'Charlie's not going to help you get a contract to come back if you don't blast Ernie. Come on, Bill, you and I have fun on the road together. Bill, you gotta do it or you won't have a job next year.' I told him one final time, 'I'm not going to do it and neither is Merle. If I don't have a job, then I won't have a job, but I'm not going to do it.'"[12]

Finley held an "Ernie Mehl Appreciation Day" between games of the A's doubleheader against the White Sox on August 20. Finley and Pat Friday mounted billboards on both sides of a flatbed truck that was driven around the playing field. The words "Ernie Mehl Appreciation Day — Poison Pen Award for 1961" were written on top of the billboards and under the words was a characterization of Mehl sitting at a typewriter. There was also a quill type pen next to a bottle labeled poison ink. As the truck circled the outfield the organist played "Who's Afraid of the Big Bad Wolf." Harmon and Grigsby refused to broadcast the event. "I told him as long as it was in good taste we probably would go along with it, but I had to know what it was before I could say for sure," Harmon recalled. "If it was in good taste we would mention it on the air, but when I saw it I didn't think it was in good taste so we didn't mention it. I thought it was in very poor taste." Harmon's refusal led to an angry confrontation with Finley in the press box.[13]

Mehl was not at the game so the "Poison Pen Award" was presented in absentia. The crowd of nearly 10,000 did not understand the significance of the event and there was little reaction from the fans. "I thought it was humorous," Finley said. Baseball commissioner Ford Frick phoned the Associated Press and asked them to run a statement that stated, "Such things do not belong in baseball and I called Mehl this morning to apologize to him both personally and in the name of baseball."[14]

Finley met with Tom Gavin, mayor pro-tem of Kansas City and several members of the city council. He convinced them to send a telegram to Frick: "The city council of Kansas City ... wish to go on record as unequivocally endorsing and supporting Mr. Charles O. Finley and his Kansas City Athletic Baseball Club," it stated. "We have always had and still have complete confidence in Mr. Finley's integrity and sincerity, and we feel that this attitude more correctly reflects the sentiments of the vast majority of the people of this city than does the unfortunate adverse publicity of recent date. Furthermore, if any apologies are due to anyone, they are certainly due to Mr. Finley and to no one else. It is our feeling that baseball should be praising rather than criticizing Mr. Finley for his courage, for his sacrifices, and for his faith in Kansas City.... It is our considered opinion that if a thorough examination of the facts had been made this unfortunate publicity would not have developed.... Mr. Finley has kept his word to Kansas City. He has done everything he said he would do and much more." Finley claimed he met with Commissioner Frick in Chicago for two hours in September "at which time he stated to me he did not apologize personally to Mr. Mehl. Mr. Frick further stated that since the press had quoted him as personally apologizing to Mr. Mehl, he would take steps to correct this misunderstanding." Frick declined to comment when asked about Finley's claim and never corrected his apology.[15]

Finley ordered his traveling secretary to discontinue making the customary arrangements for Mehl, McGuff and other *Kansas City Star* and *Kansas City Times* personnel to accompany the team on road trips and ordered the public relations personnel not to give any information to the papers. The *Star* and *Times* were the only major newspapers in Kansas City.[16]

Two days after he presented the poison pen award to Mehl, Finley invited Chicago baseball writers to a press conference in his Chicago office, an obvious affront to Mehl and McGuff, to announce he fired Frank Lane. "I've waited for him to quit to save face," he said. "But now I'm firing him.... In my book a general manager is not only a man who can make a trade over a phone — any damned fool can do that — but he must be able to oversee everything. Lane did not do this and these other responsibilities fell with Friday and myself." Finley said he tried to contact Lane but was unable to reach him. He wanted to tell Lane he was fired and not have him read it in the newspapers.[17]

"I was forced to let Gordon go because it was impossible for him and Lane to work together," said Finley. "If I had known then what I know now, Gordon would be my manager. But I gave Lane the benefit of doubt because I had hired him and I had not hired Gordon. Gordon had become field manager before I bought the club. It was Lane who poisoned my mind on Joe Gordon ... and Lane also has been knifing Hank Bauer. The biggest mistake I ever made was firing Gordon. I fired the wrong man. Lane was the man who should have been fired."[18]

Finley said Lane would be paid in full and would receive $50,000 annually for the final three years of the contract but denied reports that Lane was the highest paid general manager. "That wasn't so," Finley stated. "He got only $50,000 a year from us and there was no bonus clause attached insofar as attendance. Actually, Lane was making more money in Cleveland." The salary was the same as his salary in Cleveland, but Lane also had an attendance clause as part of the contract with the Indians.[19]

Lane was surprised when he learned he was fired. "I was making a speech in a hotel in Kansas City telling the audience that Mr. Finley was a good operator and a great fan and that we'd have a great ballclub," he said. "When I came out to get a cab to go to the ballpark the cab driver said, 'Gee, that's tough luck, Mr. Lane.' I asked him what happened — was a ballplayer hurt?' He said, 'No, you got fired. Didn't you know that?'"[20]

Lane held a press conference the following day and disagreed with Finley's version of many events, starting with Finley's desire to move the Athletics.

> This move has been in Finley's mind for some time. Now that he knows it cannot be done he is saying he never contemplated it.... Beyond the shadow of doubt Charles Finley has been considering a move of the Kansas City Athletics to Dallas.... He asked several of the A's how they would like to represent Dallas and appear in New York wearing cowboy boots and ten-gallon hats. He was considering a proposal that the Dallas-Fort Worth area build a temporary stadium to be used until a permanent stadium could be built. If this was not feasible Finley talked about using the Cotton Bowl for games.... The park they are using in Dallas for the American Association games certainly would not be satisfactory and the Cotton Bowl is out of the question. If they tried to use the Cotton Bowl it would be about 240 feet to center field and 210 feet down each foul line.... The American League even sent a representative to Dallas (Hubbard) to check on whether the Cotton Bowl could be used and discovered it was not at all suitable for baseball. I told Finley that he not only could not move to Dallas next year because of lack of facilities there, but that he was antagonizing the fans here by his efforts.[21]

> I did not fire Gordon and Finley knows it. In fact, Gordon and I got along very well. Finley fired Gordon not once, but twice. He fired him in spring training and then immediately re-hired him. Then he wanted to fire him during an eastern trip but couldn't because the A's were winning. He was looking for a chance to fire him again. The moment they had a bad day, Gordon was gone. I urged him to hold off but he was determined to go through with the firing.[22]

Lane said he tried to get either Leo Durocher or Eddie Stanky to replace Gordon because he felt the situation called for a man with some managerial experience. Neither man was interested.

> Finley wanted me on several occasions to fire him (Bauer) and I have refused. I told him that I thought Hank had been doing a better job than we could have hoped for. I will agree that Hank has made some mistakes, but who hasn't in this business? On one occasion in Chicago, Finley accused Bauer and the team of quitting and sent Hank a telegram to this effect. He has criticized the team on occasion for quitting.
>
> Finley has been talking about stopping the practice of paying traveling expenses of the *Star*'s writers and that is a lie. For his information, the *Star* called me at the start of the season and informed me that it would pay the way of any of its writers traveling with the team. Furthermore I was told that no writer of the *Star* could do any statistical work for the ballclub. I urged that the rule be changed but was told the decision was final. Finley had nothing to do with it and now he is trying to make an issue of it.[23]

"I am glad to be out. I was warned not to take the job, but I took it anyway. Now I wish I had listened to the advice. Anyone can see that this has degenerated into a sorry mess and I am relieved to be out of it. I had some high hopes when I took the job but as it developed I had no authority."[24] Lane cleaned out his desk the next day. George Selkirk resigned immediately following Lane's dismissal and joined Baltimore as field coordinator.

Finley promised to provide Lane a new car every two years when Lane was hired. "But then he told me he had a Mercedes that he didn't like," Lane said. "He said it was too damned fast. So he offered that to me instead and I took it. Must have been worth more than 13 thousand bucks." Finley did not give him the title and when he fired Lane he claimed the car went with the job and should be returned. "After I got fired I drove down to Acapulco," Lane said. "But at the end of 1961 when I'd need new license plates I had to have the bill of sale. And I couldn't get it. Charlie had it. As a consequence I put the car in my brother-in-law's garage in St. Petersburg, Florida. And three years later, Joe Brown [Pittsburgh executive] said to me at a baseball convention that he heard I had a car as good as new. I told him that I could sell him the key but that Finley had the title — and Charlie was sitting right next to us. So Charlie helped me sell the Mercedes to Brown. Finley got a thousand for the title and I got two thousand for the key."[25]

Lane filed charges in the Federal Court in Chicago on October 8, 1963, for the money he claimed Finley still owed him. He claimed his contract extended to December 31, 1964, and that he was to be retained as a consultant for four additional years. He said that his salary was reduced to $5,000 on August 29, 1962 and then discontinued altogether two months later. It took him nearly four years to recover these wages. He sought $144,166 and was granted $113,000 in the settlement.[26]

Finley appointed 37-year-old Pat Friday as the new general manager. "Mr. Finley called and said: 'I've held a press conference up here in Chicago and have decided the time has come for Frank Lane and me to have a parting of the ways. By the way, you're the new general manager.'" Friday said. "I'm just a rookie in the baseball business. But I've been in it eight months and that's long enough to know that we have a capable staff in the organization. The job is a matter of management and getting along with others in the organization. I'll have to rely on Bill Bergesch [assistant general manager] and the club scouts in making some decisions, but then Frank Lane had to do the same thing." Friday would handle the business affairs and Finley would handle the trades.[27]

Finley finally signed the provision deleting the attendance clause on August 26. "It was my idea to take the clause out and as Mr. [Herb] Hoffman [associate city counselor] pointed out, it took some time to draw up the agreement," he said. "Now it has been done and is signed. I think this should be a sufficient answer to those who have doubted my veracity.... It's a shame that when someone spends $500,000 of his own money on a city-owned stadium, works night and day and sacrifices, and then is criticized as I have been criticized. It makes me sick enough to want to take the club out of Kansas City." It was signed nearly six months after he supposedly burned the lease in the mayor's office, nine days after Mehl broke the story about Dallas, and four days after Lane was fired.[28]

Finley still claimed he had not received any invitation to move to Dallas-Fort Worth or any other city, nor had he made a proposition to any city concerning a move. He hoped to demonstrate to the fans he was serious about keeping the team in Kansas City by signing the contract to delete the attendance clause. In a statement directed toward Mehl, he added that the "unfortunate publicity" would have been avoided if anyone had bothered to contact him before the story was released.

20

1962: Let Bygones Be Bygones

Hank Bauer replaced coaches Ed Fitzgerald, John Mize and Ted Wilks after the 1961 season. Ed Lopat took over as pitching coach and Gus Niarhos was named bullpen coach. Lopat, a former teammate of Bauer's in New York, had been pitching coach for the Yankees in 1960 and the Minnesota Twins in 1961. Niarhos caught in the major leagues for eight years. This was his first coaching opportunity.

Bill Bergesch resigned at the end of the 1961 season to become minor league director for the expansion New York Mets. Finley called Hank Peters, apologized because he learned that Frank Lane had approved Bill Landis's bonus and rehired him as assistant general manager and minor league director. Ray Swallow was named assistant minor league director, replacing Walter Brock, who joined the Cleveland Indians. Jim Schaaf was named director of public relations. Former major leaguer Joe Bowman was named supervisor of scouting. He had scouted for the A's since 1955. One of his first tasks was to replace six scouts that resigned at the end of the season.[1]

New restrooms were constructed adjacent to the new left field stands at Municipal Stadium. The right field fence was replaced with a four-foot high concrete wall topped with a six-foot chain link fence. The former wood fence rotted because of a natural spring and the earth on the hill behind the fence eroded. The distance down the foul line was reduced from 353 feet to 338 feet to curve the wall and replace the sharp corner that caused problems for the right fielders. The left field fence was also changed. Just one season after increasing dimensions, the team erected a chain-link fence in front of the outer wall to cut the distance from 370 feet to 331 feet down the line. The fence curved out sharply to 364 feet in left-center.[2]

The A's changed their uniforms for the second consecutive season. Sleeveless uniforms replaced the pinstripes. The uniforms used a navy blue sweatshirt and navy blue cap at home and a crimson red sweatshirt with a gray cap on the road.

The Athletics were the last major league team to complete arrangements to broadcast their games. Schlitz wanted to continue to sponsor the broadcasts and offered to help with ticket sales and other promotional matters. Finley met with representatives from Schlitz and reportedly told them he did not want their assistance and did not like their beer. He summoned a waiter and ordered another brand.

Merle Harmon and Bill Grigsby lost their jobs when Schlitz failed to renew the contract. Finley wanted to replace them because they did not support him when he attacked Ernie Mehl. The A's signed a one-year contract to broadcast all the games on KCMO radio (810) and a network of 10 out-of-town stations on April 6. Television station KCMO-TV (Channel 5) would televise approximately 30 games. Goetz Brewing Company, a local brewery, Guy's Potato Chips and General Finance sponsored the broadcasts. Finley retained the right to name the announcers and he hired Bruce Rice and Monte Moore. Rice broadcast ABC-TV's Football Scoreboard and joined KCMO in October 1961. Moore was director of the University of Kansas sports network and play-by-play duties for the Topeka Owls minor league baseball team. He moved to Kansas City as sports director for WDAF radio and television in 1960.[3]

The A's acquired 32-year-old outfielder Gino Cimoli in the major league draft on November 27, 1961. Cimoli played in the National League for six seasons and could play all three positions in the outfield. The Athletics made two trades on December 15. They traded pitcher Bob Shaw and infielder Lou Klimchock to the Milwaukee Braves for three young prospects: Joe Azcue, Ed Charles and Manny Jimenez. Jimenez, a 23-year-old outfielder, was considered the key man as far as the A's were concerned. Azcue, a 22-year-old catcher, was a good defensive catcher with a "bazooka" arm. Charles, 27, could play all the infield positions as well as play in the outfield. In the second trade Kansas City sent catcher Joe Pignatano to the San Francisco Giants for 22-year-old outfielder Jose Tartabull. The transactions strengthened the outfield and infield but weakened the pitching.

The *Kansas City Star* had to rely on Associated Press dispatches for news about the team during the off-season. Finley ended the feud the day before the opening home game against the Minnesota Twins and asked Mehl to throw out the first pitch. Finley, wearing catching gear, caught the ball. They met halfway between the mound and home plate after the

Manny Jimenez (from Jay Publications and the Kansas City Athletics).

pitch, shook hands, and walked arm-in-arm off the field. Finley then autographed the ball with the inscription "To Ernie Mehl — Best of luck to a great guy" and presented it to Mehl.[4]

Jimenez collected three hits in four times to the plate against Camillo Pascaul, one of the league's top pitchers, in his first major league game. He led the American League in hitting during the first two months of the season and his batting average did not fall below .362 during the first 51 games. He remained among the top five hitters for most of the season, prompting Bauer to call him the best looking young hitting prospect he had seen in many years. "What makes Manny so hard to pitch to is that he hits the ball where it is pitched, and this is the mark of a truly great hitter," said Bauer.

Finley met with Jimenez in July and told him to stop concentrating on hitting for average and concentrate on hitting more home runs. "I don't pay Jimenez to hit singles," Finley told reporters. "He's going for singles and a better average." Jimenez went into a slump and lost almost 30 points on his batting average during the final two months of the season. Finley tried to deny he met with Jimenez, but when reporters reminded Finley about his previous statements he admitted he held the meeting after Bauer and the coaches unsuccessfully tried to tell Jimenez the same thing. He still finished the season with a .301 batting average with 11 home runs and 69 runs batted in. Jimenez finished ninth in the league in hitting and was one of three Kansas City batters to hit over .300.[5]

Ed Charles began the season as a utility infielder. He moved to third base when Wayne Causey injured his shoulder on May 6 and did not relinquish the position. Charles finished with a .288 average with 17 home runs and 74 runs batted in. "If Charles was a member of one of the top clubs, he would now be a leading candidate for Rookie of the Year honors," said

Bauer. "He's done a lot of things well for us and really, for a rookie, his play has been one of my most pleasant surprises." Causey ended the year as a utility infielder.[6]

Norm Siebern played first base and led the team with a .308 batting average and 25 home runs and set a new Kansas City record with 117 runs batted in. He also set Kansas City records with 114 runs scored and 110 bases on balls. He had five hits in six times at bat in the A's 18–6 win over Cleveland in Municipal Stadium on May 5. He was Kansas City's lone representative on the American League All-Star team.

Norm Siebern (from Jay Publications and the Kansas City Athletics).

Bauer rated Jerry Lumpe as the best second baseman in the league. Lumpe had at least one hit in 20 consecutive games from August 28 through September 19. He batted .301 and set a Kansas City record with 193 hits. Dick Howser broke his left thumb in a game against Chicago on June 24 and played in just 83 games at shortstop. The A's acquired 28-year-old infielder Billy Consolo from the Angels after Howser was injured. He shared the shortstop duties with Causey during Howser's absence.

Bobby Del Greco played in center field and batted .254. Cimoli appeared in 147 games in right field and had a .275 average with 71 runs batted in and set a new Kansas City record with 15 triples. He won the opening game with a three-run home run and was one of the league leaders in runs batted in during the first half of the season. Cimoli, Causey and Bill Bryan hit consecutive home runs in the seventh inning on August 19th, but the Yankees won the game 6–1. Tartabull finished with a .277 average and 19 stolen bases.

Haywood Sullivan shared the catching duties with Azcue. Azcue impressed Bauer and the coaches during spring training with his strong arm and defensive abilities. Once the season began he was plagued by injuries. He batted .229 in 72 games.

Pitching improved under coach Ed Lopat. Six pitchers, with a total of only four major league wins in 1961, won 53 games by the end of the 1962 season. Ed Rakow emerged as the best starting pitcher, leading the team with 14 wins, 11 complete games, and 159 strikeouts. He had a two-hitter, a four-hitter and a five-hitter, finishing the season with a 4.25 ERA.

Rookie Diego Segui, a 24-year-old right-hander, was not on the roster at the start of spring training. He showed potential as a later-inning relief pitcher during the exhibition games and won a spot on the team. Bauer moved him into the starting rotation and he finished with an 8–5 record and a team-leading 3.85 ERA. Rookie Dan Pfister also earned a berth in the starting rotation. He was the hard-luck victim in several close defeats during the season and finished with a 4–14 record and a 4.55 ERA.

The A's traded pitcher Bill Kunkel and outfielder Leo Posada to Toronto (AAA) to obtain Orlando Pena on August 3. They also paid the Maple Leafs $50,000 and loaned them pitcher Dale Willis for the remainder of the season. Kunkel and Posada were regulars on the team during the 1961 season but did not make the team in 1962. Pena, a 26-year-old right-hander with a forkball, finished with a 6–4 record and a 3.00 ERA for the A's. He won four games in a row and became one of the team's most dependable pitchers.

Dave Wickersham started the season in the bullpen and had several good appearances, winning three games. He moved to the starting rotation and won his first three starts before returning to the bullpen. He finished with an impressive 11–4 record, a .733 winning percentage, and a 4.25 ERA. His winning percentage was the highest since the A's moved to Kansas City.

Bill Fischer reported to spring training 25 pounds lighter and Lopat helped him develop a slow-curve to go with his sinkerball. Fischer walked only eight men in 128 innings and pitched 84⅓ consecutive innings without issuing a base on balls to break the major league record set by Christy Mathewson in 1913. The streak ended on September 30, the final day of the season, when he walked Detroit's Bubba Morton on four straight pitches in the fifth inning. He was another hard-luck pitcher. The A's were shut out five times when he pitched, and three of those were by a score of 1–0. He finished with a 4–12 record and a 4.01 ERA.

John Wyatt was not on the 40-man roster before the start of the season but won a spot in spring training. He was used in both starting and relief roles before he settled in the bullpen and became one of the top relief pitchers in the league. He appeared with 59 games and had nine saves and 99 strikeouts in 124 innings. He finished with a 10–7 record and a 4.54 ERA.

The surprising performances of the young pitchers helped overcome disappointing seasons by some of the veterans. Jerry Walker had an 8–9 record with a 5.92 ERA. Jim Archer, the A's leading pitcher in 1961, was just 0–1 in 18 games with a disappointing 9.32 ERA. Norm Bass was troubled with control problems and finished with a 2–6 record and a 6.12 ERA. Art Ditmar was released on May 25.

Jack Kralick of the Minnesota Twins became the first pitcher to pitch a no-hitter against the Kansas City A's. On August 26, he came within two outs of pitching a perfect game at Metropolitan Stadium. He retired the first 25 men in order before walking George Alusik with one out in the ninth. He retired the next two batters to preserve his no-hitter.

Cleveland outfielder Walt Bond and catcher John Romano became only the tenth pair of players to hit successive home runs twice in the same game on September 19 against the A's in Kansas City. They shelled Rakow for successive home runs in the opening inning and then duplicated the feat against Wickersham in the seventh inning. Both of Bond's home runs came with a runner on base. The two players drove in all of the Indians runs in their 10–9 victory over the A's.

Finley enjoyed his role as owner. "One day ... after we swept a series from the White Sox in Chicago, I went back to the hotel and I handed each one of the players $25 cash as they got off the bus," he said. "The coaches, trainer — everybody! I told them to go out and get a good steak. Joe Cronin once asked me if it was true I gave my players extra money like that. 'You shouldn't do that,' he told me. 'It makes it hard on the other owners.' Why, if I can't do that for my players I should get out of baseball."[7]

Bauer awaited word about his status because his contract expired at the end of the season. "When you consider all the injuries we had this season you have to agree that this club has done rather well," Bauer said. "We have had a number of very pleasant surprises and in many ways this has been a very interesting year for me. So much so I'd like to see what I could do with this group another season."

Finley did not tell Bauer if he would return. "I didn't get fired," Bauer said. "Everybody thinks I got fired; I quit. We were playing in Chicago, and we were going to California from Chicago. I got to Chicago and there was an article in the paper that Eddie Lopat would be the next manager of the Kansas City A's. So I called Finley up and said, 'What's with this rumor I read in the paper?' And he said, 'I can't answer you at this time.' So I decided before he fired me, I'm going to quit, and I had told Joe McGuff, before we went to Detroit for the last three games of the season. I said, 'I'm going to have a press conference in the morning and I'm not coming back.'"[8]

Bauer told Finley following a game with Detroit on September 27.

1962 team — Front row: Segui, Pfister, Howser, Niarhos (coach), Lopat (coach), Bauer (manager), Lodigiani (coach), White (coach), Causey, Tartabull, Consolo. Middle row: Fischer, Lumpe, Johnson, Wickersham, Siebern, Sullivan, Alusik, Cimoli, Walker, Wyatt, Keefe (traveling secretary). Back row: Sowers (assistant equipment manager), Jimenez, Rakow, Del Greco, Pena, Azcue, McDevitt, Charles, Archer, Shapanus (equipment manager), Jones (trainer). Seated in front: Woods (batboy), Turley (batboy). (From the Kansas City Athletics.)

20—1962: Let Bygones Be Bygones 163

"Charlie called me up and says, 'I'm coming to Detroit and want to talk to you about next year.'" Bauer said. "I said, 'I'm not interested in next year ... and I'm telling you right now I'm quitting at the end of the year. I have a press conference in the morning.'" Finley wanted him to wait until he got there but his plane was delayed and he showed up late. "I had it," Bauer said. "He heard it over the radio in the cab. He came in and started chewing me out. I said, 'Wait a minute; I don't work for you no more. I quit. But I'll manage the season out. That's my contract.'"[9]

Bauer resigned on September 28, effective at the end of the season. Two members of his coaching staff, Jo Jo White and Dario Lodigiani, also resigned. Finley signed Lopat to a two-year contract to manage the team and serve as pitching coach through the 1964 season. The A's won 72 games and finished 24 games behind the pennant-winning Yankees, but Bauer was unable to get the team out of ninth place after mid-season. The team had a 15–3 record against Washington and won 13 consecutive games against the Senators to enable the A's to stay out of the cellar. Home attendance plunged to just 635,675, the lowest total in eight seasons in Kansas City.

Reports indicated Finley still wanted to move to team to Dallas. Before the season started, city councilman Charles Shafer was told Finley refused to consider a two-year contract to broadcast the A's games because the team would move to Dallas after the 1962 season. Finley's daughter Sharon transferred from an exclusive girls' school in Missouri to Southern Methodist University in Dallas. He complained about the poor attendance in Kansas City and refused to begin new contract negotiations with the city for the use of Municipal Stadium, even though he told the Associated Press that as far as he knew, the team would be in Kansas City in 1963.[10]

Finley applied to move the team on May 18, but the request was ruled out of order at that time because the meeting had been called to discuss plans to aid the minor leagues. "Those goddam club owners think they can keep me from moving the team," Finley said. "I'll show them a thing or two. I've got some tricks I haven't used yet. My lawyers tell me they can't keep me in Kansas City, some kind of antitrust crap."[11]

Finley denied that he sought permission to move during that meeting. "My plans for the Athletics are indefinite," Finley stated. "When — or if and when — I decide to move the team from Kansas City, I will make a statement." He claimed the American League owners simply looked at material from Dallas. "We held discussion on the up-to-date material, as we have now and then, about various areas." Finley said. "We have also had material from Oakland and San Diego in the past."[12]

Councilman Shafer proposed that the city should purchase the team from Finley on August 24 to protect the city's $2 million investment in Municipal Stadium. The price would be set through negotiations with Finley or, if that failed, through a court decision. Funds could be raised through general obligation and revenue bonds. He felt the team's share of stadium concession revenue would support the revenue bonds. A municipally owned corporation would administer the affairs of the team. Council members agreed with his sentiments but felt it would be better if the general public supported the team with greater attendance. The proposal was re-introduced at the September 23rd meeting but it was not passed. "I believe the time has come for a more healthy, optimistic and constructive attitude toward this whole situation," said councilman Charles Royster. "Such a resolution is obviously irritating to the owner of the A's and it has no possible chance of success. There are not enough funds in Kansas City or in the city government to purchase the A's."[13]

Finley asked the American League to hold a special executive meeting in the Savoy Hilton Hotel in New York on September 18 to investigate the merits of Dallas and Fort Worth for a major league membership. Owners expected Finley intended to seek permission to move the A's to Dallas. The owners listened to a 20-minute presentation given by Amon Carter, Angus Wynne and Leonard Greene and Arlington mayor Thomas Vandergrif from the Dallas and Fort Worth delegation. "Mr. Finley told us how anxious the Dallas–Fort Worth people were to enter the American League either through expansion or by obtaining an existing franchise," American League president Joe Cronin told reporters. "However there is no sentiment, at the present time, for expansion or the transfer of a franchise. We listened politely because we didn't want to hurt the feelings of these fine people who unquestionably are sincere in their efforts to obtain an American League franchise. We fully recognize that Fort Worth–Dallas is a potential major league territory and we don't doubt they are in position to build a suitable ballpark. Our club owners like Texas very much, but...."[14]

"Finley explained his many problems [in Kansas City] and we were sympathetic," Cronin admitted. "Parking, access roads, concession problems and other griefs made him confident he would draw better crowds elsewhere."

"The Kansas City situation was discussed," Finley stated. "No official action was taken for the very good reason that no action was necessary. I made no formal request for any transfer of my franchise.... I have never at any time said I wanted to move the franchise."[15]

Finley asked the city council to submit a general obligation bond issue to the voters that, if passed, would provide funds for a new 50,000-

seat stadium with parking for 15,000 cars. "Unless Kansas City is willing to start action for a new and modern stadium, its days as a major league city are numbered," he warned. "The present stadium is the worst in the major leagues in many respects. Most of the seats are 16 inches in width whereas seats in the modern stadiums are 21 inches. I don't blame the fans for not attending more than they have.... The firm that handles my concessions tells me I have the worst stadium in the country for selling hot dogs and soda pop. The concession stands are in the wrong place, the upper deck is so steep the vendors begin to drag down about the third inning, and the distance between aisles is so great its almost impossible for a fan in the middle of a row to make a vendor hear him." He also complained the stadium was in an undesirable part of the city.[16]

"I have not made a request to the American League to move, although we have discussed the matter," he said. "But I will say that if we cannot get a new stadium, it will become necessary for me to make a request of the league to move, and I am confident I will get permission. However, I want to make it plain that I have never mentioned at any time that I wanted to move the franchise from Kansas City. The American League wants the franchise to remain, and I want it to remain, but I cannot stay and lose the money I have lost.... I made a statement when I first came to Kansas City that I would take all the profits and plow them back in and use some additional money of my own, but I can't stand the heavy losses I have already sustained.... It takes money to build a winner.... It would take a season attendance of a million persons just to break even. We in baseball have to do everything within our power to bring fans to the ballpark, and the only way you can bring them is to cater to them. We've got to make them comfortable, we've got to make them want to attend, whether we have a winning team or not. You have to entertain time and the best place to start is with a new stadium.... That's way I am asking the council to approve a stadium bond issue. If it refused, I don't think Kansas City will have major league baseball much longer."[17]

Finley said he would agree to a long-term contract to use a new stadium and suggested Swope Park as a possible location. "With the proper player facilities, Kansas City has great possibilities of being an outstanding sports city. But its like fishing — you can have all types of hooks in your tackle box but, without bait, they're no good. A new stadium is the bait."[18]

The city council studied Finley's proposal as well as the possibility of remodeling Municipal Stadium and sent Ken Krakauer, head of the Chamber of Commerce baseball committee and councilman Tom Gavin to Chicago to discuss the issue with Finley and league president Joe Cronin on September 27. The American League owners met on October 5 and asked the city to consider remodeling and adding parking facilities to Municipal Stadium if a new stadium was not feasible.[19]

Gavin told council the American League listed Municipal Stadium as having only 1,800 parking spaces while other cities in the league provided 4,300 to 12,000 parking spaces. The figures did not take into account all the surrounding parking lots in Kansas City. "There are more than 5,000 spaces within a three-block area of the stadium and the licenses purchased at city hall by parking operators will substantiate this," he said. "We had one lot two blocks south of the stadium with a 50-cent parking fee which operated at 30 percent capacity." He stated a survey indicated the present parking facilities were among the best in both major leagues and that the area around the stadium was such that additional parking could be added in a relatively short time. The new freeway from the east improved accessibility to the stadium and brought most of the areas of the city to within 16 minutes of the stadium.[20]

Earl Smith, chairman of the Chamber of Commerce baseball committee, said they would study the feasibility, cost and a possible location for a new stadium as well as the cost and feasibility of enlarging Municipal Stadium and its parking facilities, but the city did not have funds available and they recommended against any bond issue. New facilities would be provided when the A's improved and attendance increased. They felt plans should be coordinated with those of a proposed $50 million sports project that would include a stadium suitable for both baseball and football, along with facilities for hosting the Pan-American Games and a new arena for the American Royal, Kansas City's annual horse show.[21]

"When I first came to Kansas City everyone was on my side," Finley said. "Then I started working on this Texas thing and they got down on me. I don't blame them. Kansas City had a major league team and here was a threat that the team might be lost. I would have been mad and upset myself if I lived here. But on my side, I believe everyone will agree we have started building a winning ballclub. Our trades have been good ones and we have been careful not to tear down. We have tried to build. So I am asking that bygones be bygones. That the past be forgotten and that we start over again. I am convinced I can build a winner here. Contrary to what some may think I like Kansas City and I applaud the loyalty of its faithful baseball fans. Now that this season is virtually over we are going to do everything possible to get back the support we have lost. We are going to put on an intensive ticket drive. I need the support of Kansas City and to get that support we are going to do everything we can to provide Kansas City and this great area with a winning ballclub. One reason I am urging the erection of a new stadium is that I believe it will do a great deal to arouse a new interest.

"A new stadium and a winning club make an unbeatable combination. The fans here have been justified in their criticism because, understandably, they do not want to lose the Athletics. And I can't blame them. And now I want them back on my team. We'll all join forces and see if we cannot make 1963 the biggest in the history of this city."[22]

21

1963: Everything's Green and Gold

New manager Ed Lopat felt the team needed left-handed pitching, a catcher and a right-handed hitting outfielder and the A's offered Jerry Lumpe as trade bait. The Dodgers made several offers for Lumpe after the 1962 World Series and a deal appeared imminent. Cleveland also wanted Lumpe. The A's felt Wayne Causey could play second base if Lumpe was traded.[1]

Mel McGaha joined the organization during the World Series in a dual role as a coach and administrative assistant to the president and general manager. McGaha managed Cleveland in 1962 but was fired at the end of the season. Jimmie Dykes was named third base coach. Dykes played with the A's and White Sox and managed the White Sox for 13 years (1934–1946). He managed the A's (1951–1953), Orioles (1954), Reds (1958), Tigers (1959–1960), and Indians (1960–1961). He coached for the Braves in 1962. Finley's cousin Carl Finley joined the public relations department on January 7 and later became business manager. James Schaaf was promoted to the dual role as director of public relations and traveling secretary after Dave Keefe retired. Bob Wachter was fired and became a scout for the Washington Senators. He joined the Kansas City Chiefs a few months later. The A's scouting staff was trimmed from 17 scouts to 11 to cut expenses.

Finley launched a season ticket drive in November 1962 with a goal to sell 4,000 season tickets, but the team sold just 2,229 season tickets.[2] The spring training base was moved to Bradenton, Florida, from West Palm Beach. Bradenton was the former spring training base for the Milwaukee Braves.[3]

Finley changed the team colors to "Kelly green" and "Fort Knox gold" because they were his wife's favorite colors. He abandoned the traditional home white and road gray uniforms and received permission to use sleeveless, vest-type uniforms of shiny gold material trimmed in Kelly green with Kelly green sweatshirts on a one-year experimental basis. League president Joe Cronin gave Finley permission to use numerals on the sleeves as long as they were not placed on the pitchers' uniforms. Finley placed the names of the players on the back of the uniforms but abbreviated names or used nicknames such as "Cooz" for Wayne Causey and "Hawk" for Ken Harrelson. The names were dropped from the uniforms after the 1963 season. Finley unveiled the uniforms on opening day. The A's televised the game to enable the entire area to see the festivities[4].

The starting time for night games was changed from 8 P.M. to 7 P.M. on weekdays and 6 P.M. on Saturdays. The A's were the first team to offer earlier starting times for evening games. "Most of our fans come from 50 miles away," Finley explained. "We want to get them in bed at a decent hour."[5]

WDAF (610) and WDAF-TV (Channel 4) reacquired the broadcasting rights for the Athletics in 1963. WDAF carried all regular-season games and 24 pre-season contests. WDAF-TV televised the home opener and 39 road games. Monte Moore returned to the broadcasting booth, but George Bryson replaced Bruce Rice as Moore's partner. Bryson announced Cincinnati Reds games for five seasons and served as executive assistant to Los Angeles Angels general manager Fred Haney in 1961. Hamms Brewing Company replaced Goetz Brewing as the primary sponsor. Guy's Foods and General Finance continued to co-sponsor the games.

The A's made two player acquisitions during the off-season. The A's acquired 27-year-old left-handed pitcher Ted Bowsfield from the Angels on November 27, 1962. He had a 9–8 record and a 4.40 ERA with the Angels in 1962. They also reacquired outfielder Chuck Essegian from Cleveland in exchange for pitcher Jerry Walker at the start of spring training on February 27. Lopat hoped the veteran outfielder could play left field and provide right-handed power.

The A's lost their home opener 8–3 to the Yankees on April 8 before a crowd of 30,976. Finley gave former U.S. president Harry S Truman and Kansas City mayor H. Roy Bartle green ten-gallon hats. Harvey, the mechanical rabbit that popped up behind home plate, was painted green and gold. The sheep that pastured on the right field embankment were covered with green and gold blankets with a big white letter A. The ball shagger on the embankment was attired in a shepherd's outfit with a green and gold robe, a long black beard, and a long crook. The A's unveiled their new uniforms but most players did not like them. When they walked down the runway to the dugout, Gino Cimoli told a reporter, "Say one word and I'll

1963 team — Front row: Pfister, Alusik, Harrelson, McGaha (coach), Lopat (manager), Niarhos (coach), Dykes (coach), Lau, Charles. Middle row: Schaaf (traveling secretary), Edwards, Drabowsky, Wickersham, Lovrich, Siebern, Bowsfield, Cimoli, Lumpe, Wyatt, Essegian, Jones (trainer). Back row: Sigloch (clubhouse attendant), LaRussa, Tartabull, Segui, Willis, Rakow, Causey, Fischer, Pena, Del Greco, Esposito, Zych (clubhouse attendant). Seated in front: Woods (batboy). (From the Kansas City Athletics.)

deck you." The press ridiculed the uniforms and opposing players taunted the A's with comments like, "Hi there, beautiful."⁶

The A's lost 5–3 the following day to the Yankees, but then won 13 of the next 18 games and moved into first place. "Scheduled to play three games with second-place Boston in early May, Kansas City faced for the first time what might be called, if only jokingly, a crucial series," reported *Sports Illustrated*. "When the Athletics won two games of the series to lead the league by a game and a half, the *Kansas City Times* pointed out with jubilation that this was the latest date in any season that the A's had occupied first place."⁷ The A's had a 25–19 mark on the morning of June 1, and attendance showed an increase of 65,000.

Wayne Causey (from Jay Publications and the Kansas City Athletics).

Leading the A's during their early season success was 26-year-old Wayne Causey, who began the season as a utility infielder. Lopat rested shortstop Dick Howser for one game on April 21 because he was struggling at bat and in the field and replaced him with Causey. Causey had two hits and played well in the field. Howser pulled a muscle in batting practice the following day and did not play. Causey hit a triple, a double, two singles and had two runs batted in to help the A's overcome a 5–0 Detroit lead and win 6–5. By the end of the week the left-handed hitting Causey was hitting .400. He led the league in hitting with a .369 average as late as May 25 and continued to lead the league during the first few days of June. Causey's average dipped below .300 for the first time on June 12 and hit a season low of .273 on July 7 and on July 18. Over the next month he had 30 hits in 91 trips to the plate and raised his average to .285. He finished the season as the team's leading hitter with a .280 average and led the team with 32 doubles.⁸

"I never had confidence in myself as a hitter until I started playing regularly in 1963, after Dick Howser got hurt," said Causey a few years later. "No one gave my any advice or made any changes that helped me to be a better hitter. The thing that helped me most was learning to hit to left field. I had always been able to hit to left-center, but I was not a left field hitter. In 1963 I developed a little different stroke. I guess you might say a kind of an inside-out stroke. I don't know where I learned it. It was just one of those things that came to me. After I started stroking the ball this way I found I could hit to left field and I could even hit the inside pitch to left."[9]

Causey committed only 15 errors at shortstop. His range improved during the season as he became more familiar with the shortstop position and with opposing hitters. Although his arm was not strong he made quick and accurate throws. Causey's overall play at shortstop was so spectacular that Howser sat on the bench when he returned to health. He became a utility infielder before he was traded to Cleveland for catcher Doc Edwards on May 25.

Jerry Lumpe adjusted to his new partner at shortstop and they developed into one of the league's better combinations. Lumpe started slowly at the plate but finished with a .271 average. Ed Charles was a key factor in the team's early success and drove in many game-winning runs. He was the A's most consistent clutch hitter during the season. His 15 home runs and 73 runs batted in were second best on the team. Shortstop Tony LaRussa was kept on the roster to protect him from the first-year player draft. He appeared in 34 games and hit .250 in 44 trips to the plate.

Norm Siebern sought a large increase in his salary following his 1962 season. A salary dispute with Finley captured the headlines and lasted several weeks before it was resolved. He showed the strain of this dispute with a slow start. He recovered to lead the team with 16 home runs and 83 runs batted in while batting .272. He was Kansas City's lone representative on the All-Star team but did not appear in the game because Yankees manager Ralph Houk felt the green and gold uniform would embarrass the American League.

Bill Bryan started the season behind the plate but batted just .169 in 24 games before he was sent to Portland (AAA). Haywood Sullivan appeared in 40 games before being sent to Portland as a player-coach. After the A's acquired Edwards, he became the team's top receiver but was plagued with injuries and appeared in just 67 games. Kansas City acquired 30-year-old catcher Charlie Lau on waivers from Baltimore on July 1st Lou, who later gained fame as a hitting guru, finished the season with a .289 average.

Right fielder Gino Cimoli was one of the team's most dependable performers. He finished with a .263 batting average and led the team with 11 triples. Bobby Del Greco and Jose Tartabull shared center field. Tartabull led the team with 16 stolen bases. Manny Jimenez slipped to a .280 average and played in just 60 games. He was one of several players that shuttled between Kansas City and Portland. Ken Harrelson, a 21-year-old outfielder, was called up to the A's in June and hit .230 in 78 games. George Alusik led the league with 11 pinch-hit runs batted in and was second with a .474 batting average as a pinch hitter. He pinch-hit a grand slam against Boston on July 17 that won the game for the A's.

Improved pitching led to the team's early success. Orlando Pena and Dave Wickersham were the biggest winners, each registering 12 victories. Pena ended the season with 20 losses, but six of his defeats were by one run and four were by virtue of a shutout. His biggest moment of the season came on May 31 when he gave up three home runs to Washington but hit a grand slam to win the game. Wickersham emerged as one of the team's most dependable starting pitchers and finished with a 12-15 record and a 4.08 ERA.

Ed Rakow finished with a 9-10 record and a 3.93 ERA. He pitched six innings of perfect baseball, retiring 18 batters in a row on May 1. When Rakow came out to hit in the sixth inning, Finley noticed his gold pants were hanging so low that they hid his green socks. Finley reached for the phone in his box and called general manager Pat Friday. "Pat," he yelled, "look at Rakow's pants. That looks sloppy. Now I've mentioned this before. Let's take care of it." It may have been just a coincidence, but Rakow gave up eight runs when he returned to the mound in the seventh inning.[10]

Bowsfield began the season in the starting rotation. He had a no-hitter going into the ninth inning against Minnesota on May 11 and finished with a two-hitter, winning the game 5-1. He lost his bid for the no-hitter when Zoilo Versailles singled. Six days later he followed with another two-hitter in a shutout against Boston. He was injured in June and was assigned to the bullpen for the remainder of the season. He finished with a 5-7 record and a 4.45 ERA.

Diego Segui had a slow start and did not win his first game until June 11. He then became one of the most dependable starters and finished with a 9-6 record and a 3.72 ERA. He struck out 116 batters. Moe Drabowsky started the season with Portland but joined the A's in June and finished with a 7-13 record and a 3.05 ERA. He hurled a one-hitter against Washington on August 20, winning the game 9-0. The lone hit was a bunt single by Don Blasingame in the fourth inning. Drabowsky walked just two batters in the game.

Relief pitcher Bill Fischer was an early season standout. He won seven games with just one defeat by Memorial Day, but lost his effectiveness after giving up a tape-measure home run off the third deck façade to Mickey Mantle in Yankee Stadium on May 22. Mantle's ball was still rising when it

Ed Lopat (from Jay Publications and the Kansas City Athletics).

struck the façade, 109 feet above the playing field and 374 feet from home plate. It was estimated that it would have been a 620-foot home run if it had cleared the stadium. The next time the A's came to New York, Causey got a ladder and put it in front of Fischer's locker so Fischer could get the next ball Mantle hit. He finished the season with a 9–6 record and a 3.56 ERA.

John Wyatt emerged as the ace of the bullpen. He appeared in 63 games and broke the team record for appearances he set the previous year. He went 6–4 with 21 saves. He struck out 83 batters in 92 innings and had a 3.13 ERA. The A's acquired veteran right-handed reliever Tom Sturdivant on waivers from Detroit on July 23rd. The knuckleball hurler pitched one stretch of 24 consecutive scoreless innings, 13 of which came against the Yankees. Pete Lovrich, a 20-year-old right-hander, was a first year player retained on the roster due to the bonus rule. He had a 1–1 record and 7.84 ERA in 20 appearances

After the successful start of the season, the team collapsed in June. The hitting, timely in the clutch though not too potent, fell off abruptly. The team lost 27 of its next 38 games from June 1 until the All-Star break and plunged into eighth place with a 36–46 record at the All-Star break. The team's fortunes reached a low point when Detroit arrived in Kansas City on June 21. The Tigers snapped a 10-game losing streak and won three straight from the A's.

The A's finished the season in eighth place with a 73–89 record. The 73 victories equaled the Kansas City record for most wins in one season. Despite a drop in hitting from the previous season, the pitching showed great improvement. Finley extended Lopat's contract for another year, running through the 1965 season in recognition of the team's improved performance.

The final attendance for the 1963 A's was 762,364, an increase of 126,689 over the previous season. The attendance was 411,281 at the All-Star break, an increase of nearly 125,000 at the break. Had the team continued to play well the final attendance appeared certain to reach 800,000 and could have gone over 900,000. Attendance was hindered during the second half of the season by a poor record on the field and continuing rumors that Finley wanted to move the franchise.

It was not a bad season for a rookie major league manager. Lopat, a New York City native, had been one of the most effective southpaws in the major leagues, winning 166 games and losing 112 in his 12-year major league career, mostly with the Yankees. He managed Richmond (AAA) from 1956 through 1958. Lopat was the roving pitching coach in the Yankees minor league system in 1959, and was pitching coach in New York in 1960 and for the Minnesota Twins in 1961.

After one year he was the pitching coach for the Athletics in 1962, Charles Finley named Lopat manager of the Athletics when Hank Bauer resigned at the end of the season. Ken Harrelson considered Lopat "a wonderful guy, but only a fair manager. He was too nice to get mad, had trouble handling some of the guys, and wasn't sure how to run a ball game. I loved him because he was always great to me, but, like everyone else, I walked all over him.... Watching Eddie Lopat manage was an education in futility. Although he knew baseball, he couldn't run a ballgame. I guess he tried to keep everything in his head instead of writing it down, because he never remembered who played and who hadn't. By not thinking ahead, he often ran out of the ballplayers he needed most."[11]

Not surprisingly, Lopat did not last long as manager in 1964. He was offered the position as vice president of player personnel on July 3, 1964. He replaced Tom Ferrick as pitching coach on June 5, 1965. Lopat was named executive vice president in charge of the entire A's organization in a surprise announcement on October 27, 1965. Hank Peters was reassigned to the position of administrative assistant in charge of the minor league operations. Lopat's title was changed to administration assistant, Major Leagues, in 1967, though he still continued to function in the general manager's role. He resigned on October 15, 1967, three days before the Athletics moved to Oakland. Lopat died on June 15, 1992.

Ed Lopat's Managerial Record

Year	Club	League	Won	Lost	Position
1956	Richmond	AAA	74	79	5
1957	Richmond	AAA	81	73	3
1958	Richmond	AAA	71	82	6
1963	Kansas City	Major	73	89	8
1964	Kansas City	Major	17	35	10

22

Happiness Is Being Somewhere Else

Lamar Hunt announced that he would move his football team from Dallas to Kansas City on February 8, 1963. The city gave him a seven-year lease to use Municipal Stadium. The rent was $1 per year for the first two years and the city would receive half of the concession profits. After the first two years the city would receive 5 percent of the gross receipts after ticket sales reached $1.1 million. If ticket sales fell below $1.1 million, the rent would be just $1 a year. The city also agreed to provide an additional 3,000 permanent seats and 11,000 movable seats along the north sideline for the football team. This would increase the capacity of the stadium to 44,500 for football. The city would use bond money to construct an office building and a practice field in municipally owned Swope Park at a cost of $650,000.

"One of the main reason the football club came to Kansas City was because they realized it (the stadium) was such a wonderful deal," Finley declared. "Our offices were so cold my employees had to wear stadium boots and sit on heating pads in the winter and I was paying $120,000 rent for the privilege. How much rent did the Chiefs pay for the stadium —*$1 a year!*"[1]

Finley was furious and demanded a similar lease. The city council replied the city gave the A's similar benefits in 1955 and 1956 when the city reduced the stadium rental to $25,000 annually after the A's moved to Kansas City. Normal rent on the stadium since that time ranged from about $100,000 to a high of $148,000 in 1959. The A's paid $125,000 in 1963.[2]

Finley was upset he was not told about the availability of the bond money when he spent money to improve the stadium in 1961. He claimed he was promised that he would be reimbursed through a reduction in rent. He intended to seek this reimbursement when he negotiated a new lease,

Stadium Leases in 1963

A comparison of the Athletics' lease in 1963 and those in effect on other municipally-owned stadiums

Team	Basic Rent	Percent of Admissions	Concessions	Cancellation
Kansas City A's	$1,000	5%	7½%	If gate is less than 850,000
Kansas City Chiefs	$1	5% after first two years if receipts top $1.1 million	50%	Insolvency
Milwaukee Braves	-0-	5% of first one million 7% between 1-1.5 million 10% over 1.5 million	10–16%	National emergency
Cleveland Indians	$60,000	7% if greater than base rent	45%	National emergency
Baltimore Orioles	$75,000	7% if greater than base rent	10%	National emergency
Washington Senators	$65,000	7% if greater than base rent	13%	National emergency
San Francisco Giants	$125,000	5% if greater than base rent	Maximum of $25,000	National emergency
Houston Colts	$562,500–$747,000	Included in base rent	Included in base rent	Stadium loss
Minnesota Twins	-0-	7%	10%	National emergency

but when the city rented the stadium to the Chiefs for $1 he asked the city to waive his rent in 1963. The city council refused to waive the rent in 1963. They would, however, consider reimbursement under the terms of a new lease. They felt the city was not obligated to pay the entire amount Finley requested ($411,670), since many of the improvements were not vital to operate the facility. The city council and Finley later agreed on a compromise figure of $300,000.

Negotiations for a new lease began in March. Mayor H. Roy Bartle and the out-going nine-member council wanted to sign a lease before a new city council and mayor assumed office in April. They offered Finley a seven-year lease similar to the contract signed by the Chiefs. The rent was a $1 a year for the first two seasons, regardless of attendance. After the first two years the team paid 5 percent of the gross receipts if the paid admissions exceeded 950,000. The rent remained a $1 a year if the attendance did not exceed 950,000. The lease allowed Finley to cancel the lease on a 60-day notice if attendance fell below 850,000. The city would turn over its 7½ percent of the concession income to Finley until he was reimbursed $300,000 for the stadium improvements. The council approved the new lease by a 6–1 vote, with two members absent. The dissenting vote came from Charles Shafer, who battled to stall the ordinance. Finley and Bartle signed the agreement less than 10 minutes before their terms expired on April 10. The "contract was a wonderful contract," Finley said. "It was so wonderful, in fact, that no one in his right mind would have ever wanted to leave Kansas City."[3]

City counselor Keith Wilson immediately ruled the contract invalid. Wilson and acting city manager Ben Powers ruled the council had to operate under the new rules applying to a 12-man council that required seven assenting votes to approve the lease. After the newly elected 13-man council was sworn in they took immediate action to reconsider the lease by a unanimous 13–0 vote. Finley was outraged. "This was a seven-year contract with two seven-year options, making a total of 21 years," he said. "The Yankees were in town to open the season at the time I went down to the council chambers to sign this contract, so I invited Mr. Del Webb to go along with me. I've come here, I've negotiated and I've gotten no place. I want to say now that this new city council is not going to push Charlie Finley around and give him a rotten deal."

Finley contacted *Atlanta Journal* sports editor Furman Bisher. He had spoken to Finley in February 1962 about Atlanta as a possible new home for the Athletics, but Finley was not interested at that time. "Did you call me to tell me you're ready to move your franchise to Atlanta at last?" Bisher asked.

"These goddam city councilmen voted in the kind of contract I wanted for the stadium here this morning, then left office," Finley replied. "A new council took office then and these bastards just killed the contract the other council voted to accept this morning."[4]

Finley still claimed the lease he signed with the out-going council was valid. Pat Friday tried to pay for two years' rent for the stadium with a pair of $1 checks on April 15, but the city's assistant finance director refused to accept them. New Kansas City mayor Ilus Davis said the city would offer Finley the most generous lease in the major leagues but added the city wanted to be relieved of the constant threat of losing the franchise and would insist that all attendance provisions be removed. Other teams leasing municipal facilities did not have attendance provisions in their contracts. Finley refused to discuss any leases until the conclusion of the baseball season in October.

Finley and his wife Shirley went to Atlanta on April 25. Bisher and his wife met them at the Atlanta Municipal Airport and drove them by possible locations for a new stadium. Finley was not impressed with Lakewood Park, home of the Southeastern Fair and a dilapidated racetrack. Mayor Ivan Allen, Jr., and Bisher picked up the Finleys the next morning and drove them to an urban renewal area — South Expressway was on one side; the state capitol was within a quarter of a mile, and downtown Atlanta was less than a mile away. "Why, there's not a ballpark in America with a location like this," Finley said. He decided to move the Athletics to Atlanta.[5]

After Finley returned from Atlanta, Lamar Hunt and Chiefs head coach Hank Stram came to Kansas City for a speaking engagement. Finley saw Stram and said he had a proposition that might interest Hunt. Finley told Hunt Atlanta was building a new stadium and they should move their baseball and football franchises to Atlanta and leave Kansas City without any professional athletic teams. "This is a horse-shit town." Finley said. "No one will ever do any good here."[6]

Atlanta organized a stadium authority in June. The authority invited Finley to move the A's to Atlanta in 1964 and wanted to negotiate tentative rental and concession details. They planned to construct a 54,000-seat stadium at an estimated cost of $15 million and would enlarge 10,000-seat Ponce de Leon Park, home of the minor-league Atlanta Crackers, to 25,000 seats to serve as a temporary home for the team until the new stadium was completed. Bisher contacted American League president Joe Cronin. Bisher, Georgia Governor Carl Sanders, Mayor Allen and members of the stadium authority wanted to make a presentation at the American League meeting held in Cleveland during the All-Star break on July 8.[7]

The Kansas City city council offered Finley his choice of two leases on July 3, both described as similar to the contract offered the Chiefs. The city would receive $1 a year rental for the first two seasons and 5 percent of the ticket revenue during the last five years. The difference in the leases was the concession revenue. The city and the team would equally share all concession revenue in Lease "A" (listed as KC-1 in chart at the end of the chapter), but the A's would retain the city's share until $300,000 was accumulated to reimburse the team for stadium improvements. The city and team would equally share all concession revenue until the city's share of the concessions and 5 percent of the paid admissions totaled $300,000 in Lease "B" (KC-2). Once this was reached the city would receive 7½ percent of the concession sales, the same as in the previous leases. Missouri Sportservice operated the concessions for the Athletics and the A's received approximately 29½ percent of the concession income. The A's paid 25 percent of their concession income to the city because this was equivalent to 7½ percent of the total sales. In 1963 the A's paid $43,657.63 to the city. If the city received 50 percent of the revenue the concession, revenue would double to $87,315.26. Neither proposed lease contained any provisions that would waive the 5 percent in ticket revenue if attendance failed to reach a specified total, but the city indicated it would be willing to negotiate such a provision into the agreement. Finley rejected both proposals because he felt they were not comparable to the lease he signed in April.[8]

The Atlanta group attended the American League meeting in July but Finley now wanted to move to Oakland after he talked to several owners and discovered they would not approve the transfer to Atlanta. Some owners were opposed because Atlanta would increase travel and operational costs. Finley reasoned that Oakland would be acceptable because it would add another team on the West Coast to pair with the Angels and eliminate the transportation problems that currently existed. Some owners did not want Finley to move to Atlanta because they wanted to keep the city available if Cleveland or another American League franchise wanted to relocate.

Oakland had plans for a $25 million sports stadium and arena complex with a stadium seating 48,000 located adjacent to Nimitz Freeway and close to Oakland International Airport. Construction would start in the fall of 1963 and the stadium would be ready by the 1965 season. San Francisco mayor George Christopher felt some agreement could be made for the team to use Candlestick Park by renegotiating the contract with the Giants. If that could not be arranged, Oakland could enlarge the capacity of 22,000-seat Frank Youell Field in Oakland to accommodate the Athletics until the new stadium was ready.[9]

Finley discussed his problems with the lease at the meeting and expressed concern about attendance in Kansas City. The club attracted only 683,817 fans in 1961 and 635,675 in 1962; Finley claimed he lost $800,000 in cash in 1961 and $600,000 in 1962. He also complained about the radio and television revenue in Kansas City. He received only $200,000 in 1962 compared to the $1 million the Yankees made in New York. The owners were unresponsive so he made no formal request to move to Oakland or anywhere else. "I think I could have gotten permission at the All-Star meeting," Finley said, "but I didn't make a formal request. Besides, I knew there are two owners who believe I might louse up the Oakland franchise"[10]

Reporters learned Finley wanted to move the team to Oakland and contacted San Francisco Giants owner Horace Stoneham. He confirmed Finley came to see him several days earlier to request permission to share Candlestick Park until a new park could be built in Oakland. Stoneham told Finley he would not share the stadium and told the reporters "one of the reasons we (the Giants) moved from New York was that we were assured we would have the Bay area to ourselves." He admitted, however, that the Giants could not keep another team out of Oakland since Organized Baseball regarded it as open territory.[11]

"Joe Cronin told me I might be able to work out a deal to play in the Giants' park for a while in San Francisco," Finley said. "But the Giants said no. The important fact is ... I never asked the league's permission to move, but I was encouraged by the league to look around. Cronin let me take the abuse. He never had the red blood in his veins to stand up and say, 'We knew Finley had problems in Kansas City, we knew he was looking in Dallas and Oakland, we contributed financially to this.'" Finley claimed Cronin encouraged him to investigate Oakland because the league wanted a second franchise on the West Coast and Cronin even worked out a pilot schedule that included Oakland.

Cronin had a slightly different version of the events. "On Finley's request we made surveys," he said. "But those we made in Dallas, Oakland and Kansas City convinced us we weren't justified in letting Finley move. Before we abandon a city we have to consider its history—the quality of the team and its public relations and the effect they might have had on attendance."[12]

Finley complained that stadium improvements made for the Chiefs hurt the baseball team. The extension of the press box blocked the view of people in the last few rows of the lower deck along the right field line. "The football team wanted that, so the city built it and paid for it," he said. "All it does for us is to ruin a lot of our seats and louse up our public-address system. You think the city would buy us a new public-address system...? We don't ask half what the football team gets. We just want to be treated fair."[13]

Finley waited until December 20 to reopen talks with Mayor Davis and city manager Carleton P. Sharpe about a new lease. He brought two proposals to the meeting. The first (Fin-1) was a four-year contract with an annual rent of $50,000. The A's would keep all concession revenue in lieu of reimbursement for stadium improvements. It contained two four-year options under which the city would receive 7½ percent of the concession revenue but no rent unless attendance reached 900,000, the attendance he felt he needed to maintain a viable operation. (He claimed it would take an attendance of 1,100,000 for him to break even.) He felt that with the backing of the city administration and civic groups there would be no difficulty in reaching the 900,000-attendance figure. The second proposal (Fin-2) was a two-year contract with a flat rent of $125,000. Neither contract contained an escape clause, something he previously demanded. The council rejected both proposals.

"We must have a contract for at least four years," Davis said. "It's the only way to restore stability in the A's operation and regain the fan's faith," but added the city could not gamble on long-term leases that offered little promise of more than token rent. The council was willing to give Finley a 750,000-attendance minimum under which the rent would be waived but felt Finley's request of 900,000 was excessive. Finley felt he was extremely generous in his offers and accused the council of lacking confidence "in the desire of the people of Kansas City to have major league baseball."[14]

The council countered Finley's proposals with several variations of four and five year leases. The first proposal (KC-3) specified a flat rent of $25,000 a year for five years. The A's would pay the city 13 cents a ticket on all admissions above 580,000. The 13 cents would be waived on admissions under 580,000 to enable Finley to regain the money he spent on stadium improvements. The second proposal (KC-4) specified a flat rent of $65,000 a year for either four or five years. This was about $60,000 less than the A's paid to the city in 1963. The difference would enable Finley to cover money he spent on stadium improvements. Both of the proposed leases had a four-year renewal option at a flat $125,000 a year. They offered a seven-year lease (KC-5) that was virtually the same as the lease the city gave to the Chiefs with the city and team splitting the concession revenue. In the Chiefs' lease the team would pay 5 percent of its ticket sales if the ticket sale revenue reached $1,100.000. In the case of the A's the city interpreted the $1,100,000 as an attendance of 900,000. They also offered a four-year lease (KC-6) with two four-year renewal options under the same terms Finley proposed in his first proposal (Fin-1) except the rent would be waived if the attendance did not reach 750,000 instead of 900,000. Finley said none of the proposals were acceptable because they all included some rent regardless of attendance.[15]

On December 24, Finley announced that the A's would move their offices out of Municipal Stadium. He was advised that if the team remained in the stadium on January 1, they would commit themselves to at least a one-year lease because the lease expired on December 31. He said they sought permission to remain in the stadium without a lease, but the request was denied. Civic Plaza National Bank chairman Alex J. Barket offered 8,000 square feet, rent free.[16]

Mayor Davis asked Barket to withdraw his offer and granted permission for Finley to occupy the stadium until January 10 without the risk of binding himself to a new contract. Finley did not accept and set up a temporary office in Joe Bowman's garage.

"At one time we had the team's office right here in the garage for seven weeks," said Bowman. "And Finley wouldn't let them put in a telephone. They used the phone here in the kitchen. He got mad when the wife would be talking to her friends. I tried to tell him one day. I says, 'Charlie, that telephone belongs to my wife. You want a telephone in there that nobody's on, you put one in. But as long as that phone is in my kitchen and my wife is paying for it, she's going to talk on it, and you're not going to tell her how long.' He didn't say any more about it.... Hank Peters ... and all the secretaries were out here ... they wore a path going around my house. Finally I said something about putting in some new grass. Charlie bought me 15 pounds of bluegrass to spread around. He'd call the wife here while I'm on the road scouting. He'd call her one, two o'clock in the morning and have her go get something out of the garage. She had to clean it up every night.... We'd sit there and talk maybe to six o'clock, and everybody'd go home and come back the next morning at nine o'clock. We had desks and everything out there. Some people thought we were getting rich renting the garage. I didn't get a dime. Not a nickel. They didn't even pay my expenses. I didn't complain. What could I do? They had to have an office somewhere and had to have an office where people coming into town could find it, Eighty-third and State Line was no problem."[17]

"I will rent a cow pasture and put up temporary stands for the team to use next year," Finley said. "I'm talking about renting or leasing about 300 acres of land and building a temporary stadium with bleacher-type seats, lights and all modern facilities. It probably would cost me a million dollars, but I'm willing to do that if necessary.... The A's will play in Kansas City and that's definite, but they won't use the stadium unless they are given what I consider a fair lease." Pat Friday inspected several possible locations. He identified two sites, one as being on the eastern edge of Independence and another 320-acre site near Peculiar, Missouri, prompting comments that the team would be known as the "Peculiar Athletics." Sedalia, Missouri, offered the use of its baseball stadium on December 30. Sedalia is 100 miles southeast of Kansas City.[18]

Sources close to the Athletics' front office said Finley did not intend to renew the lease. He felt that if he could create an atmosphere of hostility between him and the city council he could win sympathy from owners and receive permission to move the team. He called Furman Bisher to discover how the negotiations were going between Atlanta and the Braves because Finley wanted to move the Athletics to Milwaukee if the Braves moved to Atlanta. "No other city that has lost a franchise has even been left without a major league team," Finley told Bisher (Brooklyn did not occur to him). "This would ease the pressure on baseball. Let the Athletics move from Kansas City to Milwaukee, then Milwaukee wouldn't have any kicks." When Fisher reminded him that would leave Kansas City without a team Finley replied, "That damn place don't deserve big league baseball.... It's a hick town."[19]

Mayor Davis sent a telegram to Joe Cronin on December 30: "I hereby invite you to send a committee of the American League to Kansas City to meet with the mayor and the city council on the leasing of Municipal Stadium to the Kansas City Athletics," he wrote. "We would greatly appreciate recommendations of the American League in our attempt to make a fair lease to the Athletics.... It is the desire of the city government and the city to be absolutely fair with the Kansas City Athletics ... we would welcome a review of our proposals and would be grateful for suggestions from a committee appointed by you in order to be sure we are being fair to major league baseball and our city."

Cronin termed the request as "unprecedented" and said he would wait until after January 10 before he intervened. "We (the American League) definitely will play ball in Kansas City in 1964," he said. "We have committed ourselves.... All this publicity on discussions of the stadium lease is not good for baseball. I certainly hope they get together on a new lease as quickly as possible."[20]

Finley appeared before the city council on January 4 with a new lease proposal. It was identical to his previous offer (Fin-2), a two-year lease with $125,000 annual rent, but he offered to write off the stadium improvement debt. The city council rejected Finley's proposal. "Well, that's all you're going to get," Finley shouted. "That is it."

He flew to Louisville and met with mayor William Cowger and Kentucky governor Edward Breathitt. He signed a conditional two-year contract with the state of Kentucky on January 6 to use 20,628-seat Fairgrounds Stadium, built in 1956 for the class AAA Louisville Colonels. The state would spend up to $500,000 to enlarge the stadium to 30,362 seats. Louisville was considered an open city and no indemnity would have to be paid because the city did not have a professional baseball team in 1963. The terms of the lease called for the state to receive 5 percent of the net gate proceeds and 7½ percent of the concession revenue. The "net gate proceeds" was undefined, but apparently was similar to the turnstile count. It was similar to the Kansas City lease that expired on December 31, 1963.[21]

Finley had, in effect, moved the team without league approval. "I don't expect it to be a bed of roses, but after I have had an opportunity to present all the true facts, I am sure they will be appreciative of all our problems and definitely give us approval," he said. "We have these caps that have KC on the front and we don't want to throw them away, so I think we'll call ourselves the Kentucky Colonels. Or maybe we'll just scrap the caps and call ourselves the Louisville Athletics ... or maybe the Louisville Sluggers." Finley said that before every game, after "The Star-Spangled Banner," everyone would sing, "Oh, the sun shines bright...."[22]

Finley asked Cronin to call a league meeting. "Finley is a fool," said

White Sox owner Arthur Allyn. Responses by other officials indicated Finley would not be permitted to move. Three days before the meeting Finley hinted he might take legal action. "I will take on each American League owner individually or I will take them on collectively," he said. "I have taken it on the chin from the American League long enough and I will say this: If the league pulls the rug out from under me, the league is going out with me...."[23]

The owners met in New York City's Savoy Hilton Hotel on January 16. "Finley delivered one of his better sales talks," the *Saturday Evening Post* reported. "He spoke with fire and indignation, pleading with the owners to recognize his problems and snatch him from the jaws of bankruptcy. When he had finished his presentation, there was only an embarrassed hush." The owners voted 9–1 against Finley and gave him until February 1 to conclude a stadium lease in Kansas City or face expulsion from the league. "The American League told me to stay in Kansas City for four more years or to get out of baseball," Finley said. "They sentenced me to four years of hard labor. Mayor Ilus Davis of Kansas City told owners, 'If you keep Mr. Finley in our city, we will go out and sell tickets for him.' What a con man he was. They did nothing. They wanted the team but not Finley. They figured: 'We'll starve him out.'"[24]

Finley hired famed trial lawyer Louis Nizer. "My plans will be to go to court to find out if the American League has the power they think they have to restrain me from moving my club to Louisville or any other place," Finley said. "This is still a free country and I don't believe that anybody can force me to operate my business in a city where I've lost a million dollars in three years. If I'm forced to sign, I'll sue the league and I'm sure a contract like that will not hold up in court."[25]

Finley renewed lease negotiations in Kansas City on January 25. He passed out brass tacks to members of the city council declaring it was time to get down to business. "I presume we're ready to get down to brass tacks, so I have brought some along for your lapels," he said. He proposed a two-year lease (Fin-3). The team would pay the city 5 percent of the paid admissions up to one million, and 10 percent on the portion of admissions exceeding one million. He proposed to raise the city's share of the concession revenue from 7½ percent to 10 percent and forget the $300,000 he wanted for stadium improvements. The lease, however, contained a clause that read: "This present proposal, however, is subject to the condition that in the event the American League approves a transfer of the Athletics to another territory, any lease agreement between us shall terminate."[26]

Mayor Davis rejected the proposal and said the city needed at least a four-year lease. He offered Finley a four-year lease (KC-7) with only two years' rent. The team would pay 5 percent of the paid admissions and 7½ percent of the concessions for the first two years of the contract. The rent for the remaining two years would be $1 per year. "I sincerely regret that as of the moment I cannot accept the offer of a four-year contract," Finley responded. "Due to the cloud of bad publicity that has covered Kansas City and myself in this thing, I can't enter into a four-year contract because of what might happen to me. If I had four bad years, I would expect to be bankrupt. Two bad years would hurt me, but I might be able to bail myself out financially. I was anxious to sign a four- or five-year contract before I got all of this bad publicity, but I don't see how I can now.... I am afraid to sign anything longer than a two-year lease because I might go bankrupt. Financially, I am very much afraid of the four-year lease."[27]

The city made a final proposal (Final) to Finley before the meeting ended. It was a four-year lease with two four-year options. For the first four years, the A's would pay 5 percent of the admissions and 7½ percent of the concessions. The city would keep the first $50,000 in annual rent and the balance would go to Finley for the stadium improvements. The lease also contained a four-year option with the rent based on a sliding scale. The team would pay 7½ percent of the concessions but would pay no rent until the attendance reached 575,000. The A's would pay $25,000 rent if attendance was between 575,000 and 800,000. The rent would be 5 percent of all paid admissions with attendance between 800,000 and 1,000,000. The A's would pay 10 percent on the portion of any attendance figures exceeding one million.

Finley asked for time to examine the proposal and left the room with members of his staff. Finley said he would take the proposal under advisement, although he said nothing to indicate he would sign anything longer than a two-year lease. Finley and Pat Friday went to Oakland on January 26 and 27 to meet with city government and civic leaders. They agreed to terms of a 20-year lease. The team would play at Youell Field for two or three seasons and then play in the new $25 million Coliseum at escalating rental rates starting with 5 percent of the paid attendance up to 1,000,000 and 10 percent above one million, plus a percentage of concession income. It would cost $500,000 to add lights, add 7,000 additional seats (grandstand-bleacher type seats), and reconstruct Youell Field. The city would pay $100,000 and Finley would pay $400,000. The stadium would have a capacity of 27,000 for baseball and 30,000 for football. Rent at Youell Field would be $50,000 a year. Finley would pay two years rent in advance ($100,000) and $300,000 for the parking concession to finance the A's portion of the reconstruction costs.[28]

"I think it is terrific!" Finley said. He predicted the team would draw a "million to 1.2 million in Youell Field." He requested another meeting of the league owners. Since the meeting would not be held until February, Louis Nizer requested a two-week extension of the league's February 1 deadline. The league granted Finley an extension and gave him until February 15 to negotiate a stadium lease in Kansas City.[29]

Alex Barket, president of the Metropolitan Construction Company and board chairman of the Civic Plaza National Bank met Finley on an airplane as Finley flew to Kansas City for the January 25 city council meeting. Finley offered to sell the A's to Barket for $7 million. "Isn't that about twice as much as you paid?" Barket asked. "Well, you wouldn't begrudge me doubling my money, would you?" Finley answered. Barket did not feel anyone would be interested at that price but added: "I think that some person or persons in Kansas City might be able to negotiate for purchase of the team. My theory is that there is a price tag on the ballclub."

"I never offered the club to Barket for $7 million," Finley responded. "This club is not for sale and never has been for sale."[30]

The league voted 9–1 to deny Finley's request to move the franchise to Oakland on February 19th. They held another meeting in Boston on February 21. They voted 9–1 that the Kansas City council's proposed lease was "fair and reasonable." By the same vote they authorized Cronin to call another meeting to consider expelling Finley if he did not sign the lease. Cronin sent a telegram to Finley and advised him to sign the lease or face league action.[31]

Barket and six other financial and business executives from Kansas City announced they would form a corporation to purchase the A's on February 22. If they received the option to purchase the team, they would offer stock to the public. Their primary goal was local ownership and they would offer the stock in Missouri, Kansas, Oklahoma, Arkansas, Iowa and Nebraska. Bernard Craig, a lawyer and one of the incorporators, said the articles of incorporation would be signed the following week. The group contacted Finley but they were unable to negotiate a sale. Members of the group were Bernard Craig, attorney; Alex Barket, president of Metropolitan Construction Company and chairman of the board of directors at Civic Plaza National Bank; T. S. Patti, vice president of Metropolitan Construction Company and a director at Civic Plaza National Bank; Richard Berkley, manufacturing executive; Thomas L. Davidson, furniture sales executive; Ludwell G. Gaines III, a partner in a brokerage and an investment company; and Melvin Hilliard, automobile sales executive.[32]

Finley accepted the terms of a four-year lease and sent a telegram to Mayor Davis. "We accept the offer of the city of Kansas City, Missouri, for the use of Municipal Stadium by the Kansas City Athletics for a four-year

Stadium Lease Proposals

	Date	Basic Rent	Additional Rent	Concessions	Length	Renewal	Cancel	Reimbursement
	Apr 63	$1	5% after first two years if paid admissions exceed 950,000	7½% with payment waived until the $300,000 is recovered	7-year	2 7-year options	If gate is less than 850,000	$300,000 from concession income
KC-1	July 63	$1	5% after first two years	50% with payment waived until the $300,000 is recovered	7-year	unknown	none	$300,000 from concession income
KC-2	July 63	$1	5% after first two years	50% until city's share plus 5% of the paid admissions total $300,000. Then it declines to 7½%	7-year	unknown	none	$300,000 from concession and rental income
Fin-1	Dec 63	$50,000	none during first four years	7½% with payment waived until the $300,000 is recovered	4-year	2 4-year options. No rent unless the attendance exceeds 900,000	none	$300,000 from concession income
Fin-2	Dec 63	$125,000	none	none	2-year	unknown	none	none
KC-3	Dec 63	$25,000	13 cents a ticket on all admissions above 580,000	none	5-year	4-year at a flat rate of $125,000	none	13-cent rent waived on attendance under 580,000 until the $300,000 is recovered
KC-4	Dec 63	$65,000	none	none	4- or 5-yr	4-year at a flat rate of $125,000 a year	none	Difference in rent from $65,000 to renewal rate of $125,000 to enable team to recover $300,000

KC-5	Dec 63	$1	5% after first two years if paid admissions exceed 900,000	50%	7-year	none	none	none
KC-6	Dec 63	$50,000	none during first 4 years	7½% with payment waived until the $300,000 is recovered	4-year	2 4-year options. No rent unless attendance exceeds 750,000	none	$300,000 from concession income
Fin-3	Jan 64	none	5% of paid admissions up to 1 million, 10% on admissions over 1 million	10%	2-year	none	League approval	none
KC-7	Jan 64	none	5% of paid admissions for first two years. $1 in the final two years	7½% for first two years None in the final two years	4-year	none	none	From reduced rate in final two years
Final	Feb 64	none	5% of all paid admissions	7½%	4-year No rent if attendance is under 575,000	4-year option	none	City would keep first $50,000 in rent. The balance would be used to pay the $300,000

term from January 1, 1964, to and including December 31, 1967," he wrote, "with no escape clause at an annual rental of 5 percent of paid admissions and 7½ percent of concession income the first $50,000 of said rent to be paid to the city and the excess of said sum to be applied against the $300,000 allegedly expended by Charles O. Finley & Co, Inc., for stadium improvements. At the end of the four-year period no further obligations or claims by said company will remain. The above-mentioned lease to include two 4-year options, the rent to be paid during the option period will be 7½ percent of concession income regardless of attendance. In the event attendance shall not reach 575,000 paid admissions, no rent shall be paid other than the 7½ percent of concession income. When paid admissions are from 575,000 to 800,000, a flat annual rental of $25,000 will be paid. After the total paid admissions reach one million, rent will be paid at the rate of 10 percent of that portion of the attendance exceeding one million. Paid admission under one million will be paid for at the rate of 5 percent."[33]

Finley arrived in Kansas City to sign the new contract on February 26, but three more days of negotiations were required when city officials wanted to add a clause to prevent Finley from moving the club. It was resolved in the city's favor with the wording that "the lessee agrees this is a firm, binding and noncancellable four-year lease for the playing of all home games of the Athletics at the Stadium during the term of this lease or any renewal thereof." Finley called a noon press conference but kept reporters waiting as he obtained a minor concession from city officials adding a clause stating that if his stadium improvement allowance of $300,000 was not paid off in admittances in the first four years of the contract, Finley would receive the balance under any lease renewal after 1967. Finley appeared jovial at the press conference and signed three copies of the four-year, noncancellable stadium lease on Friday, February 28, in front of more than 20 reporters. The city council approved it with a unanimous vote.[34]

"Ahead of him lay the Herculean task of convincing Kansas City fans at this late date to buy season tickets," wrote Frank Graham in the *Saturday Evening Post* after the lease was signed. "The fans' loyalty to the team may be unquestioned, but many of them hold Finley in deep distrust. At the back of their minds must lurk the fear that Finley and Nizer will somehow break the contract and flee elsewhere with the A's."[35]

Finley later complained that when the owners determined the lease was fair and ordered Finley to sign, "they tarred and feathered me.... When Cronin sent me the telegram telling me to sign, I smelled the pine box. It's one of the greatest injustices in baseball history. I'm saddled with the only noncancellable contract in the big leagues." He filed suit on May 19, 1964, to have the lease set aside in favor of the seven-year lease he signed with the outgoing city council in April 1963. The suit was dismissed on December 9.[36]

ESTIMATED RENT FROM PROPOSED LEASES
ANNUAL ATTENDANCE

		600,000	750,000	900,000	1,050,000	1,200,000
Apr 63	Year 1	1	1	1	1	1
	Year 2	1	1	1	1	1
	Year 3	1	1	1	105,001	120,001
	Year 4	1	1	1	105,001	120,001
	Year 5	1	1	1	105,001	120,001
	Five-Year Total	5	5	5	315,005	360,005
KC-1	Year 1	1	1	1	1	1
	Year 2	1	1	1	1	1
	Year 3	60,001	75,001	90,001	120,001	180,001
	Year 4	60,001	75,001	150,001	210,001	240,001
	Year 5	60,001	150,001	180,001	210,001	240,001
	Five-Year Total	180,005	300,005	420,005	540,005	660,005
KC-2	Year 1	1	1	1	1	1
	Year 2	1	1	30,001	52,501	60.001
	Year 3	30,001	112,501	135,001	157,501	180,001
	Year 4	90,001	112,501	135,001	157,501	180,001
	Year 5	90,001	112,501	135,001	157,501	180,001
	Five-Year Total	210,005	337,505	435,005	523,505	600,005
Fin-1	Year 1	50,000	50,000	50,000	50,000	50,000
	Year 2	50,000	50,000	50,000	50,000	50,000
	Year 3	50,000	50,000	50,000	50,000	50,000
	Year 4	50,000	50,000	50,000	50,000	50,000
	Renewal 1	0	0	90,000	105,000	120,000
	Five-Year Total	200,000	200,000	290,000	305,000	320,000
Fin-2	Year 1	125,000	125,000	125,000	125,000	125,000
	Year 2	125,000	125,000	125,000	125,000	125,000
	Two-Year Total	250,000	250,000	250,000	250,000	250,000
KC-3	Year 1	27,600	47,100	66,600	86,100	105,600
	Year 2	27,600	47,100	66,600	86,100	105.600
	Year 3	27,600	47,100	66,600	86,100	105,600
	Year 4	27,600	47,100	66,600	86,100	105,600
	Year 5	27,600	47,100	66,600	86,100	105,600
	Five-Year Total	138,000	235,500	333,000	430,500	528,000
KC-4	Year 1	65,000	65,000	65,000	65,000	65,000
	Year 2	65,000	65,000	65,000	65,000	65,000
	Year 3	65,000	65,000	65,000	65,000	65,000
	Year 4	65,000	65,000	65,000	65,000	65,000

		600,000	750,000	900,000	1,050,000	1,200,000
	Year 5	65,000	65,000	65,000	65,000	65,000
	Five-Year Total	325,000	325,000	325,000	325,000	325,000
KC-5	Year 1	60,001	75,001	90,001	105,001	120,001
	Year 2	60,001	75,001	90,001	105,001	120,001
	Year 3	60,001	75,001	205,001	240,001	275,001
	Year 4	60,001	75,001	205,001	240,001	275,001
	Year 5	60,001	75,001	205,001	240,001	275,001
	Five-Year Total	300,005	375,005	795,005	930,005	1,065,005
KC-6	Year 1	50,000	50,000	50,000	50,000	50,000
	Year 2	50,000	50,000	50,000	50,000	50,000
	Year 3	50,000	50,000	50,000	50,000	50,000
	Year 4	50,000	50,000	50,000	50,000	50,000
	Renewal 1	0	75,000	90,000	105,000	120,000
	Five-Year Total	200,000	275,000	290,000	305,000	320,000
Fin-3	Year 1	100,000	125,000	150,000	180,000	220,000
	Year 2	100,000	125,000	150,000	180,000	220,000
	Two-Year Total	200,000	250,000	300,000	360,000	440,000
KC-7	Year 1	100,000	125,000	150,000	175.000	200,000
	Year 2	100,000	125,000	150,000	175,000	200,000
	Year 3	1	1	1	1	1
	Year 4	1	1	1	1	1
	Four-Year Total	200,002	250,002	300,002	350,002	400,002
Final	Year 1	50,000	50,000	50,000	50,000	50,000
	Year 2	50,000	50,000	50,000	50,000	50,000
	Year 3	50,000	50,000	50,000	72,500	140,000
	Year 4	50,000	50,000	90,000	157,500	180,000
	Renewal 1	25,000	25,000	135,000	162,500	200,000
	Five-Year Total	225,000	225,000	375,000	492,500	620,000

Notes:

In order to compare the leases the attendance is assumed to remain the same during each season for all five years:

The rent and/or concession income was reduced in each example until the $300,000 was reimbursed.

The following figures were used for these comparisons:

Attendance	Rent Income	Concession at 7½%	Concession at 50%
600,000	60,000	30,000	60,000
750,000	75,000	37,500	75,000
900,000	90,000	45,000	90,000
1,050,000	105,000	52,500	105,000
1,200,000	120,000	60,000	120,000

23
1964: Rocky, Jim and a Pennant Porch

The A's added Tom Ferrick, Luke Appling and Babe Dahlgren to the coaching staff for the 1964 season, increasing the total number of coaches to six. Appling would serve as the hitting coach. Appling, who was elected to the Hall of Fame in 1964, joined the A's after coaching for Baltimore in 1963. He previously coached for Cleveland and Detroit. Dahlgren would take movies of the players so the players they could study the film when they had problems. Ferrick joined the A's as the pitching coach. He served as a pitching coach for Cincinnati (1954–1958), Philadelphia (1959) and Detroit (1960–1963). Roger Hansen replaced Max DeWeese as comptroller of the team and Jay Hankins joined the front office as ticket manager. Hankins was a former player in the A's minor league system and made brief appearances on the major league roster in 1961 and 1963.

The team continued to wear their green and gold uniforms but added two other uniforms described by Finley as "sea-foam" green and "wedding-gown" white to compliment their gold uniforms. KCMO Radio (810) and TV signed a two-year contract to broadcast the games after WDAF Radio and TV allowed their option to expire during the lease controversy. Monte Moore and George Bryson returned to the broadcast booth.

Finley felt the team needed additional power. He traded second baseman Jerry Lumpe and pitchers Ed Rakow and Dave Wickersham to Detroit for right fielder Rocky Colavito, pitcher Bob Anderson and a reported $50,000. Anderson, a 28-year-old right-hander, was considered a "sleeper" by Pat Friday. Colavito, whose departure from Cleveland had made Frank Lane available to the A's as GM in 1961, had tailed off from 45 home runs in 1961 to 22 home runs in 1963. Although he lacked speed in the

193

outfield and on the bases, he had an excellent arm and he liked to show it off.

Kansas City sent Norm Siebern to the Orioles for slugger Jim Gentile and an estimated $25,000 nine days later. Gentile hit 33 home runs in 1962 and 24 home runs in 1963. "Ed Lopat, our manager, thinks we gave up a lot of young pitching for them," Finley said. "But we had to have hitting and we had to have gate attractions."

The A's traded pitcher Fred Norman to the Chicago Cubs to obtain 22-year-old center fielder Nelson Mathews on December 15, 1963. Mathews was considered a good defensive outfielder with good speed but his hitting ability was questionable. The A's had difficulty signing Colavito and Chicago newspapers reported Pat Friday offered him to the White Sox in a two-for-one trade for outfielders Jim Landis and Dave Nicholson. The rumors ended after Colavito signed a new contract.[1]

Finley complained about the unfair advantage the Yankees had with the unusual dimensions at Yankee Stadium that gave left-handed pull hitters easy home runs. "I am convinced this is the answer to the great success of the Yankees," he said. "When our pitchers go into Yankee Stadium, they are accustomed to pitching one way in the nine other parks of the league, but in Yankee Stadium they must pitch differently.... It's great to be able to play half your total games in Yankee Stadium. Since we can't get the Yankees to conform to honest dimensions, I'll conform to Yankee dimensions. I feel that in revamping my ballpark to go along with the Yankees, I will be, for the first time, able to compete with the team on an equal basis." Finley constructed a "Pennant Porch" in right field to match the Yankee Stadium dimensions. Since, by rule, Finley could not reduce the distance down the line lower than 325 feet, the right field foul pole was moved from 338 feet to 325 feet. A 44-inch-high fence, the same height as Yankee Stadium, was built at a slight angle to a point 296 feet from the plate, matching the distance at Yankee Stadium. From that point the dimensions matched those at Yankee Stadium and angled toward center field. Bleacher seats were installed behind the new fence. Finley said the small area in fair territory down the foul line (between the 325-foot mark at the foul pole and the 296-foot mark) would remain open to make the entire project legal under existing baseball rules. Balls hit into this area would be ground-rule doubles.[2] The center field dimensions would also be changed with a 10-foot chain link fence built in front of the center field wall, reducing the distance from home plate from 421 to 408 feet.

The Pennant Porch was unveiled during two pre-season exhibition games against St. Louis. Joe Cronin and commissioner Ford Frick ordered Finley to remove the fence. "Any obstruction within 325 feet is in violation of the rules," Frick said. "There's no appeal in this. There's no hearing, no appeal, no nothing."[3] Finley said the fence would be up when the season opened on April 21st. He relented a few days later and moved the Pennant Porch back to a distance of 325 feet from home plate to conform to baseball rules and called it the "One-half Pennant Porch." From the 325-foot mark it went straight across to join the old fence at the 392-foot mark in right-center field. The new fence would be 13 feet closer to home plate than the previous fence and he claimed that would result in five additional victories during the season. There was room for about 300 bleacher seats behind the new fence.[4]

Finley emphasized the Yankees' advantage in New York throughout the season. Billboards installed in left field and right field compared the dimensions down the foul lines in New York and Kansas City with a large question mark. A chalk line was painted across the outfield to show where Finley's original pennant porch had been in right field as well as the left field dimensions at Yankee Stadium. Whenever a fly ball landed behind that line the public address announcer announced: "That ball would have been a home run in Yankee Stadium."[5]

Finley installed loud horns and flashing green and gold lights over the auxiliary scoreboard in left-center field. The lights and horns were used whenever a Kansas City player hit a home run. "When we hit a home run we've got three of the loudest horns you've ever heard in your life," Finley said. "I don't know where Mayor Davis lives, but I'll tell you one thing. He sure as hell will be woken up if he is not at the game."[6]

The team started poorly and tumbled into the American League cellar. They finished the season in tenth place with 105 defeats, although they briefly climbed to ninth at various times during the season. Despite Finley's claim that the "One-half Pennant Porch" would add five home victories, Kansas City actually lost 16 more games than in 1963. The A's won only 26 home games and had only 17 wins at home after June 1. The new dimensions at Municipal Stadium had a disastrous effect on the pitching staff. Even the experienced pitchers were hesitant to throw change-ups and slow curves because they did not want to surrender home runs. The A's pitchers gave up 220 home runs, a record that stood until 1987, when the Orioles allowed 226. The A's pitchers completed only 18 games and had the league's worst earned run average: 4.71.

The A's started the season by dropping the first two games on the road before defeating the Senators 5–1. The A's lost their home opener 5–3 to Cleveland before 28,165 fans on April 21. Diego Segui started the game and even hit a home in the losing cause. The Minnesota Twins tied a major league record in Kansas City on May 2, hitting four consecutive home runs

23—1964: Rocky, Jim and a Pennant Porch

in the eleventh inning of what had been a pitcher's battle. Tony Oliva led off the inning with a home run off Dan Pfister over the right field fence. Bob Allison followed with a blast over the left field fence. Jimmie Hall made it three-in-a-row with a home run over the right field fence. Vern Handrahan was brought in to relieve Pfister and Harmon Killebrew greeted him with a home run over the left field fence. Earl Battey, the next batter, struck out to end the spree. Before the inning ended, another Twins batter drove the ball to the wall in left field and the announcer dutifully informed the crowd: "That ball would have been a home run in Yankee Stadium." The announcement was ended the next day but the two billboards remained. The Twins won the game 7–3.

Dave Nicholson hit a tape-measure home run off Kansas City's Moe Drabowsky during the first game of a double header in Chicago on May 6. He hit it completely over the roof of Comiskey Park's second deck in left-center field. It cleared the 375-foot mark and was measured at 573 feet. Nicholson followed with two more upper deck home runs in the second game as the Sox swept the doubleheader. Boog Powell of Baltimore hit two memorable home runs in Kansas City. He had a pitch from Diego Segui off the center field scoreboard on June 3, one of only three balls to ever hit the scoreboard. He hit another tape-measure blast during the first game of a Labor Day double header on September 7. He hit the ball over both fences in center and onto the roof of the equipment shed behind the fence.[7]

The A's won just four of 12 games during a disastrous home stand from the last week in May through the first week in June. Finley gave manager Ed Lopat a vote of confidence. He said the team suffered primarily with pitching problems, although they had occasional trouble with both hitting and defense. The A's went on the road, won their first game against Washington and then lost the next three games. Lopat was fired on June 11 with the team in last place with a 17–35 record. Mel McGaha signed a two-year contract to succeed Lopat.

Although only 37 years old, McGaha had already been a major league manager and had skippered three minor league teams as well, including two to championships. McGaha, a Louisiana native, never made it to the major leagues as a player after suffering a serious injury to his right shoul-

1964 team — Front row: Pfister, Pena, Shoemaker, Dahlgren (coach), McGaha (manager), Appling (coach), Dykes (coach), Ferrick (coach). Second row: Sigloch (equipment manager), Zych (clubhouse attendant), Duncan, Stock, Alusik, Tartabull, Jones (trainer), Schaaf (traveling secretary). Third row: Mathews, Charles, Edwards, Jimenez, Harrelson, Wyatt, Green, Causey. Back row: Gentile, Segui, Santiago, O'Donoghue, Bryan, Drabowsky, Colavito, Bowsfield, Grzenda. Seated in front: Gleissner (batboy), Huey (batboy). (From the Kansas City Athletics.)

der in a 1948 bus accident. He began his managerial career with Shreveport in the Texas League in 1954 at the age of 28 and led the team to the pennant. He remained at Shreveport through 1957, when he was named manager of Mobile in the Southern Association. His Mobile club was runner-up in both 1958 and 1959. He was named manager of Toronto in 1960 and guided the team to the International League pennant.

McGaha coached in Cleveland in 1961. He became one of the youngest non-playing managers in major league history when he was named manager of the Indians at age 35 in 1962. He was fired as Cleveland manager at the end of an 80–82 season. Kansas City hired him during the World Series to fill the dual role of administrative assistant to the president and general manager and coach. McGaha served in this dual capacity until he was appointed manager of the Wytheville, Virginia, rookie league team on June 7, 1964. The A's fired manager Ed Lopat four days later and hired McGaha to replace him. McGaha later managed Oklahoma City in 1966 and 1967 and coached for Houston from 1968 until 1971. McGaha died on February 7, 2002.

Mel McGaha (from the Kansas City Athletics).

MEL MCGAHA'S MANAGERIAL RECORD

Year	Club	League	Won	Lost	Position
1954	Shreveport	AA	90	71	1
1955	Shreveport	AA	87	74	3
1956	Shreveport	AA	69	85	7
1957	Shreveport	AA	59	95	8
1958	Mobile	AA	84	68	2
1959	Mobile	AA	89	63	2
1960	Toronto	AAA	100	54	1
1962	Cleveland	Major	80	82	6
1964	Kansas City	Major	40	70	10
1965	Kansas City	Major	5	21	10
1966	Oklahoma City	AAA	59	89	12
1967	Oklahoma City	AAA	74	74	7

McGaha said he would make no major changes in the lineup but would handle the bullpen differently. He told the starting pitchers they were to work out of the bullpen if needed on any night. The change in managers, combined with good hitting and pitching, gave the A's their longest winning streak of the year. The A's won eight of their next nine games before the team returned to its losing habits. Lopat accepted a front office position and was appointed vice president in charge of player personnel on July 3.[8]

Gentile got off to a good start at first base and was batting .270 with 14 home runs before he suffered a severe leg pull on June 25th. The two-week layoff hurt his timing and he finished the season with 28 home runs, 71 runs batted in and a .251 batting average.

Rookie Dick Green replaced Lumpe at second base. He was overanxious at the plate and was hitting only .202 at the All-Star break. His defensive play kept him in the lineup. He jammed both thumbs—one diving into a base and the other when he hit a pitch off his fists—and was forced to cut down on his swing out of sheer necessity and pain. From the middle of June until the end of the season he hit at a .320 clip and raised his final batting average to .264. He committed only six errors and finished the season with a .990 fielding average. Yankees All-Star second baseman Bobby Richardson called him the best looking young second baseman to enter the league since he had been playing.

Wayne Causey had another solid season at shortstop. He got off to a hot start and for the second consecutive June found himself leading the league in hitting. He suffered a hyperextension of his left elbow in a collision at second with Bob Allison of the Twins on July 22. Causey was supposed to be sidelined for 10 days but was out of action only three days. Causey raised his average to .308 on Labor Day, but he tired during the last few weeks of the season and his final average dropped to .281.

Bert "Campy" Campaneris, a 21-year-old shortstop, was called up from Birmingham when Causey was injured and had a spectacular debut. He caught a late plane, spent the night in the air and arrived in Minnesota two hours before the start of the game on July 23. He started the game, batted leadoff and slammed the first pitch thrown by Minnesota left-hander Jim Kaat 365 feet over the left field fence in his first at bat. Subsequently he singled and bounced out before hitting another home run in the seventh inning. Bob Nieman of the St. Louis Browns was the only other player to hit two home runs in his first major league game. Campaneris also stole a base and made a brilliant defensive play as the A's won 4–3 in 11 innings. Before the game some players told Campy that Kaat was just an ordinary pitcher that did not throw hard or pitch very well. It was not until after the game that he learned that Kaat was one of the best pitchers in baseball.[9]

Ed Charles hit just .241 with 16 home runs. Despite his low batting average, he had a number of key hits and played well at third base. Campaneris played in the outfield and served as a utility infielder after Causey returned to the lineup. He also played shortstop when Causey filled in at second for the injured Green at the end of the season. Campaneris was named to the Topps All-Star Major League rookie team.

Charlie Lau and Doc Edwards shared catching duties before the A's traded Lau to Baltimore for relief pitcher Wes Stock on June 15. Edwards shared the catching duties with Bill Bryan for the remainder of the season. Edwards appeared in 97 games but batted just .224. Bryan appeared in 93 games and batted .241.

Colavito had a good season in right field and was a favorite with the fans that regularly sat behind him in the Pennant Porch. He hit 34 home runs and drove in 102 runs while batting .274. Finley decided to reward him with 300 silver dollars when he hit his 300th career home run. He had the silver dollars flown in from the Desert Inn in Las Vegas, hired a Brink's armored car at a cost of $21 a day, and put the armored car behind a section of the center field fence where it was visible through the chain-link fence. Two motorcycle policemen were on either side of the truck. When Colavito hit his 300th home run, the truck was to race to home plate accompanied by the motorcycle officers with their red lights on and sirens blaring and they would present silver dollars to Colavito on a silver tray. He went 16 days without a home run before finally hit his 300th on September 11 in Baltimore. The formal presentation of the 300 silver dollars took place during a special night honoring Colavito in Kansas City on September 25th. He was one of two Kansas City players named to the American League All-Star team in July and had one hit in two trips to the plate.[10]

Nelson Mathews played center field. He set a Kansas City record with 143 strikeouts, but he showed improvement in the second half of the season. He played well defensively and had more putouts than any other outfielder in the league. George Alusik, Ken Harrelson, Jose Tartabull and Manny Jimenez all shared the left field position. Jimenez hit three home runs in a game in Baltimore on July 4. He added a single, going 4 for 4 with five runs batted in. He missed the chance to tie the major league record of four home runs in a game when the game ended in a 6–6 tie after nine innings so the field could be cleared for the annual fireworks display.

The bullpen was the only bright spot in the pitching staff. "Big John" Wyatt appeared in 81 games, breaking the major league record set by Jim

Konstanty, and had a 9–8 record with 20 saves and a 3.59 ERA. He joined Colavito on the All-Star team, pitching one inning and giving up two runs. Wes Stock appeared in 50 games and had a 6–3 record and a 1.94 ERA. Rookie Ken Sanders appeared in 21 games for the A's and had a 0–2 record and a 3.67 ERA.

Orlando Pena was the most dependable starter and he led the team in virtually every department. He won the most games (12), and his 184 strikeouts set a new Kansas City record. He finished the season with a 12–14 record and a 4.44 ERA. Southpaw John O'Donoghue impressed team officials in spring training and won a spot in the starting rotation, becoming the first Kansas City native to win a starting job with the A's. He was the team's second leading winner with 10 victories and finished the season with a 4.87 ERA.

Rocky Colavito (from Jay Publications and the Kansas City Athletics).

Diego Segui experienced his first losing season since joining the A's in 1962. He was 8–17 with a 4.52 ERA. Moe Drabowsky reported late to spring training and his record sagged to 5–13 with a 5.25 ERA. Rookies Jose Santiago and Aurelio Monteagudo were among the 12 pitchers that came north with the team when the season began. Santiago was sidelined with a sprained ankle and missed the first two months of the season. He appeared in 34 games and had a 0–6 record with a 4.82 ERA. Monteagudo had limited experience and was over-matched in the major leagues. He had a 0–4 record in 11 games before he was optioned to Dallas (AAA) in June.

Ted Bowsfield appeared in 50 games with the A's and had a 4–7 record with a 4.17 ERA. He was nearly cut from the team in June when Jose Santiago was reactivated. "Charlie (Finley) wanted Jose Santiago to start a game instead of me in Washington just before the roster cut-down deadline," Bowsfield recalled, "and I needed just a few more days on the major league roster to get five years in for pension purposes. And Lopat says, 'I'm supposed to pitch Santiago but I'm going ahead with you.' Eddie stuck by me and I won. Three days later, Lopat was fired. And the new manager, Mel McGaha, came right out and told me I'd get one more start but that it was 'do or die.' Fortunately, I shut out the Tigers and I was kept around long enough to get my five years."[11]

John "Blue Moon" Odom agreed to a $75,000 bonus when he signed in June and was assigned to Birmingham (AA) where he posted a 6-5 record. Finley brought him up to start against the Yankees but McGaha did not know about it until he read about it in *The Sporting News*. "I was nervous as I could be," Odom said when he recalled his first start. "I walked some, and they just pounded out the rest, and I was gone after two innings. The Yankees won the game 9-7, but I was not the losing pitcher."[12]

He pitched a two-hitter in his second start on September 11th, the game in which Colavito hit his 300th home run. The A's were ahead of the league-leading Orioles 8-0 and Odom had a no-hitter going into the seventh inning. He walked the leadoff batter and Sam Bowens came to bat. "He (Bowens) hit a bouncing ball toward A's rookie third baseman Tom Reynolds, and Tommie backed up on it," wrote Monte Moore. "He plainly mishandled the ball allowing it to bounce off his chest and ruin the chance for a double play. We felt badly about that ... but what was worse was the ensuing announcement from the press box public address system. The official scorer ... had ruled the ball a HIT.... (He) had plainly blown the call that might have cost the young pitcher baseball immortality ... a no-hitter.... The Orioles did not get another hit until the ninth when once again the scorer ruled in a strange way. Brooks Robinson, a slow runner, hit a ball to the right of the mound. 'Moon' picked it up and threw wildly to first ... and once again, it was ruled a hit. That was all the Birds got and we believe to this day that 'Blue Moon' Odom pitched a no-hitter against the Orioles in his 8-0 shutout victory." Finley gave Odom a $500 bonus for pitching a no-hitter despite the scorer's rulings. Odom pitched in five games and had a 1-2 record with a 10.06 ERA.[13]

The A's purchased 24-year-old southpaw Bob Meyer from the Angels on waivers on July 29. He appeared in nine games and had a 1-4 record with a 3.86 ERA. He lost a 1-0, one-hit game in Baltimore on September 12, the day following Odom's controversial two-hitter. Orioles hurler Frank Bertaina also pitched a one-hitter, making it the seventh double-one hitter in history. Bertaina gave up the first hit, a double by Doc Edwards in the fifth inning. Meyer handcuffed the Orioles until the eighth inning when John Orsino led off with a double. Bob Saverine ran for him, moved to third on Bertaina's sacrifice and scored when Jackie Brandt hit a sacrifice fly.[14]

There were a number of unusual games during the season. The A's played Cleveland on August 18 and trailed 6–0 in the second inning. The A's then exploded with 16 hits and won the game 13–9. Kansas City fell behind Minnesota 6–0 on September 22. Dave Duncan knocked a bases loaded triple off the center field fence in the sixth inning to make the score 7–4. Green hit a home run in the seventh off reliever Al Worthington to make it 7–5. The Twins scored two more runs in the next few innings and Kansas City trailed 9–6 in the bottom on the ninth with ace reliever Al Worthington on the mound. He walked Colavito and Gentile with one out. Ed Charles hit a three-run home run over the right-center field fence to tie the game. The Twins brought in pitcher John Klippstein and McGaha brought up Bill Bryan to hit for Mathews. Klippstein quickly had two strikes on Bryan, but Bryan hit the next pitch over the right center field wall almost in the identical place where Charles hit the previous home run. The A's won the game 10–9.[15]

The A's and Twins set a major league record on September 29 when 44 players appeared in the game. The game went 15 innings and lasted four hours and 50 minutes before the A's won on a long home run by Colavito. Rookie outfielder Larry Stahl had two home runs in the game, his first major league home runs.

Finley used promotions to boost attendance. Farmers Night was held on June 20. The entire A's pitching staff rode a horse-drawn hay wagon onto the playing field and Finley gave different types of farm animals away during the game. The crowd of 25,182 was larger than anticipated and the game had to be held up nearly a half-hour to let everyone inside the park. Mathews hit a grand slam home run over both left field fences in the first inning and the A's won the game 8–2.[16]

Little League Bat Day was held on July 25. Finley gave out Kelly green bats with the A's player's names engraved on them in gold lettering. A crowd of 21,558 watched the A's lose the game to the Los Angeles Angels 18–2. Automotive Industries Day was held on August 1 and attracted a crowd of 25,003. Antique cars were driven around the park before the game and Finley drove the A's players to their positions in a green and gold fire truck. A new car, several used cars, and auto accessories were given away during the evening. Roger Ward, winner of the Indianapolis 500, raced his car around the warning track three times.[17]

Firefighters Day was held in August but was not as exciting as an event that preceded it that month. The A's ground crew drove two kelly green and gold fire trucks around the field before each game to promote Firefighters Day. George Toma and his grounds crew squirted water on the players in the Yankees dugout as they drove by on August 5. The Yankees were ready on the following day and greeted the fire truck with tomatoes, pies, mud balls and various other assorted weapons when the fire truck passed the dugout. The grounds crew in the fire truck attacked the Yankees with water. The truck circled the field and came back for another battle. Umpire Frank Umont decided that was enough and sent the truck to the shed behind the center field fence.[18]

"I had some doubts as to whether Charlie gave any importance to winning in those days rather than to showmanship," recalled Ted Bowsfield. "I wasn't sure what he was doing sometimes, because some of the things that happened definitely did not point toward trying to win every ballgame. For example, at Farmers Day Charlie asked me to drive a hay wagon with that day's pitcher, Diego Segui, aboard. I was to stick hay under my hat and under my uniform and drive Diego to the mound, pat him on the back, and then get the horses back out to Charlie. We were playing the Washington ballclub and they razzed me, called me a showboat. Next day they beat my brains out. Then another time he hired a taxicab and left it out in center field with the meter running. [Mel McGaha] said before the game that if he needed a relief pitcher, the man should wait in the bullpen until the taxicab came to pick him up. Well, we're playing the Yankees and leading 2–1. I'm trying to heat up in the bullpen because two left-handed hitters are due up. I'm called into the game and forgot all about the taxicab; I walk all the way to the mound. When I get there, McGaha says, 'My god, you forgot the taxicab.' Sure enough, it was still out there with the meter running — maybe up to $30, $40. Well, I get the two guys out, we win 2–1 and I come into the clubhouse and am told that Finley wants to talk to me on the phone right away. And he ripped me up and down one side and the other: Why didn't I ride the taxicab? That left some doubt in my mind about the importance he put on winning."[19]

Finley's largest promotion did not involve the Athletics. The Beatles scheduled a coast-to-coast concert tour and Finley wanted to bring them to Kansas City. "I first offered $50,000," Finley said, "No answer. I offered $100,000. They said they had several offers of $100,000. So I offered $150,000 because I thought if all those other places are getting the Beatles, how about a break for the Kansas City kids." They agreed to appear in Municipal Stadium on September 17. Finley said Children's Memorial Hospital would receive a $100,000 gift if he made a profit from the concert. The Beatles sang 12 songs during their 31-minute concert before a crowd of 20,280. The concert was not profitable because of the large amount paid, but Finley still donated $25,000 to the Hospital.[20]

Angels outfielder Jimmy Piersall came to plate in Kansas City wearing a Beatle wig under his baseball cap on August 26, a few weeks before the concert. Piersall did a little dance strumming his bat like a guitar in the on-deck circle. Umpire Frank Umont made Piersall take off the wig at the plate. Piersall swung and missed on the fist pitch, turned to Umont and said: "You see what you did by taking away my wig, you took away my power." Umont broke out in laughter and Piersall eventually struck out.[21]

On September 16 Finley announced that 32-year-old Betty Caywood, a Chicago weather analyst, would join the broadcasting crew. She became the first woman to broadcast a major league baseball game when she joined the broadcasting team in Yankee Stadium on September 18th.

Bryson became ill during the second game of a double header against the Twins in Kansas City on September 23. After consultation with his doctor, KCMO decided Bryson would not return to the microphone for the remainder of the season to allow him to have complete rest in the hospital. He died on October 14 in Kansas City.[22]

CBS (Columbia Broadcasting System) paid $11.2 million to Dan Topping and Del Webb to buy 80 percent of the New York Yankees. CBS held the option to purchase the remaining 20 percent for $2.8 million. Finley and White Sox owner Arthur Allyn questioned what effect a broadcasting network's ownership of a major league team would have on baseball. The American League scheduled a meeting in Boston on September 9. Finley said that if the American League approved the sale, he would sell the A's for $8 million. He reasoned if the Yankees were worth $14 million, the A's were worth $8 million. Kansas City Chamber of Commerce president Kenneth Krakauer attempted to find buyers. He found three parties, but they all felt $8 million was too high. He described one of the parties as an individual, another as a corporation and the third as a syndicate of two or more persons. He said one of the prospective buyers made an offer the previous winter when Finley attempted to move the team. (This apparently referred to Alex Barket.)[23]

The American League approved the Yankees sale by an 8–2 vote on September 9 with Finley and Allyn casting the two dissenting votes. "The ballclub can be bought by local interests now and for the next two weeks at the price of $8 million," he said. Finley added that if Kansas City interests did not buy the team it would be offered to outside interests.[24]

Two Kansas City groups offered to pay Finley substantially more than the $4 million he paid for the A's; neither met his asking price of $8 million. Krakauer did not reveal any names but added either group would be "highly acceptable" to the league and both groups were financially able to operate the franchise. "I have yet to hear from the first one," responded Finley. "About two weeks ago an individual, who has always done a lot of talking and making noise, sent me a telegram stating he was ready to buy the A's and would be contacting me [probably referring to Barket]. But as yet I haven't as much as received a telephone call from him. Other than that I haven't heard from anyone in Kansas City. I personally don't believe that there is anyone in Kansas City interested in purchasing a major league baseball team. The time is approaching for those so-called interested groups to prove their sincerity. I would suggest that these two interested groups mentioned by Mr. Krakauer might consider pooling their funds if they are financially embarrassed in being unable to raise the offering price of $8 million separately. I'm certain these individuals are the same people who were unable to raise $3,500,000 over a period of six months four years ago. I believe it is time for anyone interested in purchasing the A's to either put up or shut up.... I am not placing the club in a bidding contest. All any local group has to do is make the offer, put up earnest money and it will get the club. I would like to stay in baseball. I like baseball and will stay unless one of these Kansas City groups is willing to meet my offer."[25]

The deadline passed on September 24. Finley said he received inquiries from six different groups in Kansas City and he sent them each a telegram to the effect that $8 million was his one and only offer. One Kansas City group was willing to go as high as $5 million. He said two groups, one from the West Coast and the other from the Southwest offered to meet his asking price. *Sports Illustrated* wrote Finley's $8 million price tag was "a price that kept him in baseball after all."[26]

The 1964 season ended when the A's lost four straight games to the White Sox in Chicago. Home attendance fell to 642,478 and Finley claimed that he lost $834,356 in 1964, bringing his total deficit for four seasons to $4,628,428. Finley criticized the city's lack of support and the board of directors (consisting of his wife and children) met on October 9 to discuss moving the team. They decided to recess the meeting until October 16 because the Milwaukee Braves would meet on that day to consider moving to Atlanta and the directors of the Cleveland Indians would also meet that day to decide whether to move the franchise to Seattle, Oakland or Dallas. If either team relocated, Finley felt it would be easier to move the A's. He wanted to move the A's to Milwaukee if the Braves moved to Atlanta.

A Milwaukee group called Teams, Incorporated was organized to purchase the Braves or obtain another major league team and reportedly offered Finley $8 million. "If someone up there offered that amount, I would entertain the thought of selling," he said. The National League met in New York on October 21 to consider the Braves' request to move to Atlanta "Do you know of any other major league clubs interested in moving to Milwaukee?" Milwaukee county board chairman Eugene Grobschmidt was asked. "I am free to identify one," he answered. "That is Kansas City. There is a Milwaukee syndicate of businessmen who are willing to make an offer for that club." But Finley no longer wanted to move or sell the team. In December he announced he was dropping his suit to set aside the current lease and would definitely remain in Kansas City for the remainder of the lease that would terminate after the 1967 season.[27]

24

1965: Charlie O. — The Man or the Mule?

Veteran coach Jimmie Dykes retired at the end of the 1964 season and Babe Dahlgren was not rehired. The A's replaced them with Whitey Herzog and Gabby Hartnett. Herzog played for Kansas City for three seasons. He retired after the 1963 season and scouted for the A's in 1964, signing several players. Herzog later became manager and architect of the Kansas City Royals and won three pennants with the St. Louis Cardinals. Hartnett worked with the catchers. He was a veteran of 20 seasons in the major leagues and was elected to the Hall of Fame in 1955. He became player-manager of the Cubs on July 20, 1938, and guided the team to the pennant. Jay Hankins was the A's named traveling secretary for the 1965 season, permitting Jim Schaaf to devote full time to public relations.

The Indians tried to obtain Colavito during the winter meetings, but Finley did not want the players they offered. The Indians then tried to purchase Colavito for $300,000. The White Sox, Indians and A's completed a three-way trade on January 20. The A's traded Colavito to the Sox for outfielders Jim Landis, Mike Hershberger and pitcher Fred Talbot. The Sox then traded Colavito to Cleveland. Landis was a four-time winner of *The Sporting News* Gold Glove award as the American League's best defensive center field but was used sparingly in 1963 and 1964. Hershberger, a 25-year-old right fielder, had one of the best throwing arms in baseball and had good speed on the base paths. Talbot, a 23-year-old right-hander, divided the 1964 season between Indianapolis and Chicago.

Morris Dubiner, western judge of the Jackson County court, wanted to build a domed stadium in the downtown area. The Houston Astrodome, dubbed by some as "the eighth wonder of the world," opened on April 12, 1965. Jackson County surveyed various sites for the proposed structure and financing was studied. "It would be quite a step forward," said Lamar

24—1965: Charlie O.—The Man or the Mule?

Rendering of the proposed domed stadium in downtown Kansas City. (From the Kansas City Visitor's Bureau.)

Hunt. "Anyone who has seen the Houston stadium, well, it really makes a believer out of you." Finley was unavailable for comment.[1]

The A's changed the outfield dimensions at Municipal Stadium for the seventh time in 11 years. The left field dimensions returned to the distance of 1961, but the height of the fence was increased from 10 feet (in 1961) to 22 feet. It was now 370 feet down the left field line (instead of 331) and 408 feet in left center (instead of 364). The chain link fence in center field installed in 1964 was removed, returning the center field fence to 421 feet from home plate. The height of the fence in center field was also increased to 22 feet.[2]

The A's planted ivy along the outfield walls because Finley admired the ivy-covered walls at Chicago's Wrigley Field. A partition was removed from the third base press box to enlarge the facilities. Seats for some writers were relocated to enlarge the television facilities and a restroom was added in the press box.

Finley had a roof built over the One-half Pennant Porch that extended over the playing field to the 296-foot mark claiming the roof was "protection for the spectators against the sun." American League supervisor of umpires Cal Hubbard arrived in Kansas City three days before the start of the season and ruled the roof was illegal. It stayed in place through the weekend exhibition series against St. Louis and through batting practice on opening day, April 12. One half hour before the game two trucks rolled through the center field gate toward the roof. Spectators were removed from the area and within 30 minutes the roof was removed. The foreman of the crew estimated that the roof cost Finley $4,000 to erect and $700 to demolish. "I still think I'm right," Finley declared. "I may put it up again next year.... I'm tired of Yankee domination because of a 296-foot fence in right field." He threatened to put a statue of Connie Mack on the field in center field because the Yankees had monuments honoring Babe Ruth, Lou Gehrig and Miller Huggins in center field. "They let the Yankees have their monuments out in the playing area," Finley complained. "But if I put one up they'll probably try to run me out of baseball."[3]

A "pitchometer" was installed on the scoreboard to time the pitchers. According the baseball rules a pitcher had to throw a pitch within 20 seconds after he received the ball from the catcher when there was nobody on base. Bill Veeck installed a pitchometer on the bottom of the Comiskey Park scoreboard in 1960 but the league prohibited him from using it. Finley used his pitchometer for several weeks before it was removed. The Fan-A-Gram and public address announcer reminded people to watch the pitchometer. The rule was enforced only twice during the season and the pitchometer was not in use at the time. Plate umpire Ed Runge called balls on A's hurler Diego Segui twice during a game between Kansas City and Minnesota on May 16 because he took too long between pitches. Veteran observers said it was the first and probably the last time the rule had been enforced in a major league game.[4]

The sheep that grazed behind the right field fence were retired. Finley thought they were a good idea until a batter hit a home run that hit one of the sheep in the head and killed it. The sheep had been the target of numerous practical jokes by the players. Moe Drabowky tried to hit them with fungoes during pre-game warm-ups. "I was always taking aim at the sheep up there," he said. "You could scare the sheep.... One relief pitcher chased one of the sheep up the hill before a game.... [It] died of a heart attack." Ted Bowsfield recalled the shepherd once fell asleep and failed to ring a bell following an Athletics home run and was fired.[5]

Finley adopted a mule as a team mascot and called it Charlie O. "He is a genuine Missouri mule donated to the A's by governor Warren Hearnes of Missouri after the greatest mule search in history," Finley said. "Everybody's got to see this mule." It was kept at Benjamin Stables and brought to most of the home games in an air-conditioned trailer equipped with a record player that played "mule music" such as "The Mule Train." Finley bought Charlie O a green and gold blanket, a green and gold bridle, and a green and gold A's cap. He built a special display pen in Municipal Stadium adjacent to the left field picnic area.[6]

Governor Hearnes officially presented Charlie O to the team on opening night and Finley rode the mule around the stadium. The mule was the main attraction in a zoo installed in the picnic area, which also featured six capuchin monkeys named after Finley's father and uncles, six China gold peasants, six German checker rabbits, two peafowl and a German shorthaired pointer. The animals were the victim of practical jokes by the players. "Catfish Hunter and I would go out to the ballpark early and feed the monkeys grasshoppers. Sometimes we'd give them cough medicine and sleeping pills," said pitcher Lew Krausse. Hunter said they'd comb "the outfield grass for grasshoppers ... stuff a pill or two down the hopper's throat and toss it in the monkey cage. See the monkey catch the grasshopper ... see the monkey go running and screaming all over his cage."[7]

Charlie O. Finley riding atop Charlie O. (From the Kansas City Athletics.)

KCMO entered the final year of its two-year contract to broadcast the games on radio and television. The station carried all regular season games and 25 exhibition games on radio. KCMO-TV televised 40 regular season games. Betty Caywood did not return and Red Rush joined Monte Moore in the broadcast booth. Rush had described the play-by-play action for the San Francisco Seals (AAA) in 1957.

On March 30 Frank Lane claimed that Finley talked with Milwaukee officials and he predicted the A's would replace the Braves in Milwaukee as soon as the Braves moved to Atlanta. Finley denied the claim and said neither he nor his representatives had talked directly or indirectly about moving the A's to Milwaukee.

Finley appointed Hank Peters as general manager on April 6 replacing Pat Friday. "When I came into baseball it was on a temporary basis," Friday said. "My tenure was subject to the pressures of the insurance business. It is now necessary for me to return to the insurance business.... This move was not a sudden thing. Charlie (Finley) and I had discussed it for more than a year.... My only regret is in leaving a loser." Friday said the transition from Peters's former position would not be completed until June 1 and Friday would perform most of the general manager's duties in the interim. "I consider it a great fortune that we had in our organization a man as capable as Hank Peters," Friday said. "He is thoroughly familiar with all the business affairs of baseball."[8]

In terms of baseball knowledge and experience, Friday and Peters could not have been more different.

Pat Friday was an insurance executive who was interested in baseball because his boss was interested in baseball. Prior to his association with the Charles O. Finley Insurance Company, Friday worked for the Continental Casualty Company in Chicago.

As executive vice president and treasurer of the Athletics, Friday was involved in the business operation of the team. His first task was to renovate and remodel the stadium. Considerable improvements were made at the Kansas City stadium under his direction between his hiring on January 12, 1961, and opening day three months later. Friday replaced Frank Lane as general manager of the team on August 21, 1961. Finley felt his enthusiasm and ingenuity that he displayed since joining the organization

Stadium Leases in 1963

A comparison of the Athletics' lease in 1963 and those in effect on other municipally-owned stadiums

Team	Basic Rent	Percent of Admissions	Concessions	Cancellation
Kansas City A's	$1,000	5%	7½%	If gate is less than 850,000
Kansas City Chiefs	$1	5% after first two years if receipts top $1.1 million	50%	Insolvency
Milwaukee Braves	-0-	5% of first one million 7% between 1–1.5 million 10% over 1.5 million	10–16%	National emergency
Cleveland Indians	$60,000	7% if greater than base rent	45%	National emergency
Baltimore Orioles	$75,000	7% if greater than base rent	10%	National emergency
Washington Senators	$65,000	7% if greater than base rent	13%	National emergency
San Francisco Giants	$125,000	5% if greater than base rent	Maximum of $25,000	National emergency
Houston Colts	$562,500– $747,000	Included in base rent	Included in base rent	Stadium loss
Minnesota Twins	-0-	7%	10%	National emergency

would be invaluable in the task of rebuilding the franchise. Although he was general manager Friday candidly admitted to a pitching prospect, "I don't know much about baseball, but you look like you throw the ball pretty hard."[9] Years later Ted Bowsfield, a former pitcher on the Athletics said Friday "didn't know much about baseball ... Pat [Friday] was just a figurehead. But fortunately they had Hank Peters in the front office."[10]

The only thing Hank Peters had in common with Pat Friday is that neither played professional baseball. Regardless, Henry J. Peters started his career in professional baseball at a young age. Peters, who did play high school and semi-professional baseball in St. Louis, was offered a job by St. Louis Browns' co-owner Bill DeWitt. Peters worked under minor league director Jim McLaughlin after returning from military service in 1946. Peters became assistant minor league director in 1949 and served in that capacity until the team moved to Baltimore following the 1953 season. He was not offered a position with the Orioles and served as general manager of the Burlington, Iowa, minor league team in 1954.

He was offered a position with the Athletics in January 1955 after the team moved to Kansas City. He initially turned it down because he felt the club had a full compliment of executives and there would be no specific duties for him to perform. He reconsidered and accepted the position of assistant minor league director under Bernie Guest. Guest resigned after Peters arrived and Peters became minor league director. The A's had only a few scouts but Peters built one of the game's best scouting staffs. Peters did so well during the first year that his responsibilities were expanded.

Finley fired him during the 1961 season and he joined Cincinnati as the assistant minor league director. Finley rehired him as the assistant general manager and minor league director after the 1961 season.

The 40-year-old Peters served less than one year as general manager in Kansas City. Ed Lopat was appointed executive vice president in charge of the A's on October 27, 1965, and Peters was reassigned to administrative assistant in charge of the minor leagues. He resigned on November 28 to become the minor league director for the Cleveland Indians. His duties were expanded following the 1966 season and he was named vice president and director of player personnel. He remained with the Indians until 1971, when he was named president of the National Association, the organization governing minor league baseball. He served as president for four years.

Peters became general manager of the Baltimore Orioles on December 15, 1975. He built the Orioles into one of the strongest teams in the major leagues. The Orioles won the American League pennant in 1979 and the World Series in 1983. Peters was named Major League Executive of the

Year following both of those seasons. The Orioles fired Peters following the 1987 season after a disagreement with owner Edward Bennett Williams. Williams wanted to spend money acquiring free agents while Peters stressed building through the farm system. Without Peters, the veteran-laden Orioles lost their first 21 games to start the 1988 season.

Peters returned to Cleveland as general manager. He rebuilt the Indians organization into one of the top organizations in baseball before he retired at the end of the 1991 season. *Baseball America* named the Indians the organization of the year in 1992.

Kansas City manager Mel McGaha planned a new image for the 1965 A's built around hit-and-run plays, base stealing and strong defense. The A's responded with the worst spring training record in club history. The A's took eight first-year players with them to spring training. "Blue Moon" Odom was sent down as the A's designated player, but they kept pitchers Jim "Catfish" Hunter, Don Buschhorn and Tom Harrison, infielder Skip Lockwood, catcher Rene Lachemann, and outfielders John Sanders and Joe Rudi on the roster when the season opened to protect them from being claimed from other teams for $25,000. Rudi and Sanders were trimmed from the roster on May 3 and Harrison was sent down by the end of May. The A's kept Hunter, Buschhorn, Lachemann and Lockwood on the roster the entire season.

The A's lost 11 of their first 13 games. Peters called McGaha into his office after the A's lost 2–0 to the Twins on May 15, their seventh consecutive loss to put their record at 5–21, and fired the manager. "He couldn't get along with the players, or coaches, or the press—so he only lasted until the middle of May," said Whitey Herzog. There was speculation McGaha would be fired, but it was not expected so early in the season. "I don't feel I owe any apologies to anyone," McGaha said. "I feel I performed my job to the best of my ability. We've had some key injuries. Losing Jim Landis hurt us. Mike Hershberger hasn't been able to get started and that hurt us. In spring training we felt our defense would be the strong part of our club but it has been disappointing. I'd have to say we haven't gotten many breaks either."[11]

Peters appointed Haywood Sullivan, manager of the A's Vancouver (AAA) team, as manager in Kansas City. Sullivan was 34 years old and became the youngest manager in the major leagues.

Sullivan, an All-American quarterback at the University of Florida, had given up his final year of collegiate eligibility to sign a substantial bonus contract with the Boston Red Sox in 1952. He was drafted by Washington in December 1960 but was traded to Kansas City for pitcher Marty Kutyna before he played for the Senators. Sullivan played with the A's until midway through the 1963 season; he was sent to Portland (AAA) as a player-coach. He managed Kansas City's Birmingham minor league team and guided the team to a second place finish in the Southern League in 1964. The team was not eliminated from the pennant race until just two games remained in the regular season. He was named manager of the A's top minor league team in Vancouver for the 1965 season.

As manager of the A's, Sullivan inherited a team on which several players had been his teammates when he played for Kansas City. He signed a two-year contract to manage the team, extending through the 1966 season.

He resigned on November 28, 1965, to accept a position as vice president in charge of player personnel for the Boston Red Sox, working with scouting and player development. Sullivan, Edward LeRoux and Jean Yawkey formed a general partnership syndicate to purchase the Red Sox on September 29, 1977. Sullivan became general manager of the team on October 24, 1977 and chief executive officer in 1984. Sullivan remained with the Red Sox until November 1993, when the holders of two of the three general-partnership shares purchased the third share owned by Sullivan.

Haywood Sullivan's Managerial Record

Year	Club	League	Won	Lost	Position
1964	Birmingham	AA	80	60	2
1965	Vancouver	AAA	12	13	4
1965	Kansas City	Major	54	82	10

"I'm not planning any drastic changes right now," Sullivan said when he took over the A's. "I think it's just a matter of some guys getting going.... From what I've seen and what I've been told this club has been playing fairly well. We've been losing by one and two runs because of a mistake here and a mistake there. We've got to eliminate those mistakes and get everybody doing his best."[12]

Sullivan had a successful debut on Sunday May 16 as the A's won a doubleheader from the Twins. The A's trailed 4–2 after eight innings in the opener but came back to win 7–6 in 10 innings. Sullivan used Lachemann, one of the first year players, as a pinch hitter in the ninth. The A's trailed 4–3 with runners on first and third with one out. Lachemann lined a single to left to tie the score. Ed Charles hit a game-winning three-run home run in the tenth inning after the Twins scored two runs in the top of the inning. The A's broke a 2–2 deadlock in the seventh inning of the nightcap when Campaneris singled, stole second and came home on a bunt by Landis coupled with a throwing error. The A's won the game 4–2. The

Haywood Sullivan (from Jay Publications and the Kansas City Athletics).

success was short-lived as the White Sox crushed the A's 13–2 the following night.

Ed Lopat replaced Tom Ferrick as pitching coach on June 5. The pitching staff showed some improvement under his tutelage but still finished the season with the worst earned run average (4.24) in the American League. Ferrick became a special assignment scout. "We needed someone to scout the other major league clubs on an exclusive basis for some time," Peters said. "Tom has had previous experience in this field and should do an outstanding job for us."[13]

The A's traded catcher Doc Edwards to the Yankees for pitcher Roland Sheldon and catcher Johnny Blanchard on May 3. Sheldon, a 28-year-old right-hander, had pitched in just three games for the Yankees at the time of the trade but had a 5–2 record with a 3.62 ERA for New York in 1964. Blanchard was a left-handed hitter with power who was known for his ability to pull the ball down the right field line in Yankee Stadium.

Jim Gentile opened the season at first base. He had disagreements with McGaha and was fined on several occasions. He made an obscene gesture toward spectators in one game after hitting a home run, and in another game he permitted two easy throws to get past him at first base even though he was a good fielder. The A's traded him to Houston on June 4 for minor league relief pitcher Jesse Hickman, a reported $100,000, and a player-to-be-named later. Gentile led the team with 10 home runs at the time of the trade. Ken Harrelson, who inherited first base, hit 23 home runs with 66 runs batted in.

Second baseman Dick Green was one of the team's leading hitters during the first part of the season. He was hampered by an ankle injury in the second half of the season and his batting average dropped to .232. Third baseman Ed Charles hit only eight home runs, primarily because the new left field fence in Kansas City, but he finished with a .269 batting average.

McGaha named Wayne Causey the team captain before the start of the season. He opened the season at shortstop but was replaced by Campaneris. Causey finished the season with a .261 average. Campaneris was one of the team's most exciting players. He made sparkling defensive plays and had better range and a stronger arm than Causey but was not as consistent. He led the team in hitting (.270) and led the league with 51 stolen bases, breaking Luis Aparicio's nine-year reign as American League stolen base champion.

Campy Campaneris became the first player in modern baseball history to play all nine positions in a game. It came against the California Angels on September 8, 1965. Campy Campaneris Night was profitable as a crowd of 21,576 showed up at Municipal Stadium, but the A's lost the game 5–4 in 13 innings and also lost Campaneris to a shoulder and neck injury on a play at the plate. He started the game at shortstop. He played second base in the second inning and was credited with an assist when he handled the ball in a rundown. He moved to third base where he had no chances and to left field where he caught a fly ball. He caught a fly in center field in the fifth inning. He played in right field in the sixth inning. Jim Fregosi hit a high fly ball to right-center field with two out and a runner on first. Campaneris got under the ball but it bounced off his glove and the runner from first scored on the error to give the Angels a 2–1 lead. He moved to first base in the seventh inning and was credited with a putout on an infield fly. He gave up one run as a pitcher in the eighth inning. He retired Jose Cardenal on a pop fly, walked Albie Pearson and Jim Fregosi, gave up a run-scoring single to Joe Adcock, struck out Bobby Knoop, Fregosi was thrown out when he tried to steal second base.

Campy moved behind the plate in the ninth inning. Ed Kirkpatrick singled and stole second. Tom Egan walked and Paul Schaal flied out, with Kirkpatrick moving to third base. The Angels attempted a double steal. Campaneris threw to Green at second and Green threw back to Campaneris who took the throw on the third base side three feet in front of the plate. Kirkpatrick ran into Campaneris and knocked him to the ground. Campaneris held on to the ball for the final out of the inning. He was unable to continue and was taken to St. Luke's Hospital for X-rays of his left shoulder. He was knocked out of action for five days.[14]

Catcher Bill Bryan enjoyed his best season in his brief major league career. The 25-year-old hit 14 home runs, appeared in 108 games and finished with a .252 batting average. Rene Lachemann shared catching duties with Bryan. He was only 19 years old but had timely hitting and solid defense play.

Campy Campaneris (from the Kansas City Athletics).

Hershberger played 150 games in right field and led American League outfielders with 14 assists and seven double plays. He batted only .231 but had a 15-game hitting streak and went 5-for-5 on June 20 against Detroit in Tiger Stadium with four singles and a double. Landis played center field. He played well defensively but missed four weeks early in the season with a pulled leg muscle.

McGaha planned to move Nelson Mathews to left field after the team obtained Hershberger and Landis. Mathews lost the starting position to Tom Reynolds in spring training. Reynolds had trouble at the plate and was sent to Vancouver. The A's recalled Jose Tartabull from Vancouver. He played left field and batted .312 in 68 games for the A's with 11 stolen bases.

Fred Talbot finished with a 10–12 record and a 4.14 ERA. Roland Sheldon finished the season with a 10–8 record and a 3.95 ERA. John O'Donoghue was the staff's hard-luck pitcher. He lost three 1–0 shutouts during the season and finished with a 9–18 record and a respectable 3.94 ERA. Diego Segui was the fourth pitcher in the starting rotation. He pitched a two-hit, 5–0 shutout against California on June 15th. He finished the season with a disappointing 5–15 record and a 4.64 ERA. Orlando Pena began the season in the starting rotation but was 0–6 with a 6.88 ERA and was sold to Detroit. Moe Drabowsky had 1–5 record and a 4.38 ERA before he was optioned to Vancouver.

Jim "Catfish" Hunter was kept on the roster to protect him from the first year draft and he developed into one of the better pitchers on the staff. The 18-year-old hurler did not pitch in 1964 because he had an operation on his right foot to correct an injury. He had his first start in Cleveland because of injuries to other pitchers and gave up three home runs. Fireworks greeted each home run and teammates gave him the nickname

"Boom-Boom." He pitched an impressive two-hit shutout against Boston on September 24. Hunter led the team with two shutouts and finished with an 8–8 record, 82 strikeouts and a 4.26 ERA.

John Wyatt appeared in 65 games, led the team with 18 saves, and had 70 strikeouts in 89 innings of relief pitching. He earned two saves in a doubleheader against California on September 3. He finished with a 2–6 record and a 3.44 ERA. The A's purchased Jim Dickson in the major league draft. The 26-year-old right-hander appeared in 68 games, an American League record for most appearances by a rookie pitcher, and finished the year with a 3–2 record and a 3.45 ERA.

Wes Stock had recurring arm problems that affected his control and effectiveness. He appeared in 51 games but slumped to a 0–4 record and a 5.22 ERA. The A's signed veteran southpaw relief pitcher Don Mossi on May 28. He appeared in 51 games, did not allow any home runs in 55 innings pitched and finished with a 5–8 record and a 3.76 ERA. Jack Aker was called up from Vancouver in mid-season. The 25-year-old relief pitcher had three saves in 34 games and finished with a 4–3 record and a 3.18 ERA.

Finley signed 59-year-old Satchel Paige on September 10 to boost the sagging attendance. Paige, a legend in the Negro Leagues, made his major league debut with Cleveland in 1948 at the age of 42. He pitched for the Indians and St. Louis Browns until 1953. Finley signed Paige as a coach to help him qualify for the five years necessary to obtain a major league pension. Finley placed a rocking chair in the bullpen for Paige. Finley announced that Paige would start the game on September 25, making him the oldest player to play in a major league game. Paige pitched three shutout innings against Boston, allowing only one hit, a two-out double by Carl Yastrzemski in the first inning. He made only 28 pitches, did not allow a walk, and he struck out pitcher Bill Monbouquette. The A's led 1–0 when Segui replaced him at the start of the fourth inning, but Boston won the game 5–2. Monbouquette was winning pitcher and Mossi took the loss.

Roger Hansen resigned as comptroller of the team on August 15 and Finley hired former major league player and manager Alvin Dark to the newly created position as administrative assistant on August 27. Dark was a coach with the Cubs. "A month before the season was over I won a little golf tournament the Cubs held in Chicago and the story was in the local papers," said Dark. "Charlie Finley has an office in Chicago. He read the article and phoned me. 'I didn't know you were coaching,' he said. 'How about coming with us to be my administrative assistant…? Scout the other clubs, check into possible trades. Scout our club to see what the

Satchel Paige (with nurse) in his bullpen rocking chair. (From the Kansas City Athletics.)

other teams see.'" Many people felt Finley hired Dark to replace Haywood Sullivan at the end of the season.[15]

The A's were involved in one of the year's most confusing player transactions. The Angels placed outfielder Lou Clinton on the waiver list in early September and Cleveland claimed him. It was the third time that waivers had been asked on Clinton during the season and that made the waivers irrevocable, a fact the American League office had overlooked and failed to specify. The league office notified all the teams by teletype that Clinton would be awarded to the Indians unless he was claimed by a club lower in the standings. The A's claimed him. He joined the team on September 8 and played against the Angels, coming to bat one time in the contest. Indians president Gabe Paul protested the decision and made another claim. He said it was unfair to award him to Kansas City when Cleveland had been the only team to submit a claim. Joe Cronin notified the A's the following day that he was reopening the case and Clinton was not to be used in a game until he made a ruling. Clinton was awarded to Cleveland later that day despite protests by A's officials.

Finley held a number of special events that attracted good crowds and made up a fair percentage of the total season attendance. Farmers Night was held for the second consecutive year and Ken Harrelson represented the A's in a milking contest. Cars were given away on Automobile Industry Night and players were driven to their positions in limousines. Green and gold bats were given away on bat day. The A's starting lineup was brought on the field on a mule train on Mule Day.

Finley took Charlie O to every American League city. Charlie O traveled in his trailer pulled by a colorful station wagon and stayed at the hotels where the team stayed. Finley rode Charlie O through Times Square, waving a white western hat. He paraded the mule through the streets of several cities while players and pretty young women passed out ballpoint pens, megaphones, bats and caps, all in the team's green and gold colors. Finley asked the players if anyone knew how to ride a mule when Charlie O appeared in Yankee Stadium. Ken Harrelson said he rode a mule as a kid on his grandfather's farm. Charlie O was not saddled and when Harrelson began to bounce off he wrapped his arms around the mule's neck to hang on. Harrelson wound up upside down under the mule's neck with both arms and both legs wrapped around the mule's neck.

White Sox owner Arthur Allyn would not permit Charlie O inside Comiskey Park. "If I let Finley ride that mule around the park, I won't be able to tell which one is the jackass," said general manager Ed Short. Finley threw a luncheon at the Sheraton-Chicago hotel for the mule and hired attractive young women to picket Comiskey Park with posters that read: "White Sox unfair to Missouri Mule." He rented a vacant lot across the street from the ballpark, hired a band, and put on a show prior to the game. Police were stationed at the gates with orders to keep Charlie O out. Finley rented another mule and sneaked it into the center field bullpen. He figured it was Charlie O that was banned from the park and not the other mule.[16]

"I heard a commotion outside the [clubhouse] door, then a knock," Ken Harrelson said. "When I opened it, there was Charlie [Finley] giving orders in a stage whisper to a crew of guys a pushing a huge box, five or six feet high and so wide it wouldn't fit through the door. Panting with excitement Charlie said, 'Come on, Kenny, help us get this box open.' Inside was a mule — not Charlie O, he was too big — but a baby mule that looked just like him. 'Come on, come on,' Finley whispered, 'Let's get him out — hurry up.' Then, when we had coaxed and hauled and yanked the animal out of the box, Finley said, 'Kenny, help me get this thing on the field.'

"'You can't take him on the field, Charlie,' I said, 'It's right in the middle of the ballgame.'

"'I don't give a damn when it is,' he said. 'I got the mule this far and we're going to get him the rest of the way. Now come on. Are you going to help me or not?'"

The White Sox had men on base and were about to knock A's pitcher Jack Aker out of the game when the mule galloped around the field, ridden by Harrelson. Time was called and the umpires went after Harrelson and the mule. Harrelson was blamed while Finley pointed at Allyn and laughed.[17]

Before one game a young boy came to Finley and said: "Mr. Finley,

I've come 200 miles to see Charlie O." The mule had not been brought to the park because it was Rabbit Day and Finley was giving away 250 rabbits to illustrate how fast his outfielders were. Finley smiled and said, "Son, we weren't going to get him out today because of the rabbits."

"I don't care about the rabbits," the boy responded.

"Then out comes Charlie O," Finley said. Charlie O was brought to the stadium and Finley led Charlie O through the center field gate. The game had started and Finley and the mule nearly bumped into A's center fielder Jim Landis. Finley looked toward the infield and saw an umpire running toward him yelling: "Get the hell off the field." Finley returned through the gate to an area beyond the playing field.[18]

Finley announced a "Cellar-bray-tion" would be held if the team climbed out of last place ("cellar" because the team climbed out of the cellar and "bray" was the noise made by a mule). Kansas City climbed out of the cellar on September 3 when the A's swept a doubleheader from the Angels in California and the Yankees defeated Boston. "We were losing so many games we had a champagne party to celebrate when we escaped the cellar for a few hours one night," said broadcaster Red Rush. "Charles [Finley] came into the broadcasting booth and said, 'Red, tell 'em we're gonna win the pennant.' So I said, 'Well folks, Charlie Finley's in the booth and he says we're gonna win the pennant. And we are gonna win the pennant ... only I'm not sure when.' Well, Finley was so used to Monte Moore saying whatever he told him to say that I guess he couldn't take me and fired me." The celebration was short-lived as Boston swept a doubleheader in New York the following day and the A's lost their game in California.[19]

The A's lost 103 games and finished in the cellar for the second consecutive season. It was the ninth time in Kansas City's 11 major league seasons that the team finished in last place or next to last place in the standings. Fan disappointment was apparent as just 528,344 attended the games, the lowest total in the major leagues and the lowest total ever attracted by the A's in Kansas City.

1965 team — Front row: Campaneris, Tartabull, Hartnett (coach), Sullivan (manager), Appling (coach), Herzog (coach), Buschhorn, Sheldon, Causey. Second row: Hankins (traveling secretary), Zych (clubhouse attendant), Lockwood, Segui, Rasario, Stock, Aker, Dickson, Charles, Krausse, Lachemann, Jones (trainer), Schaaf (traveling secretary). Third row: Wyatt, Hershberger, Talbot, Hunter, Harrelson, Green, Sigloch (equipment manager). Back row: Bryan, Mossi, Reynolds, O'Donoghue, Joyce. Seated in front: Gleissner (batboy). (From the Kansas City Athletics.)

25

1966: The Dark Ages

Whitey Herzog resigned after the 1965 season. "Promotions are one thing but when you start doing things that affect the outcome of a game — like the donkey or Campaneris night — then that's something else," he said. "I told myself then that maybe I'd be better off getting out of the organization." The New York Mets hired him as a coach a few weeks later. Dodgers scouting director Al Campanis reported he was offered the A's general manager position during the World Series. Finley admitted he talked to Campanis but denied he offered him the position.[1]

Finley named Ed Lopat executive vice president in charge of the A's organization and Hank Peters was demoted to administrative assistant in charge of minor league operations on October 27. "We were shorthanded in our overall operation the last few years," Lopat said. "We're finally getting around to operating as a major league club should operate — with plenty of help in the front office."

Finley denied Peters was demoted and said Peters's authority would not be limited to minor league operations. "It may be a step down in your opinion, but in no sense is that is step down," he said. "There will be no cut in salary and Peters will work closely with Lopat. Ray Swallow, Peters and myself have tried to run the club, and it is a physical impossibility. Alvin Dark will remain as administrative assistant and, if we can find a way, financially, to add any more assistants we will do so. I don't consider this at all a shakeup.... To build a contender and eventually a championship club it is necessary to have as many capable assistants as you can surround yourself with.... At this time I do not anticipate any changes in managers. Sullivan has a contract to manage the Athletics next season."[2]

Peters was disappointed. Whitey Herzog called him, "One of the finest men I've ever worked for as well as one of the finest men I've ever known. He is bright, intelligent, always in complete grasp of the whole situation. He put together the A's teams that dominated baseball in the early '70s....

It was people like Hank Peters who built those teams. Once they got the players in the system Finley fired all the good people.... I don't think he ever appreciated the work that people did for him"³

"When the Oakland A's swept to three consecutive American League pennants in the 1970s they did so with players scouted, signed, and developed by an organization created a decade earlier by Hank Peters," wrote Jack Torrey. "Oakland owner Charles O. Finley earned raves for building the A's, but those in baseball realized that Peters quietly knew how to spot and procure talent.... Peters and Finley could not last; their styles were far too different. Peters wanted to take time to build a powerful team. Finley's impatience was legendary. As the owner, Finley felt he had every right to meddle in the daily operations of the team."⁴

Al Dark (from the Kansas City Athletics).

Peters resigned on November 28 to join the Cleveland Indians as minor league director. Haywood Sullivan resigned the same day to join the Boston Red Sox as a vice president in charge of player personnel. The A's lost two key scouts following Peters's departure. Joe Bowman resigned as scouting supervisor and joined Atlanta as a regional scouting director. Art Lily also resigned. He was the A's chief West Coast scout and had discovered and signed some of the A's most talented young players.

Dark replaced Sullivan as manager. "I think it will be a great advantage to the youngsters getting an experienced manager at the helm, even though Sullivan did a good job last season," Lopat said. "There is no substitute for experience. A manager like Dark could mean the difference of eight to 12 to 14 ballgames over an inexperienced manager."

Dark, a native of Comanche, Oklahoma, won Rookie of the Year honors with the Boston Braves in 1948 when he batted .322 and helped lead the team to the National League championship. He was traded to the New York Giants in 1950 and led National League shortstops in double plays in

1951 and 1952. He was traded to St. Louis during the 1956 season, traded to the Chicago Cubs during the 1958 season and played for both Philadelphia and Milwaukee in 1960, his final season in the major leagues.

Dark was named manager of the San Francisco Giants following the 1960 season and managed the Giants to four consecutive first division finishes between 1961 and 1964. The Giants won the 1962 pennant, but the Yankees won the World Series in seven games. He was fired following the 1964 season and coached for the Cubs in 1965.

He went from an administrative assistant for the Kansas City Athletics on August 27, 1965, to a two-year contract as manager of the A's on November 28, 1965. His 1966 team established a Kansas City record with 74 victories and the A's finished in seventh place. The team struggled during the 1967 season and Luke Appling replaced Dark as manager on August 20, 1967.

Cleveland hired Dark as manager following the 1967 season. His duties were expanded following the 1969 season and he was named general manager in addition to his managerial duties. He was fired during the 1971 season. Finley hired Dark to manage the Oakland Athletics on February 18, 1974, just a few days before the start of spring training. He led the team to the division championship, American League pennant and World Series title. He led the team to another division title in 1975, but the Athletics lost to Boston in the League Championship Series. He was not rehired. Dark managed the San Diego Padres during the 1977 season but was replaced before the start of the 1978 season.

Alvin Dark's Managerial Record

Year	Club	League	Won	Lost	Position
1961	San Francisco	Major	85	69	3
1962	San Francisco	Major	103	62	1
1963	San Francisco	Major	88	74	3
1964	San Francisco	Major	90	72	4
1966	Kansas City	Major	74	86	7
1967	Kansas City	Major	52	69	10
1968	Cleveland	Major	86	75	3
1969	Cleveland	Major	62	99	6
1970	Cleveland	Major	76	86	5
1971	Cleveland	Major	42	61	6
1974	Oakland	Major	90	72	1
1975	Oakland	Major	98	64	1
1977	San Diego	Major	69	93	5

Dark felt there was outstanding talent in the A's minor league system and was excited by the opportunity to manage the A's. "The one thing I have wanted to do in baseball, my ultimate ambition, is to start from scratch with a young team and take it to a championship," Dark stated a few years later. "I can't imagine anything more rewarding for a manager. In San Francisco we won a pennant, but I was working virtually with a veteran team.... In Kansas City, when I took the job managing Charlie Finley's Athletics in 1966, there was no doubt in my mind we could do it. Mr. Finley had them earmarked and on their way. I had something to work with in 1966 that the previous managers hadn't had, the beginning of a great pitching staff. They were the cream of the A's youth movement, fresh off the farm."[5]

Luke Appling was the only holdover on Dark's coaching staff. Cot Deal was named pitching coach. He played for St. Louis and Boston during his brief major league career. He was pitching coach for Cincinnati (1959-1960), Houston (1962–1964) and the Yankees in 1965. Al Vincent managed sixteen seasons in the minor leagues. He coached at Detroit (1943-1944), Baltimore (1955–1959), and Philadelphia (1961–1963). He scouted for Houston in 1964 and 1965. Bob Hofman spent seven years managing teams in the A's minor league system and worked with a number of the young players in the organization. Ray Swallow succeeded Peters as minor league director. He had served as Peters's assistant since 1962. Art Parrack was hired as assistant minor league director and Tom Ferrick replaced Bowman as director of scouting. Former Houston minor league director Eddie Robinson was hired as an administrative assistant. Swallow, Ferrick and Robinson exchanged positions in August. Robinson replaced Swallow as the minor league director, Swallow replaced Ferrick and Ferrick became the team's chief scout. Jim Schaaf resigned as director of public relations early in 1966 to accept a similar position with the Kansas City Chiefs. The Athletics hired former Chicago Cubs publicity director Don Biebel to replace Schaaf. Gabby Hartnett, a coach for the team in 1965, was reassigned to the public relations department.

Both the A's and Chiefs had attendance problems. "The status of Kansas City as a major league city is in jeopardy," warned councilman John Maguire. "People say they won't go out and see the Athletics because they don't like Charlie Finley. This is silly. They don't even go out to see the Chiefs. These two professional teams are just as important here as any big industry." The Greater Kansas City Sports Commission was formed to promote the sale of season tickets for both teams. The leaders set a goal to sell 5,000 season tickets for the Athletics and 20,000 season tickets for the Chiefs. They established a unique plan with area banks to sell tickets on a time-payment plan with no interest charged. They also developed a payroll deduction plan through cooperating firms. More than 100 busi-

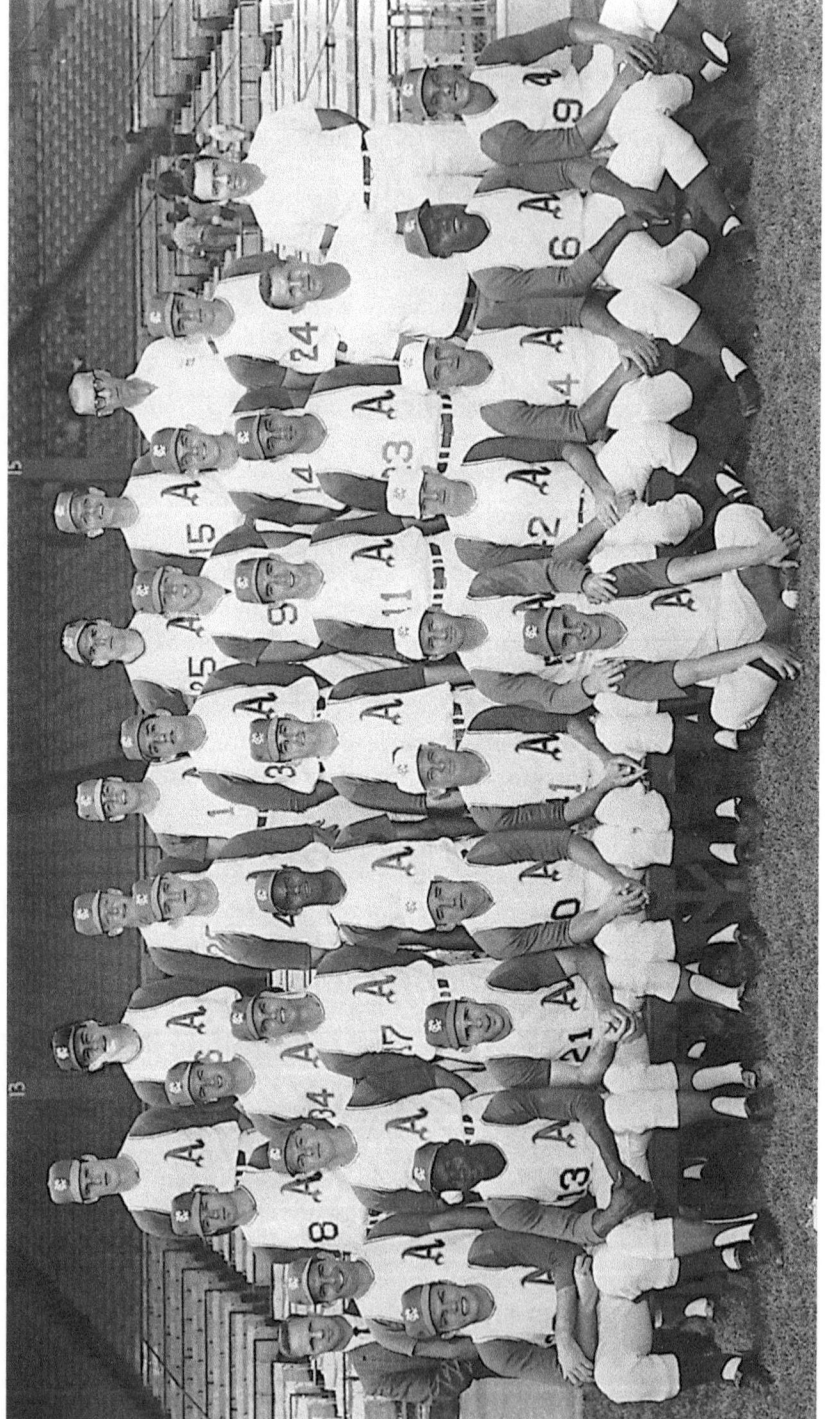

nessmen devoted several full days to the season ticket sales campaign. Finley cooperated to the extent of running several ads in newspapers encouraging people to "Jump on the A's Mule Train." The drive was successful. The Chiefs sold 21,237 season tickets and the Athletics sold 4,165 season tickets and nearly 5,500 scrip books. Each scrip book cost $50. Three and one-half scrip books were the equivalent to one season ticket. That meant the season ticket sale was 5,735, a new team record. The Sports Commission also considered the feasibility of a $65 million domed stadium located south of the downtown area and developed plans for a 60,000-seat domed stadium with an adjoining exhibition hall and field house-arena.

The A's acquired infielder Ernie Fazio from Houston on October 15, 1965, to complete the Jim Gentile trade. Fazio was the Pacific Coast League's All-Star second baseman in 1965. The A's traded outfielder Jim Landis and minor league pitcher Jim Rittwage to Cleveland for catcher Phil Roof and minor league outfielder Joe Rudi two days later. The 25-year-old Roof was a good defensive catcher who had not shown the ability to hit consistently. Rudi would not become a regular until 1970, but he was a cornerstone of the A's dynasty in Oakland in the 1970s.

Kansas City's One-Half Pennant Porch was removed and right field returned to its former dimensions, but the height of the fence was increased to 40-feet with a wire addition on top of the existing fence. KCMO radio and KCMO-TV exercised their option to broadcast the games for the 1966 season. Lynn Faris replaced Red Rush as Monte Moore's broadcast partner. Faris had broadcast games for the class AA Birmingham Barons for four seasons.

Pitcher Wes Stock was released on April 7 and signed as a player-coach for the A's Vancouver (AAA) team. The A's traded pitcher John O'Donoghue to Cleveland on the same day for pitcher Ralph Terry and a reported $25,000 in cash. The 30-year-old Terry, who had pitched in Kansas City from 1957–1959, had been a holdout during spring training. He agreed to terms for a new contract two days after the trade. He started 10 games but was used only sparingly after mid-season. He was sold to the New York Mets on August 6 after compiling a disappointing 1–5 record and a 3.80 ERA. Pitcher Diego Segui was placed on waivers on April 13 and was purchased by Washington Senators.

Front row: Nash, Odom, Gosger, Hofman (coach), Vincent (coach), Dark (manager), Deal (coach), Appling (coach), Charles, Campaneris. Second row: Hankins (traveling secretary), Fazio, Hershberger, Grzenda, Chavarria, Cater, Talton, Aker, Zych (clubhouse attendant). Third row: Blasingame, Sanders, Roof, Blanco, Repoz, Stahl, Nossek, Jones (trainer). Back row: Dobson, Hunter, Krausse, Green, Lindblad, Stock, Sigloch (equipment manager). Seated in front: Gleissner (batboy). (From the Kansas City Athletics.)

The A's played two exhibition games against St. Louis in Kansas City and then opened the regular season in Minnesota where Catfish Hunter lost the first game 2–1 on April 12. The A's won their home opener on April 19 as Chuck Dobson defeated the Twins 3–2. The A's lost 14 of their next 16 games. Dark began to use his young pitchers at every opportunity.

The A's purchased outfielder Joe Nossek on waivers from the Twins on May 11 and sold pitcher Aurelio Monteagudo to Houston on May 17. Wayne Causey was traded to the White Sox for infielder Danny Cater and cash on May 27. The 26-year-old Cater was a spray hitter that hit to all fields and the A's felt his batting style would fit in well with the large dimensions at Municipal Stadium.

Pitcher Fred Talbot and catcher Bill Bryan were traded to the Yankees on June 10 for outfielder Roger Repoz and pitchers Bill Stafford and Gil Blanco. Kansas City considered Repoz the key of the trade. He was a good defensive outfielder with a strong arm and was a power hitter with a quick bat. Stafford, a 27-year-old right-hander, won 14 games for the Yankees in 1961 and 1962 but had been hampered by sore arms and other maladies since 1963.

Three days later the A's traded pitchers Roland Sheldon and John Wyatt and outfielder Jose Tartabull to Boston for outfielder Jim Gosger and pitchers Ken Sanders and Guido Grilli. Gosger was the key player in this trade. The 23-year-old outfielder was defensive outfielder and a good hitter with the ability to hit an occasional long ball. Kansas City reacquired Sanders, a 24-year-old relief pitcher, after Boston had taken him in the major league draft at the end of the 1965 season. Grilli, a 26-year-old southpaw, was acquired to give the A's left-handed relief.

Kansas City traded first baseman Ken Harrelson to Washington for pitcher Jim Duckworth and a reported $20,000 on June 23. Duckworth was a major disappointment and was traded back to Washington when the A's reacquired pitcher Diego Segui on July 30.

The A's recovered from their slow start. From June 19 until the end of the season, the A's played at slightly better than a .500 clip with 50 victories compared to 49 defeats despite a second slump (6–12) immediately following the All-Star break. The key to this improvement was the talented and very young pitching. By the end of the season the starters averaged just 21 years old: Catfish Hunter (20), Chuck Dobson (22), Lew Krausse (22), Jim Nash (21), and John "Blue Moon" Odom (20). Paul Lindblad and relief pitcher Jack Aker were just 25 years old.

Youth was a double-edged sword for the A's. Minnesota hit five home runs in the seventh inning in a 9–4 victory against the A's in Minnesota on June 9. The A's led 4–3 when the Twins came to bat in the seventh. Earl

Battey went to first on a base on balls with one out. Pinch hitter Rich Rollins hit Hunter's first pitch into the left field stands for a 368-foot home run. Zoilo Versalles, the next batter, hit a pitch into the left field seats to give the Twins a 6–4 lead. Lindblad replaced Hunter and Sandy Valdespino grounded out for the second out of the inning. Tony Oliva and Don Mincher then tagged Lindblad for successive home runs. Dark brought in John Wyatt. Harmon Killebrew hit another home run, the team's third in a row and the fifth of the inning. Jimmie Hall hit the ball 380 feet down the line but it struck the 12-foot-high fence in right-center about 12 inches from the top of the fence and bounced back for a double. The five home runs set the American League record and matched the major league mark set by the Giants (1939 and 1961) and the Phillies (1949).

The pitchers showed their inexperience as they were victims of six steals of home by the opposition during the season. The Yankees tied a major league record when two players stole home against the A's on April 30. Roy White stole home in the third inning and Jake Gibbs repeated the feat in the fourth inning as the Yankees won the game 6–0. Tom Tresh stole home on the following day in a 10–4 Yankees victory. "Just wait," Dark said. "Just wait. Our day is coming, and it's going to be a lot sooner than most people think."[6]

Hunter was the leading pitcher during the first part of the season and was the only member of the team named to the All-Star team. He topped the staff with eight wins when he was sidelined with an appendectomy on July 26. He finished the season with a 9–11 record and a 4.02 ERA. Dobson had a shoulder injury in May and finished with a 4–6 record and a 4.07 ERA. Krausse moved into the starting rotation after Sheldon and Talbot were traded. He pitched a two-hit, 3–0 shutout against Washington on September 18 and pitched a 1–0 shutout against California on June 19. He led the A's with a 14–9 record and a 2.98 ERA

Jim Nash had a spectacular rookie season after he was recalled from Mobile (AA) on July 1. "I left Charlotte with an airplane ticket and $8," Nash said. "I didn't realize airports were so far from downtown, like it is in Detroit. I just sat in the cab and watched the meter spin. Finally, I knew I couldn't make it so I told the driver to stop when I had 50 cents left. I spent a quarter for a bus ride to the hotel, but when I got there the team bus already had gone to the ballpark. I had to ride another bus to the ballpark and that took my last quarter." Nash defeated the Tigers 10–4 on a six-hitter in his major league debut in Tiger Stadium on July 4. He won seven consecutive games before a fly ball lost in the sun and a booted ground ball helped the Yankees get four runs in the second inning of a 7–5 New York victory August 19. Nash finished the year with five consecutive victories to end the season with a 12–1 record and a 2.06 ERA. In two other games, against Baltimore and Detroit, he left with leads that relief pitchers were unable to protect. "I guess I could have been 14–1," Nash said. "But 12–1 isn't too shabby." He led the American League pitchers in percentage (.923) and was voted the American League Rookie Pitcher of the Year.[7]

Odom was brought up from Mobile a few weeks after Nash. He won games by scores of 4–1, 3–0 and 2–0, and lost games by scores of 3–0 and 1–0 in his last five starts. His best game was a one-hit, 4–1 victory over New York on August 30. The only hit by the Yankees was a double by Roger Maris in the first inning. He had a 5–5 record with a 2.50 ERA.[8]

Aker tied a league record with 26 saves and led the major leagues in saves. The side-armed pitcher added a slider to go with his sinker and curve ball and finished with an 8–4 record and a 1.99 ERA. He replaced John Wyatt as the team's closer and was named *The Sporting News* Fireman of the Year as the best relief pitcher. Wes Stock was assigned to Vancouver as pitching coach at the start of the season but was recalled by Kansas City at mid-season and had a 2–2 record, three saves and a 2.66 ERA. Sanders appeared in 38 games and had a 3–4 record and a 3.72 ERA.

Lindblad started 14 games but spent most of the season in relief and spot starting assignments. He finished the year with a 5–10 record and a 4.17 ERA.

The team was in the cellar at the start of September but began an eight-game winning streak on September 7, highlighted by a string of 45 consecutive innings scoreless innings by the pitching staff. The A's established a major league record for most pitchers used in a shutout, using seven pitchers in the 11-inning, 1–0 victory at Cleveland on September 15. Dark started rookie Bill Edgerton. He worked the first five innings and allowed six hits before he was lifted for

Jack Aker (from the Kansas City Athletics).

a pinch-hitter. Hunter worked the next two innings before he gave way to a pinch-hitter. Sanders, the A's next hurler, worked the eighth and ninth innings. Dark used Joe Grzenda and Wes Stock when the Indians threatened in the tenth. Kansas City finally broke the scoreless tie in the eleventh. Sonny Siebert, who pitched the entire game for Cleveland, walked John Donaldson. Tim Talton's single moved Donaldson to third base. He scored on Campy Campaneris's sacrifice fly. The Indians threatened in their half of the eleventh inning, forcing Dark to use Gil Blanco and Vern Handrahan to register the final two outs. The Indians collected 10 hits off the seven A's pitchers compared to just four collected by the A's off Siebert.

Ken Harrelson began the season at first base but was traded to Washington on June 23. Cater moved to first and finished the year with an overall average of .278, fifth best in the American League. Dick Green had great range at second base and teamed with shortstop Campaneris to form a dependable double play combination. Green had nine home runs and batted .250.

Campaneris had 52 stolen bases to lead the league for the second consecutive year. He also hit 10 triples and hit an inside-the-park home run on August 2. He impressed Dark with his good moves, strong arm and quick hands. He batted .267 with five home runs and 45 runs batted in. Ed Charles platooned with Wayne Causey at third until Causey was traded. Charles regained full-time status and enjoyed one of his best years. He led the A's in hitting with a .286 average with nine home runs and 42 runs batted in.

Phil Roof became the full-time catcher. Starting May 29, he missed only three of the club's last 123 games and he helped the young pitching staff develop into one of the best in the league. "If you are looking for one person who had a lot to do with their development ... it has to be their catcher, Phil Roof," said White Sox general manager Ed Short. "Roof is the glue that held us together," Dark said. "He did a terrific job of handling the pitchers." Roof hit around .240 most of the season but faded to .209 at the end of the season. Tim Talton was called up to the A's from Mobile in July and had 18 base hits in 52 at bats, nine of which came in crucial pinch-hitting roles. The 27-year-old catcher also hit two home runs and compiled a .340 batting average.[9]

Strong armed Mike Hershberger played in right field and was second in the league with 14 outfield assists. He finished with a .253 average. Larry Stahl played left field. The 24-year-old outfielder became only the second Athletics' player to hit a Brooklyn Avenue home run with a 503-foot blast over the 40-foot screen in right field that cleared the outer wall against Boston on May 11. It was the longest home run in Kansas City history. The A's won the game 6–5 in 10 innings. (Harry Simpson was the only other

A's player to clear the Brooklyn Avenue wall.) Stahl was the only A's player to steal home. He stole home on July 17 in Kansas City.

Nossek played against left-handed pitchers and was a late inning defensive replacement. His only home run was an inside-the-park home run in the first inning against Cleveland on July 10 in Kansas City. The A's won the game 4–1. Repoz played both center field and first base. He batted just .216 for the A's but led the team with 11 home runs. Gosger played all three outfield positions but hit just .224 for the A's.

When Baltimore came to Kansas City for a three-game series on May 27, Orioles hurler Moe Drabowsky played an ingenious prank on his former teammates. Coach Bobby Hofman answered when the phone rang in the A's bullpen in the second inning. "Get [Lew] Krausse hot," the voice ordered. Hoffman thought it was Dark and ordered Krausse to warm up. Moments later the phone rang again. "Okay, sit him down." The Orioles bullpen broke out in laughter because Drabowsky made the calls. He learned how to dial the A's bullpen when he played in Kansas City.[10]

George Toma's ground crew at Municipal Stadium maintained one of the finest playing fields in the major leagues. They tried to finish the job as quickly as possible when they dragged the infield during the fifth inning and when they placed the tarpaulin on the infield when it rained. They routinely dragged the infield in less than a minute. In one game they took just 39 seconds.

The A's swept the final three-game series of the season from Detroit, knocking the Tigers out of second place in the final standings. It was a season of solid progress for the A's. The most important plus was the development of solid young pitchers. The A's not only vacated the cellar for the first time in three seasons, they climbed to seventh place and finished just six games out of first division. The A's won 74 games, a new team high. The attendance, stimulated by the emergence of the young team, climbed nearly 250,000 to a final season total of 773,929.

Dark was runner-up to Hank Bauer of Baltimore, another former Finley hire, for Manager of the Year honors. Finley rewarded Dark with a new Cadillac.[11]

26
1967: "A Menace to Baseball"

The A's sold Larry Stahl to the New York Mets on October 17, 1966, and purchased the contract of pitcher Dave Roberts in the major league draft on November 28. Roberts failed to make the roster and was returned to Pittsburgh on April 7. The A's eventually regretted that decision as Roberts had a successful career with San Diego, Houston and Detroit.

The Greater Kansas City Sports Commission sold 3,812 season tickets. Finley provided little assistance as the A's merely sent out their usual form letter to previous season ticket holders.

Finley often claimed he received just $57,255.90 in radio and television revenue in 1967, but this was not accurate. "On April 27, Station KCMO sold spots to 33 more sponsors and brought the rights up to $138,664.25," Finley said. "On June 19, I heard from them again and they added 10 more sponsors, increasing the number to 43. *The amount available to me at that time was $155,478.50.* I hope that isn't the end, but I'm afraid it might be." Hamms and General Finance sponsored the broadcasts. Guys Foods no longer served as a participating sponsor but purchased commercial time during the broadcasts.[1]

Sports Illustrated ran a feature article on the Athletics in its March 13 issue with a color picture of Jim Nash on the cover. "For the first time the A's are not subject to ridicule," it stated. "Last year opposing players, managers and general managers suddenly began respecting the Athletics, and some people have been so bold as to predict a K.C. pennant may be only two years away."

"In my first four springs here we really had nothing to build on," said Ed Charles. "Now we do. These kids want to win and make money. They've come off winning minor league teams. They know how to win. And Alvin Dark does a heck of a job handling guys, young and old."[2]

Luke Appling was appointed special assignment coach, so the A's entered spring training with three coaches: Cot Deal, Bob Hofman and Al Vincent. The A's released pitcher Wes Stock on April 11 and signed him as the A's bullpen coach and batting practice pitcher. Don Biebel resigned as director of public relations and Jay Hankins resigned as traveling secretary to become a scout with Cleveland. Carl Finley, the team's business manager, assumed the added responsibilities as the public relations director. Former American League umpire Ed Hurley was hired as an administrative assistant and traveling secretary.

Jim Nash won the home opener against Cleveland 4–3. The A's added gold batting helmets and white baseball shoes made from rare albino kangaroos to their colorful uniforms. "Nash had a big, high kick," Lew Krausee said, "and right away the hitter, Jose Cardenal, called time out and said he couldn't see the ball because of the white shoes."

"But you know," added Chuck Dobson, "we liked the novelty of the white shoes when we first got 'em. We thought we looked good in them."[3]

Phil Roof had another good season behind the plate but batted just .204 in 114 games. Ken Suarez was Roof's backup.

The infield was weakened defensively when John Donaldson replaced Dick Green at second and Danny Cater replaced Ed Charles at third. Cater opened the season at first base but was challenged by 24-year-old Ramon Webster. Webster platooned with Cater until Cater was moved to third Webster finished with a .256 batting average. He moved to the outfield when the A's reacquired Ken Harrelson from Washington on June 9. Harrelson appeared in 61 games, batting .305 with six home runs and 30 runs batted in.

Shortstop Campy Campaneris led the American League with 55 stolen bases, the third consecutive year he led the league. He tied a major league record with three triples in a 9–8 loss to Cleveland on August 29 and finished the season with batting .248. Green had problems at bat. He was replaced by Donaldson at second base and ended the season at third. Donaldson, a 23-year-old rookie, finished the season as the A's leading hitter with a .276 average.

Charles started the season at third base until he was traded to the New York Mets on May 10 for minor league outfielder Larry Elliot and $50,000 in cash. Sal Bando, a 23-year-old rookie, replaced Charles, but he struggled at the plate and Cater moved to third. Cater had trouble defensively and was replaced by Green. Cater led the club in hitting most of the season and had five singles in five trips to the plate when the A's defeated Cleveland 6–5 on August 30. His season was cut short when he was hit in the head by a pitch. It was the third time he had been hit in the head during the season and doctors recommended that he not play during the final two weeks.

Rick Monday, a 21-year-old center fielder, impressed Dark during spring training. One morning Dark put him in the batting cage and stood behind him hollering out situation plays. "Shortstop's covering second, Rick," he yelled. Monday hit the ball through short. "Second baseman's covering," he yelled. He hit the ball through the hole between first and second. "Middle," Dark said and Monday hit a line drive through the pitcher's box and into center field. Monday, the first player selected in the first-ever amateur draft, had been signed out of Arizona State for $104,000 in 1965. He made the major league roster in 1967 and finished with 14 home runs and 58 runs batted in while batting .251. He tied for the league lead with six double plays by an outfielder despite missing over 50 games because of injuries and military duty. He was named to the Topps Major League Rookie All-Star team at the end of the season.[4]

Mike Hershberger led the league's outfielders with 17 assists with his strong arm and finished with a .254 average. Jim Gosger batted .242. Joe Nossek appeared in 87 games, mostly as a defensive replacement or pinch-hitter. Roger Repoz appeared in 40 games and was batting .241 when he was traded to the California Angels on June 15 for veteran pitcher Jack Sanford and minor league outfielder Jack Warner. Rookie Reggie Jackson was another Arizona State outfielder; he was taken by the A's with the second overall pick in the 1966 amateur draft. He was added to the roster on June 9 but batted just .178 in 35 games and struck out 46 times. After the brief trial in Kansas City, Jackson returned to Birmingham and helped the team win the Southern League and Dixie Series championships.

Allan Lewis, a 25-year-old outfielder that Finley nicknamed the "Panamian Express," had minimal talent, but Finley wanted him as a designated runner. "Charlie thought it was a good promotion idea," Bando said. "But from a player's point of view it's a terrible idea. It takes good men out of close ballgames. And Allan Lewis couldn't even run that well. He had no knowledge of running the bases." He had 14 stolen bases and was caught stealing five times.[5]

Hunter, just 21 years old, was the ace of the pitching staff and pitched five shutouts. He won a pair of 1–0 games, against Washington on May 2 and against Baltimore on June 13. He ended the season with a three-hit shutout over Chicago. He lost six shutout games and the A's scored only one run in four other starts. He struck out 12 Boston batters in one game to tie a Kansas City record and broke K.C. records for innings pitched (260), shutouts (five) and strikeouts in a season (196). He finished the season with a 13–17 record and a 2.80 ERA. He pitched 4⅓ innings in the 15-

Catfish Hunter (from the Kansas City Athletics).

inning All-Star game in Anaheim. He shut out the power-laden National League team before Tony Perez hit a home run to win the game in the fifteenth inning.

Hunter, who went on to 224 wins in 500 career starts, went from a docile teenager who agreed to Finley's concocted nickname of Catfish, to a shrewd veteran who became baseball's first free agent when Finley failed to make an insurance fund payment. In between, he pitched a perfect game, won a Cy Young award and earned seven postseason victories for the Oakland A's.

Nash won 12 games and had two shutouts in 1967. One of his shutouts was a 1–0 victory over Boston on April 30. He also lost a pair of 1–0 games. He pitched a two-hit, 2–1 victory over Minnesota on May 12. He twice tied Hunter's team record with 12 strikeouts in a game and finished the year with a 12–17 record, a 3.77 ERA and 186 strikeouts.

Dobson's last three losses were all by shutout. His first major league shutout was a 2–0 victory over Cleveland. He also pitched a three-hit, 5–2 victory against Chicago during the last week of the season that helped knock the White Sox out of the pennant race. He finished with a 10–10 record and a 3.68 ERA,

Krausse opened the season losing four games in a row. He won two straight and then lost his next three starts. Krausse had a 2–7 record and the A's had not scored more than one run in any of the seven games he lost. He was placed in the bullpen during the first week in August to change his luck. He appeared in 21 games, gave up runs in only five of the games, and had five saves and three wins. He finished the season with a 7–17 record and a 4.28 ERA. Blue Moon Odom opened the season in Kansas City but had control problems and finished with a 3–8 record and a 5.02 ERA.

Jack Aker had a 3–8 record and 10 saves with a 4.30 ERA. He entered a game in Boston in the seventh inning on April 29 with Boston leading 9–8. The A's tied the game and it went into extra innings. Aker pitched 8⅓ innings, his longest stint in the major leagues, and allowed only two runs. Both runs came in the fifteenth inning and Boston won the game 11–10.

Paul Lindblad was a spot starter and relief pitcher. He had a three-hit shutout over Chicago on July 16, the only complete game in his career. He added five saves to his 5–8 record and 3.57 ERA.

Tony Pierce, a 21-year-old southpaw, worked primarily out of the bullpen but finished the year with four impressive starts. He lost games by scores of 1–0, 2–1 and 3–2. In his other start he allowed only two runs in seven innings before leaving for a pinch-hitter. He finished with a 3–4 record and a 3.03 ERA. Veteran Diego Segui lost only one game after June 17. He appeared in 36 games and had a 3–4 record. Jack Sanford appeared in just 10 games before the A's released him on August 15th.

The A's and Detroit set a record for the longest double header ever played on June 17. It took nine hours and five minutes to complete. Detroit won a rain-delayed first game 7–6. The second game went 19 innings before Dave Duncan hit a home run to give Kansas City a 6–5 victory.

The A's had an 18–18 record on May 25 and were just three games under .500 with a 31–34 record on June 19. The A's lost five straight and nine of their last 10 games before the All-Star break to drop into last place with a 35–49 record. There were rumors Dark would resign, the players grumbled over travel arrangements (Finley used commercial flights instead of charter flights to save $50,000 a year) and legal entanglements from a paternity suit prevented Campy Campaneris from playing any games in California. "The trouble with ... committing yourself to a youth movement is growing pains," Dark explained "Young players require great patience. We had a lot of growing pains in 1967. The team languished in the second division.... I have to say this for Charlie Finley. He never once interfered with my field managing those two years."[6]

Pitching coach Cot Deal resigned during the All-Star break for personal reasons. "[Dark] treated me royally," he said. "And I enjoyed working with him. I enjoyed my experience in Kansas City and I want to thank all the people who treated me so kindly." Wes Stock replaced Deal as pitching coach.[7]

Losses increased and some players had drinking problems. Detroit pounded Krausse 11–1 in the first game of a double header in Kansas City on June 6. He stopped for a drink before going to his room at the Bellerive Hotel. "I just got wasted," Krausse recalled. "I was discouraged, depressed, everything ... so I just raised the window and got my gun, an old police

.38 special an uncle had given me. I stuck the pistol out the window and shot it off twice, just maybe to get something out of my system — maybe hearing the noise or whatever. Then I put the window down and went to sleep."[8]

Finley called Krausse at seven the next morning and asked whether he shot a gun. Krausse admitted he had and Finley told him to take the gun, go to the train station and put it in a storage locker, then call him when he got back. "I thought I'd killed somebody," Krausse recalled. "I put on a raincoat so I can carry the gun under it and it's about a hundred degrees outside. I go to the train station, put the gun in a little locker and then come back to the Bellerive. And there's all kinds of detectives in my room.... They had different kinds of measuring devices—angle type things—trying to check the trajectory of a bullet.... The police told me there were reports from the room next door that gunfire had come last night from my room. They said the shots went into an office building, the Phillips Petroleum Building, across the way but that no one was injured.... When the police left, I called Finley back.... All he said was, 'This is it. This is your last chance.' I don't know how he found out about it, probably from somebody in the hotel. When he talks about the shooting, he says I came close to hitting a cleaning woman." Police tests indicated one of the bullets might have come from Krausse's room and Finley placed him on probation.[9]

The A's lost an extra-inning fame to Boston on August 3 and returned to Kansas City on TWA flight 85 with stops in Baltimore and St. Louis. "The whole back of the plane was ours almost because there were hardly any regular passengers," Krausse recalled. " I remember there was a crew change in, I guess, Baltimore. And the new crew of stewardesses were based in Kansas City. Ken Harrelson and I and a couple of other players who were single knew these girls. And when the girls got on they asked if we wanted drinks. We said we did, but that we'd rather not pay for them. So they just handed us a tray of drinks and everybody had a couple."

"I was sitting in the back with Krausse and Lindblad," Aker said. "I remember that the stewardesses parked the little drink cart in the aisle between our seats and told us we could have as many as we wanted, which they shouldn't have done, because two or three of us got carried away. We were kidding amongst ourselves and telling stories and there were probably some swear words that were heard farther up the plane by the regular passengers. But other than that, I didn't see anything that was out of the way."[10]

Dark sat in the front of the plane with his coaches and traveling secretary Ed Hurley. Monte Moore walked to the front of the plane to complain to Dark and he went back to see what was happening. "As soon as I saw their faces I suspected they were up to something," Dark recalled. "They were like kids with innocent looks, staring straight ahead." Dark asked the flight attendant is she had any trouble with the players and she answered, "Oh no, they're a great bunch of guys." He returned to his seat. Harrelson said there was "no yelling back and forth, no monkeying around with the stewardesses, no unsolicited conversations with the passengers" during the trip. It was a routine flight with no evidence of drunkenness or bad behavior. The plane landed in Kansas City around 10:30.[11]

The team traveled to Chicago, Washington and Baltimore two weeks later. Finley called Dark when the team arrived in Washington on August 18. "I want you to fine Lew Krausse $500 and suspend him," Finley demanded. "Because he was drunk getting off the plane after the last road trip and used bad language around a woman passenger." He said he had been informed about the players' boisterous behavior on the flight in which players had gotten drunk. Krausse used deplorable language that was overheard by a woman with a small child, stewardesses had been abused and other passengers had been bothered. "We thought [Moore] was involved," said Krausse. "He was the guy who opened his mouth and told the whole story — who was drinking, who wasn't." Dark told Finley he could not support the fine and suspension because Harrelson was always in the middle of that kind of thing and he told him "it didn't happen." [12]

"My phone rings at eight in the morning there in Washington," Krausse said. "Finley ... he said, 'I'm fining you $500 for carrying on and drinking on that flight.' And seriously, I had to wait and think what flight it was.... Finley and I are screaming and hollering at one another and I'm denying everything. And I slammed down the phone on him. I went into the bathroom to get of drink of water and tried to wake up and came back into the bedroom where the phone was ringing again. Finley. He says, 'As of today, you're suspended indefinitely without pay. You're to go directly to Kansas City.' And this time, he hung up on me."[13]

Finley called Hurley and dictated a statement that was placed on the clubhouse bulletin board. "Effective immediately and for the balance of the season, all alcoholic drinks will no longer be served on commercial airlines to members of the Kansas City Athletics," it said. "The Kansas City Athletics will no longer tolerate the shenanigans of a very few individuals who obviously do not appreciate the privilege of playing in the major leagues and being treated like gentlemen. The attitude, actions and words of some of you have been deplorable. As a member of Organized Baseball, you have certain responsibilities and obligations to yourself, your family, your club and most important of all — the fans. To the vast majority of you who have always conducted yourselves as gentlemen on and off the playing field, I sincerely regret the necessity of this action."[14]

The players were upset because it insinuated that all 25 players had a drunken brawl on the plane. They asked player representative Jack Aker to call Finley and request the statement be kept from the press until they could discuss the situation with him, but he had already released the story to the AP and UPI and it was printed in the early editions of the next day's sports pages. The players met in various hotel rooms and decided to draft a statement to publicly reply to Finley. Aker sat in the bullpen before the next game on Saturday afternoon and made a rough draft on a small piece of paper. Aker, Harrelson and a couple of other players went to Dark's room after the game to tell him they might release a statement. "All right," Dark replied, "But it might get you in trouble. Before you do let me see the final draft."[15]

Finley anticipated trouble and flew to Washington. After he arrived at 7 P.M., he summoned Dark to his suite at the Shoreham Hotel. Finley asked for Dark's support and wanted Dark to tell the players that Finley's action against Krausse was correct. Dark refused to support him. "Alvin, I'm going to have to let you go," Finley said. "I want my manager to back me on this and you're not doing it."

"We talked and talked," Dark said. "And I found myself telling him what a terrific bunch of boys he had, that with them and the ones he had coming up—Reggie Jackson, Sal Bando, Joe Rudi—he would win a pennant for sure, and it wouldn't take long, maybe as early as 1971. We talked for two and a half hours."

"How'd you like to manage two more years?" Finley asked.

"Fine, Charlie, but you just fired me," Dark answered. "You going to hire me back?"

"How about two more years? Finley said. "With a raise."[16]

Finley called in Ed Lopat, Ed Hurley, Monte Moore, Wes Stock and Bob Hofman. They talked about the future of the club until *Kansas City Star* reporter Paul O'Boynick knocked on the door. He had been waiting for Finley in the lobby and was pressed by a deadline. "Do you have any comment on the players' statement?" he asked. Finley did not know what O'Boynick was talking about so the reporter explained how the players issued a statement. He read it to Finley: "In response to Charles O. Finley's statement of August 18, we, the players of the Kansas City Athletics, feel that an unjust amount of pressure has been brought to bear on several members of the club who had no part whatsoever in the so-called incident on the recent plane trip from Boston to Kansas City. The overwhelming opinion of the players is that the entire matter was blown out of proportion. Mr. Finley's policy of using certain unauthorized personnel in his organization as go-betweens has led to similar misunderstandings in the past and has tended to undermine the morale of the club. We players feel that if Mr. Finley would give his fine coaching staff and excellent manager the authority they deserve, these problems would not exist."[17]

Finley turned to Dark and asked: "Did you know about this?"

"About what?" Dark asked. He had not seen the final draft and thought the players would show it to him before they released it. Finley assumed this meant Dark denied any knowledge about the statement.

"Get Jack Aker," Finley ordered. Aker was not in his room because he was visiting a friend in Baltimore and broke the midnight curfew. He returned at 2:30 A.M. and walked into Finley's suite. Finley fined him $200 for breaking curfew and demanded an immediate retraction of the players' statement. Aker refused because he acted as the players' representative and had to follow their unanimous vote.

"Did Alvin see the statement?" Finley asked.

"Yeah," Aker answered.

"You knew they were working on this?" Finley asked.

"Yes I did," answered Dark.

Finley accused Dark of disloyalty and asked Dark why he had not told him about the statement. Dark said Finley had not asked. The meeting ended at 5 A.M. Finley left the suite saying he was going out for coffee and Dark returned to his room.

Thirty minutes later Finley called Dark. "Alvin," he said. "I have decided to make a change." Luke Appling would manage for the remainder of the season. Finley intended to fire Dark when he flew to Washington because Appling had checked into the hotel at the same time Finley did.[18]

"I released Alvin Dark as manager because I am convinced he had lost control of his ball players," Finley stated in the press release. "During my meetings with Dark and my coaching staff from Saturday at 7 P.M. until 4:30 A.M. on Sunday, Dark stated several times that the contents of the statement made by the ballplayers had come as a complete surprise to him. He said that had the player representative consulted him or the players he would have made every effort to prevent it because it had no basis in fact. However, when we located player representative Jack Aker at 1:30 A.M. in Baltimore, and he arrived at our meeting at 2:30 A.M., he stated in the presence of Dark and the coaching staff that Dark not only knew of the statement but also had approved it. In view of this and other developments it is obvious to me that Dark was no longer operating in the best interests of the Kansas City ballplayers or owner."[19]

The players talked about what they could do on the bus trip to the stadium. The game was delayed by rain and finally postponed. Dark came in to say goodbye as the players sat in the clubhouse. "I'm not upset about being fired," he told his players. "That's part of baseball. I hate to leave you kids—good luck. I really wish I could have stuck around to see you guys win." The players issued a second statement expressing "deep personal loss" over Dark's dismissal. They also discussed the possibility of striking.[20]

"I have believed and will always believe that management difficulties should remain within the confines of a ballclub but when the integrity of my ballplayers, whom I greatly admire, is at stake, I must set the record straight," said Dark responding to Finley's press release. "I want to point out that I disagreed with Mr. Finley about the Krausse fine. This was a case of singling out one ballplayer and making him look bad. It was also a reflection on the entire team.... At no time did I make the remark attributed to me by Mr. Finley that the players' statement of August 19 had no basis in fact. When I went to Mr. Finley's room at 7 P.M. Saturday, he told me he was going to fire me. We discussed the team at length and later he offered me a two-year contract. We were discussing the contract when Paul O'Boynick came to the room and asked Mr. Finley if he had seen the players' statement. I knew the players were drafting a statement. They did it with my approval but I did not instigate it. They were making revisions in the statement Saturday. I had not seen the final draft and I thought they were not going to release it until Sunday. When Paul showed the statement to Mr. Finley and me, I said, 'Paul, I wish you had given me this at 6:30.' I had expected the players to go over it again Sunday and possibly temper it a little. This may have given Mr. Finley the impression I did not know of the statement. I did know of it, but I had not seen the final draft. I want to say that I think the actions of the players is the most courageous thing I have ever seen. I will never forget the way they have stood up for me."[21]

The players returned to the hotel after the rain out. "I could hardly talk and when a writer came to me all I could think of was what Finley had done, not only to Alvin, but to the whole club," Ken Harrelson said. "Because of something that never happened on an airplane trip nearly three weeks before, he had made a fool of himself, a scapegoat of Krausse, alleged drunks out of all of us, and an apparently ineffectual manager out of Dark. 'The only thing I know,' I said, 'is that Charlie Finley's actions of the last few days have been bad for baseball. I think they have been detrimental to the game.'"

A reporter from a Washington newspaper misquoted Harrelson as saying, "Charlie Finley is a menace to baseball." Later that evening as Harrelson and his roommate Mike Hershberger rested on their beds and watched television they heard a sports announcer report Harrelson called Finley a menace to baseball. Several players rushed to the room and felt it was funny; Harrelson did not. He did not use the word menace and he wondered what Finley would do.[22]

Harrelson left instructions with the hotel operator that no calls whatsoever were to be put through to his room. The phone rang at 9 A.M. "Kenny, this is Charlie. Did you make those statements in the papers?" Finley asked.

"I said everything except you were a menace," Harrelson answered. "What I actually said to the reporter was that I thought your actions of the last few days were bad for baseball."

"I've been good to you.... I want you to write a public retraction and give it to the papers," Finley said.

"Charlie, I'll be glad to retract the word 'menace,' but I won't retract anything else."

Finley threatened to suspend or release him. He hung up but called back less than a half an hour later and said: "You have your unconditional release from the Kansas City Athletics. As of this moment, you are no longer a member of the Kansas City Athletics." The Athletics could have received about $50,000 if he was sold to another club in a waiver transaction but Finley said, "It would have been blood money." He added, "I'd rather lose the $50,000 than take money like that."[23]

Harrelson said he would have remained with the Athletics if Finley called him back that morning and told him he'd changed his mind. He was afraid he would be blacklisted, but as soon as the news of his free agent status was announced the Twins, Tigers, White Sox and Red Sox contacted him and began bidding for his services. Chicago called first and Harrelson asked for $50,000. Paul Richards of Atlanta offered $100,000 and Harrelson asked for $125,000. They settled on $112,000.[24]

Finley realized he made a mistake and asked Appling to contact Harrelson. Appling invited him to his office. "Hawk, sit down," he said, "Charlie didn't mean to fire you. You know how he is—he lost his head this morning. He wants you back. I want you back. We all want you back."

"If Charlie wanted me back, he'd have called and asked me," Harrelson replied. "And maybe I'd have gone back. But instead of calling me, he called the commissioner's office and put me on the irrevocable waiver list. Luke, there's no way now that I'm coming back to play for this man. I don't care what he might offer me—I wouldn't take it. I will not play for Charlie Finley."

Ken Harrelson (from the Kansas City Athletics).

Appling shrugged and said, "Well, if that's the way you feel, I guess there isn't anything anyone can do." The Red Sox offered him an estimated $75,000 signing bonus and a salary package estimated at $75,000 for the remainder of the 1967 season and for the 1968 season. Richards could not match the offer. Harrelson joined the Red Sox with five weeks remaining in the season and helped them win the pennant.[25]

The A's players wanted a hearing with baseball commissioner William Eckert and threatened to strike. They met before their next game against Baltimore and unanimously voted to stand by their statement. Finley flew to Baltimore to meet with the players after the game and removed Krausse's suspension the following day. Finley claimed Krausse agreed that he deserved the fine and Finley was justified for taking the action he did. Eckert called a hearing for September 28 in New York City. After Eckhart scheduled the hearing, some players complained they were being "intimidated and coerced" by Finley. They claimed he threatened to publicly reveal unflattering episodes from their private lives. Hunter said a "bunch of guys we'd never seen before seemed to be following us players around everywhere we went." He did not have any proof they were private detectives "but they sure acted like it."[26]

The Major League Players Association filed a charge of unfair practices with the National Labor Relations Board on September 5 because of Finley's coercion. Eckert did not want to see the NLRB involved, so he moved up the hearing to September 11 at 10 A.M. The parties met in his office 14 hours and 40 minutes before a compromise was reached. Finley agreed to provide a written statement assuring he would not coerce or intimidate his employees in their right to obtain a hearing and that there would be no discrimination against any of his employees as a result of this dispute. The meeting before the NLRB was not held because the players voted 14–9 to withdraw the charge. Krausse wanted his case heard by the commissioner on an individual basis and Finley agreed as part of the settlement. The hearing was scheduled for September 28th, but Krausse later withdrew his request, possibly because he was vulnerable because his father was still a scout for the team. Even though he promised not to retaliate, Aker's salary was cut 10 percent for the 1968 season. He said, "Finley offered no explanation for the cut." Finley traded away some of the players that opposed him.[27]

The White Sox played a twi-night double header in Kansas City on September 27. If the Sox swept the doubleheader they would move into first place a half-game ahead of Boston and Minnesota and would finish the season playing the seventh-place Senators in Chicago. The Sox arrived at Municipal Stadium with their ace pitchers, Gary Peters and Joel Horlen, ready to pitch. Peters lasted only 5⅔ innings in the opener and Horlen lost the second game. The Sox collected only seven hits off Dobson and Hunter in the double header. At the end of the second game the Sox were in fourth place, 1½ games back with only three games left to play.

Appling managed the team to a 10–29 record in the final weeks of the season. During one critical point in a meaningless game in September 1967 Appling wasn't even in the dugout. "He'd gone upstairs for another sandwich," said a player. The A's finished in last place, winning just 62 games and losing 99, nine and a half games behind the ninth-place Yankees. Attendance plunged during the final month of the season but the A's still drew a respectable 726,639 fans. Appling realized there was little chance he would be retained. "Whatever Mr. Finley decides will be all right with me," he said. Appling was fired shortly after the season ended.[28]

Ed Lopat resigned as administrative assistant on October 15th. "After long and serious considerations I have decided to resign my position as administrative assistant with the Kansas City Athletics with the request the resignation take place immediately," he said. "This has not been a snap decision nor has it been an easy one to make. Yet I sincerely feel I have done the right thing for my family, myself and the Athletics since I have not always been in complete agreement with Mr. Finley and his policies ... the action which I am taking is in the best interests of all concerned." He informed Finley about his resignation earlier in the day and said their parting was amicable "Mr. Lopat's successor was selected two weeks ago," Finley said when asked to comment on the resignation, "and the announcement will be made in a few days." Finley hired Joe DiMaggio after the team moved to Oakland.[29]

Ed Robinson, administrative assistant in charge of the minor leagues,

was fired and joined the Atlanta Braves. Ed Hurley was not retained as traveling secretary. Monte Moore accepted a position with the Athletics in Oakland in a public relations capacity and as announcer, but Lynn Faris was not retained because he had been critical of Finley on the radio during the final weeks of the season.

Appling, who played with the Chicago White Sox from 1930 until 1951, was one of the most popular players to ever wear a White Sox uniform. He served as a minor league manager from 1951 through 1955 and again in 1959 and 1962. He coached for Detroit in 1960 up to August 8, when he traded jobs with Jo-Jo White of the Cleveland Indians. Appling and White were part of the famous Joe Gordon–Jimmie Dykes trade when Detroit and Cleveland traded managers. Appling coached in Cleveland for the remainder of the 1960 season and also during the 1961 season. He coached for Baltimore in 1963.

He coached for Kansas City from 1964 through 1966 and did special assignment work for the A's following the 1966 season. He took over the A's amid controversy and, other than their sweep of the White Sox to keep Chicago from the pennant, the A's showed little life, going 10–29 in his only major league managerial stint.

LUKE APPLING'S MANAGERIAL RECORD

Year	Club	League	Won	Lost	Position
1951	Memphis	AA	79	75	4
1952	Memphis	AA	81	74	4
1953	Memphis	AA	87	67	1
1954	Richmond	AAA	60	94	7
1955	Richmond	AAA	58	95	8
1959	Memphis	AA	76	77	4
1962	Indianapolis	AAA	89	58	1
1967	Kansas City	Major	10	29	10

1967 team — Front row: Campaneris, Suarez, Hershberger, Stock (coach), Appling (manager), Vincent (coach), Webster, Donaldson, Pierce, Lindblad. Middle row: Hurley (traveling secretary), Odom, Nossek, Talton, Aker, Kubiak, Krausse, Segui, Jones (trainer). Back row: Zych (equipment manager), Hunter, Rodriguez, Cater, Stafford, Monday, Nash, Roof, Green, Gosger, Sigloch (clubhouse attendant). Seated in front: Popham (batboy). (From the Kansas City Athletics.)

27

"Luckiest City Since Hiroshima"

Plans for a multi-purpose domed stadium for the A's and the Chiefs were unveiled in 1966. Governor Warren E. Hearnes appointed people to the newly formed Jackson County Sports Complex Authority in September. They determined a domed multi-purpose stadium in downtown Kansas City was impractical because of the high daily operating costs and the cost of acquiring land. They released a 12-page report to the public on January 5, 1967, recommending that twin stadiums should be built in eastern Kansas City because it was "unwise to recommend housing for two major league franchises in the same facility." The total cost of both stadiums was estimated to be $54 million:

COST ESTIMATES FOR STADIUM COMPLEX IN KANSAS CITY (1967)

50,000-seat baseball stadium	$20,000,000
75,000 football stadium with a roof	
(cost without a roof $15 million)	$20,000,000
Cost of land	$2,005,000
Site improvement and development	$10,080,000
Parking for 18,750 autos	$2,000,000
	$54,000,000

The concept for twin stadiums originated with Lamar Hunt and Jack Steadman of the Kansas City Chiefs after Finley refused to discuss the plans for a multi-purpose stadium. The Chiefs suggested twin stadiums to break the stalemate. The football stadium could be built first and a baseball stadium could be added later. Both stadiums would be tailored to the exact specifications needed by the teams. The baseball stadium would seat 45,000 but could be expanded to seat 57,000. The football stadium would seat 75,000. The complex would be part of a $102 million bond package that would be presented to Jackson country taxpayers on June 27. Mayor Ilus Davis, authority chairman Dutton Brookfield and Bishop G. Leslie DeLapp, a member of the authority, tried to contact Finley. He did not respond.[1]

Various people expressed interest in purchasing the A's to assure the team would remain in Kansas City. Ewing Kauffman, head of Marion Laboratories, called Ernie Mehl on August 19, 1966. "About this Finley situation," he said. "I have never been to a baseball game and I never played as a boy, but I would like to see about buying the ballclub." Cleveland Indians president Gabe Paul set up a three-way phone conversation. "Unless he's [Kauffman] willing to start the discussion at $25 million, he might as well not even come up to see me," Finley said. Kauffman told Finley that he would like to see the books so he could get an idea what was involved in owning a major league team. "Which set of books do you want to see?" Finley asked. That ended the conversation and Finley denied rumors that the A's would be sold to a local group headed by Kauffman.[2]

Oakland completed its $30 million, 50,000-seat stadium in mid–1966. Finley looked at the construction site as the stadium neared completion and returned to watch the Oakland Raiders football team play the Kansas City Chiefs before a crowd of 50,746 on September 18, 1966, the first game played in the stadium.[3]

On May 7, 1967, the *New York Daily News* and *New York Times* reported that Finley wanted to move the A's to Oakland. The *Daily News* article accused Kansas City of being indifferent to the fate of the A's, while the *Times* reported there was a mutual lack of interest shown by both Finley and the sports authority. Finley refused to comment. Kansas City officials complained the articles were not accurate because Kansas City had done everything possible to support the team. The Greater Kansas City Sports Commission sold 4,100 season tickets in 1966 and 3,800 in 1967. The said "lack of interest" was one-sided. Joe McGuff sent a well-documented letter to American League owners accusing Finley of deliberately neglecting to promote the A's in order to depress attendance and move the team. He complained that Finley had not acted in good faith and cited the numerous attempts to move the team, the lack of cooperation with the season ticket sales and his "nonattempt" to sell radio and television rights.[4]

McGuff and Ernie Mehl divided the names of the team owners and spoke to them about Kansas City and its support of major league baseball. "Knowing Charlie's lease ran out after the '67 season we knew we could be facing a crisis," recalled McGuff. "We knew we had certain clubs on our side. Lee McPhail, who had once been in Kansas City as the general manager of the minor league Blues, was in Baltimore. George Selkirk, who had been a manager with the Blues and later an assistant general manager with the A's, was in Washington. And we had some ties with the Yankees and Angels. But Ernie felt we needed to enlist other people as we traveled that summer. He became friendly with Arthur Allyn, who owned the White Sox. I decided I would zero in on Tom Yawkey, the owner of the Red Sox.... Every time we went to Boston I made it a point to go by and see Yawkey.... He had a very strong opinion that an owner should be able to do what he wanted with his ballclub. I told him I agreed with that — if the owner was on the level, if he was trying to operate a good ball club. But in Kansas City we had an owner who was trying to sabotage the club in order to get it out of town. Yawkey understood that. The trouble was, Charlie was feeding stuff to the owners all the time, so it was important for us to get our side of the story out there."[5]

Mayor Davis and Brookfield still attempted to contact Finley. Although the current lease expired at the end of the 1967 season, Finley held two four-year options. They indicated the city would be happy to work out an attractive lease if Finley wanted to exercise his options to use the present stadium. They felt it was unlikely an owner would prefer an old stadium instead of the new one. Some people wanted to postpone the vote on the bond issue until the baseball situation was resolved, but supporters felt approval would be a powerful argument to retain major league baseball. County officials and the complex authority pledged the baseball stadium would not be built without a long-term commitment from a major league team.[6]

Finley broke his silence on May 17, 1967. "I have continuously considered it to be unethical and unfair for me to express my opinion on this bond issue," he said. Jackson County voters approved the $43 million bond issue for the complex in the June 27 election. The sports complex, one of seven proposals on the ballot, passed 61,872 to 27,878. It received 68.9 percent of the vote, exceeding the two-thirds majority necessary for passage. "I have no comment whatsoever," Finley said after the election.[7]

Finley met with members of the Jackson County Sports Complex Authority in Chicago on July 18. "As of the moment, I don't know what I want to do," he said but added he would not seek permission to move the team when the owners met in Chicago on August 2. Finley stated the two key factors influencing his final decision would be the type of lease offered and some assurance that he would receive a better radio and television contract in Kansas City. "We came away feeling there was a genuine spirit of cooperation on Mr. Finley's part," said Brookfield. "We hope to come back with a more concrete proposal. I must say he has some very good reasons to be critical of the Kansas City situation. We hope these problems can be remedied.... The instability of our situation affected radio and television revenues." Finley met with the group two weeks later. "I did not present any proposal," he said. "I requested they make me a proposal in writing ... and I will give it consideration. It will be around the first of October before I know what I want to do. If I decide to move, I will request permission of the American League at that time. Through last year my losses in Kansas City were $4,283,000. The average attendance was 670,000, turnstile count."[8]

Brookfield sent Finley a lease proposal for the new stadium in August. It was for 20 years, with three five-year options. The Authority would receive 7 percent of net revenues from baseball ticket sales and 10 percent of net revenues from concessions. He stated the proposal was similar to the proposal made to the Kansas City Chiefs for the use of the football stadium at the new complex. Mayor Davis stated that if the A's owner wanted to enter into a lease with the Jackson County sports complex for the use of the planned stadium, "The city would negotiate for an interim lease which would cover him in Kansas City at the Municipal Stadium during the time the new stadium is under construction."[9]

Richard J. Stern, president of Stern Brothers & Company investment bankers in Kansas City, announced that his organization wanted to purchase the A's. "We have investigated in detail the possibility of purchasing the A's and have been working with the members of the sports complex authority and the Greater Kansas City Sports commission," he said. "We would hope to have a broad-based ownership of the club in Kansas City. The purpose of this would be to make sure that the Athletics remain permanently in Kansas City." He had not met with Finley and did not reveal the amount he would offer, but he emphasized that it would be substantial.[10]

Brookfield said two other Kansas City parties expressed interest in purchasing the team. He refused to identify the potential owners, but it is assumed one was Ewing Kauffman and the other was a group headed by Alex Barket. Kaufman expressed an interest in buying the team the previous summer and Barket tried to purchase the team in 1964. Stern and Barket attended the league meeting when the A's were permitted to move to Oakland in October. They came with offers in case Finley was forced sell the team or the team was forced to remain in Kansas City and Finley wanted to sell the team. The Stern and Barket groups and Ewing Kauffman became the three leading candidates when Kansas City was granted an expansion franchise. The new team was eventually awarded to Kauffman.[11]

Finley visited Oakland, Seattle, Milwaukee and New Orleans during the season as possible sites for his team. He quickly eliminated New Orleans. The city planned to build a $65 million domed stadium (Superdome) that would seat 57,000 for baseball, but it would not be completed until 1972. The lack of a suitable playing facility in the interim made a move to New Orleans impractical.

The Sporting News reported that Finley wanted to move to Milwaukee. He reportedly met with Milwaukee County executive John Doyne and was offered a favorable lease to use Milwaukee County Stadium. The team would pay no rent during the first year unless attendance exceeded 900,000. The payment point would be 750,000 in the second year and it would decrease on a sliding scale over the remainder of the lease. Finley would get all the concession profit, but the county would keep the parking receipts. Schlitz Brewing Company would help finance the move by offering Finley $500,000 for broadcasting rights. Finley needed seven votes from the American League owners to approve a transfer. The Angels, White Sox, Indians and Twins reportedly would approve a move to Milwaukee. The Yankees, Tigers and Senators would vote no. The Red Sox and Orioles held the pivotal votes because both teams would have to vote for the move. Finley placed a value of $8 million on the team and was willing to sell 49 percent of his stock. Milwaukee had bad experiences with absentee owners after losing the Braves following the 1965 season and the Milwaukee group wanted to buy 51 percent, leaving Finley as a minority stockholder. The negotiations ended when Finley refused to sell the majority ownership.[12]

Oakland officials contacted Finley and offered to lease Oakland Coliseum to the team for $125,000 a year or 5 percent of the gate up to an attendance of 1,450,000. He would also receive 27 cents of every dollar from parking revenue and 25 percent of the concession revenue. They also pledged radio and television income over $1 million a season, compared to $155,000 Finley received in Kansas City and $500,000 reportedly promised by Schlitz in Milwaukee. "I'm very much impressed," Finley said.[13]

Seattle officials also contacted Finley. The Seattle metropolitan area had 1.4 million people and a large radio and television network could be established because it would be the only major league team in the Pacific Northwest. Seattle did not have a suitable stadium. Voters failed to pass a bond issue for a new stadium in 1960 and another stadium bond issue received a bare majority of 52 percent of the vote in 1966 (it needed 60 percent). A $40 million bond issue for construction of a domed stadium was scheduled for February 1968 and city officials were confident it would pass. Seattle mayor J.D. Braman and Washington governor Dan Evans made verbal commitments to Finley to spend between $1.5 and $2 mil-

27—"Luckiest City Since Hiroshima"

lion to increase the capacity of Sicks Stadium from 12,000 to 25,000 seats as an interim facility. They also discussed the possibility of turning the job of enlarging the stadium over to Finley. Finley visited Seattle on August 1. "I have known for a long time that the Seattle area would be a great area for major league baseball," he said.[14]

Finley met with the Seattle city officials and the board of King County commissioners on August 7. He called Seattle "the best place I have seen" and told them that he planned to request permission to move the team in October. Finley and Mayor Braman discussed possible playing sites and reached an informal agreement to enlarge Sicks Stadium to 25,000 seats. "I'm optimistic over my league's thinking if I have to leave Kansas City, but I cannot make predictions," Finley said.

"Seattle and the northwest territory is the prime territory," said one owner, "and the league that wins it really will have something to shout about.... The league has said 'no' to Charles so many times that I don't see how we can turn him down again. We'd much rather have him move to Seattle than Oakland."[15]

Finley sent a telegram to Kansas City manager Carleton F. Sharpe. "Pursuant to paragraph four of our lease dated February 28, 1964; this is to advise you that it is our present intention not to exercise our option to renew the lease on Municipal Stadium," Finley wrote. Finley lost his claim to $50,000 for stadium improvements when he did not renew. He had recaptured $250,000 of the $300,000 in stadium improvements during the four years of the lease and would have recaptured the remainder during the renewal options.[16]

Joe Buzas, owner of class AA franchises in Knoxville, Tennessee, and Pittsfield, Massachusetts, wired Finley on August 22 and offered to buy the Athletics for $7 million and keep the team in Kansas City. He was part of a syndicate that included former Boston Red Sox star Ted Williams. If Finley accepted their offer, Buzas said he would become general manager and Williams would become field manager.[17]

Joe Cronin announced that a league meeting would be held following the World Series in October. He did not reveal the specific purpose, but the United Press International reported Finley wanted the meeting to consider his application to move the team. Dave Cohn, vice chairman of the State Stadium Commission in Washington said Finley asked for permission to move the A's to Seattle and Governor Evans, Mayor Braman, and senators Warren Magnuson and Henry M. Jackson would attend the October meeting. Finley hired the firm of Booz, Allen and Hamilton to survey the Kansas City, Seattle and Oakland territories to determine their value and potential as major league markets. The report would be ready for study by league owners after October 1st. Kansas City hired the Midwest Research Institute to make a market survey of Kansas City that they would present to the American League meeting to offset Finley's survey.[18]

Mayor Davis received a letter from Alexander H. Hadden, an attorney representing the American League, inviting Davis and other city officials to the league meeting on October 18 in Chicago to "discuss an application which is expected to be filed shortly, to transfer the Kansas City Athletics to another location effective for the 1968 championship season." The American League also invited Senator Symington and Dutton Brookfield. Members of the sports committee and councilmen John Maguire, Vic Swyden and Sal Capra would accompany them. Representatives from the Richard Stern group and the Alex Barket group would also attend in case Finley would be forced to stay in Kansas City and wanted to sell.[19]

There was increasing probability the American League would expand to 12 teams to solve the Kansas City problem. White Sox owner Arthur Allyn contacted Mehl and indicated that if Kansas City interests permitted Finley to move the Athletics, Kansas City would be guaranteed an expansion team by 1970. Allyn said he had seven expansion votes lined up in his pocket. Mehl said he had no authority to speak for Kansas City interests but would let them know about Allyn's proposal. Two groups emerged in Kansas City. The hawks represented city hall and were led by Davis and councilman John Maguire. They wanted to keep the Athletics and did not want an expansion team. Senator Stuart Symington was willing to apply congressional pressure, if necessary. The doves were led by Earl Smith and represented the business community. There were willing to work out a compromise to keep baseball in Kansas City, whether it meant the city would immediately be granted an expansion franchise or promised an expansion team at an undetermined future date.[20]

Finley sent a letter to city manager Carleton Sharpe on September 28 formally stating that he did not plan to return to Kansas City. "Thank you for your letter of September 18, 1967 expressing an interest in discussing with me the advantages of staying in Kansas City," he wrote. "During recent years I have given a great deal of consideration to the question of what action should be taken with respect to our franchise upon the expiration of our present lease of Municipal Stadium. As you know, I have had many discussions with you and other representatives of Kansas City over the years. More recently I have sought and obtained expert advice as to what course of action would best serve the interest of the American League as well as the interest of the Athletics. I sincerely believe that consideration has been given to all significant aspects of the experiences of the Athletics in Kansas City. Based on that consideration and that advice I have decided to take the steps necessary to transfer the Athletics' franchise to another city."[21]

Finley formally announced his plans to move the Athletics to Oakland on October 11. "I have informed the other owners in the league of my intentions," he said. "I based my choice of Oakland on four points: the Oakland–Alameda County Coliseum sports complex provides the finest facilities for all-round sports in the world, the climate in the area is very ideal for baseball and second to none, the population growth in the area is the fastest of any major league area in either league, and the enthusiasm for sports in the area is overwhelming."[22] It was unlikely the American League would leave Kansas City without baseball. The league had three options:

1. It could force the Athletics to remain in Kansas City. This appealed to the hawks representing city hall, but this would not solve the problem because Finley would still own the team. The league could not force him to sell, he would probably sue the league and he would not sign a long-term lease, making it impossible to start construction on the new stadium.

2. Local ownership could buy the team from Finley for a fair price. In turn, Finley would be granted an expansion franchise in Oakland. Kansas City representatives who publicly preferred the first alternative actually hoped for this solution. Expansion was seen as inevitable and Kansas City preferred to keep the A's rather than obtain an expansion team. This would not appeal to Finley and precedent was on his side because Calvin Griffith moved the Washington Senators to Minnesota in 1961 and Washington was given the expansion team.

3. Finley could move the A's to Oakland, and Kansas City would be assured of receiving an expansion team within one to four years. This appeared to be the likely solution, but it created a problem: who would be the lame duck — Finley or Kansas City? Kansas City would temporarily be without baseball if Finley immediately moved the team. If Finley was forced to remain in Kansas City until expansion became a reality, that would leave Oakland assured of a team but with an empty stadium for a few years.[23]

"I'm very hopeful," Finley said before the meeting. "I'm sure that all the owners will come into the meeting with open minds." The meeting was scheduled to begin at 9:30 in the morning but was delayed a few minutes when Finley showed up late. He made the first presentation. He claimed to have lost more than $4 million in his seven years of operation in Kansas City and contended he would be forced into bankruptcy if he were required to remain in that city.[24]

Finley presented the results of the survey made by the Booz, Allen and Hamilton. It was not impartial because he instructed them to favor Oakland. Oakland had a new stadium located adjacent to a major expressway that was superior to Candlestick Park in San Francisco. Both Kansas City and Seattle would build new stadiums, but only Kansas City had adequate facilities that could be used until the new stadiums were completed. If the A's moved to Seattle they would be forced to play in Sicks Stadium for an indefinite period until the new stadium was completed and the approval of the bond issue to build a stadium was not guaranteed. The climate in Oakland was ideal for baseball. Kansas City often had cool, wet springs and hot summers. The rainy spring weather in Seattle would create problems until the domed stadium was completed. Finley would not be required to pay territorial payments or indemnities in Oakland because it was classified as an "open" city. If the A's moved to Seattle no fewer than three teams in the Pacific Coast League would demand territorial payments: Seattle, Vancouver and Tacoma. (The PCL demanded $1 million from the Seattle Pilots in 1969 and probably would have demanded a similar amount from Finley.) Both Seattle and Oakland would provide a substantial boost over the radio and television income Finley received in Kansas City. Atlantic Richfield Oil Company was ready to offer a contract for radio and television rights that would net Finley $1.1 million annually for five years if Finley moved the team to Oakland. The population in the Oakland–San Francisco area was larger than both Kansas City and Seattle. The population in the Bay Area ranked as the sixth largest in the nation with the majority of the people living on the east side of the Bay with easy access to the Oakland Coliseum. Finley felt the Bay Area could easily support two major league teams.[25]

City	1960 Population Figures		1970 Population Figures		1966 Attendance
	City Proper	Metro Area	City Proper	Metro Area	
Oakland–San Francisco	367,548	3,275,000	361,561	4,109,519	1,657,192 Giants
Seattle	557,087	938,400	530,831	1,421,869	138,862 AAA team
Kansas City	475,539	1,025,900	507,330	1,253,916	726,639 Athletics

The survey concluded that baseball had to be force-fed in Kansas City and that of the three cities, Oakland was clearly the best location for the team. Some owners questioned the results. "Very frankly, we felt the A's had not done the proper market studies to look at the various places that were available," said Frank Cashen of the Baltimore Orioles. "And we thought it would certainly hurt the San Francisco Giants to put another team into the Bay Area."[26]

Oakland's delegation appeared in mid-morning, headed by Robert T. Nahas, president of the Oakland–Alameda County Coliseum complex; William F. Knowland, former senator and publisher of the *Oakland Tribune*; and George Loors, president of an Oakland construction firm. They emphasized that Oakland had one of the finest stadiums in the country and that Oakland had proved itself as one of the best areas in the country for major sports. "It was an excellent meeting," Nahas said. "We brought maps and charts and weather reports and explained our complex will be ready for an April opening. We have a population of 2.5 million in the East Bay area."[27]

Oakland was followed by the Kansas City group. Davis and Jackson county judge Charles E. Curry spoke about attendance, sports interest and the radio and television market. Chamber of Commerce president Robert Ingram discussed growth and expansion of the metropolitan Kansas City area, its economy and the transportation available in the city. Dutton Brookfield described the sports complex, its potential and the lease proposal they made to Finley. Symington told the owners they had an obligation to see that Kansas City retained a major league franchise. "All we want is continuation of our franchise with or without Finley," they said after their presentation. "Even though Kansas City was never out of the second division in 13 years, we still drew more than 12 million admissions."[28]

The owners broke for lunch and listened to Seattle and Dallas groups in the afternoon. Johnny O'Brien, chairman of the King County commissioners and a former baseball and basketball player, headed the Seattle delegation. Lamar Hunt and Dick Butler represented Dallas. They arrived at mid-afternoon and stated they were just as interested in a National League franchise. After they met with the league owners, Hunt joined the Kansas City's representatives to await the league's decision. He told them he was asked to appear on short notice and was surprised when he received the invitation.[29]

The league started their deliberations about 5:30. There had been reports that the league would vote to permit Finley to move to Oakland and then discuss expansion at another meeting, but Arthur Allyn knew the transfer would not be approved unless it was accompanied by immediate assurance that a franchise would be reactivated in Kansas City. The owners wanted to wait until Seattle built a new stadium, but this meant Kansas City could be without a team for as long as four years. The meeting lasted until 10 P.M. There were six votes in favor of the combined package of expansion and transfer on the first ballot. Baltimore voted against and Cleveland, New York and Washington abstained. Joe Cronin ordered a second ballot. The Yankees switched to give Finley the seven votes necessary to move the team. There was no motion for a third ballot in an attempt for unanimity.[30]

"The American League today voted to allow Charles O. Finley to move the Kansas City Athletics to Oakland, California, effective for the 1968 baseball season," stated the press release issued at 10:30. "The league also voted to adopt its expansion plan under which the league would expand to 12 clubs as soon as practical, but not later than the 1971 season, and awarded these two expansion franchises to Kansas City, Missouri and Seattle, Washington. The awards will be subject to applicable baseball rules and procedures and to other terms acceptable to the league, and, in the case of Seattle, to that city being able to provide suitable stadium facilities. Details which remain to be worked out include the coordinating of expansion plans with the commissioner of baseball and the National League."[31]

Cronin, Yankees president Michael Burke, and Angels president Bob Reynolds met with the Kansas City delegation. Symington and Davis did not want Kansas City to be without a major league team for as long as three years. Symington threatened federal legislation that would upset baseball's anti-trust laws and walked out of the meeting. "Finley deliberately sabotaged the Kansas City franchise to get out of town," Davis told them. "He's rewarded by getting permission to move elsewhere and we're penalized by having to wait four years for another ballclub. We were prepared to sit out one year but we're not going to be without baseball for three years because of Finley. We'll fight it all the way." Davis threatened to return to Kansas City and file an injunction to prevent Finley from moving. Brookfield and Curry reminded them that the stadium had been approved as part of the sports complex on June 27 with the understanding that construction would not begin until a long-term lease was signed with a major league team. March 1, 1968 had been set as the deadline date for such a lease arrangement.[32]

Ernie Mehl and Joe McGuff saw Red Sox owner Tom Yawkey in the hotel lobby. "I guess you guys got what you wanted," Yawkey said.

"No, Tom, we did not get what we wanted," they answered. They were afraid the owners could always find a reason not to expand and years might pass before Kansas City obtained a team.

"Yawkey he said he'd go back upstairs and see what he could do, although the meeting had actually broken up," McGuff said. "There was no longer a quorum upstairs but he did go up. He talked to Cronin and

I'm not sure who else. So about midnight we get word there's another meeting, but without a quorum." Some owners already checked out of the hotel. Cronin returned to the meeting room, rounded up the five owners that had not left (Boston, New York, California, Detroit and Cleveland), and held a second meeting. (Cronin claimed he thought six owners were present.) He ruled the previous meeting had not adjourned but merely recessed. He explained that Kansas City wanted a firm commitment for an expansion franchise no later than 1969.[33]

The owners were reluctant to expand until Seattle passed the stadium bond issue, even though it was likely Kansas City would take the case to court if the league refused to alter its position. The league decided to agree to do everything possible to expand in 1969, but would make no commitment. Cronin called Davis, Curry and Brookfield into the meeting to discuss the compromise. "They told us that it had been settled, that for sure they would give us an expansion team at the end of two years," said McGuff. The Kansas City group had been informed of the proposal before they entered the meeting room and already decided it was unacceptable.[34]

The Seattle delegation assured league officials that Sicks Stadium could be used until the new stadium was ready and insisted that only five months would be required to increase the capacity. The league agreed to put expansion franchises in Kansas City and Seattle in 1969. Cronin then called reporters into the room and issued the following statement: "Following a later session to the meeting, the league agreed that the first step to the implementation of the expansion plan for the new Kansas City franchise would be to comply with a baseball rule requiring a joint major league meeting to he held under the auspices of the commissioner with the National League to discuss the matter and the league thereafter would take all action within its power to: 1). Select the new ownership of the Kansas City club prior to March 1, 1968, in order that the Jackson County Sports Complex Authority would be able to obtain a commitment on a long-term lease on the proposed stadium in Kansas City; and 2). To enable the new club to field a team for the 1969 championship season."[35]

"George Selkirk (from the Washington Senators) told us he didn't know about any of this until the next morning when he read in the paper that all of this had happened," McGuff said. "We felt it had been an extraordinary situation and even though Symington had a great effect, Yawkey was the one who upped the scales in favor of us getting another club."[36]

Symington returned to Washington D.C., took the floor of the Senate and described Finley as "one of the most disreputable characters ever to enter the American sports scene." Even though Kansas City would be without baseball for one year he said: "This loss is more than recompensed for by the pleasure resulting from our getting rid of Mr. Finley.... Oakland is the luckiest city since Hiroshima."[37]

Sportservice filed a $10 million suit on November 15, 1967, and asked the court to issue a restraining order to prevent Finley from signing an agreement with Volume Service Company for the concession rights at the Oakland Coliseum. Attached to the suit were documents that were originally signed by the Philadelphia Athletics on September 25, 1950. Sportservice acquired exclusive home stadium concession rights for 25 years "regardless where such franchise is exercised." The contract covered exclusive rights for scorecards, programs, advertising, refreshments, novelties and other concession rights. Finley inherited the contract when he purchased the team in 1960. The court ruled in favor Sportservice and Finley was forced to either honor the contract or arrange a settlement.[38]

28

A Bad Marriage

"My intentions are to keep the A's permanently in Kansas City," said Finley after he purchased the team in December 1960. This was his original intent. He did not choose Kansas City but he chose to move the A's to Oakland. Many of the things he did in Oakland repeated things he did in Kansas City after he purchased the team. Bill Dauer, who was executive vice president of the Kansas City Chamber of Commerce in 1961, held a similar position with the San Francisco Chamber of Commerce in 1968. He said Finley's promotion in Oakland was so similar to Kansas City in 1961 that "everything he has said and done in Oakland is like a record being played back to me."[1]

One of Finley's promotional efforts was personal appearances, of which he made at least 125 during the first three months in Kansas City. These appearances decreased when he became disenchanted and wanted to move the team. He spoke to civic groups and organizations throughout the East Bay area during his first year in Oakland but rarely spoke to these groups in the following years.[2]

Finley said he might move his family to Kansas City in 1961, but that he would not do it until his oldest son graduated from high school in two years. He promised to move his family to Oakland in 1968. Finley did not move to either city. "The similarities between his early speeches in Kansas City and what he said to us [in Oakland] are amazing," said Bill Cunningham.[3]

As another promotional move, Finley invested $411,670.74 for stadium improvements in Kansas City. "It looked like a pigpen," Finley said. "So ... I dig into my pocket and I spend $550,000 (actually $411,670) out of my own pocket to beautify a ballpark out there ... for a stadium owned by the city, not me-e-e-e! And I'll tell you another thing. If I had that to do over again, I'd have never spent that money. I'd have kept playing in the pigpen." Finley added a $1 million scoreboard at municipally owned

Oakland Coliseum after he moved the team. "The original contract he had with the Coliseum required him to put in the scoreboard," said Bill Cunningham. "And it did cost him about a million. The scoreboard becomes the property of the Coliseum after the expiration of his contract."[4]

Finley would not spend money to improve municipally owned stadiums in Kansas City and Oakland if he did not intend to remain at the stadium. "The sum he has spent on the [Municipal] stadium — that would not [provide] evidence of any possibility of moving," said J.W. Putsch when rumors surfaced in 1961 that Finley wanted to move the team to Dallas. Putsch was chairman of the Kansas City group that attempted to purchase the team in 1960.[5]

Finley also used promotions similar to those used by Bill Veeck to boost attendance in Kansas City and Oakland. Veeck set attendance records with the Indians and White Sox and Finley anticipated similar results. When attendance did not meet his expectations in Kansas City and Oakland, he stopped promoting the team. "When the public doesn't support his teams the way he thinks they should, he loses interest in spending money of promotions," said John O'Reilly, Finley's director of promotions in Oakland.[6]

Hiring a locally popular general manager was usually a good public relations move. Finley hired Frank Lane as general manager in 1961 because Lane was popular in Kansas City. Finley hired Joe DiMaggio as executive vice president when the team moved to Oakland in 1968, a position similar to the one Lane held in Kansas City. DiMaggio lived in Oakland and had been a popular player with the San Francisco Seals (AAA) before he became an All-Star player with the Yankees.[7]

Civic leaders encouraged Finley to eliminate the Municipal Stadium attendance clause that permitted him to cancel the lease as a gesture of good faith and a pledge to keep the team in Kansas City. Finley would have ignored their request if he intended to move the team, but he held a press conference in February where he supposedly burned the lease. "It was my idea to take the clause out, and as Mr. [Herb] Hoffman [associate city counselor] pointed out, it took some time to draw up the agreement," Finley said, explaining why he did not sign a new lease until August. "Now it has been done and is signed. I think this should be a sufficient answer to those who have doubted my veracity." (This last statement was directed toward Mehl.) The delay probably occurred because Finley no longer wanted to remove the clause when season ticket sales and early season attendance failed to meet his expectations.[8]

Finley's enthusiasm for Kansas City diminished when attendance failed to reach the levels he expected. Finley concluded the novelty of major league baseball had worn off and the city was too small to support major league baseball. At various times he stated six reasons why he thought it was necessary to move the team.

The first reason was the size of the city. "I am not certain that Kansas City has the metropolitan population to support major league baseball year after year," said Finley even though the population was comparable to Milwaukee, Cincinnati, Baltimore, Houston, Atlanta and Minneapolis–St. Paul. "You only draw crowds in a small area when you have a championship team or when your team is a novelty. Kansas City has drawn well in the past. Now we have gone down because the novelty wore off."[9]

The novelty of the major league baseball in Kansas City wore off by 1957, when attendance dropped to 901,067. Attendance increased during the next two seasons when the team improved. Attendance was good considering the teams that represented the city during the years the Athletics operated in Kansas City. Before the Athletics moved to Kansas City, *Philadelphia Bulletin*'s Hugh Brown stated, "No city, no matter how large and charitable, can be whipped or cajoled into supporting a team that has finished in the cellar eight times in the last 13 years." The Athletics finished in last place six times during the years they operated in Kansas City (even with the addition of two expansion teams in 1961), similar to the record the Athletics had in their final seasons in Philadelphia that prompted Brown's statement.[10]

Joe McGuff wrote that during the first eight seasons the A's operated in Kansas City (1955–1962) no city in the majors, with the possible exception of Washington, had been subjected to worse teams than Kansas City. The total ticket sales, a far more accurate measure than turnstile count because it included tickets sold but not used, totaled 8,034,725, an average of more than one million each season.[11]

	Turnstile Count	*Total Ticket Sales*
1955	1,393,054	1,477,967
1956	1,015,154	1,029,766
1957	901,067	1,001,542
1958	925,090	1,030,000*
1959	963,683	1,042,075
1960	744,944	894,000*
1961	683,817	775,000*
1962	635,675	730,000*
1963	762,364	870,000*
1964	642,478	725,000*
1965	528,344	597,667
1966	773,929	882,667
1967	726,639	756,062

*estimated, exact total unknown

An inadequate ballpark was Finley's second reason. Finley claimed Municipal Stadium was the most "inadequate, obsolete stadium in either league." Finley wanted a new 50,000-seat stadium with parking facilities for 15,000 cars because attendance and concession income would improve at a new stadium. "I would be willing to sign a long-term lease for use of the [new] stadium." Finley said. "If this could be accomplished all of our problems would be over." A new stadium was in the city's long-range plans but not in the immediate future when Finley made his demand in 1962. City officials felt the seating capacity at Municipal Stadium could be enlarged when needed and a new stadium would be built in the future. Finley interpreted this as forcing him to lose money in an inadequate stadium.[12]

Plans for a new domed stadium immediately south of the downtown area were unveiled in 1965. The Jackson County Sports Authority recommended a pair of stadiums rather than the domed stadium in 1967. The bond issue passed and Finley was offered a lease. He was not interested because he had already decided to move the team to another city.

Finley also felt that the team's income from radio, television and advertising was too low. He added billboards to the stadium walls to increase advertising income but could rent only a few. The team used some unsold billboards to compare foul line dimensions at Kansas City with those at Yankee Stadium. Finley said the firm that handled his billboard advertising claimed advertisers shied away from Kansas City because of its comparatively small consumer market.[13]

"In metropolitan Kansas City I get about $200,000 for my radio and television rights," Finley said. "The Yankees get about $1,000,000. That gives them a big edge on me. Anybody in the game will tell you that no team makes money on its admissions—they make it on concessions and radio-TV."[14] Kansas City was a small market and radio and television income was less than other major league cities. The income during the Athletics tenure in Kansas City is as follows:

Year	Radio-TV Income	Year	Radio-TV Income
1955	$210,000 +	1962	$200,000
1956	$210,000 +	1963	$350,000
1957	$210,000 +	1964	$300,000
1958	$210,000 +	1965	$325,000
1959	$210,000 +	1966	$250,000
1960	$300,000	1967	$155,478
1961	$300,000		

+It was actually $250,000 each year between 1955–59 but was reduced when the A's received a five-year advance.

Arnold Johnson signed a five-year contract with Schlitz Brewing Company before the 1955 season and received an advanced payment that he used to purchase the team. Schlitz increased the broadcasting rights to $300,000 for the 1960 and 1961 seasons. Finley severed the contract with Schlitz in 1962 and sold rights to local radio stations. The money he received was contingent on the amount of advertising sold to sponsor the games, but Finley usually waited until after the first of the year to sell rights and this did not provide them with enough time to sell advertising.

The expansion Kansas City Royals signed a three-year contract to sell their rights to Schlitz in 1969 and received $400,000 each season. Finley probably could have obtained a similar amount if he negotiated a guaranteed contract with Schlitz or another major sponsor or sold the rights to local stations early enough to provide the originating station with ample time to sell advertising and build a network of out-of-town stations. Schlitz Brewing Company built a network of 33 stations in 1955, 47 in 1956 and 51 stations in 1957. This declined to 33 in 1958, seven stations in 1959 and eight stations in 1960. During the Finley years the originating stations had a network of 10 stations in 1962, 17 stations in 1963 and 11 in 1964 and approximately 10 stations during Finley's final three years in Kansas City. The Kansas City Royals began with a network of 48 stations in their first season (1969) and increased their network to 106 stations by 1979. The potential for a large network remained untapped during the Finley years.

Finley had similar problems in Oakland. He signed a five-year, $5.5 million contract with Atlantic Richfield (ARCO) for broadcasting rights in 1968. This dropped to $650,000 a year after the contract expired in 1973 despite the team's success on the field. Before he sold the team it was virtually impossible to find a local station to carry the games. The only station that agreed to carry the games in Oakland in 1978 was a 10-watt FM station and Finley had to pay them for the broadcasting rights.[15]

Large losses were another reason for Finley's desire to move the team. The Athletics were profitable when Arnold Johnson owned the franchise, but Finley claimed large losses. "I never wanted to make money in baseball, but I think I should have a chance to break even," Finley said. "My problem is real." Unfortunately it is impossible to determine how real it was as Finley quoted different figures. During the 1962 season he claimed a tax loss of $812,000 in 1961: $200,000 was the cash loss and the remainder ($612,000) was player depreciation expenses. The figures changed one year later when he said the player depreciation cost in 1961 was $619,000, but the cash loss in 1961 was $803,000 — making the total loss $1,422,000.[16]

Finley claimed he lost $1,694,000 in 1962, with a cash loss of $676,000 and player depreciation costs of $1,018,000. "The losses by the baseball club have been enormous, despite what you believe about write-offs," Finley stated about the 1961 and 1962 losses. "The significant thing, however, is that the losses have not been offset by the very excellent profits of my insurance business.... For the last two years, 1961 and 1962, my tax returns will show you that even in balancing the insurance profits against the ballclub losses, I'm out $45,000 in capital. That's money I don't want to lose. All I ask is a chance to break even."[17]

Finley claimed he lost $834,356 in 1964, making a total deficit of $4,628,428 from 1961 through 1964. This apparently included both the cash losses and player depreciation expenses. He claimed a total loss of $4,283,000 during the first six seasons in Kansas City in 1967. This conflicts with the total loss figure he quoted in 1964, but this *may* be just the cash loss. He claimed he lost $400,000 in 1967, making a total loss of approximately $4,683,000 during his seven years in Kansas City.[18]

Finley paid almost $4 million for the team. If he allocated $250,000 of that for the cost of the team and the remainder for player depreciation, he gained a tax deduction of $3,750,000 spread over a five-year period. The tax of corporate earnings was 52 percent, making this worth approximately $2 million in tax savings. Finley was not able to take advantage of this and the reported losses may include these lost tax deductions.

Finley added further confusion to his claims of substantial losses in Kansas City in 1984, after he sold the franchise. "In 19 out of 20 years the A's were profitable," he said. "I ain't saying I made a hell of a lot of money, but that's doing pretty good to finish in the black 19 out of 20 years." The one season he likely lost money was 1979, when the team attracted just 306,723 fans in Oakland. Even if the loss occurred in Kansas City, it meant he now claimed to have made money during six of the seven years he operated the team in Kansas City. Finley actually made money in Kansas City, but he felt the A's would be more profitable in another location.[19]

According to Finley, another problem with Kansas City was a lack of cooperation from the local media. "I have no quarrel with the Kansas City fans," Finley said in 1964. "The way newspapers and the city council there have smeared me I can sympathize with the way the average fan feels about me." Reporter Ernie Mehl was suspicious of outsiders and worked hard to organize the local group that tried to purchase the team in 1960 before being out-bid by Finley. During Finley's first year in Kansas City Mehl reported Finley did not actually burn the lease with the attendance clause, criticized Finley when he fired Joe Gordon and Frank Lane, and broke the news that Finley wanted to move the Athletics to Dallas. Finley felt Mehl was too critical and retaliated by presenting the "poison pen award" to Mehl. He refused to release information to either the *Kansas City Times* or *Star* because he felt it was impossible to get fair coverage in papers owned by the same corporation. "What do I have here [to present his side of the story]?" he asked. "My Fan-A-Gram and the Poison Pen Award."[20]

"I didn't totally dislike Finley," said Mehl. "There are a lot of things to like about him.... Unfortunately, many of the things he does are outrageous. He hurts people and then tries to laugh it off. If I reported his activities inaccurately he would have had every reason to complain. The fact is, as almost everyone knew then and everyone else found out later, I reported his activities absolutely accurately.... He said he was a man of his word and then broke his word.... He came in and within a few months he was trying to take the team out of town. We had to fight him on it out of responsibility to our community. Once the community found out it could not trust him, it turned on him. He couldn't seem to understand this. Somehow, men like Finley do not consider themselves responsible for their own actions. They blame everyone but themselves for what goes wrong."[21]

"Some people say that Charlie had a lot of problems with the press in Kansas City," said Herb Michelson. "If McGuff and veteran Kansas City baseball writer Ernie Mehl chose to scrutinize the owner and general manager, they were well within their professional rights. Another newspaperman close to the situation told me, 'There was no policy on the *Star* to get Charlie.' McGuff and Mehl were working to keep a viable major league baseball franchise in Kansas City.... They did not want Finley to move the club."[22]

Finley also had problems with the media in Oakland. He did not pay for travel, hotel and food expenses for local writers just as he refused in Kansas City. After *Oakland Tribune* writer Ron Bergman wrote an article criticizing the A's radio announcers, Finley told A's traveling secretary Tom Corwin to physically remove Bergman from any charter flights if he tried to board the plane and ordered Corwin not to speak to Bergman or make any hotel reservations for the writer, as was the customary practice. "Finley's treatment of Bergman typified his stormy relationship with the Oakland media," said author Bruce Markusen. "When local reporters wrote negatively of the A's and Finley, the owner responded vindictively. If a reporter described Finley in a positive light, he became an instant friend."[23]

Clashes with city officials were Finley's sixth reason for wanting to leave. For example, in 1961, Finley wanted to use fireworks after home runs in Kansas City just as Bill Veeck was doing in Chicago. The city council refused to grant a permit because the stadium was in a residential community. A compromise was reached and Finley spent $32,000 to purchase fireworks and aerial bombs and hired a company to shoot them off. Citizens who lived near the stadium complained about the noise but Finley refused to curtail the aerial bombs even when games continued late into the evening. By the end of May the city council banned the use of fireworks after night games. "I have tried to do everything I can think to make baseball more attractive here," Finley responded, "but if this sort of cooperation is any indication, it makes me wonder whether the city wants the ballclub." Finley placed a poignant message on his new Fan-A-Gram: "Thirty thousand dollars' worth of fireworks for sale, cheap."[24]

Finley wanted to improve the stadium, but the city was unwilling to spend public funds. When Kansas City obtained the Chiefs in 1963 the city provided funds for stadium improvements, a practice field, training headquarters and office space. The extension of the press box to accommodate football writers and broadcasters blocked the view from seats in the upper rows of the lower deck down the right field line. "The football team wanted that, so the city built it and paid for it," he said. "All it does for us is to ruin a lot of our seats and louse up our public address system. You think the city would buy us a new public address system? Naw, we don't play football. We don't want to be treated as well as the football team. We don't ask half what the football team gets. We just want to be treated fair."[25]

Finley demanded a lease similar to that given to the Chiefs. (The A's had received similar benefits to those the Chiefs received with reduced rent at Municipal Stadium in 1955 and 1956.) The outgoing city council met Finley's demands and Finley signed a seven-year lease to rent the stadium for $1 a year with an escape clause that permitted him to cancel the lease if attendance failed to reach 850,000. Finley was satisfied, but the new city council voided the lease. They wanted a long-term lease without an escape clause. Finley ultimately signed a new contract that bound the team to Kansas City through the 1967 season. He moved the team when the contract expired.

Had the new council accepted the lease, the ill feelings could have been avoided. City officials took a hard-line approach because they did not trust Finley, but they would not have been as insistent if Finley had not tried to move the team. History somewhat vindicates Finley because Kansas City lost two other major league franchises within the next 20 years because they refused to make compromises that ultimately resulted in the loss of these teams.

The National Hockey League granted an expansion team to a group of Kansas City investors in 1974. The group paid $6 million for the franchise, but they were under-financed. The Kansas City Scouts had a $4 million debt by 1976. Officials from the Kansas City Kings basketball team offered to purchase the hockey team for $2 million and assume the debt.

28—A Bad Marriage

They wanted to manage Kemper Arena and operate both teams but wanted an escape clause in the lease to allow them to sell the Scouts if the hockey team continued to lose money. City officials refused to consider an escape clause. The Kings chose not to purchase the team and no other local buyers were interested. The Scouts were sold to Denver interests and moved to that city (the franchise later moved to New Jersey). "The city staff ... with the apparent agreement of the council and the mayor, to be candid — blew the hockey franchise," said Bill Clarkson, chairman of the Jackson County Sports Complex Authority.[26]

The city lost the Kings 10 years later. The team was sold to an out-of-town syndicate headed by Frank and Greg Lukenbill in 1982. "Their goal was to keep this team successful," said Kings general manager Joe Axelson, "and then get an expansion team in Sacramento. An expansion team would have satisfied them 100 percent. No doubt about it." A dispute arose over advertising rights and concession income. The Kings were given exclusive advertising rights in Kemper Arena for all events under the terms of their lease. After the city obtained an indoor soccer team, it gave the Kansas City Comets the right to sell advertising on the nights they played. The Kings claimed they lost $450,000 a year in advertising income because the city did not enforce their exclusive rights. The city claimed the Kings were the only franchise using the Arena when they signed their lease and the exclusive rights did not apply when another franchise shared Kemper Arena. The Kings also wanted a percentage of the concession income. Kansas City officials refused to give the Kings exclusive advertising rights or any concession revenue in a new lease. On January 21, 1985, the Kings announced they would move to Sacramento after the season. City officials claimed the owners' lack of marketing kept attendance low because they wanted to move the team to Sacramento. McGuff explained: "In reality, the Kings are leaving principally because of bungling at city hall."[27]

Finley ultimately moved the team because he did not like Kansas City and Kansas City did not like him. "Human nature then spawned personality clashes that even Solomon could not have refereed," wrote David Condon. "These molehills melded into a mountain until no party could retreat." Neither Finley nor Kansas City was totally blameless and it was unlikely that the problems could be resolved. League officials felt the only solution was to permit Finley to move to Oakland and place an expansion team in Kansas City. Detroit owner John Fetzer summarized the relationship between Kansas City and Finley as a "bad marriage."[28]

Finley had similar problems in Oakland. The A's became one of the best teams in baseball history but attracted one million spectators in just two seasons. An interesting comparison is made between the Finley years in Oakland (1968–1980) and the expansion Royals in Kansas City during those years. The two teams had approximately the same record (the Royals average record was 85–77, the A's was 84–77) but the average attendance in Kansas City (1,435,274) was nearly twice the attendance in Oakland (777,274).

Three years after Finley moved the A's to Oakland, there were rumors he wanted to move the team to Toronto, New Orleans, Dallas, Seattle or Washington D.C. Leonard Koppett reported Finley was preparing to move out of Oakland in "the strikingly similar pattern" that preceded his departure from Kansas City. Koppett cited attendance and television problems that Finley inflicted upon himself "to prove that this area [Oakland] can't or won't support baseball." Finley could not move because he signed a 20-year lease to use Oakland–Alameda County Coliseum in 1968. He ultimately sold the team to the Levi Strauss family for $12.7 million in August 1980.[29]

Finley became disenchanted in Kansas City and in Oakland when the attendance did not meet his expectations. "The hunch is that he thought he gave them all he could and that when they failed to respond to his giving, Charlie lost interest in responding to them," wrote Herbert Michelson. "He must have felt that he did so much — and received ... so little in return. The surface sullenness has always obscured the inner need for adulation and attention and affection. A million people buying tickets in one season could have bought this man's heart."[30]

Finley said his operating loss at Oakland in 1977 was $1.2 million and $800,000 the year before. "I realized (we were in trouble in Oakland) in 1972, '73 and '74," Finley said. "We won world championships all three years. We drew 921,000, 1,000,000 and 845,000 — and in each of those years the figures included 150,000 at half price."

"Are you sorry you left Kansas City?" he was asked. "I made a big mistake," he answered. "With the new stadium they built there, with their baseball weather, I would have drawn 2,000,000. In most baseball towns on summer nights, people come to the game in a light sweater. In Oakland they need overcoats." Finley made a similar statement in 1985. "The biggest mistake I ever made was moving the team from Kansas City to Oakland," he told a reporter. "I shouldn't have moved away from the greatest baseball fans in the world in Kansas City."[31]

Despite Finley's change of opinion about Kansas City, it is doubtful the A's would have matched the attendance achieved by the Royals. Kansas City was not a bad baseball city and neither was Oakland. Attendance was low in both cities when Finley owned the team and increased significantly in the post–Finley years, especially after the Royals moved into their new stadium in 1973. The American League changed their official attendance figures from turnstile count to total paid attendance in 1969. Using total paid attendance it is possible to compare attendance between the Finley years in Kansas City and attendance in Kansas City and Oakland.

Why was attendance poor during the Finley years in Kansas City and Oakland? Finley had poor marketing skills and operated with minimal front office personnel. "Despite his reputation as a promotional genius, Finley actually knew very little about what it took to build attendance," wrote Glenn Dickey about Finley's operation in Oakland. "Finley had no marketing director, nor any marketing staff. Since there was nobody out in the community marketing season tickets, very few were being sold. That meant that the A's depended on walk-up sales. But when they had big games this caused a problem because Finley never had enough ticket sellers. Fans would wait in long lines to buy tickets and then not get into the game until the third or fourth inning. Few of them returned for other games."[32]

Between 1955 and 1959 the A's sold approximately 5,000 season tickets each season. This meant 400,000 tickets were sold and this provided nearly $1 million in cash before the season started. Season ticket sales dropped to 4,091 in 1960 and that was the primary reason it became necessary to sell 150,000 tickets to meet the 850,000-attendance minimum. The Athletics' front office personnel, following the patterns of previous seasons, began selling season tickets in October 1960, but the unsettled ownership caused sales to fall behind previous seasons. After Finley purchased the team, staff personnel and four players who lived in Kansas City began to sign up season ticket holders. The players were paid $400 for the month of January to obtain renewal contracts and find new business. The staff planned to travel the seven-state trade area as in the past, show World Series movies, distribute 1961 schedules and work with civic groups—actions that had been successful since 1957. The direct contact established by having a representative of the team call upon clients to obtain their season ticket contract and check had been very successful in the past.[33]

After Finley bought the team he planned to sell season tickets and a nine-game ticket package through direct mail, an approach that had been successful in the insurance business. He had dinner with Mehl and McGuff. "He kept boasting that he was going to sell out every game at Municipal Stadium," McGuff said. "I recall asking him how he was going to do it and he said the same way he sold insurance: mail order. I knew we were in trouble at that point." Finley stopped all season ticket promotional appearances, including the appearances by the four players who had been paid to do that work. All sales were to be made through the mail and neither

Year	Pos.	Won	Lost	Turnstile	Total Paid Attendance	Pos.	Won	Lost	Attendance
	Kansas City (Finley Years)								
1961	9th	61	100	683,817	775,000				
1962	9th	72	90	635,675	730,000				
1963	8th	73	89	762,364	870,000				
1964	10th	57	105	642,478	725,000				
1965	10th	59	103	528,344	597,667				
1966	7th	74	86	773,929	882,667				
1967	10th	62	99	726,639	756,062				
	Kansas City (Post-Finley)						**Oakland (Finley Years)**		
1968	4th	69	93		902,414	6th	82	80	837,466
1969	4th	65	97		693,047	2nd	88	74	778,232
1970	2nd	85	76		910,784	2nd	89	73	778,355
1971	4th	76	78		707,656	1st	101	60	914,933
1972	2nd	88	74		1,345,341	1st	93	62	921,325
1973	5th	77	85		1,173,292	1st	94	68	1,000,763
1974	2nd	91	71		1,151,836	1st	90	72	845,693
1975	1st	90	72		1,680,265	1st	98	64	1,075,518
1976	1st	102	60		1,852,603	2nd	87	74	780,593
1977	1st	92	70		2,255,493	7th	65	98	495,599
1978	2nd	85	77		2,261,845	6th	69	93	526,999
1979						7th	54	108	306,763
1980	1st	97	65		2,288,714	2nd	83	79	842,259
							Oakland (Post-Finley)		
1981	5th	50	53		1,279,403	2nd	64	45	1,304,054
1982	2nd	90	72		2,284,464	5th	68	94	1,735,489
1983	2nd	79	83		1,963,875	4th	74	88	1,294,941
1984	1st	84	78		1,810,018	4th	77	85	1,353,281
1985	1st	91	71		2,162,717	4th	77	85	1,334,599
1986	3rd	76	86		2,320,794	3rd	76	86	1,314,646
1987	2nd	83	79		2,392,471	3rd	81	81	1,678,921
1988	3rd	84	77		2,350,181	1st	104	58	2,287,335
1989	2nd	92	70		2,477,700	1st	99	63	2,667,225
1990	6th	75	86		2,244,956	1st	103	59	2,900,217

28—A Bad Marriage

personal appearances nor telephone sales were to be used to accept or commit season ticket sales. One employee stopped by a person's office to pick up a check for $1,520 for season tickets. Finley reprimanded him and told him not to make any additional calls.[34]

Finley's primary sales technique was $100,000 worth of brochures mailed to 600,000 people in the area. This resulted in the sale of $20,000 worth of tickets. Customers that bought tickets from direct sales campaigns in the past did not respond to the mail campaign. The decline in the number of season ticket sales was dramatic. Only 2,000 season tickets were sold each season from 1962 through 1965 and that was the primary factor in the drop in attendance during those seasons. Season ticket sales increased in 1966 and 1967 and that resulted in a sizeable increase in attendance.[35]

Year	Season Tickets
1955	4,436
1956	5,422
1957	5,060
1958	4,600
1959	4,800
1960	4,091
1961	3,668
1962	2,039
1963	2,229
1964	2,018
1965	2,073
1966	5,735 +
1967	3,411 +

+The increase in season ticket sales was the result of the sales campaign by the city council and Chamber of Commerce.

"Finley has done nothing to promote season ticket sales," wrote McGuff. "He has never had one salesman on the street. The A's do not have a ticket outlet outside of Greater Kansas City. Promoters who formerly promoted bus and train trips to the A's games for groups report they get no cooperation from the A's. In 1964 and 1965 it was assumed here we [*Kansas City Star*] would help the club conduct its season ticket sale. The club did nothing other than send out a form letter to previous season ticket holders. In 1966 a group known as the Greater Kansas City Sports Commission was formed.... More than 100 of the leading businessmen in Kansas City devoted several full days of selling A's tickets. A similar drive was conducted this year [1967]. Mr. Finley's actions are most significant. The A's did not assist in the drive in any way other than to send out their usual form letter. Finley ran no ads.... Under these extremely difficult circumstances, 3,800 season tickets were sold. Again there was no expression of appreciation on Finley's part. The major civic clubs in Kansas City held a luncheon for the A's at the outset of the 1967 season. Mr. Finley, who was in town the previous night, not only did not stay over, but did not even have the courtesy to send a message to be read at the luncheon."[36]

"I talk to cabdrivers and bartenders because these are the people who deal in conversation," wrote Bill Veeck. "They know how the average guy in town really feels about baseball, about the team and about the current operator." Finley wanted to follow Veeck's example and said he would give away over 300,000 tickets to cab drivers, construction workers, barbers, bartenders, teachers and nurses in 1961. The A's distributed only 76,000 tickets and only 46,000 people used these tickets to attend a game.[37]

Finley also eliminated popular youth programs. The Athletics had booster clubs for high school students and membership cards were sent to more than 250 high schools in Missouri, Kansas, Oklahoma and Nebraska. A high school student could present his card at the gate and get in the game for just 50 cents. The A's also had a youth program through the YMCA in which 10,000 children were invited to attend five games each year. The YMCA provided supervisory personnel and each child had a membership card at the cost of 15 cents a year. Finley tried to discontinue these youth programs during the spring of 1961. The booster club was eliminated but commitments made earlier with the YMCA prevented him from discontinuing the program in 1961. It was eliminated after the season.[38]

Attendance increased in Kansas City and Oakland in the post–Finley years. The Kansas City Royals had a large marketing and sales staff. They also organized a team of civic leaders called the Royals Lancers to sell season tickets. The Oakland Athletics also increased their marketing staff after Finley sold the team

Finley antagonized fans. He wanted to follow Bill Veeck's example. Fans loved Veeck, but they did not like Finley and did not want to support his team at the box office. "Charlie lacked Veeck's flair, sense of humor, subtlety," wrote Herbert Michelson. Bruce Markusen's evaluation of Finley's attendance problems in Oakland also applies to Kansas City: "Many fans in the Bay Area seemed turned off by Finley's brash, outlandish style of running the team," he wrote. "People resent him because he overshadows the team and because he doesn't live here."[39]

29

Just a Yankees Farm Team

The general impression is that the A's essentially served as a farm club for the New York Yankees during Arnold Johnson's ownership because they traded valuable young players to the Yankees and did not receive comparable talent in return. Johnson negotiated most of these trades. "Until Arnold Johnson died," said Bill Veeck, "Kansas City was not an independent major league team at all. It was nothing more than a loosely controlled Yankee farm club." In the five years that Johnson owned the team the A's and Yankees made 16 trades involving 59 players and many trades were beneficial to the Yankees judging solely in terms of short-term results.[1]

A better evaluation measures long-term results. What seems to be a bad trade may become good as players develop and have productive careers. Bill James developed a method to determine the value of players in his book *Win Shares*. A player's long-term value can be determined using James's win shares for each season the player played in the major leagues after the trade was made (regardless of the team). The win shares system is a method of statistical analysis that allows for player evaluation across positions, teams and eras, while measuring all of a player's contributions with a single number. The win shares for each player involved in Kansas City A's transactions is listed following his name with the value of the players purchased or sold shown in brackets. The final column evaluates only players involved in trades and not players purchased or sold.[2]

The A's made only one trade during their first season in Kansas City, primarily because infielder Jim Finigan and pitcher Arnold Portocarrero were the only players sought by other teams. Kansas City traded Sonny Dixon and $20,000 to the Yankees on May 11 for Johnny Sain and Enos Slaughter, but this was essentially a purchase of two veterans rather than a trade. Slaughter made a valuable contribution to the A's in 1955 with 16 pinch hits. Johnson spent nearly $400,000 to purchase Ewell Blackwell,

1955 Transactions[3]

Date	Acquired	From	In Exchange For	Win Shares A's	Other
Mar. 30, 1955	Dick Kryhoski, 1b (0) Ewell Blackwell, p (0) Tom Gormon, p (38)	New York Yankees	$50,000		
Apr. 28, 1955	Lou Sleater, p (10)	New York Yankees	cash		
May 11, 1955	Johnny Sain, p (1) Enos Slaughter, of (33)	New York Yankees	Sonny Dixon, p (0) and $20,000	34	0
May 11, 1955	Ray Herbert, p (96)	Detroit Tigers	cash		
May 11, 1955	Harry Simpson, of (48)	Cleveland Indians	cash		
Sept. 12, 1955	Glenn Cox, p (1)	Brooklyn Dodgers	waiver price		
Sept. 14, 1955	Tom Saffell, of (0)	Pittsburgh Pirates	waiver price		

Tom Gormon, Lou Sleater, Vic Raschi, Ray Herbert, Dick Kryhoski, Harry Simpson and Tom Saffell. Most of these players were veterans close to retirement that Johnson hoped would improve the team in the short term.

The A's were more active in the trading mart in 1956. The team had more players with trade value, but the A's still purchased players and most of the trades included cash. Kansas City acquired Lou Skizas in a trade with New York and then made one of its best trades on August 17, trading Joe Ginsberg to Baltimore for Hal Smith. Smith became the team's starting catcher and batted .300 in 1957.

The A's held a considerable 119–16 advantage in win shares from the players Johnson acquired in trades in 1955 and 1956. The A's gave up little talent in trades but spent considerable sums of money to purchase surplus players from the Yankees and other teams.

1956 Transactions

Date	Acquired	From	In Exchange For	Win Shares A's	Other
Apr. 16, 1956	Johnny Groth, of (16)	Washington Senators	cash		
Apr. 16, 1956	Tim Thompson, c (8)	Brooklyn Dodgers	Leroy Wheat, p (0) Tom Saffell, of (0) and cash	8	0
May 16, 1956	Jose Santiago, p (0)	Cleveland Indians	cash		
June 14, 1956	Lou Skizas, of (18) Eddie Robinson, 1b (1)	New York Yankees	Moe Burtschy, p (0) Bill Renna, of (2) and cash	19	2
June 23, 1956	Jack McMahan, p (1)	Pittsburgh Pirates	Spook Jacobs, 2b (0)	1	0
Aug. 17, 1956	Hal Smith, c (57)	Baltimore Orioles	Joe Ginsberg, c (14)	57	14
Aug. 25, 1956	waiver price	New York Yankees	Enos Slaughter, of (16)		

1957 Transactions

Date	Acquired	From	In Exchange For	Win Shares A's	Other
Oct. 11, 1956	Ryne Duren, p (39) Jim Pisoni, of (3)	Baltimore Orioles	Art Ceccarelli, p (3) Al Pilarcik, of (34)	42	37
Oct. 15, 1956	Ben Flowers, p *(0)*	Philadelphia Phillies	waiver price		
Oct. 16, 1956	Bob Cerv, of *(66)*	New York Yankees	$40,000		
Dec. 5, 1956	Ned Garver, p (40) Gene Host, p (0) Virgil Trucks, p (15) Wayne Belardi, 1b (0) $20,000	Detroit Tigers	Jim Finigan, if (6) Jack Crimian, p (0) Bill Harrington, p (0) Eddie Robinson, 1b (0)	55	6
Feb. 19, 1957	Billy Hunter, ss (7) Rip Coleman, p (4) Tom Morgan, p (41) Mickey McDermott, p (4) Milt Graff, 2b (2) Irv Noren, of (14) Jack Urban, p* (10)	New York Yankees	Art Ditmar, p (45) Bobby Shantz, p (71) Jack McMahan, p (0) Wayne Belardi, 1b (0) Curt Roberts, 2b* (0) Clete Boyer, 3b* (158)	82	274
June 15, 1957	Billy Martin, 2b (24) Ralph Terry, p (103) Woodie Held, of (153) Bob Martyn, of (9)	New York Yankees	Ryne Duren, p (39) Jim Pisoni, of (0) Harry Simpson, of (16) Milt Graff, 2b (0)	289	55
Aug. 1, 1957	cash	Detroit Tigers	Johnny Groth, of *(10)*		
Aug. 27, 1957	Al Aber, p *(0)*	Detroit Tigers	waiver price		
Aug. 31, 1957	waiver price	St. Louis Cardinals	Irv Noren, of *(13)*		

*New York received Roberts on April 4, 1957, and Boyer on June 4, 1957; Kansas City received Urban on April 5, 1957

Johnson's trade philosophy changed following the 1956 season because the A's now had players with trade value. During 1957 and 1958 he made numerous trades and the A's generally benefited from them. He made his first major trade on December 3, 1956, sending Jack Crimian, Bill Harrington, Eddie Robinson and Jim Finigan to Detroit in exchange for Ned Garver, Virgil Trucks, Gene Host and Wayne Belardi. The A's held a 55–6 advantage in win shares because Garver and Trucks were important additions to the pitching staff.

The A's made two major trades with New York. They traded Art Ditmar, Bobby Shantz, Jack McMahan, Wayne Belardi, Curt Roberts and a player-to-be-named-later to the Yankees on February 19 in exchange for Mickey McDermott, Tom Morgan, Rip Coleman, Jack Urban, Milt Graff, Billy Hunter and Irv Noren. The Yankees gained a large 274–82 advantage in win shares as Ditmar and Shantz played important roles in the Yankees' championship reign. Shantz won eight straight games, finished with an 11–5 record and led the league with a 2.45 ERA. Ditmar was part of the Yankees' starting rotation for four years and led the Yankees with 15 victories in 1960.

Clete Boyer, the A's first bonus player, was the player-to-be-named-later. Hank Peters signed him for a $40,000 bonus on May 31, 1955. At that time any player that received a bonus in excess of $4,000 was required to remain with the major league team for at least two seasons before he could be optioned to the minor leagues. The A's tried to include Boyer in February, but baseball commissioner Ford Frick ruled that Boyer would have to stay with the A's until he completed the bonus period. He completed his two-year period of bench sitting on May 31. Instead of being sent to the minor leagues, he was sent to the Yankees as the player-to-be-named-later from that trade. Reports later indicated the Yankees actually provided the bonus money to sign Boyer with an understanding that he would be turned over to the Yankees as soon as his two-year bonus period ended.[4]

The trade appeared one-sided even *before Boyer* was included. Hank Greenberg and Chuck Comiskey questioned what they described as a suspiciously close alliance between the A's and the Yankees and some writers began to refer to the A's as a Yankees farm club. Johnson thought it was an unfair interpretation of the efforts he made to improve the club that had almost no talent two years earlier. He answered his critics in an interview in *The Sporting News*:

> *Question:* Arnold, because of the numerous player deals which have been made with the Yankees, some of the writers are referring to Kansas City as a farm club of the Yankees. Do you feel that comment is justified?
>
> *Answer:* I certainly do not…! The Yankees have the players on both a major league level and youngsters coming up in the farm system. Isn't it logical to deal with an organization this rich in playing talent?
>
> *Question:* Do you believe that in your last deal, in which you gave up Art Ditmar and Bobby Shantz, you got back value received in players?
>
> *Answer:* My only purpose in making the deal was to strengthen the Athletics. I'm not particularly concerned about the results for the Yankees. The deal was made for only one reason, namely: I am going to build a winner!
>
> *Question:* The comment has been said and written that these deals with the Yankees have been influenced by your business relationship as well as friendship for Dan Topping and Del Webb, the Yankee co-owners. Is this true?
>
> *Answer:* Can I help it that some of my business associates happen to

be connected with baseball...? In the recent A's-Yankee deal, you must remember that there is a wide divergence of opinion among big league managers and baseball experts as to who got the better of the deal. This is now one good reason which leads me to believe we made a good deal.

Question: Have you made the same attempt to deal with other clubs in the American League that you have with the Yankees?

Answer: I have contacted every club in the American League many times and also talked to certain National League clubs in an effort to make deals.... In two years we have made deals with Cleveland, Baltimore, Washington, Detroit and New York in the American League; with Brooklyn, Pittsburgh, Philadelphia and New York in the National League. That represents nine of 15 other major league clubs. I do not know of any other major league club which has dealt on such a broad scale.[5]

The Yankees had a significant advantage in the February trade, but the A's evened the score when the two teams completed another major trade in June 15. The A's traded Harry Simpson, Jim Pisoni, Milt Graff and Ryne Duren to New York for Billy Martin, Ralph Terry, Woodie Held and

1958 Transactions

Date	Acquired	From	In Exchange For	Win Shares A's	Other
Nov. 20, 1957	Bill Tuttle, of (49) Jim Small, of (0) Duke Maas, p (16) John Tsitouris, p (27) Frank House, c (8) Kent Hadley, 1b (7) Jim McManus, 1b* (0)	Detroit Tigers	Billy Martin, 2B (22) Gus Zernial, of (6) Tom Morgan, p (35) Lou Skizas, of (1) Mickey McDermott, p (2) Tim Thompson, c (0)	107	66
Apr. 17, 1958	Bud Daley, p (47)	Baltimore Orioles	Arnold Portocarrero, p (17)	47	17
May 14, 1958	Whitey Herzog, of (37)	Washington Senators	cash		
June 12, 1958	Chico Carrasquel, ss (9)	Cleveland Indians	Billy Hunter, ss (2)	9	2
June 15, 1958	Roger Maris, of (205) Dick Tomanek, p (7) Preston Ward, 1b (7)	Cleveland Indians	Woodie Held, of (139) Vic Power, 1B (91)	219	230
June 15, 1958	Bob Grim, p (18) Harry Simpson, of (9)	N.Y. Yankees	Duke Maas, p (12) Virgil Trucks, p (1)	27	13
June 23, 1958	waiver price	Cincinnati Reds	Alex Kellner, p *(13)*		
Aug. 22, 1958	Zeke Bella, of† (0) and cash	N.Y. Yankees	Murry Dickson, p (2)	0	2

*A's received McManus on April 3, 1958
†A's received Bella on September 29, 1958

Bob Martyn. Billy Martin was essentially "banished" to Kansas City after an incident at the Copacabana nightclub in New York. He was considered the key player in the trade, but he contributed little to the A's and was traded to Detroit at the end of the season. Terry was considered one of the best young pitching prospects in the league. He had an 11–13 record for Kansas City in 1958. Held became the A's center fielder and hit 20 home runs with the A's during the second half of the 1957 season. These players gave the A's a significant 289–55 advantage in win shares even though the Yankees acquired a valuable relief pitcher in Duren. He had six wins, 20 saves and a 2.01 ERA in 1958.

The A's sent Billy Martin, Gus Zernial, Lou Skizas, Tom Morgan, Mickey McDermott and Tim Thompson to Detroit in exchange for Bill Tuttle, Jim Small, Duke Maas, John Tsitouris, Frank House, Kent Hadley and a player-to-be-named-later on November 20. This improved the A's outfield because neither Zernial nor Skizas were good defensive players but Bill Tuttle was one of the best defensive center fielders in the league. "We have progressed from a fairly old club to a young one and that means improvements each year," said Johnson following the trade. "Held, Martyn, Bill Tuttle, Joe DeMaestri, Vic Power, Jack Urban, Hector Lopez, Ralph Terry, Duke Maas, Walt Craddock, Harry Taylor, Howard Reed and many others are young. We have changed from a slow club to a fairly fast one. We now have enough speed so that manager Harry Craft can manipulate. We have improved our outfield defense; we think we will have more effective pitching."[6]

Kansas City completed one of its best trades on April 17, sending Arnold Portocarrero to Baltimore for Bud Daley. Daley became one of the league's best pitchers, leading the A's with 16 victories in both 1959 and 1960 and giving Kansas City a 47–17 advantage in win shares. The A's made another valuable acquisition when they purchased Whitey Herzog from Washington.

The A's sent Vic Power and Woodie Held to Cleveland for Roger Maris, Preston Ward and Dick Tomanek. Power and Held were starters in Kansas City while Maris was considered one of the best prospects in baseball. "Frank Lane knew he was sending Roger Maris on a one-stop trip to the Yankees when he traded him to Kansas City," claimed Bill Veeck. "Everyone in baseball knew it; the sportswriters knew it, and any well-informed 15-year-old boy in Des Moines knew it. I called Frank and asked him what in the world he was doing. 'I know I'm handling him over to the Yankees,' Frank said, 'but it's a trade I have to make for my own ball club.'" Cleveland holds a slight 230–219 advantage in win shares because Held and Power had successful careers in Cleveland.[7]

The Murry Dickson trade for a player-to-be-named-later was typical of the maneuvering that took place between the A's and the Yankees. Dickson was 42 years old when the A's signed him in the fall of 1957 after he had been released by St. Louis. He became one of the A's most dependable pitchers and had an 8–3 record and a 3.27 ERA when he was traded to New York. The A's were in sixth place, only 2½ games out of fourth place and just 6½ games out of second. Dickson helped the Yankees win the pennant while the A's finished seventh without Dickson. The A's obtained Zeke Bella as the player-to-be-named-later at the end of the season. His most memorable achievement for the A's occurred in Baltimore in 1959 when, after popping up, he angrily raced back to the dugout, hit his head on the roof and knocked himself out.[8]

1959 TRANSACTIONS

Date	Acquired	From	In Exchange For	Win Shares A's	Other
Oct. 2, 1958	Dick Williams, of (34)	Baltimore Orioles	Chico Carrasquel, ss (6)	34	6
Apr. 8, 1959	Mark Freeman, p (1)*	N.Y. Yankees	Jack Urban, p (0)	1	0
Apr. 12, 1959	Russ Snyder, of (47) Tommy Carroll, ss (0)	N.Y. Yankees	Mike Baxes, if (0) Bob Martyn, of (0)	47	0
May 2, 1959	Ray Boone, 3b (5)	Chicago White Sox	Harry Simpson, of (1)	5	1
May 9, 1959	Murry Dickson (2)	N.Y. Yankees	cash		
May 26, 1959	Johnny Kucks, p (8) Tom Sturdivant, p (30) Jerry Lumpe 2b (114)	N.Y. Yankees	Hector Lopez, of (70) Ralph Terry, p (84)	152	154
Aug. 20, 1959	Ray Jablonski, 3b (1)	St Louis Cardinals	waiver price		
Aug. 20, 1959	waiver price	Milwaukee Braves	Ray Boone, 1b (1)		
Sept. 6, 1959	waiver price	Baltimore Orioles	Rip Coleman, p (1)		

*Freeman was returned to the Yankees on May 8, 1959

The A's were not as active in the trade mart following the 1958 season because the team won 73 games in 1958 and Johnson felt the team had the nucleus of talent to compete with other teams. Kansas City acquired Dick Williams from Baltimore in exchange for Chico Carrasquel on October 2, 1958. The A's gained a 34–6 advantage in win shares because Williams became a valuable utility infielder and a good hitter for the A's. Kansas City traded Make Baxes and Bob Martyn to New York on April 12 for Russ Snyder and Tom Carroll. The A's earned a 47–0 edge in win shares in this trade because Snyder became a regular for the A's and later for the Orioles.

Kansas City made a major trade with the Yankees on May 26, sending Ralph Terry and Hector Lopez to New York for Johnny Kucks, Tom Sturdivant and Jerry Lumpe. The Yankees gained a slight 154–152 advantage in this trade. Lumpe developed into a steady second baseman in Kansas City and batted .301 in 1962. Terry returned to the Yankees after he developed into a good pitcher, bringing charges that the Yankees merely sent Terry to Kansas City for fine-tuning with the promise he would eventually return to New York. Terry won 10 games with the Yankees in 1960, 16 in 1961, 23 in 1962 and 17 in 1963 and appeared in four straight World Series. The Yankees also benefited from Lopez's bat in their explosive batting order.

1960 Transactions

Date	Acquired	From	In Exchange For	Win Shares A's	Other
Oct. 12, 1959	Bob Trowbridge, p (2)	Milwaukee Braves	cash		
Nov. 21, 1959	Tom Acker, p (0)	Cincinnati Reds	Frank House, c (1)	0	1
Dec. 3, 1959	Pete Daley, c (7)	Boston Red Sox	Tom Sturdivant, p (28)	7	28
Dec. 9, 1959	Ken Hamlin, ss (22) Dick Hall, p (101) Hank Foiles, c* (18)	Pittsburgh Pirates	Hal Smith, c (23)	141	23
Dec. 11, 1959	Hank Bauer, of (6) Don Larsen, p (31) Norm Siebern, of (136) Marv Throneberry, 1b (16)	New York Yankees	Roger Maris, of (176) Joe DeMaestri, ss (1) Kent Hadley, 1b (1)	189	178
Apr. 5, 1960	Leo Kiely, p (3)	Cleveland Indians	Bob Grim, p (4)	3	4
May 11, 1960	Bob Giggle, p (0)	Milwaukee Braves	George Brunet, p (63)	0	63
May 19, 1960	Andy Carey, 3b (18)	New York Yankees	Bob Cerv, of (12)	18	12
May 31, 1960	Danny Kravitz, c (2)	Pittsburgh Pirates	Hank Foiles, c (17) and cash	2	17
July 26, 1960	cash	Detroit Tigers	Harry Chiti, c (1)		
July 30, 1960	Johnny Briggs, p (0)	Cleveland Indians	cash		
Oct. 15, 1960	Dutch Dotterer, c (1)	Cincinnati Reds	Danny Kravitz, c (0)	1	0

*Foiles sold to A's on December 15, 1959 to complete the deal

The Athletics had a disappointing season in 1959 and made numerous trades following the season. The A's completed only the second inter-league trade in baseball history on November 21, 1959, sending Frank House to Cincinnati for Tom Acker. The barrier on inter-league trading had been eliminated earlier that day. Kansas City made another inter-league trade three weeks later, trading Hal Smith to Pittsburgh for Ken Hamlin and Dick Hall. Hamlin was considered a top shortstop prospect and was considered the key player in the trade for Kansas City. Although Hamlin was a major disappointment Kansas City earned a 141–23 advantage in win shares because Hall emerged as a dependable major league relief pitcher.

The A's completed their most controversial trade with New York two days later, sending Roger Maris, Joe DeMaestri and Kent Hadley to New York for Hank Bauer, Norm Siebern, Don Larsen and Marv Throneberry. The *New York Post* evaluated the trade, determined the Yankees received far more in the trade than they gave up, and rekindled rumors that the A's would move to Los Angeles.

Wise money Saturday was on the next Kansas City deal being a move to Los Angeles. The lads in the American League believe the A's abdicated their franchise when they let Roger Maris go to the Yankees in a seven-man deal Friday in what was the fifteenth trade between the two clubs.

Maris is the second slugger the A's traded to the Yankees in less than a year. The other is Hector Lopez, who came to the Yankees last summer and proved to be a big man with a bat and a small man with a glove.... Mickey Mantle ... will be in center, but it'll be Lopez in right and Maris in left, a state of affairs which the Yankees might have been maneuvering toward for months now. Maris is 25 years old and a left-handed hitter with good power which is just what the Yankees have been looking for. He was hitting .344 last June and owned Kansas City when an attack of appendicitis knocked him out just before the trade deadline time. The story then was that the Yankees were about to get him but settled for Lopez when Maris went to the hospital. Now they have them both.... The short porch in right field at the Stadium is just tailored for his talents.

...The big man for the A's in the deal for Maris, the man everybody said was supposed to represent half the franchise, was Siebern. He was a marked man since the 1958 World Series when he showed that the left field in the Stadium is too much for him. Still, it's believed he's a natural hitter who let his troubles go to his head. That's supposed to explain his hangdog look and .271 batting average last season.... "We hated to part with Maris," Carroll said, "but I don't think we hurt ourselves. Siebern batted .300 last year (actually the 1958 season) and I like him."

But the good people of Kansas City liked Roger Maris.... The theory is that Carroll would like to move the franchise to Los Angeles and has stopped being afraid of the K.C. fans. Probably the kindest thing they could do for him is stay away from the ballpark. Besides, Siebern would be a hell of a left fielder in the Coliseum.[9]

"The New York Athletics and the Kansas City Yankees pulled another heist yesterday," wrote Jack Lang in the *Long Island Press*, "in which the

New York team got what it wanted ... and the Kansas City team got what New York didn't want.... In exchange for four players who did not figure in their plans for the future, the New York second-story artists succeeded in kidnapping from Kaycee one of the most promising young sluggers in the game today."[10]

Bill Veeck asked for a full-scale investigation of the situation. "I know of nothing of their connection," said Veeck. "But I do know that if the Yankees continue doing business only with Kansas City, it can be injurious to the American League and to baseball. Before the Yankee–Kansas City deals were just a joke; it is funny no longer ... the unusually close alliance between the Yankees and A's creates an unhealthy alliance."[11]

Frank Lane felt the trade was preordained. "They had their eye on him [Maris] for years," Lane said. "I figured Maris would be going to the Yankees all the time. I'm not all certain they didn't tell Johnson to get Maris from me. I even made Carroll promise he'd keep him at least a year." Lane admitted the only problem with his theory was that at the start of the negotiations with the Indians, Johnson said he wanted to obtain Rocky Colavito. Lane wanted to trade Maris who was sitting on the Indians bench. Colavito was a powerful home run hitter but he was right-handed and hit to the wrong field to be an effective long-ball hitter in Yankee Stadium. "OK," Lane said to Johnson, "You can have him [Colavito]. But if you're smart, you'll take Maris. He's a better all-around player, faster runner. He's got the more accurate arm. He's a better outfielder. They tell me he'll be one of the great hitters." Lane convinced Johnson to accept Maris but now felt the A's actually wanted Maris from the beginning of the negotiations. "It's just the kind of thing they would have done," he said. "Why come out and say right off who the guy is you want? Hurts your bargaining position." Lane felt the Yankees were behind both the trade of Maris from Cleveland to Kansas City and from Kansas City to New York. "The only theory about the whole thing which makes any sense at all — and then only in a wacky, impossibly Machiavellian way — is that it was the Yankees who were at the root of both trades," he said.[12]

Johnson insisted the A's traded Maris only after they discussed trades involving Maris with Pittsburgh (for shortstop Dick Groat) and other teams. He said the only reason that had been so many trades with the Yankees was that he was able to get more for what he had to offer from New York than from other teams. He reminded critics that the A's also made several trades with Detroit and Cleveland.[13]

This trade became even more controversial during the 1960 season when Maris emerged as an All-Star player. He won the American League Most Valuable Player award in both 1960 and 1961 and set a new major league record when he hit 61 home runs in 1961. Despite the one-sided appearance, the A's actually gained a 189–178 advantage in win shares. Siebern had several good years for Kansas City. In 1962 he batted .308 with 25 home runs and 114 runs with 117 runs batted in. In the team's 13 seasons in Kansas City, Siebern held the single-season marks for RBI (1962), runs (1962, walks (110 in 1962), and doubles (36 in 1961).

This was the last trade made by Johnson. He died two months later and Parke Carroll operated the teams during the 10-month interim period until Charlie Finley purchased the A's. The general consensus was that Johnson made bad trades with the Yankees and New York used Kansas City as a farm team. "While a few unwise trades may have resulted from imprudent decisions by the Athletics' gullible front office," wrote Francis Kinlaw, "and while the Yankees' deep talent pool placed the New Yorkers in strong negotiating positions, Johnson cannot be excused for repeatedly exchanging players with men who had committed numerous acts of arson upon his organization by burning it over and over again!"[14]

The consensus was based on short-term results and is contradicted by the long-term results. Johnson gained an 840–678 advantage in win shares in the trades with the Yankees, a figure that is even higher (956–694) if it includes players purchased from or sold to the Yankees. "Despite the popular feeling that the Yankees gained the upper hand in their dealings with the A's, the facts do not bear this out," wrote Ernie Mehl. "The only trade which created far more censure than any other was the one which sent Maris to the Yanks. The fact that Roger had his banner year invited a storm of criticism over the steady stream of trades."[15]

Johnson's overall trade record (1,572–1,109 advantage in win shares) was impressive. The team improved as he made many successful trades. Carroll's record was not nearly as good as Johnson's, but he served as chief executive for less than a year and his role during this time was to maintain the team until it was sold to a new owner. He made five trades and gained 24 wins shares while trading away 96. Despite Carroll's previous ties to the Yankees, he made only one trade with New York, sending Bob Cerv to New York for Andy Carey. Both players were near the end of their playing careers.

Since Johnson's trade record is better than previously assumed, the inability of the team to produce winning teams cannot be blamed on poor trades. Some of the blame can be placed on the rapid turnover of players, especially in 1956 and 1957, that made it difficult to create continuity and build team unity. Some of the players that came to Kansas City from the Yankees were upset they would miss the bonus checks from the World Series and were not thrilled to play on a team with a losing record. The major cause was the inability of the A's minor league system to produce players that advanced to the major leagues. An interesting comparison can be made between the 1957 Athletics and the 1971 Royals. The Royals were an expansion team in 1969 and both the Royals and the A's were in comparable positions during their first two seasons in Kansas City because their upper-level minor league teams did not produce major league talent and both teams used trades to improve their teams. The players acquired in trades enabled the Athletics to compete for the first division in 1958 and the Royals to finish second in their division with an 85–76 record in 1971.[16]

Johnson knew the A's had to develop minor league players to continue to improve. Following the 1957 season he felt the A's had as many as 20 or 25 players in the minor leagues capable of reaching the major leagues. "Obviously, all will not make it, but if five or six do we will be helped greatly. We've known all along we could not build a winning club by trades or major league purchases. We had to develop our own stars. At the same time I wanted to do everything I could to make the Athletics themselves as presentable as possible and that's the reason for all the trades we have made. After all, when you're down as far as we were you can hardly hurt yourself by making moves."[17]

The comparison between the A's and Royals ends abruptly. The teams made similar progress through trades, but the A's fell into the cellar in 1959 and 1960, while the Royals continued to improve and won their first division championship in 1976. The difference was player development. The Royals built a productive minor league system and developed players that advanced to the major leagues; the A's did not. This became apparent during each team's third year in Kansas City (1957 and 1971). The Royals already had two pitchers on their 1971 roster (Paul Splittorff and Jim York) that had been signed and developed in their minor league system. Four additional minor league graduates joined the team in 1973: Doug Bird, Steve Busby, Frank White and Jim Wohlford. George Brett, Al Cowens and Mark Littell debuted with the club in 1974. During the Royals' first six years the team developed nine players that made significant contributions to the major league team.

During this same period of time the Athletics produced only one player, Lou Klimchock, who became an everyday player in the major leagues. When Johnson needed to make changes in the roster during the 1959 season he had no other choice than to continue to trade players to obtain other players — filling one hole while creating another. These trades, especially the trades with the Yankees, were blamed for the team's poor record, but the real reason the team failed to improve during the Johnson era was the failure of the Athletics minor league system to produce major league players.

30

No More Trades with the Yankees

Charlie Finley announced he would end the Yankees trades after he purchased the team. "We will have no alliances with any other club in the American League," he said. "There will be no such trades as have been made in the past.... One of the first things I'm going to do is prove that Kansas City isn't a Yankee farm team." Finley purchased an old school bus to symbolize the shuttle bus to Yankee Stadium and burned it in a parking lot at Municipal Stadium. "A trade could help in certain instances," he said. "But, as I see it, the only manner in which the Athletics can be improved is by spending money, and I mean a lot of money, to both acquire and develop stars."[1]

Finley hired Frank Lane as general manager. This virtually guaranteed Kansas City would be active in the trade mart.

The A's first trade during the Finley era occurred before Frank Lane joined the team. The A's obtained Haywood Sullivan from Washington to replace two catchers lost in the expansion draft.

Lane made his first trade on January 24, sending Russ Snyder, Whitey Herzog and a player-to-be-named-later to Baltimore for Clint Courtney, Jim Archer, Al Pilarcik, Bob Boyd and Wayne Causey. Courtney was returned to Baltimore three months later as the player-to-be-named-later. Lane called Finley after he made the trade. "I blew my top," Finley said. "I told him that I wanted to know about the deals before they were made, not after."[2]

Lane completed his worst trade on April 12, acquiring Jerry Walker and Chuck Essegian form Baltimore in exchange for Dick Hall and Dick Williams. Baltimore gained a 101–38 advantage in win shares because Hall became a dependable relief pitcher with Baltimore. Lane made his best trade on June 14th, trading Bud Daley to New York for Art Ditmar and Deron

The Kansas City Athletics

1961 Transactions

Date	Acquired	From	In Exchange For	Win Shares A's	Other
Dec. 29, 1960*	Haywood Sullivan, c (15)	Washington Senators	Marty Kutyna, p (11) and cash	15	11
Jan. 24, 1961	Wayne Causey, 3b (89) Jim Archer, p (15) Bob Boyd, 1b (0) Al Pilarcik, of (0) Clint Courtney, c†	Baltimore Orioles	Whitey Herzog, of (21) Russ Snyder, of (83)	104	104
Jan. 25, 1961	Joe Nuxhall, p (54) John Briggs, p (0)	Cincinnati Reds	John Tsitouris, p (25)	54	25
Jan. 31, 1961	Joe Pignatano, c *(9)*	L.A. Dodgers	cash		
Mar. 30, 1961	Ed Rakow, p (33)	L.A. Dodgers	Howie Reed, p (28) and cash	33	28
Apr. 12, 1961	Jerry Walker, p (13) Chuck Essegian, of (25)	Baltimore Orioles	Dick Hall, p (93) Dick Williams, of (8)	38	101
May 3, 1961	cash	Cleveland Indians	Chuck Essegian, of *(25)*		
June 1, 1961	Paul Giel, p§ Reno Bertoia, 3b (2)	Minnesota Twins	Bill Tuttle, of (7)	2	7
June 7, 1961	Gene Stephens, of (8)	Baltimore Orioles	Marv Throneberry, 1b (7)	8	7
June 10, 1961	Wes Covington, of (52) Bob Shaw, p (77) Gerry Staley, p (3) Stan Johnson, of (0)	Chicago White Sox	Ray Herbert, p (56) Don Larsen, p (30) Andy Carey, 3b (7) Al Pilarcik, of (0)	132	93
June 10, 1961	cash	Milwaukee Braves	Bob Boyd, 1b *(0)*		
June 14, 1961	Art Ditmar, p (1) Deron Johnson, 3b (144)	N.Y. Yankees	Bud Daley, p (13)	145	13
July 2, 1961	Bobby Del Greco, of (23)	Philadelphia Phillies	Wes Covington, of (52)	23	52
July 21, 1961	Mickey McDermott, p *(0)*	St Louis Cardinals	cash		
July 21, 1961	cash	Cincinnati Reds	Ken Johnson, p *(89)*		
July 31, 1961	Bill Fischer, p (17) Ozzie Virgil, 3b (2)	Detroit Tigers	Reno Bertoia, 3b (1) Gerry Staley, p (1)	19	2

*Trade made before Frank Lane became general manager
†Courtney was returned to Baltimore on April 14 to complete trade
§Giel was returned to Minnesota for a cash payment

Johnson despite Finley's promise the A's would not trade with the Yankees. Lane orchestrated the trade but Finley said he approved it. Lane gained a 145–13 advantage in win shares in this transaction because Johnson had a productive major league career with Cincinnati and Philadelphia.

30—No More Trades with the Yankees

Lane was fired in August. His trades weakened the team in the short-term and he admitted the team was "at least 25 percent inferior to the one which began the season." The pitching staff had improved, but the other parts of the team were not as strong and the outfield was considerably weaker than at the start of the season. Lane's long-term success, however, showed a 558–432 advantage in win shares from the trades he made during his short tenure.[3]

Finley became the general manager of the team, in deed if not in title, after he fired Lane. Finley negotiated the trades while the general manager, Pat Friday, ran the business affairs of the team. "He's a good front office man who can go out and get the ballplayers you need at the right time," said Dick Green of Finley. "He'll spend anything for that, and there's a lot of owners who don't. I think he knows more about the game that 85 or 90 percent of the other owners and general managers." Finley "really is a good trader," said sportswriter Ron Bergman. "I think he knows players pretty well, he knows who to get and who's good. Obviously he understands a player's ability. He's a good general manager."[4]

Finley purchased players during the 1962 season to improve the team. Finley's first trade was one of his best. He traded Bob Shaw and Lou Klim-

1962 Transactions

Date	Acquired	From	In Exchange For	Win Shares A's	Other
Oct. 11, 1961	cash	Baltimore Orioles	Johnny Kucks, p *(0)*		
Dec. 15, 1961	Joe Azcue, c (82) Ed Charles, 3b (108) Manny Jimenez, of (23)	Milwaukee Braves	Bob Shaw, p (70) Lou Klimchock, inf (10)	213	80
Dec. 15, 1961	Jose Tartabull, of (37)	San Francisco Giants	Joe Pignatano, c (2)	37	2
Apr. 10, 1962	Danny McDevitt, p (0)	Minnesota Twins	cash		
May 7, 1962	George Alusik, of (17)	Detroit Tigers	cash		
May 15, 1962	Marlan Coughtry, 3b (0)	Los Angeles Angels	Gordon Windhorn, of (1)	0	1
June 26, 1962	Billy Consolo, inf (2)	Los Angeles Angels	cash		
July 2, 1962	cash	Cleveland Indians	Marlan Coughtry, 3b (0)		
July 21, 1962	Ted Bowsfield, p* (10)	Los Angeles Angels	Dan Osinski, p (26)	10	26
Aug. 13, 1962	Moe Drabowsky, p (76)	Cincinnati Reds	cash		

*A's obtained Bowsfield on November 27, 1962 to complete the trade chock to Milwaukee for Joe Azcue, Ed Charles and Manny Jimenez. The A's earned a 213–80 advantage in win shares because Azcue was the A's catcher in 1962, Charles became one of the better third basemen in the league and Jimenez was one of the American League's leading hitters in 1962. Finley also acquired Jose Tartabull from San Francisco in exchange for Joe Pignatano. The A's enjoyed a 37–2 advantage in win shares as Tartabull became a regular outfielder with Kansas City.

The A's traded pitcher Dan Osinski to the Los Angeles Angels on July 21 for $25,000 and a player-to-be-named-later. The A's would receive Bo Belinsky to complete the trade. Belinsky, a 25-year-old southpaw, began the season with a 5–0 record including a no-hitter against Baltimore. His record reached 6–1 before he lost six of his next seven decisions. The Angels warned him about his nightlife and fined him for missing curfews, but Finley felt he was the type of player that could attract fans and bring exposure to the A's. Belinsky learned about the trade from Hank Bauer. After a game in New York he announced: "I've been traded to the A's as the player-to-be-named-later in the Osinski deal and I'm not going." The Angels spent the remainder of the day making denials. They placed Belinsky on waivers to send him to Kansas City but withdrew his name when Washington claimed him. It was agreed by the teams that Belinsky would be sent to Kansas City after the season. Commissioner Ford Frick investigated on September 6 and said he would not approve the trade because it was unethical for Belinsky to pitch for the Angels if he would be traded to Kansas City after the season. The Angels substituted pitcher Ted Bowsfield and sent him to the A's on November 27 to complete the trade. Belinsky spent another two years in Los Angeles before joining the National League in 1964.[5]

Finley's philosophy changed during the 1963 season. He spent money in player development and many trades were made with a profit motive in mind. In a period of three years he made six deals that brought him $425,000 in cash. The trades enabled Finley to trade veterans and open

1963 Transactions

Date	Acquired	From	In Exchange For	Win Shares A's	Other
Feb. 27, 1963	Chuck Essegian, of (3)	Cleveland Indians	Jerry Walker, p (2)	3	2
May 25, 1963	Doc Edwards, c (12) and $100,000	Cleveland Indians	Dick Howser, ss (47) Joe Azcue, c (79)	12	126
July 1, 1963	Charlie Lau, c (21)	Baltimore Orioles	cash		
July 23, 1963	Tom Sturdivant, p (3)	Detroit Tigers	cash		

spots on the roster for young players. Finley made one of his worst trades on May 23rd, sending Dick Howser and Joe Azcue to Cleveland for Doc Edwards and $100,000 in cash. The Indians had a 126–12 advantage in win shares because Howser and Azcue assumed starting positions for the Indians. Edwards contributed little on the major league level in Kansas City.[6]

1964 Transactions

Date	Acquired	From	In Exchange For	Win Shares A's	Other
Nov. 18, 1963	Rocky Colavito, of (84) Bob Anderson, p (0) and $50,000	Detroit Tigers	Jerry Lumpe, 2b (36) Ed Rakow, p (8) Dave Wickersham, p (41)	84	85
Nov. 27, 1963	Jim Gentile, 1b (32) and $25,000	Baltimore Orioles	Norm Siebern, 1b (47)	32	47
Dec. 15, 1963	Nelson Mathews, of (11)	Chicago Cubs	Fred Norman, p (0)	11	100
June 15, 1964	Wes Stock, p (17)	Baltimore Orioles	Charlie Lau, c (13)	17	13
June 29, 1964	Bob Meyer, p (2)	L.A. Angels	cash		

Finley made two of his biggest trades at the end of the 1963 season, acquiring home run hitters Rocky Colavito and Jim Gentile. Finley traded Jerry Lumpe, Ed Rakow and Dave Wickersham to Detroit on November 18, 1963, for Colavito, Bob Anderson and a reported $50,000 cash. Nine days later he sent Norm Siebern to Baltimore for Jim Gentile and $25,000. Colavito had a good year for the A's, but they gave up too much pitching and tumbled into the American League cellar.

Finley acquired Mike Hershberger, Jim Landis and Fred Talbot from Chicago in exchange for Colavito in a three-way trade that included Cleveland on January 20, 1965. The A's obtained three starters: Landis started in center field, Hershberger started in right field and Talbot became a starting pitcher.

The A's tried to protect first-year players John Sanders and Joe Rudi but lost the rights to them when they were claimed by other teams as Kansas City tried to send them to the minor leagues on May 3. Rudi was in effect traded to Cleveland for pitcher Jim Rittwage, a first-year player that Cleveland wanted to protect. The teams agreed to trade them back at the end of the season.[7]

Finley began to slowly phase out older players and replace them with prospects from the minor league system. The A's traded first baseman Jim Gentile to Houston on June 4 for pitcher Jesse Hickman, infielder Ernie Fazio and $100,000. Hickman was a disappointment and Fazio made only minimal contributions to the team, but this trade enabled the A's to move Ken Harrelson to first base. Dick Green, Catfish Hunter and Campy Campaneris also joined the starting lineup.

1965 Transactions

Date	Acquired	From	In Exchange For	Win Shares A's	Other
Jan. 20, 1965	Jim Landis, of (19) Mike Hershberger, of (48) Fred Talbot, p* (21)	Chicago White Sox	Rocky Colavito, of (62)	88	62
Feb. 15, 1965	waiver price	Cleveland Indians	Bill Edgerton, p *(1)*		
Apr. 9, 1965	Bill Edgerton, p *(1)*	Cleveland Indians	waiver price		
May 3, 1965	John Blanchard, c (1) Roland Sheldon, p (11)	N.Y. Yankees	Doc Edwards, c (4)	12	4
May 3, 1965	waiver price	Boston Red Sox	John Sanders, of *(0)*		
May 3, 1965	waiver price	Cleveland Indians	Joe Rudi, of *(173)*		
May 3, 1965	Jim Rittwage, p *(2)*	Cleveland Indians	waiver price		
May 7, 1965	Bill Schlesinger, of *(0)*	Boston Red Sox	waiver price		
June 4, 1965	Jess Hickman, p (0) Ernie Fazio, 2b† (1) and $100,000	Houston Astros	Jim Gentile, 1b (13)	1	13
June 23, 1965	cash	Detroit Tigers	Orlando Pena, p *(31)*		
Sept. 8, 1965	cash	Milwaukee Braves	John Blanchard, c *(0)*		

*A's received Talbot on February 10, 1965 to complete the trade
†A's received Fazio on October 15, 1965 to complete the trade

1966 Transactions

Date	Acquired	From	In Exchange For	Win Shares A's	Other
Dec. 1, 1965	Phil Roof, c (49) Joe Rudi, of (173)	Cleveland Indians	Jim Landis, of (10) Jim Rittwage, p (2)	222	12
Apr. 6, 1966	Ralph Terry, p (4) and cash	Cleveland Indians	John O'Donoghue, p (19)	4	19
Apr. 13, 1966	cash	Washington Senators	Diego Segui, p *(73)*		
May 11, 1966	Joe Nossek, of *(6)*	Minnesota Twins	cash		
May 17, 1966	cash	Houston Astros	Aurelio Monteagudo, p *(5)*		
May 27, 1966	Danny Cater, inf (91)	Chicago White Sox	Wayne Causey, inf (15)	91	15
June 10, 1966	Gil Blanco, p (0) Roger Repoz, of (64) Bill Stafford, p (1)	N.Y. Yankees	Fred Talbot, p (13) Bill Bryan, c (6)	65	19
June 13, 1966	Jim Gosger, of (30) Ken Sanders, p (54) Guido Grilli, p (0)	Boston Red Sox	John Wyatt, p (24) Roland Sheldon, p (1) Jose Tartabull, of (12)	84	37

30—No More Trades with the Yankees

1966 TRANSACTIONS (cont.)

Date	Acquired	From	In Exchange For	Win Shares	
				A's	Other
June 23, 1966	Jim Duckworth, p (0)	Washington Senators	Ken Harrelson, 1b (66)	0	66
July 30, 1966	Diego Segui, p (73)	Washington Senators	Jim Duckworth, p (0)	73	0
Aug. 2, 1966	Don Blasingame, 2b *(0)*	Washington Senators	cash		
Aug. 6, 1966	cash	N.Y. Mets	Ralph Terry, p *(2)*		

Finley sent Jim Landis and Jim Rittwage to Cleveland on December 1, 1965, for Phil Roof and Joe Rudi. This was one of Finley's best trades and earned the A's a 222–12 advantage in win shares. Rudi became one of the stars on the team in Oakland and Roof was credited for the improved performance of the A's young hurlers.

The A's traded infielder Wayne Causey to the Chicago White Sox for infielder Danny Cater on May 27, 1966. The trade was completed late in the afternoon but officials from both teams agreed it would not go into effect until after the games played that evening. The White Sox played in New York and the A's hosted Baltimore. One half hour after the Kansas City game began, news of the trade was announced on the radio. Causey went to the clubhouse and began packing when he found out about the trade. Dark called him back to the bench and used him as a pinch hitter in the seventh inning. Causey finished the game at shortstop. Major league rules were changed following the season so that once a club notifies the news media about a trade the club may no longer use those players in a game. The A's gained a 91–15 advantage in win shares as Cater was a good hitter who enjoyed several successful major league seasons.

After a slow start in the 1966 season, manager Al Dark decided to use young pitchers developed in the minor leagues. Catfish Hunter, Chuck Dobson, Lew Krausse, John Odom and Jack Aker pitched well and this enabled Finley to trade some veteran pitchers. The A's made two major trades in June. The A's traded Fred Talbot and Bill Bryan to the Yankees on June 10 for Roger Repoz, Gil Blanco and Bill Stafford. Repoz and Blanco were regarded as outstanding prospects and earned the A's a 65–19 advantage in win shares. The A's traded John Wyatt, Roland Sheldon and Jose Tartabull to Boston three days later for Ken Sanders, Guido Grilli and Jim Gosger. Gosger was considered a good prospect and the A's gained a 84–37 advantage in win shares as he played for the A's for a number of seasons.

Finley traded first baseman Ken Harrelson to Washington for pitcher

Jim Duckworth on June 23, 1966 in one of Finley's worst trades. Washington gained a 66–0 advantage in win shares, but the trade was primarily banishment for Harrelson because he owed money to Finley. Duckworth was ineffective and later returned to Washington in exchange for Diego Segui on July 30. Segui was a dependable hurler for the A's, giving Kansas City a 73–0 advantage in win shares.

1967 TRANSACTIONS

Date	Acquired	From	In Exchange For	Win Shares A's	Other
Oct. 17, 1966	waiver price	New York Mets	Larry Stahl, of *(26)*		
May 10, 1967	Larry Elliot, of *(0)* and $50,000	New York Mets	Ed Charles, 3b *(25)*	0	25
June 9, 1967	Ken Harrelson, 1b *(58)*	Washington Senators	cash		
June 15, 1967	Jack Sanford, p *(0)* Jackie Warner, of *(0)*	California Angels	Roger Repoz, of *(51)*	0	51
Aug. 14, 1967	cash	New York Mets	Joe Grzenda, p *(15)*		

The A's traded third baseman Ed Charles to the New York Mets for outfielder Larry Elliott and $50,000 on May 10, 1967. The Mets earned a 25–0 advantage in win shares but the trade was actually an attempt to provide opportunities for some of the A's young talent such as Sal Bando. The A's traded Roger Repoz, who had been a major disappointment, to California for Jack Sanford and outfielder Jack Warner. The Angels gained a 51–0 advantage in win shares because Sanford was ineffective and Warner never appeared in an A's uniform. Finley reacquired Ken Harrelson from Washington on June 9 to provide additional power. Harrelson was released on August 28 after he was quoted as calling Finley "a menace to baseball."

Finley's overall trade record is impressive. He held a 1,059–805 advantage in win shares. Finley developed young players in the A's minor league system and when these players were ready to move to the major league level he phased out veterans to provide an opportunity for the young players to join the major league roster. He considered these players the core of future championship teams, carefully guarded them and rarely traded them away.

Kansas City fans watched the young players as they moved into the lineup and began to play regularly for the A's. By the time the time the franchise moved to Oakland Sal Bando, Dick Green, and Campy Campaneris were regulars in the infield, Rick Monday was the team's center fielder, and Chuck Dobson, Catfish Hunter, Lew Krausse, Paul Lindblad

30—No More Trades with the Yankees

and John Odom were emerging as star pitchers. Catcher Dave Duncan and outfielders Joe Rudi and Reggie Jackson also appeared in a Kansas City uniform during the 1967 season. These players became part of the core of players that formed the nucleus of the great Oakland teams in the early 1970s.

31

Crop Failure

There were few prospects in the Athletics minor league system when Arnold Johnson purchased the team. Only 11 players eventually advanced to the major leagues and only three, George Brunet, Hector Lopez and Ken Johnson, made significant contributions. "We are ready to spend $1 million in the next three years," said Johnson. "We intend to strengthen our farm system. I am going to work this year to build up a strong farm club organization that will help us in providing good your players in the years ahead." By 1956 the minor league system had revived to the point where it became somewhat respectable and they could become more selective.[1]

Bernie Guest was the A's minor league director in Philadelphia and was the only official familiar with the limited talent in the minor league system. He accepted the same position in Kansas City but resigned a few months later and was replaced by Hank Peters. The team had just three full-time scouts when Johnson purchased the team. Nine scouts were added within the next few months. There was a rapid turnover among the scouts during the first three years as the team replaced some scouts and added new scouts. This stabilized in 1957 as Peters built a strong scouting staff.

Year	Scouts	Scouts from Previous Season	Carryover
1955	12	3 (of 3)	100%
1956	16	6 (of 12)	50%
1957	19	9 (of 16)	56%
1958	22	17 (of 19)	89%
1959	20	18 (of 22)	82%
1960	19	15 (of 20)	75%

The A's placed an ad in *The Sporting News* in 1955 to acquire players. "There must be an awful lot of youngsters around the country whom the scouts never have a chance to see," said Johnson. "I know they have records on a majority of the better ones. But a great many of the stars of the game were once youngsters overlooked by the scouts or passed up by them. Suppose we insert an advertisement in *The Sporting News* and if out of it get even one player with some major league potential, I would say the campaign would be worthwhile." Publisher J.G. Spink wrote a story about the plan and more than 1,000 letters were received. The A's had trial camps run by scouts in various sections of the East, South, Southwest and Midwest in July and August and a number of players were signed.[2]

Nonetheless, the minor league system failed to produce major league players during the Johnson era. It took an average of nearly five years for a player to reach the major league level and there should have been players ready to make the major league roster by 1959 or 1960. Measuring its effectiveness by using Bill James win shares, players developed by the A's produced 162 wins shares in 1955, 74 in 1956 and just 23 in 1957. The only player signed during 1955 to appear regularly in the major leagues was infielder Clete Boyer. None of the players signed in 1956 played on the major league level on a regular basis, although two minor leaguers purchased from other organizations (John Wyatt and Leo Posada) made the team. Infielder Lou Klimchock signed in 1957. He played in the major leagues for a number of seasons and was acknowledged as the first player produced by the Kansas City Athletics minor leagues to help the team.

Some of the blame lies with scouting. The rapid turnover among scouts during the first three years indicates the team was not pleased with the performance of some scouts. More major league players were developed after 1957. Most of the blame, however, must be placed on the failure to sign bonus players. An interesting comparison can be drawn between the Orioles and the Athletics. The St. Louis Browns had few minor league prospects when the franchise moved to Baltimore in 1953. Orioles general manager Paul Richards initiated an aggressive program to sign bonus players. At that time major league rules stipulated that these bonus players had to be kept on the major league roster and could not be sent to the minor leagues for three season. The Orioles had many bonus players on the roster and struggled with losing records, but this policy enabled the team to become one of the best teams in the league.

The A's signed Clete Boyer to an estimated $40,000 bonus contract and kept him on the major league roster. They signed only one other bonus player (Dave Hill, a 19-year-old pitcher, signed for an estimated $35,000 bonus on August 12, 1957). The rule was changed after the 1957 season. The failure to sign bonus players meant the team did not acquire the prospects with the greatest potential. Every other major league team, with the exception of the Yankees and Dodgers, who already had flourishing minor league systems, spent considerable amounts to sign bonus players.

An interesting comparison is made with what other major league teams spent during 1955 and 1956 when the figures were made available to the Congress:

Team	Bonuses 1955–1956
Cleveland	$363,676
Milwaukee	$344,341
Chicago Cubs	$215,625
Pittsburgh	$123,743
Baltimore	$92,738
Boston	$87,500
NY Giants	$48,383
St. Louis	$46,666
Washington	$41,519
Chicago White Sox	$41,200
NY Yankees	$31,650
Kansas City	$10,000
Brooklyn	$9,000

Figures not available from Detroit, Cincinnati or Philadelphia[3]

The A's began to spend more money to sign players in 1958 and the minor leagues began to produce more players, and consequently, more win shares, but the team still did not spend the money to sign the most outstanding prospects. "The Athletics at their very best, will never be anything more than a .500 club until their farm system starts producing," wrote Joe McGuff in 1959. "Frankly we have been disappointed at what we have seen in the farm system. In four years, or five if you prefer to be technical, the A's have not produced one regular — pitcher, infielder, outfielder or catcher — in their own farm system. The only truly outstanding prospect we have observed who has a chance to make the majors next year is Lou Klimchock, who has been playing second base through the closing days of the season. Somehow it seems the Athletics are not getting the youngsters with truly outstanding physical ability. It is our opinion that the men running the farm system are both competent and vigorous but judging from what we have gathered in talking with various baseball people the Athletics simply are not spending the money that other organizations are. Johnson has been operating on the theory that it is better to sign 10 boys for $4,000 apiece than to sign one for $40,000. It is a wonderful theory, but we feel it is totally impractical. Of the 100 outstanding youngsters who are signed each year we would guess that all of them get $20,000 or more. And the price goes up steeply for the few individuals with exceptional talent. By the time you get down to the $4,000 class, there isn't a great deal left. The Athletics have paid some bonuses in excess of $25,000 this year but they ... have never gone after any of the big money prospects. As long as the other clubs are paying them the Athletics must either keep pace or settle for second line talent."[4]

Three players signed in 1958 eventually reached the major leagues: pitchers Norm Bass and Howard Reed and shortstop Dick Howser. Howser was an American League All-Star and was named team captain as a rookie in 1961. The A's signed more bonus players in 1959 and 1960 and more graduates from these classes reached the major league level: pitcher John O'Donoghue, Jose Santiago, Dave Wickersham, Diego Segui, and Ken Sanders, catcher Bill Bryan, infielders Ken Harrelson, Dick Green and Ossie Chavarria, and outfielder Larry Stahl. "[A's scout] Clyde Kluttz pointed out the advantages of going to Kansas City and said the Athletics would give me a sizable bonus," said Ken Harrelson. "We didn't talk specific figures. Most of Kluttz's argument was that I'd move up faster with the Athletics, which was true. They needed so much help that a kid really did have a better opportunity with them than anyone else."[5]

The Baltimore Orioles conducted a major league wide survey in 1960 to evaluate the number of players that reached or were on the verge of reaching the major leagues covering the years 1954 through 1960. It included players signed by one organization that played with another major league team. Kansas City had the fewest players to reach either the major league or AAA level.[6]

PLAYERS, DEVELOPED, 1954–1960

Team	Major Leagues	AAA Leagues	Total
St Louis	8	23	31
Milwaukee	5	25	30
Baltimore	11	14	25
Los Angeles	6	17	23
Pittsburgh	6	17	23
San Francisco	9	14	23
Cincinnati	10	12	22
Chicago Cubs	11	10	21
Boston	5	13	18
Chicago White Sox	6	11	17
Philadelphia	8	9	17
Cleveland	7	7	14
Detroit	4	9	13
New York Yankees	3	8	11
Washington	3	8	11
Kansas City	2	4	6

Hank Peters, minor league director under both Johnson and Finley, was asked why the A's had so much trouble building a winning team during the

Players That Advanced to the Major Leagues

Players in the Philadelphia Athletics organization when Johnson acquired the team in 1954 that eventually made the major leagues.
(Numbers preceding names indicate career win shares; numbers following names indicate seasons played)

Brief Appearance	Moderate Contribution	Major League Regular
(0) Walt Craddock, p (56, 58)	*(5)* Bill Harrington, p (55, 56)	*(63)* George Brunet, p (56–71)
(0) Carl Duser, p (56, 58)		*(136)* Hector Lopez, inf (55–66)
(0) Bill Kern, of (62)		*(95)* Ken Johnson, p (58–70)
(0) John Kume, p (55)		
(0) Don Pilarski, of (55)		
(0) Bill Stewart, of (55)		
(0) Oscar van Bryant, p (55)		

Class of 1955: 162 Win Shares

(2) Bob Davis, p (58, 60)
(0) Alex George, inf (55)
(0) Evans Killeen, p (59)

(160) Clete Boyer, inf (55–71)

Class of 1956: 74 Win Shares

(0) Chet Boak, inf (60)	*(9)* Leo Posada, of (60–62)	*(65)* John Wyatt, p (61–69)
(0) Gordon MacKenzie, c (61)		

Class of 1957: 23 Win Shares

(1) Jay Hankins, of (61, 63)	*(9)* Dan Pfister, p (61–64)	*(12)* Lou Klimchock, inf (58–70)
(0) David Hill, p (57)		
(1) Harry Taylor, p (57)		

Class of 1958: 111 Win Shares

(7) Norm Bass, p (61–63)

(30) Howard Reed, p (58–60, 64–71)
(74) Dick Howser, ss (61–68)

Class of 1959: 397 Win Shares

(0) Ray Blemker, p (59)	*(5)* Ossie Chavarria, inf (66–67)	*(73)* Jack Aker, p (64–74)
(0) Dave Theis, p (63)		*(88)* Ken Harrelson, 1b (63–71)
		(31) John O'Donoghue, p (63–71)
		(32) Jose Santiago, p (63–70)
		(103) Diego Segui, p (62–75, 77)
		(65) Dave Wickersham, p (60–69)

Class of 1960: 247 Win Shares

(0) Frank Cipriani, of (61)	*(26)* Bill Bryan, c (61–68)
(0) Hector Martinez, inf (62–63)	*(117)* Dick Green, 2b (63–74)
(0) Ruperto Toppin, p (62)	*(65)* Ken Sanders, p (64–76)
(1) Dale Willis, p (63)	*(38)* Larry Stahl, of (64–73)

Johnson era. "When Arnold Johnson acquired the Athletics in 1955, he took over a defunct organization," answered Peters. "I think the Philadelphia club had three scouts and about 50 players in its farm system. We tried to build things up, but we were handicapped because we had to operate on a very limited budget. In fact, our budget wasn't just limited, it was extremely strict. We did come up with a few players, but we weren't really competitive. When Mr. Finley bought the club he was willing to spend more money."[7]

MINOR LEAGUE STANDINGS 1955–1960

1955

Class	Team	Won	Lost	Pct	GB	Place
AAA	*Columbus	64	89	.418	30½	7 (of 8)
A	Savannah	61	79	.436	28	6 (of 8)
B	Lancaster	72	54	.571	3½	2 (of 8)
C	†Hot Springs	57	62	.479	20	4 (of 6)
C	*Burlington	65	64	.504	20½	3 (of 6)
D	*Welch-Marion	45	77	.369	39	8 (of 8)
D	*Seminole	56	83	.403	39	8 (of 8)
	Totals	420	508	.453		

1956

Class	Team	Won	Lost	Pct	GB	Place
AAA	*Columbus	69	84	.451	17½	7 (of 8)
A	*Columbia	64	76	.457	23	5 (of 8)
B	*Abilene	73	67	.521	10	5 (of 8)
C	*Crowley	63	60	.512	13	3 (of 8)
C	*Pocatello	51	81	.386	23	8 (of 8)
D	*Fitzgerald	47	92	.338	47	8 (of 8)
D	Grand Island	35	28	.556	6	2 (of 8)
D	*Seminole	74	66	.529	9½	3 (of 8)
	Totals	476	554	.462		

1957

Class	Team	Won	Lost	Pct	GB	Place
AAA	†Buffalo	88	66	.571	½	2 (of 8)
AA	*Little Rock	64	88	.421	22	7 (of 8)
A	*Columbia	59	95	.383	39	7 (of 8)
B	*Abilene	61	66	.480	15½	4 (of 6)
C	*Crowley	63	47	.573	4½	2 (of 6)
C	*Pocatello	64	62	.508	15	3 (of 8)
D	Mattoon	45	82	.344	33	8 (of 8)
D	Grand Island	33	22	.600	—	1 (of 8)
D	*Seminole	46	79	.368	28	8 (of 8)
	Totals	521	.607	.462		

1958

Class	Team	Won	Lost	Pct	GB	Place
AAA	†Buffalo	69	83	.454	20½	7 (of 8)
AA	†Little Rock	74	80	.481	17½	6 (of 8)
A	*Albany	57	70	.449	15½	7 (of 8)
B	*Rochester	57	73	.438	20	5 (of 6)
C	*Pocatello	70	63	.526	7½	3 (of 7)
D	*Selma	71	49	.592	—	1 (of 8)
D	Grand Island	33	30	.524	8	3 (of 8)
D	*Plainview	50	70	.417	22	6 (of 6)
	Totals	481	518	.482		

1959

Class	Team	Won	Lost	Pct	GB	Place
AAA	*Portland	75	77	.493	9	6 (of 8)
AA	*Shreveport	75	79	.487	17½	5 (of 8)
A	*Albany	54	85	.388	30½	8 (of 8)
B	*Sioux City	58	68	.460	20	5 (of 8)
C	*Pocatello	58	70	.453	23	5 (of 6)
D	Grand Island	32	30	.516	11	3 (of 6)
D	*Olean	57	69	.452	23	6 (of 8)
D	*Plainview	60	65	.480	29½	4 (of 8)
	Totals	469	543	.463		

1960

Class	Team	Won	Lost	Pct	GB	Place
AAA	*Dallas-Ft. Worth	64	90	.416	24	8 (of 8)
AA	*Shreveport	86	67	.562	½	2 (of 8)
AA	†Monterrey	66	79	.455	12	4 (of 6)
B	†Lewiston	78	63	.553	6½	3 (of 6)
B	*Sioux City	71	68	.511	11½	3 (of 8)
C	*Visalia	54	85	.388	34½	6 (of 6)
D	*Sanford	77	60	.562	8½	3 (of 8)
D	*Albuquerque	57	72	.442	19½	5 (of 6)
	Totals	553	584	.486		

*General Working Agreement
†Limited Working Agreement
All other teams owned outright

32

Growing a Championship Team

"We had some good players in the organization when Mr. Finley bought the club," Hank Peters said. "We had signed [Dick] Howser, [Dave] Wickersham, [John] Wyatt, [Diego] Segui and Cletis Boyer. We just didn't have enough good prospects, however." Finley promised to do everything possible to build the team into a winner after he purchased the team. "All the profits will be poured back into the club and if that isn't enough, I will use more of my own money," he promised.[1]

Finley retained Peters to head the minor league operations, although Finley fired him during the 1961 season and replaced him with Bill Bergesch. Finley rehired Peters after the season and he served as minor league director through 1965. "Guys like Hank Peters ... have to come in for some of the credit for the A's success," said Baltimore vice president Frank Cashen. "I think some people may labor under the illusion that Charlie went out to the highways and byways and found people like Vida Blue and Catfish Hunter himself. But he had to have somebody at the top to identify the personnel. He did have the imagination and the pocketbook to sign them."[2]

The A's also had good scouts. "Finley realized that he was a relative novice at baseball," wrote Bruce Markusen. "He listened intently to his scouts—people like Joe Bowman, Dan Carnevale, Tom Giordano, Clyde Kluttz, Art Lilly, Don Pries, Jack Sanford and others—who told him which amateur players to pursue as free agents and which ones to draft. As a result, the A's developed future stars like Catfish Hunter, Vida Blue, Blue Moon Odom, Rollie Fingers, Campy Campaneris, Sal Bando and Reggie Jackson." Six scouts resigned following the 1961 season and the scouting staff was cut from 22 scouts in 1961 to 11 in 1963 as an economy measure, but the scouts that remained helped Finley acquire some of the top prospects in baseball.[3]

Year	Scouts	Scouts from Previous Season	Carryover
1961	22	16 (of 19)	84%
1962	17	8 (of 22)	36%
1963	11	9 (of 17)	53%
1964	16	9 (of 11)	82%
1965	12	12 (of 16)	75%
1966	11	7 (of 12)	58%
1967	16	9 (of 11)	82%

Finley demonstrated his willingness to spend money to sign top prospects during his initial season in Kansas City signed players that produced 218 wins shares. A's scouts signed pitchers Aurelio Monteagudo, Bill Landis and Fred Norman, outfielder Allan Lewis and Ted Kubiak, a slick-fielding 18-year-old shortstop from New Jersey. Finley signed Lew Krausse for an estimated $125,000 bonus, the largest bonus Finley ever paid to a player.[4]

"Before there was a draft my job was to meet Finley wherever we were going to sign a kid," said Joe Bowman, describing the negotiations. "I'd have the report. I'd meet him. I'd take him out to talk to the kid. We'd walk in the house. Finley would just let me alone. Finley would take off his necktie and coat. He'd go to the refrigerator and get something to drink, wander around the house, go to the bathroom. And all this time I'm talking, see. I'd talk about our organization, about Finley and what a great opportunity the kid would get by signing with our organization. He would. Because Finley would bring them up at any age. Finally, when Finley comes in and sits down and starts talking money, I'd shut up and keep writing down what he's offering. We didn't miss many, because when it's all over with, he'd say. 'Okay, what in the hell do you want?' The kid'd name some outrageous price like $100,000 or $125,000. Finley'd say, 'Okay, Joe. Write it up. Let's get out of here....' Then we would hit spots where he wouldn't give a kid another nickel. The kid'd say something to him that turned him off, and he just wouldn't go for it. That's all there was to it. There was a kid by the name of Fazio, who lived out on the coast and never did go anywhere. We went in to talk to this kid, and he was way up over the price that he should've been offered. Finley said something to the kid: where he would send him, what he would do with him. And the kid's father said, 'When you sign him, you can say what you're going to do with him. But right now, he's my kid, and I'll say what I'm going to do with him.' Finley just cut it off, just like that, and finally got up and left. Left me with the figures and everything. I said, 'Well, what do I do, Charlie? Do I tell him they don't get this either?' He says, 'No, I said I'd give it to them. But don't you give them one nickel more. A nickel, he said. And the guy tried to come down to where it was only a difference of about $2,500, and I said, 'I'm sorry. I can't give it to you.'"[5]

The A's signed Tony LaRussa to a modest bonus in 1962 and kept him on the roster during the 1963 season to protect him from the draft. Felix Delgado discovered a 20-year-old, 140-pound catcher from Cuba named Campy Campaneris, and signed him for a $500 bonus. He pitched both right-handed and left-handed in two innings of relief in a minor league game for Daytona Beach on August 13, 1962, giving up one run and one hit while walking two and striking out four batters. He eventually settled in at shortstop.[6]

The A's signed pitchers Jim Nash and Paul Lindblad and catcher Dave Duncan in 1963. A dozen scouts watched Nash pitch his final high school game. He had a poor game as he pitched several innings the previous day and only two scouts remained interested: Mercer Harris from Kansas City and a scout from the Mets. Nash told them he was not interested in signing because he was going to college, but his car broke down the following day and he decided to accept the modest $1,000 bonus that was offered. He tried to contact the Mets scout, but when he could not contact him he called Harris and signed with the A's.

The A's sent Nash to Daytona Beach and Hank Peters ordered manager Bobby Hofman not to use him in any games. Peters hoped if Nash did not pitch any games it would be possible to sneak him through the first year draft without protecting him on the major league roster. "Seventy games without pitching an inning," Nash recalled. "I worked in the mornings with Hofman, threw batting practice and ran.... It gave me time to work on pitches."[7]

Jim Gleeson signed left-handed pitcher Paul Lindblad. Lindblad lived in the Kansas City area and pitched at the University of Kansas. Art Lilly scouted Dave Duncan, a catcher from San Diego. Finley signed the 18-year-old to a $65,000 bonus and assigned him to Daytona Beach.[8]

Baseball officials became alarmed at the large bonus contracts required to sign players and wanted to initiate an amateur player draft. Finley

Jim Nash (from the Kansas City Athletics).

decided to sign as many quality players as he could before the draft went into effect. He spent $662,000 to sign 80 players in 1964, the most spent by one team in a single season. These players produced 734 win shares.

"I had a giant six-state territory—Missouri, Arkansas, Kansas, Oklahoma, Nebraska and northern Texas—and worked it like a Show-Me mule on speed," said scout Whitey Herzog. "I signed 12 ballplayers from that territory for a total of $125,000. Seven made big league rosters inside of a year. A few—like pitcher Chuck Dobson—played parts in the three Oakland championships of the 1970s.... The year I joined them, 1964, Finley made a huge profit in his insurance business.... He came barging into the office of Hank Peters one day, 'Hank,' he said, 'I have to spend $900,000 by July 15, so lets sign some ballplayers'.... Hank had wonderful scouts in place for him—not a lot of guys—but good ones; Tom Giordano on the East Coast, Clyde Kluttz in the Carolinas, Jack Sanford in Florida, Art Lily on the West Coast. We fanned out all over the country. We signed Blue Moon Odom, Catfish, Skippy Lockwood, Joe Rudi.[9]

Jim Hunter, an 18-year-old right-hander from Hertford, North Carolina, had a 26–2 record in high school and threw five no-hitters. "He knew instinctively how to pitch," said Kluttz. "There was no way you could give that to him. Those kind of guys are just born, and not very often." Hunter was an all-state end and linebacker in football. He injured his foot in a hunting accident. His brother's shotgun accidentally fired and Hunter's little toe on his right foot was blown off, filling the foot with 60 buckshot pellets. The boys walked to a hospital. The doctor decided to leave the pellets in Hunter's foot. He won 12 games during his senior year but many scouts were concerned about the injury. Finley admitted that Hunter's foot "scared the hell out of me. I already had offered him a contract. But that day he went out and won the state high school championship, pitching one of the most tenacious games I've ever seen."[10]

Finley and Kluttz drove to the Hunter farm in a black limousine, preceded by a police escort. "Mr. Finley started passing out green warm-up jackets and green bats and orange baseball and it sort of scared off the other scouts," said Hunter. "They figured Mr. Finley had me all sewed up.... The money they offered me was fine but I kind of felt I could get a new car, too. I said I'd call up the other scouts to see if they'd top his offer. He got mad and said I take the money then or not at all. I took it." Finley signed Hunter to a $75,000 contract and instructed Kluttz to take him to Mayo Clinic where surgeons removed 45 pellets and some bone fragments from his foot. He missed the entire 1964 season after the surgery. Finley nicknamed him "Catfish" and told him to tell people he ran away as a boy, went fishing, and returned with a string of catfish slung over his shoulder. "I did fish a lot as a boy," he said, "But I didn't think much of my name. But I also didn't want to cross this man who was spending so much money on me so I said all right. I didn't think the name would stick."[11]

Finley also gave a colorful nickname to pitcher John "Blue Moon" Odom. He supposedly was given the nickname "moon" because of his round face. It became "Blue Moon" because he seldom smiled and always seemed sad. Odom was an all-around athlete at Ballard-Hudson High School in Macon, Georgia, but excelled in baseball. He had a 42-2 record in high school with eight no-hitters.

"My father died when I was five and there was just me and my mother living in this place in a housing project," said Odom. "I was almost 19 years old when the baseball scouts came around. The San Francisco Giants offered me about $40,000. The A's offer was real low. So their scout, Jack Sanford, got on the phone with Finley and Finley came down to see me personally.... When he got to my house he waited for his turn to talk to me, just like the other scouts. And before I knew it there was a truck outside with all kinds of fruits and vegetables and stuff. He just got all the neighbors to come up to the truck ... and he passed out Kansas City A's jackets to them, too, after I had signed. I got $75,000. I was happy that an owner had come to see me, because I could bargain more with him than I could with a scout.... What he doesn't know is I'd have signed for as little as $35,000."[12]

Whitey Herzog signed pitcher Chuck Dobson for an estimated $25,000 bonus. He pitched for the University of Kansas and played for a United States Amateur All-Star team that toured the Far East and performed at the opening of the 1964 Olympics in Tokyo. The A's also signed Olympians Joe Bosworth, Dick Joyce and Ken Suarez. Don Pries signed Joe Rudi from Downey High School in Modesto, California. Rudi impressed several major league scouts until he was hit by a pitch that fractured his left hand during his senior year. Pries was the only scout that remained interested and he even set up medical treatment for Rudi's hand. Rudi rewarded Pries's loyalty by signing a contract with the A's.[13]

Bill Enos signed Skip Lockwood, a 17-year-old infielder from Boston, for a $100,000 bonus, the second highest bonus paid by the A's. (Lockwood later converted to pitcher and appeared in 420 games, none with the A's.) The A's also signed pitchers Tony Pierce and Don Buschhorn, catcher Rene Lachemann and infielders Syd O'Brien and Felix Millan. Millan batted .291 at Daytona Beach but was not placed on the A's roster and was claimed by the Braves.

Finley would have reached his $900,000 goal if he signed Rick

Reichardt and Willie Crawford. Reichardt was a 21-year-old outfielder from the University of Wisconsin. Finley offered him more than any other team, but Reichardt told Finley that even if Finley offered him $1 million, "I still won't sign because I want to play in an area like Los Angeles or New York." The Angels eventually signed him for a reported $200,000 bonus in June 1964. Crawford batted .600 for his high school team and representatives from every major league team visited his Los Angeles home. Finley offered him $200,000, bought him a tuxedo for his senior prom, a gown for his date and rented a Thunderbird for him to drive. The Dodgers raised their offer to $100,000 and sent Tommy Lasorda to Crawford's home. Crawford signed with the Dodgers while Finley sat outside the house waiting for another chance.[14]

Major league baseball initiated a free-agent draft on May 1, 1965. The clubs drafted players in reverse order of their standings from the previous season. Kansas City finished in last place in the American League in 1964 and had the first choice in the draft. Kansas City selected 19-year-old outfielder Rick Monday. He batted .356 with 11 home runs at Arizona State and was chosen college player of the year. Finley came to Omaha and signed him to an estimated $100,000 bonus at the conclusion of the College World Series. He also gave Monday a $4,000 car. Finley was impressed by Arizona State's third baseman Sal Bando when he scouted Monday at the College World Series. Hank Peters signed Bando for an estimated $30,000 bonus.[15]

Dan Carnevale discovered Gene Tenace. Tenace impressed Carnevale with a model swing and great determination. He signed with the A's and played various positions before he was converted to a catcher. Art Lilly signed right-handed fastball pitcher Roland Fingers from California for a $20,000 bonus. He led his Upland American Legion Post Number 73 team to a national championship in 1964 with an 11–3 record and a .450 batting average.[16]

The players signed in the 1965 free-agent draft produced 1,065 shares. Finley spent $1.6 million in five years to build what he called the strongest minor league system in baseball. "It takes a man like Charlie Finley to get a club to the threshold that quickly," wrote Alvin Dark. "It takes somebody with guts, foresight and a willingness to put money into areas where there isn't much glory returned on the investments. That means investing in the farm system, in scouting.... It has to be a tremendous satisfaction for Finley to realize that with few exceptions the guys who won three world championships back to back were houseplants who came up through the A's system: Joe Rudi, Sal Bando, Bert Campaneris, Dick Green, Reggie Jackson, Rollie Fingers, Vida Blue, Catfish Hunter, Blue Moon Odom—

32—Growing a Championship Team

every one of them were originals, players Mr. Finley went out and offered bonuses to and signed. Finley was willing to pay large bonuses to sign the top prospects and Peters and his scouts find a number of players that eventually became major league All-Stars. Almost any scout could name the top players in the country, but it took good scouts to find the players nobody else knew about and then see the player wind up in the major leagues."[17]

Finley promoted Peters to general manager of the team on April 6, 1965, but the owner replaced him six months later. Peters resigned and became the minor league director of the Indians. The A's lost director of scouting Joe Bowman and chief West Coast scout Art Lilly after Peters left. Bowman joined Atlanta as regional scouting director. The loss of these men signaled a change in the team's philosophy. Finley spent less money on player procurement and concentrated on developing players already signed by the organization.[18]

The A's finished in last place in the American League in 1965 and had the second pick in the 1966 free-agent draft. Kansas City chose Reggie Jackson, an outfielder from Arizona State. The Dodgers, Phillies, Giants, and Twins offered him bonus contracts after he graduated from high school, but he did not feel the bonuses were large enough and he attended Arizona State. He hit 15 home runs in his only varsity season and became the first college player to hit a ball out of Phoenix Municipal Stadium, a drive estimated to be over 500 feet. Finley and scout Bob Zuk signed Jackson following the College World Series in Omaha for an estimated $85,000 bonus and a new car. "He came driving up in a big Cadillac," said Jackson. "He kept talking about what a big star I was going to be and how we were going to be champions. He really overwhelmed me."[19]

Reggie Jackson made his major league debut with the Kansas City A's in 1967. (From the Kansas City Athletics.)

Don Lindesberg signed

outfielder Joe Keough, a four-sport star at Ganesha High School in Pomona, California. He helped his team win the state baseball championship and was an All-American in football. The A's also signed pitcher Dave Hamilton and outfielders Robert Brooks and Pete Koegel. The draft produced 510 win shares.

Connie Ryan scouted 18-year-old pitcher Vida Blue and the A's selected him in the second round of the 1967 draft. He once pitched a no-hitter and struck out 21 men in a seven-inning game at DeSoto High School in Mansfield, Louisiana, but lost because of walks, missed third strikes and passed balls. He lost only two games in three years and pitched his team to two district titles. Blue was also a football star and passed for 3,400 yards, threw 35 touchdown passes and ran for 1,600 yards during his senior year. Ryan offered him a $25,000 bonus. Blue's high school coach tried to get Ryan to increase the offer. When Ryan declined Blue became angry and refused to sign. Finley fired Ryan, telephoned Blue and offered him the $25,000 bonus with an additional $8,000 set aside in a trust if he wanted to attend college. A's scouting director Ray Swallow flew to Louisiana to complete the deal.[20]

By 1968 *Life Magazine* reported Finley spent $2.5 million on bonus contracts and built the best minor league system in baseball. The magazine said Finley "has one of the youngest and most promising teams in baseball" largely because of the success in the minor league system. The players signed by Finley became the core of three championship teams.

PLAYERS THAT ADVANCED TO THE MAJOR LEAGUES

Players in the Philadelphia Athletics organization when Johnson acquired the team in 1954 that eventually made the major leagues.
(Numbers preceding names indicate career win shares; numbers following names indicate seasons played)

Brief Appearance	Moderate Contribution	Major League Regular
	Class of 1961: 218 Win Shares	
(0) Allan Lewis, of (67–73)	(6) Bill Landis, p (63, 67–69)	(53) Lew Krausse, p (67–74)
(1) Charles Shoemaker, if (61,62,64)	(7) Aurelio Monteagudo, p (63–70)	(46) Ted Kubiak, inf (61, 64–76)
	(4) John Wojcik, of (62–64)	(101) Fred Norman, p (62–78)
	Class of 1962: 287 Win Shares	
(0) Pete Lovrich, p (63)	(3) Tony LaRussa, inf (63, 68–73)	(280) Campy Campaneris, ss (64–83)
	(4) Ron Tompkins, p (65, 71	
	Class of 1963: 253 Win Shares	
(0) Jim Driscoll, inf (70, 72)	(7) Marcel Lachemann, p (69–71)	(71) Dave Duncan, c (64, 67–76)
(1) Bill Edgerton, p (66–67, 69)	(4) Roberto Rodriguez, p (67, 70)	(79) Paul Lindblad, p (66–78)

32—Growing a Championship Team

Class of 1963: 253 Win Shares (cont.)

Brief Appearance	Moderate Contribution	Major League Regular
		(56) Jim Nash, p (66–72)
		(17) Tom Reynolds, of (63–72)
		(18) Ramon Webster, 1B (67–71)

Class of 1964: 734 Win Shares

Note: This is the last year before the free-agent draft. Finley spent $634,000 for 80 players.

(1) Don Buschhorn, p (65)   (4) Rene Lachemann, c (65–68)   (29) John Donaldson, inf (66–70, 74)
(0) Dick Joyce, p (65)   (6) Tony Pierce, p (67–68)   (206) Catfish Hunter, p (65–80)
(1) Santiago Rosario, inf (65)   (79) Skip Lockwood, inf-p (65, 69–79)
(0) Frederico Valazquez, c (69)   (14) Syd O'Brien, inf (69–72)
(69) Blue Moon Odom, p (64–76)
(152) Felix Millan, 2B (66–77)
(173) Joe Rudi, of (67–82)

Class of 1965: 1065 Win Shares

Note: This is the first year under the free-agent draft.

(2) George Lazerique, p (67–70)   (6) Dwain Anderson, inf (71–74)   (283) Sal Bando, 3b (66–81)
(0) Bill McNulty, of (69, 72)   (48) Chuck Dobson, p (66–75)
(0) Don O'Riley, p (69–70)   (188) Roland Fingers, p (68–85)
(0) Randy Schwartz, 1B (65–66)   (31) James Holt, of (68–76)
(258) Rick Monday, of (66–84)
(18) Ken Suarez, c (66–72)
(231) Gene Tenace, c (69–83)

Class of 1966: 510 Win Shares

(0) Pete Koegel, of (70–72)   (6) Robert Brooks, of (69–70, 72–73)   (42) Dave Hamilton, p (72–80)
(1) Gonzalo Marquez, inf (72–74)   (444) Reggie Jackson, of (67–87)
(17) Joe Keough, of (68–70)

Class of 1967: 566 Win Shares

(0) Warren Bogle, p (68)   (202) Vida Blue, p (69–83)
(1) Jim Panther, p (71–73)   (363) Darrell Evans, inf (69–89)

MINOR LEAGUE STANDINGS 1961–1967

The classification of minor league teams changed in 1963. Class A and AA teams became AA teams and Class B, C, and D teams became A teams.

1961

Class	Team	Won	Lost	Pct.	GB	Place
AAA	*Hawaii	68	86	.442	29	6 (of 8)
AA	*Shreveport	69	84	.451	21½	7 (of 8)
A	†Portsmouth	66	72	.478	21½	6 (of 8)

1961 (cont.)

Class	Team	Won	Lost	Pct.	GB	Place
B	*Lewiston	84	56	.600	—	1 (of 6)
C	*Visalia	60	79	.432	36½	4 (of 6)
C	†Pocatello	57	72	.442	16	5 (of 6)
D	*Sarasota	79	60	.568	13½	2 (of 7)
D	*Albuquerque	64	63	.504	14	3 (of 6)
	Totals	547	572	.489		

1962

Class	Team	Won	Lost	Pct.	GB	Place
AAA	*Hawaii	68	86	.442	29	6 (of 8)
AAA	*Portland	74	80	.481	19	6 (of 8)
AA	*Albuquerque	70	70	.500	10	3 (of 6)
A	*Binghamton	60	80	.429	23	6 (of 6)
B	*Lewiston	66	75	.468	12½	5 (of 6)
C	*Minot	44	80	.355	28	8 (of 8)
D	*Daytona Beach	61	61	.500	10½	5 (of 8)
	Totals	375	446	.457		

1963

Class	Team	Won	Lost	Pct.	GB	Place
AAA	*Portland	74	84	.465	24½	7 (of 12)
AA	*Binghamton	65	75	.464	18	4 (of 6)
A	*Daytona Beach	51	71	.418	29	7 (of 8)
A	*Burlington	72	52	.581	11	2 (of 10)
A	*Lewiston	77	63	.550	7	3 (of 6)
	Totals	338	345	.495		

1964

Class	Team	Won	Lost	Pct.	GB	Place
AAA	*Dallas	53	104	.338	42½	12 (of 12)
AA	*Birmingham	80	60	.571	1	2 (of 8)
A	*Daytona Beach	63	71	.470	18	5 (of 8)
A	*Burlington	63	59	.516	17	4 (of 10)
A	*Lewiston	70	70	.500	8	4 (of 6)
Rookie	Wytheville	38	33	.535	9	2 (of 4)
	Totals	367	397	.480		

1965

Class	Team	Won	Lost	Pct.	GB	Place
AAA	*Vancouver	77	69	.527	14½	5 (of 12)
AA	*Birmingham	54	85	.388	25½	8 (of 8)
A	*Leesburg	53	80	.398	17	9 (of 10)
A	*Burlington	82	40	.672	—	1 (of 10)

32—Growing a Championship Team

1965 (cont.)

Class	Team	Won	Lost	Pct.	GB	Place
A	*Lewiston	86	53	.619	—	1 (of 6)
A	*Shelby	55	68	.443	17½	6 (of 8)
	Totals	407	395	.508		

1966

Class	Team	Won	Lost	Pct.	GB	Place
AAA	*Vancouver	77	71	.520	8	6 (of 12)
AA	Mobile	88	52	.629	—	1 (of 8)
A	*Modesto	88	53	.624	—	1 (of 8)
A	*Leesburg	87	44	.664	1½	2 (of 10)
A	*Burlington	77	48	.616	6	3 (of 10)
A	*Lewiston	27	56	.325	29½	4 (of 4)
	Totals	444	324	.578		

1967

Class	Team	Won	Lost	Pct.	GB	Place
AAA	*Vancouver	77	69	.527	7	4 (of 12)
AA	Birmingham	84	55	.604	—	1 (of 6)
A	*Peninsula	74	64	.536	1	2 (of 12)
A	*Leesburg	64	71	.474	30	6 (of 10)
A	*Burlington	56	59	.487	14	5 (of 10)
Rookie	Sarasota	35	22	.614	—	1 (of 6)
	Totals	390	340	.534		

*General Working Agreement
†Limited Working Agreement
All other teams owned outright

Notes

1—BIG LEAGUE DREAMS

1. Ernest Mehl, *The Kansas City Athletics* (New York: Henry Holt, 1956), 35; *Sporting News*, July 22, 1953; James Miller, *The Baseball Business* (Chapel Hill: University of North Carolina Press, 1990), 33.
2. *Kansas City Star*, Sports Section, April 6, 1986, 2; Mehl, *Athletics*, 26.
3. David Jordan, *The Athletics of Philadelphia* (Jefferson, NC: McFarland & Company, Inc., 1999); Lanse McCurley, "House of Mack—A House Divided," *The Sporting News*, November 10, 1954; and Harry T. Paxton, "The Philadelphia A's Last Stand," *Saturday Evening Post*, June 12, 1954. These sources were used for the information on the Philadelphia Athletics.
4. Paxton, *Saturday Evening Post*, 31.
5. *Ibid.*, 136.

2—A CLEVER BUSINESSMAN

1. Arthur Mann, "How to Buy a Ball Club for Peanuts," *Saturday Evening Post*, April 9, 1955, 106.

3—QUEST FOR THE A'S

1. Mehl, *Athletics*, 49–50.
2. Charles Johnson, "How Major League Baseball Came to Minnesota," *Metrodome Souvenir Book* (Minneapolis: MSP Publications, 1982), 48.
3. Mehl, *Athletics*, 46.
4. *New York Times*, August 7, 1954; August 11, 1954; August 16, 1954.
5. Mehl, *Athletics*, 46, 57, 76.
6. *Ibid.*, 66.
7. *New York Times*, October 9, 1954.
8. Mehl, *Athletics*, 68.
9. *Ibid.*, 47, 72.
10. Bill Veeck, *Veeck—As in Wreck* (New York: G.P. Putnam's Sons, 1962), 266–268.
11. *Ibid.*, 247; *New York Times*, October 13, 1954.
12. Mehl, *Athletics*, 70.
13. *Ibid.*, 73.

14. *Ibid.*, 70; Herbert Michelson, *Charlie O* (Indianapolis: Bobbs-Merrill Company, Inc., 1975), 85.
15. Veeck, *Veeck*, 324.
16. Mehl, *Athletics*, 69.
17. Johnson, *Metrodome*, 48.
18. Veeck, *Veeck*, 247; *New York Times*, October 16, 1954.
19. Veeck, *Veeck*, 267–268.

4 — LAST-MINUTE MANEUVERING

1. Mehl, *Athletics*, 77.
2. *New York Times*, October 16, 1954; Mehl, *Athletics*, 79.
3. Mehl, *Athletics*, 83.
4. *Ibid.*, 91–92.
5. *Ibid.*, 93–94.
6. *Ibid.*, 93–94.
7. *Ibid.*, 100.

5 — GOING TO K.C.

1. Mehl, *Athletics*, 102.
2. Art Morrow, "Inside Story of the Race for Possession of Athletics," *The Sporting News*, November 10, 1954, 6; Mehl, *Athletics*, 103.
3. Bill Libby, *Charlie O. and the Angry A's* (Garden City, NY: Doubleday & Company, Inc., 1975), 45–46.
4. Mehl, *Athletics*, 106.
5. Morrow, "Inside," 6.
6. Mehl, *Athletics*, 110.
7. *Ibid.*, 110.
8. *Ibid.*, 114.
9. Charles Johnson, "Minnesota," 48; *Omaha World Herald*, November 12, 1954.
10. Mehl, *Athletics*, 114–115.
11. *Ibid.*, 116–117.
12. *Ibid.*, 119–120.
13. *Ibid.*, 115.
14. *Ibid.*, 123–124.
15. *Ibid.*, 124.
16. Bruce Kuklick, *To Every Thing a Season* (Princeton, NJ: Princeton University Press, 1991), 124.

6 — HOW TO BUY A BALLCLUB FOR PEANUTS

1. Mann, *Saturday Evening Post*, 25.
2. *Ibid.*, 108.
3. Mehl, *Athletics*, 192–193.
4. Joe McGuff, "The Royals," *Trade Him* (Chicago: Follett Publishing Company, 1976), 196. Boston paid $250,000 to purchase the Milwaukee AAA franchise in 1946 and $50,000 to the American Association in 1953 for the loss of the Milwaukee franchise. The Orioles paid $350,000 to acquire the AAA franchise and paid $48,749 to the International League for the loss of the Baltimore franchise in 1953.

5. Kuklick, *To Every Thing*, 123–124. Kuklick wrote: "Roy and Earle Mack took over a weak franchise in 1950 for $2,000 a share. In four years they had run it into the ground, dismissed what might have helped them, demanded that someone else save them.... When they sold out to Johnson, they did so at an effective price of $2,250 a share."

6. Bill Veeck usually took 10 percent of the stock as a finder's fee for "putting together the syndicate, finding the club and closing the deal" (Veeck, *Veeck*, 89). If Johnson took a similar fee, his investment would drop to $468,000 for 52 percent of the stock.

7. *Kansas City Star*, November 23, 1959.

8. Mehl, *Athletics*, 193; James Quirk and Rodney Fort, *Pay Dirt* (Princeton, NJ: Princeton University Press, 1992), 92.

7 — ARNOLD JOHNSON'S ULTIMATE PLAN

1. Hal Lebovitz, "Tribe G.M. Regards Several Cities as Better Locations Than Baltimore and K.C.," *The Sporting News*, November 17, 1954.

2. Veeck, *Hustler's*, 275.

3. Paul Zimmerman, *The Los Angeles Dodgers* (New York: Coward-McCann, Inc., 1960), 67.

4. Dan Daniel, "How Close to California," *The Sporting News*, November 17, 1954; Johnson, *Metrodome*, 48.

5. Mann, *Saturday Evening Post*, 106–108.

6. *Ibid.*, 107–108.

7. Paul O'Neal, *The American Association* (Austin, TX: Eakin Press, 1991), 122.

8. Quirk and Fort, *Pay Dirt*, 91–93; Bill Veeck, *The Hustler's Handbook* (New York: G.P. Putnam's Sons, 1965), 250.

9. Veeck, *Veeck*, 267–268.

10. *Kansas City Times*, March 28, 1957.

8 — THE 90-DAY WONDER

1. Mehl, *Athletics*, 31–33.

2. *Kansas City Star*, November 10, 1954.

3. *Kansas City Times*, November 19, 1954; *Kansas City Star*, December 6, 1954; *The Sporting News*, January 26, 1955, 15.

4. *Kansas City Times*, November 19, 1954.

5. Mehl, *Athletics*, 147–149; *Kansas City Star*, November 19, 1954.

6. Veeck, *Veeck*, 267. The total mortgage was actually $3 million: $2.9 million for Yankee Stadium and $100,000 for Blues Stadium.

7. Mehl, *Athletics*, 139–140.

8. *The Sporting News*, January 26, 1955, 15.

9. *Kansas City Times*, January 22, 1955, *Kansas City Star*, January 28, 1955.

10. *Kansas City Times*, January 23, 1955.

11. Mehl, *Athletics*, 145.

12. *The Sporting News*, March 2, 1955, 11; Mehl, *Athletics*, 193.

13. Mehl, *Athletics*, 151–152.

14. *Ibid.*, 150; "Stadium Mystery Is Solved," *Kansas City Star*, August 5, 1958.

9 — 1955: BIG LEAGUE BASEBALL COMES TO K.C.

1. Mehl, *Athletics*, 216
2. Jack Torrey, *Endless Summers* (South Bend, IN: Diamond Communications, Inc, 1996), 184.
3. Torrey, *Endless*, 184; Mehl, *Athletics*, 185.
4. Boudreau, *Covering*, 163–164; *Kansas City Star*, September 11, 1955; Dan Daniel, "Johnson Earmarks $1,000,000 for Three-Year Player Buying," *The Sporting News*, November 17, 1954, 6.
5. Tim Cohane, "Baseball's Most Exciting Owner," *Look*, March 22, 1955, 71; Mehl, *Athletics*, 159–160
6. *Ibid.*, 168.
7. *Kansas City Star*, April 7, 1985.
8. *Kansas City Star*, April 7, 1985.
9. Mehl, *Athletics*, 171; Boudreau, *Covering*, 167; *Kansas City Star*, April 7, 1985.
10. Mehl, *Athletics*, 170.
11. *Ibid.*, 198.
12. *Kansas City Star*, April 7, 1985; Jack Etkin, *Innings Ago* (Kansas City: Normandy Square Publications, 1987), 59.
13. Etkin, *Innings*, 59.
14. *Kansas City Star*, April 7, 1955.
15. *Ibid.*, Mehl, *Athletics*, 199–200.
16. Etkin, *Innings*, 96.
17. Boudreau, *Covering*, 166–167.
18. Mehl, *Athletics*, 175.
19. *Kansas City Star*, April 7, 1955.
20. *Ibid.*
21. *Ibid.*
22. Mehl, *Athletics*, 188.
23. *Kansas City Star*, April 7, 1985.
24. *Kansas City Star*, April 7, 1985.
25. Mehl, *Athletics*, 202.
26. *Ibid.*
27. *Kansas City Star*, April 7, 1955.
28. Mehl, *Athletics*, 203.

10 — 1956: LISTLESS AND BAD

1. Mehl, *Athletics*,195–196
2. *Kansas City Times*, September, 24, 1955.
3. *Kansas City Times*, November 5, 1955.
4. Fritz Kraisler, "Dimensions at Stadium Change Again," *Kansas City Star*, April 11, 1965.
5. Mehl, *Athletics*, 208.
6. *Ibid.*, 214.
7. Etkin, *Innings*, 96.
8. *Kansas City Star*, July 1, 1956; Boudreau, *Covering*, 168.
9. *Sports Illustrated*, April 15, 1957, 60.

11—1957: BIG TRADES BRING NEW FACES

1. Veeck, *Veeck*, 155; *Sports Illustrated*, April 14, 1958, 75.
2. *Kansas City Star*, February 19, 1957.
3. *Sports Illustrated*, April 15, 1957, 60.
4. *The Sporting News*, August 21, 1957.
5. Boudreau, *Covering*, 169; *The Sporting News*, August 21, 1957.
6. *Kansas City Times*, August 7, 1957.
7. Boudreau, *Covering*, 169.
8. "Hats Off," *The Sporting News*, n.d.
9. *The Sporting News*, n.d.
10. Etkin, *Innings*, 97.
11. *Kansas City Star*, April 17, 1966
12. *Kansas City Star*, August 16, 1957.
13. *Ibid.*

12—1958: CERV'S AMAZING SEASON.

1. *Kansas City Star*, November 21, 1957.
2. *Sports Illustrated*, April 14, 1958, 74.
3. Jerome Holtzman, "Brooks Once Killed Roster Swap," *The Sporting News*, September 10, 1977, 25.
4. *Sports Illustrated*, April 13, 1959, 68.
5. Bob Cerv, "I Played Without Eating," *Saturday Evening Post*, July 19, 1958, 56.
6. *Ibid.*
7. *Sports Illustrated*, April 14, 1958, 74.
8. *Kansas City Star*, September 29, 1958.
9. *Kansas City Star*, August 16, 1958.
10. Barry Gottehrer, "Bud Daley and Ray Herbert," *Baseball Stars of 1961*, Ray Robinson, editor (New York: Pyramid, 1961), 140.
11. Joe McGuff, "Of Baseball, Charlie Finley, 10-Gallon Hats, and the Old A's," *Kansas City Star Magazine*, April 10, 1983, 12.

13—1959: GREAT EXPECTATIONS

1. *Kansas City Star*, September 29, 1958.
2. Gene Fox, *Sports Guys* (Lenexa, KS: Addax Publishing, 1999), 40.
3. *Kansas City Star*, September 29, 1958.
4. *Kansas City Times*, January 27, 1959.
5. Tom Marshall, "Press Box Ready for New Season," *Kansas City Star*, 1965; Bill Moore, "Press Box Longer and, It Is Hoped, Drier," *Kansas City Star*, February 27, 1959.
6. Bill Richardson, "Little Boy Still in Cerv at Age 55," *Kansas City Star*, April 6, 1980.
7. Leonard Shecter, *Roger Maris, Home Run Hero* (New York, 1961), 63, 67.
8. *Ibid.*
9. Gottehrer, *Baseball Stars*, 135.
10. *Ibid.*, 135–136.
11. Jack Newcombe, "Bud Daley," *Baseball Stars of 1960*, Ray Robinson, editor (New York: Pyramid, 1960), 141.
12. *Kansas City Times*, August 29, 1959, *Kansas City Star*, August 30, 1959.

13. *Kansas City Star*, n.d.
14. *The Sporting News*, October 7, 1959, 28.

14 — 1960: A VERY DIFFICULT YEAR

1. Shecter, *Maris*, 80–82; *The Sporting News*, November 4, 1959, 16.
2. *The Sporting News*, November 4, 1959, 16.
3. *Kansas City Times*, January 9, 1960.
4. *The Sporting News*, November, 1960.
5. *Ibid.*, 78–79.
6. Shecter, *Maris*, 85.
7. *Ibid.*, 79.
8. *Kansas City Star*, March 10, 1960.
9. Rex Lardner, "Charlie Finley and Bugs Bunny in K.C.," *Sports Illustrated*, June 5, 1961, 25.
10. Gottehrer, *Baseball Stars*, 135.
11. *Ibid.*, 141–142.
12. *Kansas City Star*, October 3, 1960.

15 — WHO WILL BUY THE TEAM?

1. *New York Times*, March 24, 1960.
2. *Kansas City Star*, June 23, 1960.
3. *Kansas City Times*, July 8, 1960; *Kansas City Times*, July 1, 1960.
4. *Kansas City Times*, July 8, 1960; *Kansas City Times*, July 1, 1960.
5. *Kansas City Times*, July 22, 1960.
6. *Ibid.*
7. *Ibid.*
8. *Kansas City Times*, August 4, 1960.
9. *Ibid.*
10. *Kansas City Times*, September 15, 1960.
11. *Kansas City Star*, August 3, 1960.
12. *Kansas City Times*, September 23, 1960.
13. *The Sporting News*, November 23, 1960.
14. *The Sporting News*, November 16, 1960.
15. *Kansas City Times*, November 16, 1960.
16. *Ibid.*
17. *Kansas City Times*, November 19, 1960.
18. Veeck, *Veeck*, 357.
19. *The Sporting News*, November 30, 1960.
20. *Ibid.*
21. *The Sporting News*, December 28, 1960, 14.
22. *Kansas City Star*, December 8, 1960.
23. *The Sporting News*, December 28, 1960.
24. Joe McGuff, *Why Me? Why Not Joe McGuff?* (Prairie Village, KS: Joe McGuff, 1992), 158–159.

16 — CHARLES O. FINLEY — THE "O" STANDS FOR OWNER

1. Michelson, *Charlie O*, 26, 29; Libby, *Angry*, 42.
2. Michelson, *Charlie O*, 30.

3. Don Kowet, *The Rich Who Own Sports* (New York: Random House, 1977), 125.
4. Michelson, *Charlie O,* 84–85. The Goldblatt family owned a chain of Chicago-area department stores. The Armour family formed the Armour Packing Company, one of the largest meat-packing companies in the country.
5. *Ibid.,* 86.
6. Veeck, *Veeck,* 324.
7. Michelson, *Charlie O,* 89.
8. Veeck, *Veeck,* 363. Bill Veeck felt Ford Frick favored the National League because he did not require the Mets to pay the Yankees for the New York City territorial rights. In fairness to Frick, the National League had two franchises (the Giants and Dodgers) in New York City until 1957, whereas O'Malley purchased the territorial rights to Los Angeles for approximately $1 million in 1957. Gene Autry agreed to these terms when he obtained the Los Angeles franchise. The Angels played in Wrigley Field in 1961 and Autry agreed to a four-year lease to use Dodger Stadium beginning in 1962 with an option to renew for three years.
9. Libby, *Angry,* 47.
10. Michelson, *Charlie O,* 90.

17 — TRYING TO OUTDO VEECK

1. Michelson, *Charlie O,* 91; *The Sporting News,* January 11, 1961, 2, *The Sporting News,* July 27, 1963.
2. *The Sporting News,* December 28, 1960, 7; Joe McGuff "The Finley Story," *Kansas City Star,* 1980.
3. *The Sporting News,* December 28, 1960, 7; *The Sporting News,* n.d.
4. *The Sporting News,* December 28, 1960, 14.
5. *The Sporting News,* January 11, 1961, 1–2. The actual salary was a total of $200,000 spread over eight years.
6. *Ibid.*; *Kansas City Star,* August 23, 1961.
7. Jack Torrey, *Endless,* 58.
8. *The Sporting News,* January 11, 1961.
9. *The Sporting News,* December 28, 1960, 7.
10. *The Sporting News,* January 25, 1961.
11. *Kansas City Star,* January 13, 1961.
12. Kowet, *Rich,* 128.
13. *The Sporting News,* October 14, 1967, 30.
14. *Kansas City Star,* February 16, 1961.
15. Libby, *Angry,* 51.
16. *Kansas City Star,* January 11, 1961, 2.
17. Lardner, *Sports Illustrated,* 26; Michelson, *Charlie O,* 128.
18. Lardner, *Sports Illustrated,* 26.
19. *Kansas City Star,* April 8, 1962.
20. Lardner, *Sports Illustrated,* 26.
21. Tom Clark, *Champagne and Baloney* (New York: Harper & Row, 1976), 11.
22. McGuff "Finley Story."
23. Lardner, *Sports Illustrated,* 25; Libby, *Angry,* 48.

18 — 1961: GORDON, LANE AND CHARLIE O.

1. *The Sporting News,* January 11, 1961, 6.
2. *Ibid.*

3. *Sports Illustrated,* June 5, 1961, 26.
4. Joe McGuff, "The Finley Story," *Kansas City Star,* 1980; *The Sporting News,* August 30, 1961, 5.
5. *The Sporting News,* January 11, 1961, 6; *Sports Illustrated,* June 5, 1961, 26.
6. Libby, *Angry,* 60–61.
7. *Ibid.,* 60.
8. Torrey, *Endless,* 185
9. Fox, *Sports Guys,* 42; Libby, *Angry,* 154.
10. *Sports Illustrated,* June 5, 1961, 29.
11. *Ibid.*
12. Libby, *Angry,* 60.
13. *Sports Illustrated,* June 5, 1961, 24; Libby, *Angry,* 60.
14. Libby, *Angry,* 57; *The Sporting News,* August 30, 1961, 6; *Kansas City Star,* August 23, 1961.
15. Joe McGuff, "The Royals," *Trade Him,* 198.
16. Michelson, *Charlie O,* 100–101.
17. *Kansas City Star,* July 17, 1961.
18. *The Sporting News,* August 30, 1961, 5; Libby, *Angry,* 160; Frank Graham, "Happiness Is Being Somewhere Else," *Saturday Evening Post,* April 4, 1964, 76; *Kansas City Star,* June 19, 1961.
19. Michelson, *Charlie O,* 95; *The Sporting News,* August 30, 1961, 6.
20. Libby, *Angry,* 155; Etkin, *Innings,* 23; *Kansas City Star,* June 19, 1961.
21. Libby, *Angry,* 154.
22. Etkin, *Innings,* 24
23. Joe Donnelly, "Dick Howser," *Baseball Stars of 1962,* Ray Robinson, editor (New York, Pyramid, 1962), 126.
24. *Ibid.,* 126–127.
25. *Ibid.,* 127.
26. *News of the Athletics,* November 1961.
27. *Kansas City Star,* August 17, 1961; Michelson, *Charlie O,* 95.

19 — COURTING DALLAS

1. *Kansas City Times,* August 16, 1961; *The Sporting News,* October 14, 1967, 13.
2. Fox, *Sports Guys,* 68.
3. *The Sporting News,* 1964.
4. *Kansas City Times,* August 17, 1961.
5. *Kansas City Star,* August 17, 1961.
6. Libby, *Angry,* 66.
7. *Kansas City Times,* August 18, 1961.
8. *Dallas Times,* August 18, 1961.
9. *Kansas City Star,* August 23, 1961, Libby, *Angry,* 64.
10. *Kansas City Star,* August 23, 1961.
11. *Ibid.*
12. Fox, *Sports Guys,* 69.
13. Libby, *Angry,* 64; Michelson, *Charlie O,* 296.
14. Libby, *Angry,* 64.
15. *The Sporting News,* September 6, 1961, p. 22; Libby, *Angry,* 64–65.
16. Libby, *Angry,* 64–65.
17. *Kansas City Star,* August 23, 1961.
18. *Ibid.*

19. *The Sporting News*, August 30, 1961, 5; September 6, 1961, 22. Ernest Mehl reported the contract called for an annual salary of $25,000 a year spread over eight years. Lane was to serve as general manager during the first four years and as a consultant during the last four years.
20. Michelson, *Charlie O*, 96.
21. *Kansas City Star*, August 23, 1961.
22. *Ibid.*; *The Sporting News*, August 30, 1961, 6.
23. *Ibid.*; *Kansas City Star*, August 23, 1961.
24. *Kansas City Star*, August 23, 1961.
25. Michelson, *Charlie O*, 92–93.
26. *Ibid.*
27. *Kansas City Star*, August 23, 1961.
28. *Kansas City Star*, August 26, 1961.

20 — 1962: LET BYGONES BE BYGONES

1. Torrey, *Endless*, 185.
2. *Kansas City Star*, April 8, 1962.
3. Michelson, *Charlie O*, 123; Libby, *Angry*, 223.
4. Libby, *Angry*, 65.
5. *Kansas City Athletics Official Scorebook 1962*, 12; McGuff, *Why Me*, 3.
6. *The Sporting News*, September 29, 1962, 16.
7. Graham, "Happiness Is," 74.
8. *The Sporting News*, September 29, 1962, 16; Etkin, *Endless*, 24.
9. *Ibid.*, 24–25.
10. *Kansas City Times*, December 1961.
11. Michelson, *Charlie O*, 125; *The Sporting News*, July 27, 1963, 2; Furman Bisher, *Miracle in Atlanta* (Cleveland, OH: World Publishing Company, 1966), 13.
12. *Kansas City Star*, May 10, 1962.
13. *Kansas City Times*, August 25, 1961; *Kansas City Times*, September 24, 1962. The A's received approximately $150,000 a year from concession revenue.
14. *Kansas City Times*, September 19, 1962; *The Sporting News*, September 29, 1962, 16.
15. *Ibid.*, *Kansas City Times*, September 19, 1962; *Kansas City Star*, September 19, 1962.
16. *The Sporting News*, September 29, 1962, 16; *Kansas City Star*, September 19, 1962; Graham, *Saturday Evening Post*, 74.
17. *Kansas City Star*, September 19, 1962; *The Sporting News*, July 23, 1963; *The Sporting News*, September 29, 1962, 16.
18. *The Sporting News*, September 29, 1962, 16.
19. *Kansas City Times*, September 20, 1962; *Kansas City Star*, October 6, 1962.
20. *The Sporting News*, n.d.
21. *Kansas City Star*, n.d., *The Sporting News*, n.d.
22. *Kansas City Star*, September 30, 1962.

21 — 1963: EVERYTHING'S GREEN AND GOLD

1. *The Sporting News*, n.d.
2. Libby, *Angry*, 67.
3. *Ibid.*
4. *The Sporting News*, April 20, 1963.

5. Walter Bingham, "Everything's Green & Gold in Kansas City," *Sports Illustrated*, 1963, 26.
6. *Ibid.*, 29–30.
7. *Ibid.*, 24.
8. *Ibid.*, 26.
9. *The Sporting News*, April, 1965.
10. *Ibid.*, 29
11. Ken Harrelson, *Hawk* (New York: Viking Press, 1969) 90, 107–108, 116–117.

22 — HAPPINESS IS BEING SOMEWHERE ELSE

1. Joe McGuff, *Winning It All* (Garden City, NY: Doubleday & Company, 1970), 72–73; Michelson, *Charlie O*, 128.
2. *New York Times*, January 12, 1964.
3. *Kansas City Star*, April 10, 1963; *The Sporting News*, January 1964.
4. *Kansas City Star*, April 10, 1963; *The Sporting News*, January 1964; Bisher, *Miracle*, 13–14.
5. Bisher, *Miracle*, 16.
6. Fox, *Sports Guys*, 70; McGuff, *Winning*, 73.
7. Bisher, *Miracle*, 28–29.
8. *The Sporting News*, July 20, 1963, 6; *Kansas City Star*, December 10, 1963.
9. *The Sporting News*, July 20, 1963, 3; Michelson, *Charlie O*, 126.
10. *The Sporting News*, July 20, 1963, 8; *The Sporting News*, July 27, 1963, 1, 4.
11. *The Sporting News*, July 20, 1963, 3.
12. Graham, *Saturday Evening Post*, 76.
13. Libby, *Angry*, 68.
14. *The Sporting News*, January 11, 1964; Graham, *Saturday Evening Post*, 76.
15. *The Sporting News*, January 11, 1964.
16. *Kansas City Times*, December 25, 1963.
17. Etkin, *Innings*, 126–127.
18. Michelson, *Charlie O*, 129; *New York Times*, December 31, 1963.
19. Bisher, *Miracle*, 63–64, 79.
20. *The Sporting News*, January 11, 1964.
21. *New York Times*, January 12, 1964; Michelson, *Charlie O*, 129.
22. *Kansas City Times*, January 7, 1964; "Louisville Sluggers?" *Newsweek*, January 20, 1964.
23. Michelson, *Charlie O*, 131.
24. Graham, "Happiness Is," 76–77; Libby, *Angry*, 70.
25. Michelson, *Charlie O*, 132.
26. *The Sporting News*, February 8, 1964.
27. *Ibid.*
28. *Ibid.*
29. *Ibid.*
30. *Kansas City Star*, February, 1964.
31. *New York Times*, February 18, 1964; February 20, 1964.
32. *Kansas City Times*, February 22, 1964.
33. *Kansas City Times*, February 24, 1964.
34. *Kansas City Times*, February 29, 1964.
35. Graham, *Saturday Evening Post*, 77.
36. *Ibid.*

23 — 1964: ROCKY, JIM AND A PENNANT PORCH

1. Michelson, *Charlie O*, 134.
2. *Kansas City Star*, April 1964.
3. *Kansas City Star*, April 12, 1964.
4. *Kansas City Star*, April 1964.
5. Libby, *Angry*, 56.
6. *Kansas City Star*, April 21, 1964.
7. Monte Moore, *Highlights*, 3.
8. *Kansas City Star*, June 11, 1964.
9. Moore, *Highlights*, 11.
10. Joe McGuff, "Of Baseball, Charlie Finley, 10-gallon Hats, and the Old A's," *Kansas City Star Magazine*, April 10, 1983, 19.
11. Michelson, *Charlie O*, 99.
12. William Leggett, "Dark's Outlook Is Young and Bright," *Sports Illustrated*, March 13, 1967, 52.
13. Moore, *Highlights*, 18.
14. *Ibid.*, 19.
15. *Ibid.*, 20.
16. *Ibid.*, 6–7.
17. *Ibid.*, 12.
18. *Ibid.*, 13.
19. Michelson, *Charlie O*, 96–97.
20. McGuff, "Of Baseball," 19.
21. Moore, *Highlights*, 16.
22. *Ibid.*, 19–21.
23. *Kansas City Star*, September 10, 1964; *Kansas City Star*, September 9, 1964.
24. *Kansas City Star*, September 10, 1964; *Kansas City Times*, September 1964.
25. *Kansas City Star*, September 18, 1964; *Kansas City Times*, September 19, 1964; *Kansas City Star*, September 20, 1964.
26. Michelson, *Charlie O*, 135.
27. *Kansas City Star*, October 15, 1964; Bisher, *Miracle*, 105.

24 — 1965: CHARLIE O. — THE MAN OR THE MULE?

1. *The Sporting News*, May 29, 1965, 15.
2. *Kansas City Star*, April 11, 1965.
3. *Ibid.*; Libby, *Angry*, 57.
4. Veeck, *Hustler's*, 18; Libby, *Angry*, 70; *The Sporting News*, May 29, 1965, 15.
5. Michelson, *Charlie O*, 99.
6. Libby, *Angry*, 54–55.
7. Michelson, *Charlie O*, 99; Jim "Catfish" Hunter, *Catfish* (New York: McGraw-Hill Book Company, 1988), 256.
8. *Kansas City Star*, April 6, 1965.
9. Torrey, *Endless*, 186.
10. Michelson, *Charlie O*, 97.
11. *The Sporting News*, May 29, 1965, 15; Whitey Herzog, *White Rat* (New York: Harper & Row, Publishers, 1987), 74.
12. *The Sporting News*, May 29, 1965, 15.
13. *Kansas City Star*, June 6, 1965.
14. *Omaha World Herald*, September 9, 1965.

15. Al Dark and John Underwood, *When in Doubt Fire the Manager* (New York: E.O. Dutton, 1980), 116.
16. Libby, *Angry*, 75–76.
17. Harrelson, *Hawk*, 145–146.
18. Michelson, *Charlie O*, 310.
19. Libby, *Angry*, 227.

25 — 1966: THE DARK AGES

1. Herzog, *White Rat*, 70, 74.
2. *The Sporting News*, November 6, 1965; November 13, 1965.
3. Herzog, *White Rat*, 70, 74.
4. Torrey, *Endless*, 178, 186.
5. *Kansas City Star*, November 29, 1965; Dark, *Doubt*, 111, 124.
6. Leggett, "Dark's Outlook," 51.
7. *Kansas City Star*, n.d.
8. Leggett, "Dark's Outlook," 52.
9. *Ibid.*, 57.
10. *Official Baseball Guide — 1967* (St. Louis, MO: The Sporting News, 1967), 254.
11. Dark, *Doubt*, 124.

26 — 1967: "A MENACE TO BASEBALL"

1. *The Sporting News*, July 29, 1967, 15.
2. Leggett, "Dark's Outlook," 51, 57.
3. Michelson, *Charlie O*, 231.
4. Leggett, "Dark's Outlook," 57.
5. Michelson, *Charlie O*, 235.
6. Dark, *Doubt*, 126.
7. *The Sporting News*, July 29, 1967, 15.
8. Michelson, *Charlie O*, 102.
9. *Ibid.*, 102–103.
10. *Ibid.*, 104–105.
11. *Ibid.*, 127–128.
12. *Ibid.*; *The Sporting News*, September 2, 1967, 18; Hunter, *Catfish*, 73, 108; Dark, *Doubt*, 127. Former A's announcer Jim Woods felt Campy Campaneris was the snitch. "Monte [Moore] couldn't have done that if he'd wanted to — he didn't know what the players were doing, he was off by himself. Bert Campaneris was really the guy who was Finley's stooge. He'd tell Finley everything. But Monte, for some reason, got blamed for everything." Curt Smith, *Voices of the Game* (Diamond Communications, South Bend, IN, 1987), 329 .
13. Michelson, *Charlie O*, 106–107.
14. *The Sporting News*, September 2, 1967, 16.
15. Michelson, *Charlie O*, 106–108; Dark, *Doubt*, 129.
16. Dark, *Doubt*, 129–130.
17. *Official Baseball Guide — 1968*, 196; Dark, *Doubt*, 130.
18. Dark, *Doubt*, 131.
19. *The Sporting News*, September 2, 1967, 16, 18.
20. *Ibid.*, 16.
21. *Ibid.*, 18.
22. Harrelson, *Hawk*, 187; Libby, *Angry*, 83–84.

23. Harrelson, *Hawk*, 191; Libby, *Angry*, 84-85.
24. Harrelson, *Hawk*, 191.
25. *Ibid.*, 196-197, Libby, *Angry*, 85.
26. *The Sporting News*, September 2, 1967, 16; *Official Baseball Guide—1968*, 196; Michelson, *Charlie O*, 113-114.
27. *Official Baseball Guide—1968*, 196; Ron Bergman, *Mustache Gang* (New York: Dell Publishing, 1973), 34; Michelson, *Charlie O*, 114.
28. Michelson, *Charlie O*, 163.
29. *The Sporting News*, October 28, 1967, 19; *Kansas City Times*, October 16, 1967.

27 — "LUCKIEST CITY SINCE HIROSHIMA"

1. *Kansas City Fan*, September, 1972, p 21; *The Sporting News*, January 1967.
2. Twyman, *Kansas City Star*, n.d.
3. Michelson, *Charlie O*, 136.
4. *The Sporting News*, May 27, 1967, 8; Michelson, *Charlie O*, 134.
5. Fox, *Sports Guys*, 73.
6. *The Sporting News*, May 27, 1967, 8.
7. *Kansas City Star*, May 17, 1967; *The Sporting News*, July 13, 1967, 15.
8. *The Sporting News*, July 29, 1967, 15.
9. *Omaha World Herald*, September 1967.
10. *Kansas City Times*, July 15, 1967.
11. *Ibid.*; Twyman, *Kansas City Star*.
12. *The Sporting News*, July 22, 1967, 9; *The Sporting News*, July 29, 1967, 15.
13. *The Sporting News*, July 29, 1967, 15; *Kansas City Star*, July 21, 1967.
14. *Official Baseball Guide—1967*, 180; *Kansas City Star*, August 1, 1967; and August 8, 1967.
15. *Kansas City Star*, August 8, 1967; *Chicago American*, October 18, 1967.
16. *The Sporting News*, n.d.
17. *Kansas City Star*, August 29, 1967.
18. *The Sporting News*, n.d.
19. *The Sporting News*, October 14, 1967, 13.
20. *The Sporting News*, October 7, 1967, 39.
21. *The Sporting News*, October 14, 1967, 13.
22. *Chicago Tribune*, October 12, 1967.
23. David Condon, "In the Wake of the News," *Chicago Tribune*, October 18, 1967.
24. *Chicago Sun Times*, October 18, 1967.
25. Kowet, *Rich*, 128; *Chicago Sun Times*, October 19, 1967; *Chicago American*, October 18, 1967; Michelson, *Charlie O*, 146; Libby, *Angry*, 92. The Seattle Pilots played in Sicks stadium in 1969 and drew just 677,944 fans. The inadequate stadium facilities were a major reason the team was a financial failure during its only season in Seattle.
26. *Kansas City Star*, October 18, 1969; Michelson, *Charlie O*, 137.
27. *Chicago American*, October 18, 1967.
28. *Chicago Tribune*, October 19, 1967; *Chicago American*, October 18, 1967.
29. *Chicago Tribune*, October 19, 1967.
30. *Official Baseball Guide—1968*, 176.
31. *Kansas City Times*, October 19, 1969.
32. Michelson, *Charlie O*, 137; *Kansas City Star*, October 19, 1969; *Chicago Sun Times*, October 19, 1969; *Official Baseball Guide—1968*, 177.

33. Sid Bordman, *Expansion to Excellence* (Walsworth Publishing, 1985), 4; Fox, *Sports Guys*, 74; *The Sporting News*, November 4, 1967.
34. *Chicago Tribune*, October 20, 1967, Fox, *Sports Guys*, 74.
35. *Kansas City Star*, October 19, 1969.
36. Fox, *Sports Guys*, 74.
37. Clark, *Champagne*, 39.
38. *Chicago Tribune*, November 16, 1967.

28 — A BAD MARRIAGE

1. *Kansas City Star*, December 21, 1960; Libby, *Angry*, 92.
2. *The Sporting News*, October 14, 1967, 13.
3. Libby, *Angry*, 92; Michelson, *Charlie O*, 136.
4. Mike DeArmond, "In 22 years, Charlie Finley Hasn't Grown Apologetic," *Kansas City Star*, November 26, 1989; Michelson, *Charlie O*, 146–147.
5. *Kansas City Times*, August 16, 1961.
6. Fox, *Sports Guys*, 68; *Kansas City Star*, August 17, 1961; Libby, *Angry*, 34–35.
7. Libby, *Angry*, 94.
8. *Kansas City Star*, August 26, 1961.
9. *The Sporting News*, July 27, 1963, 1.
10. Kuklick, *Every Thing*, 123.
11. *The Sporting News*, August 1963.
12. *The Sporting News*, January 1964; *Kansas City Star*, September 19, 1962; *The Sporting News*, August 29, 1962, 16.
13. Graham, "Happiness Is," 74.
14. *The Sporting News*, July 27, 1963, 4.
15. Michelson, *Charlie O*, 147.
16. Graham, "Happiness Is," 74; *Kansas City Star*, September 19, 1962.
17. *The Sporting News*, July 27, 1963, 4.
18. *Official Baseball Guide — 1965*, 160.
19. *The Sporting News*, May 28, 1984.
20. Graham, "Happiness Is," 74; Libby, *Angry*, 65.
21. Libby, *Angry*, 65–66.
22. Michelson, *Charlie O*, 122.
23. *Ibid.*, 289; Bruce Markusen, *Baseball's Last Dynasty* (Indianapolis, IN: Masters Press, 1998), 121–122.
24. *Kansas City Star*, March 24, 1961; *Kansas City Star*, May 24, 1961; *New York Times*, January 12, 1961; Libby, *Angry*, 68.
25. Libby, *Angry*, 68.
26. *Kansas City Star*, n.d.
27. *Kansas City Star*, January 24, 1985, 4; *Kansas City Star*, April 14, 1985, 1.
28. Condon, *Chicago Tribune*, October 18, 1967; *Chicago Sun Times*, October 19, 1967.
29. Michelson, *Charlie O*, 142, 321, 330–331.
30. *Ibid.*, 117
31. *The Sporting News*, April 29, 1978, 29; *USA Today*, October 1985.
32. Glenn Dickey, *Champions — The Story of the First Two Oakland A's Dynasties* (Chicago: Triumph Books, 2002), 13.
33. *Kansas City Star*, August 17, 1961.
34. Fox, *Sports Guys*, 68.
35. *The Sporting News*, October 14, 1967, 13.

36. Michelson, *Charlie O*, 133–134.
37. Veeck, *Veeck*, 88; *The Sporting News*, October 14, 1967, 30.
38. *The Sporting News*, October 14, 1967, 30.
39. Michelson, *Charlie O*, 228; Markusen, *Dynasty*, 50

29 — JUST A YANKEES FARM TEAM

1. Veeck, *Veeck*, 269.
2. Bill James and Jim Henzler, *Win Shares* (Morton Grove, IL, Stats Publishing, 2002).
3. In the tables that follow, both the "Acquired" and "In Exchange for" columns have numbers in parentheses for the win shares for each of the individual players involved in a trade. The total win shares in the right column indicates the total for all players acquired or traded away in each trade. The numbers in italics are for players purchased or sold with no other players exchanged. Note that in these instances there are no win shares in the right column.
4. McGuff, "The Royals," 194–195.
5. *The Sporting News*, March 20, 1957.
6. *Kansas City Star*, April 13, 1958.
7. Veeck, *Veeck*, 269.
8. McGuff, "The Royals," 194.
9. Shecter, *Maris*, 81–82.
10. *Ibid.*, 82–83.
11. *The Sporting News*, December 23, 1959, 6.
12. Shecter, *Maris*, 82–86.
13. *The Sporting News*, December 23, 1959, 6.
14. Francis Kinlaw, "Arnold Johnson's Railroad to New York," *Union to Royals*, 1996.
15. *The Sporting News*, January 11, 1961, 4.
16. *The Sporting News*, August 21, 1957, 10.
17. *Kansas City Star*, April 13, 1958.

30 — NO MORE TRADES WITH THE YANKEES

1. *The Sporting News*, December 28, 1960, 7; *The Sporting News*, January 11, 1961, 4, 6; Libby, *Angry*, 57.
2. *The Sporting News*, August 30, 1961, 5.
3. *Kansas City Star*, August 17, 1961.
4. Michelson, *Charlie O*, 223.
5. Ross Newman, *The California Angels* (New York, Simon and Schuster, 1982), 49.
6. McGuff, "The Royals," 198.
7. Hunter, *Catfish*, 41–42.

31 — CROP FAILURE

1. *Kansas City Times*, April 5, 1955.
2. Mehl, *Athletics*, 186–187.
3. *The Sporting News*, n.d.
4. *Kansas City Star*, September 25, 1955.
5. Harrelson, *Hawk*, 97.
6. *The Sporting News*, November 9, 1960.
7. *Kansas City Star*, April 6, 1965.

32 — GROWING A CHAMPIONSHIP TEAM

1. *Kansas City Star,* April 6, 1965; *The Sporting News,* December 28, 1960, 7.
2. Torrey, *Endless,* 185; Michelson, *Charlie O,* 98.
3. Markusen, *Dynasty,* 403.
4. Clark, *Champagne,* 20, 100.
5. Etkin, *Innings,* 127–128. Fazio probably refers to Ernie Fazio, the player-to-be-named-later acquired in the Jim Gentile trade in 1965. Fazio was from Oakland, California, and played for Santa Clara in the 1962 College World Series.
6. Libby, *Angry,* 193; Clark, *Champagne,* 20; Markusen, *Dynasty,* 196–198.
7. Leonard Koppett, *A Thinking Man's Guide to Baseball* (New York: E. P. Dutton, 1967), 212–213; *Kansas City Star,* n.d.
8. Clark, *Champagne,* 20.
9. Whitey Herzog, *You're Missing a Great Game* (New York: Berkley Books, 2000), 37, 49–50.
10. Hunter, *Hawk,* 27–28; Clark, *Champagne,* 22.
11. Libby, *Angry,* 181–182.
12. *Ibid.,* 189; Michelson, *Charlie O,* 152–153.
13. Clark, *Champagne,* 23–24; Markusen, *Dynasty,* 25, 37.
14. Newman, *California,* 71; Michelson, *Charlie O,* 152.
15. Libby, *Angry,* 10; Clark, *Champagne,* 25.
16. Clark, *Champagne,* 25–26.
17. Dark, *Doubt,* 111–112.
18. Clark, *Champagne,* 27.
19. Libby, *Angry,* 100; Clark, *Champagne,* 27; Markusen, *Dynasty,* 9.
20. Libby, *Angry,* 124–125; Clark, *Champagne,* 28.

Bibliography

BOOKS

Bergman, Ron. *Mustache Gang.* New York: Dell Publishing, 1973.
Bisher, Furman. *Miracle in Atlanta.* Cleveland, OH: World Publishing Company, 1966.
Bordman, Sid. *Expansion to Excellence.* Walsworth Publishing, 1985.
Boudreau, Lou. *Covering All the Bases.* Champaign, IL: Sagamore Publishing, 1993.
Clark, Tom. *Champagne and Baloney.* New York: Harper & Row, 1976.
Dark, Al, and Underwood, John. *When in Doubt Fire the Manager.* New York: E.O. Dutton, 1980.
Dickey, Glenn. *Champions — The Story of the First Two Oakland A's Dynasties.* Chicago: Triumph Books, 2002.
Etkin, Jack. *Innings Ago.* Kansas City: Normandy Square Publications, 1987.
Fox, Gene. *Sports Guys.* Lenexa, KS: Addax Publishing, 1999.
Harrelson, Ken. *Hawk.* New York: The Viking Press, 1969.
Herzog, Whitey. *White Rat.* New York: Harper & Row, Publishers, 1987.
_____. *You're Missing a Great Game.* New York: Berkley Books, 2000.
Hunter, Jim. *Catfish.* New York: McGraw-Hill Book Company, 1988.
James, Bill, and Henzler, Jim. *Win Shares.* Morton Grove, IL: Stats Publishing, 2002.
Jordan, David. *The Athletics of Philadelphia.* Jefferson, NC: McFarland & Company, Inc., 1999.
Koppett, Leonard. *A Thinking Man's Guide to Baseball.* New York: E. P. Dutton & Co, 1967.
Kowet, Don. *The Rich Who Own Sports.* New York: Random House, 1977.
Kuklick, Bruce. *To Everything a Season.* Princeton, NJ: Princeton University Press, 1991.
Libby, Bill. *Charlie O. and the Angry A's.* Garden City, NY: Doubleday & Company, Inc., 1975.
Markusen, Bruce. *Baseball's Last Dynasty.* Indianapolis, IN: Masters Press, 1998.
McGuff, Joe. *Why Me? Why Not Joe McGuff?* Prairie Village, KS: Joe McGuff, 1992.
_____. *Winning It All.* Garden City, NY: Doubleday & Company, 1970.
Mehl, Ernest. *The Kansas City Athletics.* New York: Henry Holt, 1956.
Michelson, Herbert. *Charlie O.* Indianapolis: Bobbs-Merrill Company, Inc, 1975.
Miller, James. The *Baseball Business.* Chapel Hill: University of North Carolina Press, 1990.
Newman, Ross. *The California Angels.* New York: Simon and Schuster, 1982.
Official Baseball Guide (various years). St. Louis: The Sporting News.

O'Neal, Paul. *The American Association.* Austin, TX: Eakin Press, 1991.
Quirk, James, and Fort, Rodney. *Pay Dirt.* Princeton, NJ: Princeton University Press, 1992.
Shecter, Leonard. *Roger Maris, Home Run Hero* New York: 1961.
Smith, Curt. *Voices of the Game.* South Bend, IN: Diamond Communications Inc., 1987.
Torrey, Jack. *Endless Summers.* South Bend, IN: Diamond Communications, Inc., 1996.
Veeck, Bill. *The Hustler's Handbook.* New York: G.P. Putnam's Sons, 1965.
____. *Veeck — As in Wreck.* New York: G.P. Putnam's Sons, 1962.
Zimmerman, Paul. *The Los Angeles Dodgers.* New York: Coward-McCann, Inc., 1960.

ARTICLES AND PERIODICALS

Bingham, Walter. "Everything's Green and Gold in Kansas City." *Sports Illustrated,* 1963.
Cerv, Bob. "I Played Without Eating." *Saturday Evening Post,* July 19, 1958.
Cohane, Tim. "Baseball's Most Exciting Owner." *Look,* March 22, 1955.
Daniel, Dan. "How Close to California." *The Sporting News,* November 17, 1954.
____. "Johnson Earmarks $1,000,000 for Three-Year Player-Buying." *The Sporting News,* November 17, 1954.
DeArmond, Mike. "In 22 Years, Charlie Finley Hasn't Grown Apologetic." *Kansas City Star,* November 26, 1989.
Donnelly, Joe. "Dick Howser." *Baseball Stars of 1962.* Ray Robinson, editor. New York: Pyramid Books, 1962.
Gottehrer, Barry. "Bud Daley and Ray Herbert." *Baseball Stars of 1961.* Ray Robinson, editor. New York: Pyramid Books, 1961.
Graham, Frank. "Happiness Is Being Somewhere Else." *Saturday Evening Post,* April 4, 1964.
Holtzman, Jerome. "Brooks Once Killed Roster Swap." *The Sporting News,* September 10, 1977.
Johnson, Charles. "How Major League Baseball Came to Minnesota." *Metrodome Souvenir Book.* Minneapolis: MSP Publications, 1982.
Kinlaw, Francis. "Arnold Johnson's Railroad to New York." In Lloyd Johnson (ed.), *Union to Royals.* A publication of the Kansas City chapter of SABR. New York: AG Press, 1996.
Kraisler, Fritz. "Dimensions at Stadium Change Again." *Kansas City Star,* April 11, 1965.
Lardner, Rex. "Charlie Finley and Bugs Bunny in K.C." *Sports Illustrated,* June 5, 1961.
Lebovitz, Hal. "Tribe G.M. Regards Several Cities as Better Locations Than Baltimore and K.C." *The Sporting News,* November 17, 1954.
Leggett, William. "Dark's Outlook Is Young and Bright." *Sports Illustrated,* March 13, 1967.
Mann, Arthur. "How to Buy a Ball Club for Peanuts." *Saturday Evening Post,* April 9, 1955.
Marshall, Tom. "Press Box Ready for New Season." *Kansas City Star,* 1965.
McCurley, Lanse. "House of Mack — A House Divided." *The Sporting News,* November 10, 1954.
McGuff, Joe. "Of Baseball, Charlie Finley, 10-gallon Hats, and the Old A's." *Kansas City Star Magazine,* April 10, 1983.
____. "The Finley Story." *Kansas City Star,* 1980.

Bibliography

_____. "The Royals," *Trade Him*. Jim Enright, editor. Chicago: Follett Publishing Company, 1976.
Moore, Bill. "Press Box Longer and, It is Hoped, Drier." *Kansas City Star*, February 27, 1959.
Moore, Monte. "Highlights of the 1964 Season." Kansas City: KCMO Radio and Television, 1964.
Morrow, Art. "Inside Story of the Race for Possession of Athletics." *The Sporting News*, November 10, 1954.
Newcombe, Jack. "Bud Daley." *Baseball Stars of 1960*. Ray Robinson, editor. New York: Pyramid Press, 1960.
Paxton, Harry T. "The Philadelphia A's Last Stand." *Saturday Evening Post*, June 12, 1954.
Richardson, Bill. "Little Boy Still in Cerv at Age 55." *Kansas City Star*, April 6, 1980.

NEWSPAPERS

Chicago American
Chicago Sun Times
Chicago Tribune
Dallas Times
Kansas City Fan
Kansas City Star
Kansas City Times
New York Times
Newsweek
Omaha World Herald
Sports Illustrated
The Sporting News
USA Today

Index

Acker, Tom 102, 284
Adcock, Joe 108, 217
Aker, Jack 219, 221, 230, 232, 238–240, 242–243, 247, 295
Alexander, Babe 6
All-Star Game (1960) 107–108
Allen, Ivan 178–179
Allen, Mel 91
Allis, Barney 115
Allison, Bob 197, 199
Allyn, Arthur 121, 185, 205, 221, 252, 256, 259
Alusik, George 161, 173, 200
American Association 30, 126
Anderson, Bob 193, 293
Aparicio, Luis 97, 144, 217
Appling, Luke 193, 226, 227, 236, 245–247, 249; A's manager 243
Archer, Jim 135, 138, 145, 161, 289
Astroth, Joe 57, 60
Atwell and Company 10
Austin, William 44
Automatic Canteen Corporation 9, 11
Autry, Gene 122
Axelson, Joe 271
Azcue, Joe 157, 159, 292–293

Baker, Frank "Home Run" 56
Bando, Sal 236, 242, 296, 305, 310
Banks, Ernie 108
Barket, Alex 110, 182, 187, 205–206, 253, 256
Barry, Jack 56
Bartle, H. Roy 128, 132, 169, 177
Bass, Norm 138, 145, 161, 301
Battey, Earl 197, 230, 231

Bauer, Hank 72, 103–105, 144–145, 147–149, 153–155, 159–163, 234, 285; A's manager 140–142
Baxes, Mike 65, 86, 91, 283
Baxter, Charles 113
Belardi, Wayne 71, 279
Beatles 204
Belinsky, Bo 292
Bella, Zeke 89, 283
Benson, Robert 3
Berg, Kenneth 109
Berg, Leonard 109
Bergesch, Bill 110, 127, 137, 155–156, 305
Bergman, Ron 269, 291
Berkley, Richard 187
Berra, Yogi 72
Bertaina, Frank 202
Bertoia, Reno 142–144
Biebel, Don 227, 236
Bird, Doug 288
Bisher, Furman 178–179, 183
Blackwell, Ewell 52–53, 278
Blair, James 52
Blanchard, John 216
Blanco, Gil 230, 233, 295
Blasingame, Don 173
Blue, Vida 305, 308, 310, 312
Blues Stadium 10–11, 14, 42
Boak, Chester 135
Bollweg, Don 53
Bond, Walt 161
Boone, Ray 95, 97, 102
Booz, Allen and Hamilton 255, 258
Bosworth, Joe 309
Boudreau, Lou 51–53, 55, 61–62, 73; A's manager 49, 64, 69

Bowens, Sam 202
Bowman, Joe 156, 182–183, 225, 305–306, 311
Bowsfield, Ted 169, 173, 201–202, 204, 210, 213, 292
Boyd, Bob 135, 142, 289
Boyer, Clete 66, 70, 280, 299, 305
Boyer, Cloyd 48
Bradford, Bill 65
Braman, J.D., 254–255
Brandt, Jackie 202
Breathitt, Edward 184
Brett, George 288
Briggs, John 135
Briggs, Joseph 27–28, 31
Briggs, Walter "Spike," 13, 18, 25, 27–28, 52, 65
Brock, Walter 156
Brookfield, Dutton 251–253, 256, 259–261
Brooks, Robert 312
Brown, Hugh 265
Brown, Joe 102, 154–155
Brown, Kenyon 122
Brucker, Earle 4
Brunet, George 97, 298
Bryan, Bill 159, 172, 200, 203, 217, 230, 295, 301
Bryson, George 169, 193, 205
Buhl, Bob 108
Burke, Michael 160
Burnett, Dick 12, 15
Burnette, Wally 69, 77
Burtschy, Ed 66–67
Busby, Jim 89
Busby, Steve 288
Busch, August 126
Buschhorn, Don 214, 309
Butler, Dick 259
Buzas, Joe 255

Callison, Johnny 97
Campaneris, Bert "Campy" 199–200, 215, 217, 233, 236, 239, 293, 305, 307, 310
Campanis, Al 224
Capra, Sal 256
Cardenal, Jose 217, 236
Carey, Andy 105, 142, 144, 287
Carnevale, Dan 305, 310
Carpenter, Bob 28–29, 36

Carrasquel, Chico 85, 91, 283
Carroll, Parke 69, 73, 98–99, 102–104, 108, 112–113, 124–125, 127, 134, 285–287; A's business manager 31, 48; A's general manager 90; death of 128
Carroll, Tom 91, 284
Carter, Amon 164
Cashen, Frank 258, 305
Cater, Danny 230, 233, 236, 295
Causey, Wayne 135, 144, 158–159, 168, 171–172, 174, 199–200, 217, 230, 233, 289, 295
Caywood, Betty 205, 211
Ceccarelli, Art 48
Cerv, Bob 71, 76–77, 83–85, 89, 92–93, 105, 287
Chandler, Spurgeon "Bud" 71, 90
Challinor, Dick 102, 127
Charles, Ed 157–159, 172, 200, 203, 215–217, 233, 235–236, 292, 296
Charlie O (mule) 210–211, 220–223
Chavarria, Ossie 301
Chicago Blackhawks 8
Chiti, Harry 82, 87, 95, 105
Christophers, George 180
Cimoli, Gino 157, 159, 169–172
Clark, Joseph 12
Clarke, James 5
Clarkson, Bill 271
Clinton, Lou 220
Cochrane, Mickey 5, 56
Cohn, Dave 255
Colavito, Rocky 86, 125, 193–194, 200–201, 203, 208, 286, 293
Coleman Rip 72, 279
Colt, John 151
Comiskey, Chuck 14, 28, 121, 126, 280
Condon, David
Connie Mack Stadium 5; mortgage on 5, 15–16, 20, 25, 29, 31, 36; sold to Phillies 28–29, 31, 36
Consolo, Billy 159
Continental League 109, 111
Cook, Jack Kent 12
Cookingham, L.P., 45–46
Cooper, Milton 110, 116
Cooper, Walker 102
Corwin, Tom 269
Courtney, Clint 135, 289
Covington, Wes 142–143
Cowens, Al 288

Cowger, William 184
Cox, John 34
Craddock, Walt 282
Craft, Harry 49, 64, 67, 71, 92, 96, 98–99, 282; A's manager 73–74, 90
Craig, Bernard 187
Crandall, Del 108
Crawford, Willie 310
Crimian, Jack 65, 69, 71, 279
Crisconi, John 20, 23, 25
Cronin, Joe 49, 117, 165, 169, 179–181, 183–184, 187, 194, 220, 255, 260–261
Crown, Henry 15, 17
Crown, Lester 113
Cunningham, Bill 263–264
Curry, Charles 259–261

Dahlgren, Babe 193, 208
Daley, Bud 82, 88, 96, 105, 108, 135, 138, 145, 282, 289
Daley, Pete 102, 105, 135
Dark, Al 219–220, 224, 225–227, 231–234, 235, 239–244, 295, 310; A's manager 225–226
Dauer, Bill 263
Dautch, Jerry 110
Davidson, Thomas 187
Davis, Bob 135
Davis, Ilus 178, 181–185, 187, 251–253, 256, 259–261
Deal, Cot 227, 236, 239
Delapp, G. Leslie 251
Delgado, Felix 307
Del Greco, Bobby 143, 145, 159, 172
Del Webb Construction Company 3, 38, 45
DeMaestri, Joe 56–57, 66, 70, 75, 87, 92, 95, 97, 102–103, 282, 285
DeOrsey, C. Leo 16, 19
DeWeese, Max 193
DeWitt, Bill 134, 213
Dick, Eddie 79
Dickey, Glenn 273
Dickson, Jim 218
Dickson, Murry 82, 88, 97–98, 283
DiMaggio, Joe 247, 264
Ditmar, Art 60–61, 67, 72, 138, 145, 161, 279–280, 289
Dixon, Sonny 277
Dobson, Chuck 227, 230, 231, 236, 238, 247, 295, 308–309

Dolin, Nate 125
Donaldson, John 233, 236
Dorish, Harry 56
Dotterer, Henry 135
Doyne, John 254
Drabowsky, Moe 173, 197, 200, 210, 218, 234
Dubiner, Morris 208
Duckworth, Jim 230, 295–296
Duncan, Dave 203, 239, 271, 297, 307
Dunne, Judge Robert 113, 116–117
Duren, Ryne 72, 281–282
Durocher, Leo 133, 154
Dykes, Jimmy 4, 6, 126, 134, 168, 208, 249

Eckert, William 246
Edgerton, Bill 232
Edwards, Doc 172, 200, 202, 216, 293
Edwards, Ed 71, 90
Egan, Tom 217
Elliott, Bob 103–104, 108, 112; A's manager 101–102
Elliott, Larry 236, 296
Enos, Bill 309
Essegian, Chuck 142, 169, 289
Estrada, Bill 108
Evans, Dan 254–255
Ewell, Jim 85

Fain, Irwin 114–115
Faris, Lynn 229, 249
Fazio, Ernie 229, 293
Ferrick, Tom 175, 193, 216, 227
Fetzer, John 271
Fingers, Rollie 305, 310
Finigan, Jim 50–51, 56–57, 66, 71, 277, 279
Finkelstein, Saul 110
Finley, Carl 168, 236
Finley, Charles O. 32, 118–124, 126–132, 136–140, 151–155, 157–158, 161–163 168–169, 173–174, 176–187, 190–191, 193–195, 197, 200–207, 208–213, 219–226, 227, 234–235, 237, 239–247, 251–276; Atlanta 148, 178–180; attempt to purchase A's (1954) 16, 19, 23–25, 120; attempt to purchase White Sox 120–121; Burns Stadium lease 128, 148, 264; copies Bill Veeck 131, 264, 269, 276; Dallas 148–150,

153, 155, 163–164; financial losses in Kansas City 180, 206, 253, 267–268; initial promises 123, 263; Louisville 184–185; Milwaukee 183, 206–207, 211, 253–254; New Orleans 253–254; Oakland 180–181, 186–187, 251, 253–254, 257–259; personal appearances 124, 129; player development 301, 303, 305–312; purchases A's (1960) 116–117; purchases minority stock 127–128; San Diego 148; Seattle 253–255, 258; seeks new stadium 164–167; stadium improvements 129–131, 176–177, 179, 181–182, 186, 190, 255, 263–264, 270; ticket sales 124; trades 136, 138, 289–297
Finley, Fred 127–128
Finley, Shirley McCartney 118–119
Fischer, Barney 20
Fischer, Bill 143, 147, 160, 173–174
Fitzgerald, Ed 134–135, 156
Fitzsimmons, Fred 102
Flaherty, Vincent 17–18
Foiles, Hank 104–105
Ford, Whitey 69, 72, 88
Fox, Nellie 97
Foxx, Jimmie 56
Freeman, Mark 91, 97
Fregosi, Jim 217
Frick, Ford 26, 52–53, 121, 152, 194–195, 280, 292
Friday, Pat 126–128, 139, 151, 173, 178, 183, 186, 193, 211–213, 289; A's general manager 155
Friedlund, J. Arthur 9

Gaines, Ludwell 187
Gallagher, Arthur 20
Gardner, Billy 89
Garver, Ned 53, 71, 76, 88–89, 92, 96–97, 107, 135, 279
Gavin, Tom 152, 165–166
Gehrig, Lou 210
Geiger, Gary 145
general finance 157, 169
Gentile, Jim 194, 199, 203, 216, 229, 293
Gibbs, Jake 231
Giel, Paul 142
Ginsberg, Joe 65–66, 70, 144, 278
Giordano, Tom 308

Gleeson, Jimmy 74, 81, 307
Goetz Brewing 157, 169
Goldberg, Samuel 24–25
Gordan, Joe 123, 126, 133–140, 142, 151, 153–154, 249; A's manager 112
Gorman, Tom 52, 55, 61, 68, 77, 88, 97, 278
Gosger, Jim 230, 234, 237, 295
Gould, Sam 42–43
Graff, Milt 72, 75, 86, 279, 281
Green, Dick 199–200, 203, 216–217, 233, 236, 293, 296, 301, 310
Greenberg, Hank 26–27, 116, 121, 280
Greene, Leonard 164
Greenfield, Albert 13
Griffith, Calvin 15–16, 37, 120, 257
Griffith, Clark 13, 17–18, 25–26, 37
Grigsby, Bill 90–91, 132, 137, 151, 157
Grilli, Guido 230, 295
Grim, Bob 86, 88, 92, 97
Grimes, Burleigh 49, 64
Groat, Dick 102, 286
Grobschmidt, Eugene 207
Groth, Johnny 65
Grove, Lefty 56
Grzenda, Joe 233
Guest, Bernie 48–49, 213, 298
Guys Potato Chips 157, 169

Haas, Mule 56
Hadden, Alexander 256
Hadley, Kent 81–82, 93, 103, 282, 285
Hall, Dick 103–104, 107, 142, 285, 289
Hall, Fred 52
Hall, Jimmie 197, 231
Hallahan, Katherine 4
Hamilton, Dave 312
Hamlin, Ken 102–103, 105, 135, 285
Hamms Brewing 169
Handrahan, Vern 197, 233
Haney, Fred 169
Haniff, Ted 20, 23
Hankins, Jay 193, 208, 236
Hansen, Roger 193, 219
Harmon, Merle 50, 90–91, 132, 151, 157
Harrelson, Ken 173, 175, 200, 216, 220–221, 230, 233, 236, 240–242, 244–246, 293, 295–296, 301
Harridge, Will 14, 18, 20–22, 25, 27, 53
Harrington, Bill 71, 279

Index

Harris, Mercer 307
Harrison, Tom 214
Harshman, Jack 89
Hartnett, Gabby 208, 227
Hayes, Thelma 37
Hearnes, Warren 210, 250
Heffner, Don 81, 90, 102
Held, Woodie 72–73, 76, 85–87, 281–282
Herbert, Ray 60, 88, 92, 96, 105–107, 135, 142, 145, 278
Herridge, Bill 65, 69
Hershberger, Mike 208, 214, 218, 233, 237, 245, 293
Herzog, Whitey 87, 105, 135, 208, 214, 224, 282, 289, 308–309
Hickman, Jesse 216, 293
Higgins, Miller 210
Hill, Dave 299
Hilliard, Melvin 187
Hilton, Conrad 15, 17, 39
Hoffman, Herb 155, 264
Hofman, Bob 227, 234, 236, 242, 307
Hogan, Margaret 3
Hogueland, Ed 115
Holdener, Lou 102
Horlen, Joel 247
Host, Gene 71–72, 279
Hough, Frank 4
Houk, Ralph 142, 172
House, Frank 81–82, 95, 102, 282, 284
Howser, Dick 143–144, 159, 171, 293, 301, 305
Hubbard, Cal 148, 210
Humes, Carmen (Johnson) 8, 104, 114–116; desire to retain ownership of A's 109, 113; purchases option to buy shares 113; withdraws bid to buy shares 116
Hunt, Lamar 176, 179, 208–209, 250, 259
Hunter, Billy 72, 75, 85, 280
Hunter, Jim "Catfish," 211, 214, 218–219, 230–231, 233, 237–238, 247, 293, 295–296, 305, 308–310
Hurley, Ed 236, 240–242, 249

Ingram, Robert 115, 259

Jackson, David 115
Jackson, Henry 255

Jackson, Reggie 237, 242, 297, 305, 310–311
Jacobs, Louis 12
Jacobs, Spook 50, 66
Jacobs Brothers *see* Sportservice
James, Bill 277
Jensen, Jackie 85
Jimenez, Manny 157–158, 173, 200, 292
Johnson, Arnold 8–13, 48, 50, 63, 69, 73, 82, 86, 90, 103, 107, 127, 150, 267; cost of purchasing the A's 29–34; death of 104, 109; player development 298–303; profits in Kansas City 32–34, 38–41; purchases A's (1954) 11–12, 16, 19–28; purchases Blues Stadium 10, 37–38; relocation rumors 39–42, 79–80, 100, 285; trades by 277–288
Johnson, Bob 102, 135
Johnson, Carmen *see* Humes, Carmen
Johnson, Charles 26
Johnson, Deron 138, 144, 289–290
Johnson, Earl 10, 27–28, 31, 109, 127–128
Johnson, Jeffrey 113
Johnson, Ken 107, 137–138, 298
Johnson, Stan 142
Jones, Sam 4
Joyce, Dick 309

Kaat, Jim 199
Kaline, Al 53, 56–57, 65, 108
Kansas City: attendance 62, 64, 70, 79, 89, 98, 100, 104, 110–111, 163, 174–175, 180, 206, 223, 233, 247, 265, 272–274; attendance clause 38, 40–41, 44, 100, 110, 128, 149, 155, 177–178, 181–182, 264; attendance guarantee 15–16, 27–28, 32, 38; bond issue (1954) 12, 42, 44–45; 1955 stadium lease 27, 32, 38, 44, 132; 1960 stadium lease 40, 100, 132; 1964 stadium lease 177–179, 181–182, 184–186, 190, 270; proposed stadium (1947) 12, 42; proposed stadium (1965–67) 208–209, 227, 250–251, 266; purchased Blues Stadium 3, 29, 38; radio and television 30–31, 50, 90–91, 132, 149, 157, 169, 180, 193, 205, 211, 227, 235, 254, 266–267; rent paid by A's 32, 44, 176; season tickets sold 90, 168, 226–227, 235, 251, 273, 275; ticket campaign (1960) 111

Kansas City Athletics: board dissolves (1961) 127; cities seeking team (1960) 109–112; concession income 179; elephant emblem changed 48; incorporated (1954) 31; minor leagues 48; nickname change considered (1954) 48; spring training 50; uniforms 131, 157, 168–169, 193, 236
Kansas City Blues 30, 38, 71, 74, 125, 141, 251
Kansas City Chiefs 176, 181, 250, 270
Kansas City Comets 271
Kansas City Kings 270
Kansas City local ownership groups (1960) 110, 112, 114–116; purchases option to buy minority shares 114; receives conditional league approval 115; waives option to buy minority shares 127; withdraws offer for majority shares 117
Kansas City Municipal Stadium 10; Braves Field scoreboard 30, 46; cost to rebuild stadium 47; Fan-A-Gram 130; improvements (1956) 64; improvements (1960) 101, 108; improvements (1961) 129–131, 176–177; improvements (1962) 156; outfield dimensions 64, 91, 129, 156, 194, 209, 227; parking 42–43, 166; press box renovation 91–92; reconstruction 14, 42–47
Kansas City Royals 272, 288
Kansas City Scouts 270–271
Kansas City Stadium Association 44–47
Karp, Morris 110
Kauffman, Ewing 251, 253
Keane, Thomas 127
Keefe, Dave 48, 127, 168
Kellner, Alex 53, 59–61, 68, 77
Kemmerer, Russ 88
Kemp, William 3, 46
Kennedy, Ray 48, 65
Keough, Joe 312
Killebrew, Harmon 197, 231
Kinlaw, Francis 287
Kirkpatrick, Ed 217
Klimchock, Lou 157, 288, 291, 299–300
Klippstein, John 203
Kluttz, Clyde 301, 305, 308
Knoop, Bobby 217

Knorr, Fred 120
Knowland, William 259
Koegel, Pete 312
Koerper, Karol 3
Konstanty, Jim 200
Krakauer, Ken 165–166, 205–206
Kralick, Jack 161
Krausse, Lew 139–140, 145, 147, 210, 230, 231, 234, 236, 238–242, 244, 246–247, 295–296, 306
Kravitz, Danny 105, 135
Kretlow, Lou 65, 69
Kryhoski, Dick 278
Kubiak, Ted 306
Kucks, Johnny 72, 95, 97, 284
Kuenn, Harvey 126
Kunkel, Bill 145, 147, 160
Kutyna, Marty 107, 135, 214

Lachemann, Rene 214–215, 217, 309
Landis, Bill 137, 156, 306
Landis, Jim 97, 194, 208, 214–215, 218, 223, 229, 293, 295
Lane, Frank 14, 85–86, 124–126, 133–143, 147, 151–156, 193, 211, 264, 282, 286, 289–291; A's general manager 124
Lang, Jack 285
Lannan, J. Patrick 8, 27–28, 31, 109, 127–128
Larsen, Don 89, 103, 107, 142, 285
LaRussa, Tony 172, 307
Lasorda, Tom 68, 310
Latham, Barry 93
Lau, Charlie 172, 200
LeRoux, Edward 215
Leverone, Louis 9
Leverone, Nathaniel 9, 26, 28, 31, 104, 109, 111, 127–128
Levi, Alex 3
Levi Strauss Company 122
Lewis, Allan 237, 306
Liebman, Morton 20, 23, 25
Lily, Art 225, 305, 307–308, 310–311
Lindblad, Paul 230–232, 239–240, 296, 307
Lindesberg, Don 311
Littell, Mark 288
Littrell, Jack 56
Lockwood, Skip 214, 308–309
Lodigiani, Dario 134–135, 163

Index

Lollar, Sherman 43, 97
Loors, George 259
Lopat, Ed 156, 160–161, 168–169, 171, 174, 197, 199, 201–202, 213, 216, 242, 247; A's manager 163, 175; A's vice president 175, 224
Lopez, Hector 56–57, 66–67, 70, 75–76, 86–87, 92, 95, 97, 282, 284–285, 298
Lovrich, Pete 174
Lukenbill, Frank 271
Lukenbill, Greg 271
Lumpe, Jerry 95, 105, 144, 159, 168, 172, 193, 284, 293

Maas, Duke 81–82, 86, 88, 282
MacFarland, Benny 4
MacFarland, Frank 4
Mack, Connie 3–6, 14, 21, 23–25, 29, 31, 52–53, 56, 65, 210
Mack, Connie, Jr., 4–5
Mack, Connie, III 21, 48, 102
Mack, Earle 4–6, 13–16, 19–21, 23–25, 29, 31
Mack, Margaret 1–09, 128
Mack, Marguerite 4
Mack, Roy 4–6, 13–15, 18–23, 25–31, 104, 109, 127
MacPhail, Bill 48, 64
Magnuson, Warren 255
Maguire, John 227, 256
Mann, Arthur 29–30, 38
Mantle, Mickey 60, 72, 85, 173–174, 285
Marion, Marty 74
Maris, Roger 77, 86–87, 89, 92–93, 97, 102–103, 232, 282, 285–286
Markusen, Bruce 269, 276, 305
Martin, Billy 72, 75–76, 81, 281–282
Martyn, Bob 72, 76, 91, 282–283
Mathews, Nelson 194, 200, 203, 218
Matthewson, Christy 160
Mays, Willie 108
Mazeroski, Bill 108
McCloskey, Matthew 13
McCormick, Mike 108
McDermott, John 3, 44
McDermott, Mickey 72, 77, 81, 279, 282
McGaha, Mel 168, 199, 202–203, 214, 217; A's manager 197–198
McGillicuddy, Margaret see Mack, Margaret

McGuff, Joe 150–152, 161, 251, 260–261, 265, 269, 271, 273, 275, 300
McLaughlin, Jim 213
McLish, Cal 77
McMahan, Jack 65–66, 70, 279
McManus, Jim 81–82
McPhail, Lee 251
McShain, John 5, 13, 15
Mehl, Ernest 3, 11, 30, 38, 109, 112, 148–152, 155, 157–158, 251, 256, 240, 268–269, 287
Melillo, Oscar 49, 64, 71
Melton, Dave 65, 86
Meyer, Bob 202
Michelson, Herb 269, 272, 276
Midwest Research 255
Miles, Clarence 14, 28
Milgram, Lester 3, 44
Millan, Felix 309
Miller, Bing 56
Mincher, Don 231
Mize, John 142, 156
Monbouquette, Bill 108, 219
Monday, Rick 237, 310
Monteagudo, Aurelio 201, 230, 306
Moore, Monte 157, 169, 193, 202, 211, 229, 240–242, 249
Morgan, Tom 72, 76, 81, 279, 282
Morris, Bill 115
Morton, Bubba 160
Mossi, Don 219
Muehlebach, George 42
Murchison, Clint 12, 15–17
Murtaugh, Danny 102
Musial, Stan 126

Nahas, Robert 259
Nash, Jim 230–232, 235–236, 238, 307
Neville, Jim 46
New York Yankees 3, 30
Niarhos, Gus 156
Nicholson, Dave 194, 197
Nieman, Bob 199
Nizar, Louis 185, 187
Nolan, Joe 3
Noren, Irv 72, 76, 280
Norman, Fred 194, 306
Nossek, Joe 230, 234, 236
Nuxhall, Joe 135, 145

O'Boynick, Paul 242

O'Brien, Johnny 259
O'Brien, Syd 309
O'Dell, Bill 89
Odom, John "Blue Moon" 202, 214, 230, 232, 238, 295–296, 305, 308–310
O'Donoghue, John 201, 218, 229, 301
Oliva, Tony 197, 231
O'Malley, Walter 79, 121
O'Reilly, John 264
Osinski, Dan 292

Pacific Coast League 36
Paige, Satchel 219
Pappas, Milt 89
Parrack, Art 227
Patterson, Guy 115
Patti, T.S., 187
Paul, Gabe 220
Pearson, Albie 217
Pena, Orlando 160, 173, 200, 218
Perez, Tony 238
Perini, Lou 46
Peters, Gary 247
Peters, Hank 48–49, 127, 137, 156, 175, 183, 212–214, 216, 224–225, 227, 280, 298, 301, 303, 305, 307–308, 310–311; A's general manager 211–213
Peterson, Jim 6
Pfister, Dan 160, 197
Philadelphia Athletics 3–7, 11–13; American League meeting (first) 14; American League meeting (second) 15–18; American League meeting (third) 21–22; American League meeting (fourth) 25–28; cities seeking team 7, 12, 15–18, 26–27; financial problems 6, 13, 15, 35; local groups seek team 6, 12–16, 19–25; Macks' ownership 4–5, 13
Philadelphia Phillies 5
Phillips, Bubba 97
Pierce, Tony 239, 309
Piersall, Jimmy 204–205
Pignatano, Joe 135, 145, 157, 292
Pilarcik, Al 135, 142, 289
Pisoni, Jim 72, 281
Pless, Rance 65
Portocarrero, Arnold 50, 60, 77, 82, 277, 282
Posada, Leo 145, 160, 299
Powell, Boog 197

Power, Vic 53, 56, 66–67, 75, 85–86, 282
Powers, Ben 178
Pries, Don 305, 309
Putsch, J.W., 109–110, 114, 128, 264

Rakow, Ed 142, 145, 147, 160–161, 173, 193, 293
Rashi, Vic 60, 278
Ray, Larry 50, 71
Reed, Howard 282, 301
Reichardt, Rick 309–310
Renna, Bill 57–58, 66
Rensel, Jack 16, 19–20
Repoz, Roger 230, 234, 237, 295–296
Reynolds, Bob 122, 260
Reynolds, Tom 202, 218
Rice, Bruce 157, 168
Richards, Paul 69, 82, 89, 96, 143, 245, 299
Richardson, Bobby 199
Richardson, Tommy 14–16
Rigney, Dorothy Comiskey 120–121
Rittwage, Jim 229, 293, 295
Rivera, Jim 142
Roberts, Chuck 21–22, 24
Roberts, Curt 66, 279
Roberts, Dave 235
Robinson, Brooks 82, 202
Robinson, Eddie 66, 71, 227, 247, 279
Rogers, Roy 122
Rollins, Rich 230
Romano, John 161
Roof, Phil 229, 233, 236, 295
Rosenberg, Arthur 20
Royster, Charles 164
Rudi, Joe 229, 242, 293, 295, 297, 308–310
Runge, Ed 210
Rush, Red 211, 223, 229
Ruth, Babe 210
Ryan, Connie 312

Saffell, Tom 65, 278
Sain, John 60, 90, 96, 98, 277
St Louis Browns 3
Salkeid and Company 10
Sanders, Carl 179
Sanders, John 214, 293, 301
Sanders, Ken 201, 230, 232, 233, 295
Sanford, Jack (player) 237, 239, 296,

Index

Sanford, Jack (scout) 305, 308–309
Santiago, Jose 201, 301
Saverine, Bob 202
Schaaf, James 127, 156, 168, 208, 227
Schaal, Paul 217
Schaalook, Vic 56
Schirk, Gordon 113
Schlipp, Frank 24
Schlitz Brewery 30, 50, 115, 132, 157, 254, 267
Schlitz-Skelley Network 90
Schoendienst, Red 126
Schwall, Don 143
Segui, Diego 160, 173, 195, 197, 200, 204, 210, 218, 229, 230, 239, 296, 301, 305
Selkirk, George 71, 87, 127, 137, 154, 251, 261
Shafer, Charles 40, 163–164, 177
Shantz, Bobby 6, 59–60, 68, 72, 279–280
Shantz, Wilmer 57
Sharpe, Carleton 181, 255–256
Shaw, Bob 97, 142–143, 145, 157, 289
Sheldon, Roland 216, 218, 230, 231, 295
Shibe, Benjamin 4
Shibe, John 4
Shibe, Tom 4
Shibe Park *see* Connie Mack Stadium
Short, Ed 233
Siebern, Norm 103–105, 144–145, 159, 172, 194, 285, 287
Siebert, Sonny 232
Simmons, Al 4, 56
Simpson, Harry 58–59, 66–67, 72, 86, 92–95, 233, 278, 281
Skelley Oil 90, 132
Skinner, Bob 1098
Skizas, Lou 66–67, 81, 97, 278, 282
Skowron, Moose 103
Slaughter, Enos 57–59, 61, 67, 70, 277
Sleater, Lou 52, 278
Sley, Isadore 20, 23–25
Small, Jim 81–82, 282
Smith, Al 77, 97
Smith, C. Arnold 148
Smith, Earl 128, 166, 256
Smith, Gordon 65, 127
Smith, Hal 59, 66, 76, 85, 87, 92, 95, 97, 103, 278, 285

Snyder, Russ 91, 93, 105, 135, 284, 289
Sommers, Bill 61
Spencer, Byron 112, 115–117, 128
Spicer, Robert 49
Spink, J.G., 299
Splittorff, Paul. 288
Sportservice 5–6, 12, 29–30, 44, 179, 262
Stafford, Bill 230, 295
Stahl, Larry 67, 203, 233, 234, 235, 301
Staley, Gene 142–143, 147
Stanky, Eddie 154
Steadman, Jack 250
Stein, Elliott 113–114
Stengel, Casey 112, 121–122
Stephens, Gene 142
Stern, Richard 253, 256
Stock, Wes 200–201, 218, 229, 232, 233, 236, 239, 242
Stoneham, Horace 79, 180
Stover, Harry 112
Stram, Hank 179
Strauss, Levi 272
Sturdivant, Tom 95, 97, 102, 174, 284
Suarez, Ken 236, 309
Sudar, Pete 56
Sullivan, Haywood 135, 145, 159, 172, 220, 225, 289; A's manager 214–215
Susce, George 49, 64, 71
Susquehanna Corporation 9
Swallow, Ray 156, 224, 227, 312
Swift, Bob 71, 90
Swyden, Vic 256
Sylk, Harry 13, 19
Symington, Stuart 256, 259–262

Talbot, Fred 208, 218, 230, 231, 293, 295
Talton, Tim 233
Tartabull, Jose 157, 159, 172–173, 200, 218, 230, 292, 295
Taylor, Harry 282
Tenace, Gene 310
territorial rights: Kansas City 3, 30–31, 38; Los Angeles 36, 40; Seattle 258
Terry, Ralph 72–73, 76, 88, 92, 95–96, 229, 281–282, 284
Thompson, Charley "Tim" 65–66, 76, 81, 282
Throneberry, Marv 103–104, 142, 144, 285

Toma, George 79, 203, 234
Tomanek, Dick 86, 88, 282
Topping, Dan 9–11, 16, 37–38, 205, 280
Torgeson, Earl 97
Tresh, Tom 231
Trowbridge, Bob 102
Trucks, Virgil 71, 75–76, 86, 279
Truman, Harry 53, 169
Tsitouris, John 81–82, 97, 135, 282
Tucci, Joe 16
Tuttle, Bill 81–82, 86–87, 92–93, 105, 142–143, 145, 282

Umont, Frank 204–205
Urban, Jack 72, 76–77, 88, 91, 279, 282

Valdespino, Sandy 231
Valo, Elmer 53, 57–59, 61, 67
Vandergrif, Thomas 164
Veeck, Bill 3, 39–40, 71, 114, 116, 120–121, 131, 210, 264, 269, 276–277, 282, 286; attempt to purchase A's (1954) 12, 15–17, 27; tax shelter (depreciation) 32, 36, 39
Versailles, Ziolo 173, 231
Vincent, Al 227, 236
Virgil, Ozzie 143
Vollers, Ed 13, 19–20, 25–27, 109, 111–113, 115–116, 127

Wachter, Bob 48, 127, 130, 168
Walker, Jerry 142, 145, 161, 169, 289
Ward, Preston 86–87, 282
Ward, Roger 203
Warner, Jack 237, 296
Washington Senators 40, 79
Wayne, Angus 164
Webb, Del 3, 9–11, 16–18, 37–39, 52, 121–122, 178, 205, 280

Webb-Winn-Senter Corporation 45
Webster, Ramon 236
Weiss, George 103, 124
Western League 30, 38
Wheat, Leroy 65
White, Frank 288
White, Jo Jo 134–135, 137, 163
White, Roy 231
Wickersham, Dave 145, 147, 160–161, 173, 193, 293, 301, 305
Wilks, Ted 134–135, 147, 156
Williams, Dick 91, 95, 105, 142, 283, 289
Williams, Edward Bennett 214
Williams, Ted 85, 255
Willis, Dale 160
Wilson, Bill 53, 57–58
Wilson, Keith 178
Wilson, Red 83
Win Shares (defined) 277
Winn-Senter Company 45
Wohlford, Jim 288
Woodling, Gene 77, 89
Worthington, Al 203
Wrigley, Phil 15, 36
Wrigley Field (Los Angeles) 36, 121
Wyatt, John 160, 174, 200–201, 219, 230–231, 295, 299, 305

Yankee Stadium 10, 26–27, 34
Yastrzemski, Carl 219
Yawkey, Bill 252, 260–261
Yawkey, Jean 215
York, Jim 288

Zarilla, Al 137
Zerniel, Gus 55, 57–59, 67, 70, 76, 81, 282
Zuk, Bob 311

www.ingramcontent.com/pod-product-compliance
Ingram Content Group UK Ltd.
Pitfield, Milton Keynes, MK11 3LW, UK
UKHW041922140426
5217IPUK00014B/273